PRESCRIBING CULTURES AND PHARMACEUTICAL POLICY IN THE ASIA-PACIFIC

Edited by Karen Eggleston

 THE WALTER H. SHORENSTEIN
ASIA-PACIFIC RESEARCH CENTER

THE WALTER H. SHORENSTEIN ASIA-PACIFIC RESEARCH CENTER (Shorenstein APARC) is a unique Stanford University institution focused on the interdisciplinary study of contemporary Asia. Shorenstein APARC's mission is to produce and publish outstanding interdisciplinary, Asia-Pacific–focused research; to educate students, scholars, and corporate and governmental affiliates; to promote constructive interaction to influence U.S. policy toward the Asia-Pacific; and to guide Asian nations on key issues of societal transition, development, U.S.-Asia relations, and regional cooperation.

The Walter H. Shorenstein Asia-Pacific Research Center
Freeman Spogli Institute for International Studies
Stanford University
Encina Hall
Stanford, CA 94305-6055
tel. 650-723-9741
fax 650-723-6530
http://APARC.stanford.edu

Prescribing Cultures and Pharmaceutical Policy in the Asia-Pacific may be ordered from:
The Brookings Institution
c/o DFS, P.O. Box 50370, Baltimore, MD, USA
tel. 1-800-537-5487 or 410-516-6956
fax 410-516-6998
http://www.brookings.edu/press

First printing, 2009.
13-digit ISBN 978-1-931368-16-2

PRESCRIBING CULTURES AND PHARMACEUTICAL POLICY IN THE ASIA-PACIFIC

SHORENSTEIN APARC STANFORD

THE WALTER H. SHORENSTEIN
ASIA-PACIFIC RESEARCH CENTER

CONTENTS

Acknowledgments

This book represents the inaugural work of the Asia Health Policy Program (AHPP) at the Walter H. Shorenstein Asia-Pacific Research Center (Shorenstein APARC) at Stanford University. AHPP seeks to foster rigorous and policy-relevant comparative analysis of health policies in the Asia-Pacific region. By focusing on specific components of health-care systems (such as pharmaceutical policy) rather than comparative systems as a whole, researchers and policymakers can seek common ground as they tackle specific health system challenges. At the same time, this directed approach ensures that the distinctive contours of each system—contours that shape policy choices—are acknowledged.

AHPP thanks the Council for Better Corporate Citizenship for its support of the Asia Health Policy Program.

Many thanks to Dr. Gi-Wook Shin, director of Shorenstein APARC, for encouraging this project, and to Ambassador Michael Armacost for welcoming it into the center's series for distribution through Brookings Institution Press. Neeley Main, our senior event coordinator, was instrumental in making the coauthors' meeting in April 2008 possible and memorable. I extend sincere gratitude to all the contributors for cheerfully committing their time and effort to this project, and for their enthusiastic endeavors in the field of comparative health policy. I thank my research assistants, Crystal Zheng and Ting-Ting Wu, for excellent assistance with the health system overviews, and Victoria Tomkinson for her cheerful and professional shepherding of the manuscript through the Shorenstein APARC and Brookings publication process. Fayre Makeig did a superb job copyediting the final manuscript.

Finally, I thank my husband, Kesi, and our children, Adrian and Alanna, for their love and support.

Karen Eggleston
Stanford, CA
June 2009

Editor's Note: In August 2009, as this book was going to press, John H. Barton—a contributor to this volume and longtime Stanford law professor—passed away. Professor Barton devoted his academic career to the examination of questions at the intersection of science and the law, and his chapter in this book explains how the global pharmaceutical market fails to meet global medical needs. We mourn the passing of our brilliant and distinguished colleague.

FOREWORD

Michael R. Reich

The pharmaceutical sector—one of the most conflict-ridden areas of any health system—promises great benefits and also poses enormous risks. This book examines how pharmaceuticals play, in editor Karen Eggleston's words, an "often contentious role in the health-care systems of the Asia-Pacific." Indeed, this is an understatement. Conflicts abound over public policies, industry strategies, payment mechanisms, professional associations, and dispensing practices—to name just a few of the regional controversies covered in this excellent book. While many of the authors are economists, they recognize that an analysis of pharmaceutical policy must address politics as well. Each chapter covers important aspects of the pharmaceutical sector's political economy, which in turn captures many of the core conflicts affecting health systems. Taken as a whole, the book points to three key lessons.

First, the pharmaceutical sector needs to be viewed within the context of a national health system. This book covers eight major health systems of the Asia-Pacific, ranging from poor (India) to rich (Japan), including countries with universal coverage (Taiwan, South Korea, and Japan), countries with highly regulated markets (Japan), and others with chaotic regulation (China). The two most populous countries in the world (India and China) have huge regional variation within their borders. Yet all of these countries are struggling with how to make the pharmaceutical sector contribute in positive ways to the ultimate goals of their health systems. It is helpful to think about three ultimate goals for a health system: the *health status* of the population, citizens' *satisfaction* with the system, and the capacity to provide *financial risk protection* to individuals (Roberts et al. 2004:24). Each of these goals is deeply influenced by the role of pharmaceuticals in the health system, including which products are available, where they are available, at what cost to individuals and to the system, who provides them and under what conditions, the quality of the products, and what patients know about the products. Questions about access to pharmaceuticals are addressed in each of the various—in fact, very different—health systems studied in this book. In short, national context matters.

A second lesson is that certain conflicts emerge in all kinds of national health systems and must be confronted by those societies. Such conflicts take various forms, and the solutions vary as well. Comparing national trends can help advance our understanding of contested issues. This book is structured around two basic conflicts: (1) the trade-offs of separation versus integration in the dispensing and prescribing of pharmaceuticals, and (2) tension between promoting innovation versus access to pharmaceuticals. The first conflict is especially important in Asia because of its long cultural tradition of medical practitioners who both prescribe and dispense, a practice that became embedded in modern health systems and payment and reimbursement policies. This book provides a long-needed analysis of how different Asian countries are struggling with the separation of dispensing from prescribing and what kinds of results (both intended and unintended) are being achieved by system reform. Meanwhile, the tension between emphasizing innovation versus access is examined in several chapters, which go on to propose policies that may be able to achieve both goals. This tension represents a topic of hot debate on today's global health policy agenda—especially when asking how to promote the development of new medicines (and devices and diagnostics) for conditions that affect poor people in poor countries where market incentives are insufficient to stimulate private research efforts (Frost and Reich 2008).

A third lesson is that health systems around the world are struggling to contain costs and that this often generates conflicts over policy. Many pharmaceutical policy reforms described in this book were adopted by governments seeking to contain rising health-care costs, as discussed in the chapters on Japan, South Korea, Taiwan, China, and Australia. The government goal of cost containment often leads to a focus on pharmaceuticals, which frequently represents the largest area of government spending after health workers and is thus a politically attractive target. This focus then leads to policies that use listing and pricing decisions as mechanisms to control costs and that promote the economic analysis of new medicines. Author Hans Löfgren notes that in Australia in the early 1960s, "drugs formed the largest single item of government expenditure under national health benefits, and costs became a political concern." Australia subsequently became the first country to adopt mandatory cost-effectiveness analysis for all medicines listed on the public reimbursement formulary. In Thailand, as described by Sauwakon Ratanawijitrasin, the government adopted all sorts of policies in its pursuit of cost containment—what she calls "multiple policies, one aim." The government has adopted policies for procurement, production, pricing, payment, and patents, with varying results (including some unintended consequences)—a theme that appears in other chapters as well. This and other chapters demonstrate that problems arise in both market-oriented and state-based efforts to address the policy dilemmas around cost containment; there is no simple fix.

This book makes a special contribution to our understanding of the pharmaceutical sector in China through the six chapters of analysis devoted to this country. Qiang Sun and Qingyue Meng underscore the importance of medicine in the Chinese health system, citing the fact that in 2005, China spent 4.7 percent of its gross domestic prodct (GDP) on health care—of which 44 percent was for pharmaceuticals, with about half of total health costs paid by individuals out of pocket. China's health policymakers are now focused on cost containment, which depends critically on what happens in the pharmaceutical sector. The government has shifted back and forth in its pricing policies on medicines (indeed, it has introduced nine different policies since 2000 and is preparing yet another one). But cost control is not the only elusive goal in China. As Mingzhi Li and Kai Reimers report, "Many researchers and industry analysts now ascribe the overall chaos of China's health-care sector to the government's rapid opening of the industry to market forces without the establishment of sufficient and enforceable regulations." This chaos includes high prices, poor quality, counterfeit medicines, official kickbacks to hospitals and secret kickbacks to doctors, ineffective regulation, lax drug approval, and more. Michael A. Santoro and Caitlin M. Liu report that in May 2007, China executed the former director of the China State Food and Drug Administration for receiving "$850,000 in bribes to facilitate the approval of myriad new drugs, including some that contained substandard or counterfeit ingredients." China's ineffective regulations continue to have global consequences through an increasingly connected network of medicines and food products. As Santoro and Liu write:

> Perhaps the most significant regulatory gap concerns chemical companies, which are neither certified nor inspected by Chinese drug regulators. Chemical companies from China supply active ingredients and, in some cases, finished products to drug manufacturers and distributors worldwide. There are approximately 80,000 chemical companies in China, and no one knows how many of these are involved in manufacturing drug ingredients.

Globalization is galloping forward, with Chinese producers pushing the pace at breakneck speed. More and more, our safety depends on China's ability to get its regulatory act together, especially since it is increasingly difficult to determine the production source of many medicines and food products. The crisis resulting from contaminated infant formula and milk products made by Chinese firms (reported in September 2008) highlights the risks of lax Chinese regulation combined with high global connectedness (Yardley and Barboza 2008). We all depend on the Chinese government to effectively regulate its producers and markets.

In conclusion, this book contributes to our knowledge of how the pharmaceutical sector operates in the Asia-Pacific—including public policies, industrial strategy, and market issues. The countries discussed offer many different political and economic contexts, as governments, companies, and societies struggle with the many contentious questions raised by pharmaceutical products. The book contains nuggets of wisdom for academics as well as policymakers. I hope that similar studies can be conducted for other parts of the world—such as Latin America, Sub-Saharan Africa, and the Middle East. Each region shares certain structural and cultural traits that would bear regional analysis and cross-national comparisons. At the same time, regional studies like this one can help lead us toward a more general understanding of how to address the problems at the heart of the pharmaceutical sector—the promises of better health and cost-effective care, compounded by the risks of economic costs, adverse health effects, and fraudulent claims. Neither a market-based system nor a state-based system alone can provide the right mix of constraints and incentives, hence the need for cross-sectoral approaches and public-private interactions.

Michael R. Reich
Brookline, MA
October 1, 2008

References

Frost, Laura J., and Michael R. Reich. 2008. *Access: How do good health technologies get to poor people in poor countries?* Cambridge, MA: Harvard Center for Population and Development Studies, distributed by Harvard Univ. Press.

Roberts, Marc J., William Hsiao, Peter Berman, and Michael R. Reich. 2004. *Getting health reform right: A guide to improving performance and equity.* New York: Oxford Univ. Press.

Yardley, Jim, and David Barboza. 2008. Despite warnings, China's regulators failed to stop tainted milk. *New York Times*, September 27, p. A1.

INTRODUCTION

Karen Eggleston

The Asia-Pacific is arguably the most diverse region in the world. Home to deep-rooted cultural traditions and all the world's major religions, the Asia-Pacific also encompasses a wide array of political systems governing countries both large and small, wealthy and poor, rapidly growing and stagnant. Health-care systems in the region, also diverse, face challenges common around the globe: safeguarding public health, expanding health-care coverage, and improving quality while controlling costs and balancing government and market roles in the health sector.

Pharmaceuticals and their regulation play an increasingly important and often contentious role in the health-care systems of the Asia-Pacific. For example, drug expenditures account for an extraordinarily high percentage of total health expenditures in China, while India and a few other countries host thriving domestic pharmaceutical industries of global importance. At the same time, controversy surrounds patents, trade-related aspects of intellectual property (TRIPS), and pharmaceutical pricing within bilateral trade agreements (Australia–United States, Republic of Korea–United States). Nations throughout the region struggle to regulate drugs appropriately, from patents to evidence-based purchasing (for example, the Australian government's Pharmaceuticals Benefit Scheme) and direct-to-consumer advertising. Meanwhile, strong traditions of indigenous medicine are becoming integrated into broader health-care systems, and new policies that separate drug prescription from dispensation are rewriting the professional roles of physicians and pharmacists. Throughout the Asia-Pacific, effective pharmaceutical prescription and use will be central to controlling infectious diseases both old and emerging, protecting the efficacy of antibiotics around the world, and treating the growing burden of chronic disease.

This book seeks to explore these issues in detail, using a multidisciplinary approach. Each contributor focuses on a specific area of expertise, while touching on two overarching questions. First, what institutional forces are driving pharmaceutical use, industry trends, and medical policies in the Asia-Pacific? Second, what lessons can the economies of the Asia-Pacific learn from one another and from other regions to improve pharmaceutical policies? The first section of the book features chapters on pharmaceutical policy in seven health-care systems of the Asia-Pacific: South Korea, Japan, Thailand, Taiwan, Australia, India, and China. The second section focuses on the cross-cutting themes of prescribing cultures and access versus innovation. Taken as a whole, the contributors aim to provide an evidence base for policies even as they acknowledge the historical and cultural contexts that distinguish them.

3

The book targets several audiences. Policymakers will find it a useful reference not only for understanding other nations' domestic health-care systems but also for learning about U.S. policy toward Asia. In addition, the book explores potential policy solutions to the global dilemma of how to provide incentives for innovation—especially in the creation of drugs to treat neglected diseases—while ensuring access to life-saving medicines. Researchers will find the collection useful for defining what we know and what we need to know about pharmaceutical policy in this region and for examining these issues from multiple perspectives. For government analysts and nongovernmental organizations investing in global health, the book seeks to show how the process of research and producing "evidence" can and should be policy based. Industry insiders will find the analyses useful for putting market developments in a broader context. Finally, professors and students will find the book an important resource in the learning process.

The chapters assembled here analyze the forces that have shaped industry development, regulatory structures, and other policy decisions to date, as well as the likely trajectories and uncertainties ahead for this region. Using pharmaceutical policy as a window into the economic trade-offs, political compromises, cultural legacies, and historical institutions that shape health-care systems, the book facilitates cross-country comparisons of policymaking processes and industry structures. It also illustrates how cultural legacies shape and are shaped by the forces of globalization, and thus may be of interest to social scientists beyond the confines of pharmaceutical and health policy.

Because no single volume can provide a comprehensive overview of all aspects of pharmaceutical policy in the Asia-Pacific, the most populous region in the world, we have chosen a select group of economies from northeast, southeast, and south Asia, as well as Oceania, which vary in per capita income, health-system structure, and approach to pharmaceutical industry development, procurement, and regulation. In addition to the seven systems highlighted individually, Anita Wagner and Dennis Ross-Degnan provide an extended example from the Philippines in chapter 18. As F. M. Scherer notes in the book's conclusion, the covered jurisdictions were "home to some 2.6 billion individual human beings in the year 2000, or 42.8 percent of the world's population." A cluster of six chapters—chapter 9 by Yiyong Yang, chapter 10 by Mingzhi Li and Kai Reimers, chapter 11 by Qiang Sun and Qingyue Meng, chapter 12 by Yanfen Huang and Yiyong Yang, chapter 13 by Wei Wilson Zhang and Xue Liu, and chapter 14 by Michael A. Santoro and Caitlin M. Liu—provides a case study of Chinese pharmaceutical policy, ranging from domestic industry structure and distribution channels to prescribing incentives, price regulation, product safety, and the relationship to overall health-sector reforms.

At least two central themes emerge in the chapters that follow: first, the crucial role that differences in "prescribing cultures" and policies play in delineating the functions of prescribing and dispensing medications; second, the perennial balancing act of providing access to medications and incentives for innovation. In this introduction, I provide an overview of these two key themes, which cut across the different contributions in the book. I then offer a brief description of the seven selected health-care systems and a preview of the main arguments presented in each chapter.

Prescribing Cultures and Physician Dispensing

The physician-patient dyad lies at the heart of medical care. Economists often conceptualize this as one example of a "principal-agent relationship," in which the patient (principal) "hires" the medical-care provider (agent) to supply expertise such as diagnosis and treatment. Providers may be able to exploit their superior information for profit. The asymmetry of information between patient and provider is often compounded by differences in social status and power as well as the feelings of urgency and discomfort (or even incapacity and defenselessness) associated with illness.

Health-care systems differ in the incentives and assumptions that govern the physician-patient relationship, including use of pharmaceuticals. In many herbal medicine traditions, for example, doctors prepare, prescribe, and dispense drugs to their patients. This tradition seems alien to practitioners of other systems, especially Western systems of biomedicine, in which pharmaceutical firms produce medications, physicians prescribe them, and pharmacists dispense them to patients.[1]

Economic theory suggests some possible advantages of integrating prescription with dispensation. First, fixed costs (patient search and travel costs, provider diagnosis costs) may imply less expense when a single provider both diagnoses and treats the patient. In economic models such as that of Wolinsky (1993), the fixed costs of search and diagnosis imply the advantage of integration, all else equal.[2] Second, even if another provider treats a given diagnosis more efficiently, there may be nontrivial costs associated with accurately communicating the diagnosis and its nuances. Third, if barriers to timely, accurate feedback between diagnosis and treatment hamper the development of appropriate human capital in each skill set, then integrating diagnosis and treatment provides better incentives for improving their quality over time, compared with separating them.

Conversely, separation may bring several advantages. First, integration implies a strong economic incentive for oversupplying profitable goods and services. This potentially severe supply-side "moral hazard" problem has also been referred to as "supplier-induced demand" (see, for example, Gruber and Owings 1996). Separation can remove this incentive. Second, separation subjects a diagnosis and treatment decision to two experts, who may check the safety and quality of each other's decisions. True, to err is human, but medical error can lead to tragedy. A monitoring role may justify additional costs even if we do not suspect either expert of any systematic bias or deficiency. The benefit of this role increases when there is reason to suspect substantial heterogeneity

5

in diagnosis skill, unobserved by patients, which a second expert's systematic review can rectify cost-effectively (such as by checking for drug interactions with decision-support tools). Third, patients may value different opinions, especially when a variety of appropriate treatments are available in which doctors have varying levels of expertise. Fourth, insofar as the two roles—diagnosing and managing disease on the one hand and preparing and dispensing medications on the other—require distinct skill sets, separating them may lead to greater safety, quality, and efficiency over time.

Economic theory clearly does not indicate that separation is inherently superior to integration. Given this theoretical ambiguity, relative efficiency is largely an empirical question. To date, few empirical studies have examined the relative benefits of separating versus integrating diagnosis and treatment; notable exceptions are Iizuka (2007) and Afendulis and Kessler (2007). As several chapters in this book illustrate in detail, Asia-Pacific systems with traditions of integration have attempted, to varying degrees, to separate prescribing from dispensing. Such policies include instituting a fee for prescribing (which South Korea later abolished); paying an extra fee for pharmacy dispensing (which in Japan in 2008 was linked to the prescription of generic drugs); closing inpatient pharmacies (South Korea); establishing formulas for regulating pharmaceutical retail prices (Japan); and bundling forms of provider payment, such as capitation and case-based payment (Thailand), which encourages providers to reduce drug spending along with overall spending.

The results show that although separation may bring benefits, it is not a silver bullet for reducing overall health-care spending, particularly as the capabilities—and costs—of medicine continue to expand. In some cases, the reforms were watered down, with so many loopholes that they appear to have had little substantial effect on behavior (as in Taiwan). In other cases, sweeping change succeeded but did not slow the pace of spending increases (South Korea). Generous but bundled case payments for inpatient episodes appear to complement separation policies.

Moreover, separation and pricing policies appear to affect the industrial organization of domestic pharmaceutical industries. Although one might think that branded pharmaceuticals have an advantage in offering price-cost markups to doctors, in many systems a large number of small-scale generic drug firms thrive by offering generous price-cost margins to hospitals and doctors. Such an industrial structure—with a large number of small-scale generic drug firms—suffers from its lack of economies of scale in research and development (R&D) for innovative drugs, and substantially complicates efforts to regulate quality and safety. Whether separation policies do in fact complement efforts to foster larger-scale, research-based pharmaceutical firms is an important area for further research.

Access and Innovation

Globalization affects virtually all segments of society, including health care. Pharmaceutical policies in particular are interlinked globally not only by multinational and domestic firms that sell to global markets, but also by pricing policies that spill over into international price comparisons and parallel trade (importing drugs from low-price economies to high-price ones; see Danzon 1997). Moreover, prices are a key determinant of pharmaceutical access and innovation, two goals that are often in conflict.

Producing innovative, research-based pharmaceuticals involves high R&D costs but low production costs for each pill or dose (Danzon 1997; Sloan and Hsieh 2007). This cost structure presents challenges in allocating the high R&D costs across products and users. Moreover, these joint sunk costs are increasingly global, so that their payment does not clearly fall to a single country or region. As Patricia Danzon (1997:11) notes, "it is the *global* nature of the sunk, joint costs of pharmaceuticals that makes the regulation of drug prices potentially more distortionary than the regulation of traditional utilities," another industry characterized by high fixed costs and low user-specific marginal costs.

Herein lies a fundamental dilemma. At a given point in time, it is efficient and equitable to provide access to therapeutically beneficial drugs to all patients for whom the benefit exceeds the low user-specific marginal cost. But maximizing access in this way is also myopic. Over time, it is efficient (and, many would argue, equitable) to invest in innovations that bring benefits to patients in the future. Indeed, without past innovation, there would be no current access. The dilemma arises because promoting innovation—dynamic efficiency—requires a price high enough to cover the joint sunk costs of R&D and some return on investment, whereas promoting access—static efficiency—requires a price low enough to cover only user-specific marginal costs. No pricing policy can achieve both goals simultaneously.

This access-versus-innovation dilemma is not an equity-versus-efficiency trade-off, even though some observers frame it as such. While one can argue that promoting access is efficient and promoting innovation is equitable, the reverse is equally true.[3] The policy challenge is to design systems that promote appropriate access, constrain inappropriate access, and cooperate at the global level to stimulate innovation, particularly for drugs targeted at diseases that disproportionately afflict the poor (or "neglected" diseases).[4] Several chapters in this book, especially in the final section on access and innovation (including chapter 19 by John H. Barton; chapter 20 by Henry G. Grabowski, David B. Ridley, and Jeffrey L. Moe; and the conclusion by F. M. Scherer), explore the contours of this debate and propose promising ways forward.

Compulsory licensing vividly illustrates the controversies that surround access and innovation. In chapter 4, Sauwakon Ratanawijitrasin describes Thailand's compulsory licensing policies, which have made access to life-saving drugs possible in her country. As F. M. Scherer notes in the conclusion, "I was shocked to read, in chapter 4 (Ratanawijitrasin), that the U.S. government put Thailand on a priority watch list in 2007 for its compulsory licensing activities. A similar patent-linked action by the United States in 1991 led to proposed legislation in the Thai parliament precipitating a no-confidence vote and dissolution of the government. Will we Americans ever learn to let other governments make their own decisions freely, within the latitude allowed by international law?"

The United States figures prominently in other pharmaceutical policy controversies as well. U.S. health spending, at 15.3 percent of the gross domestic product (GDP) in 2006, far exceeds that of other regions; the closest economies in terms of percent of GDP allocated to health were Switzerland (11.3 percent), France (11.1 percent), and Germany (10.6 percent) (OECD Health Data 2008). The United States is also the largest market for pharmaceuticals in the world. U.S. policies shape innovation incentives, and U.S. policymakers thus have a special responsibility to promote access to the fruits of that innovation. Numerous chapters in this book focus on issues of importance for U.S. policymakers. For example, Grabowski and his colleagues discuss priority review vouchers, a new U.S. policy designed to promote R&D for drugs targeting neglected diseases. Scherer discusses drug exports to the U.S. market. And multiple chapters examine global public health problems that require multilateral solutions, from TRIPS to regulation of supply chains so that drug safety and quality are assured.

Policymakers and analysts in the United States and elsewhere often use Europe as a frame of reference (see, for example, Mossialos, Mrazek, and Walley 2004), but they may benefit from exploring the experiences of the Asia-Pacific as well. Indeed, pioneering work has been done in this region, as in the case of adopting economic evaluation in purchasing—for example, Australia's Pharmaceutical Benefits Scheme—and, more recently, in developing performance measures that include medicines, also in Australia, as noted in chapter 18 (Wagner and Ross-Degnan). Thailand has achieved the remarkable feat of offering universal health coverage despite relatively low per capita income.

For these and other topics examined in this book, we hope that the value of a comparative approach to health policy will be apparent and compelling.

Seven Health-care Systems of the Asia-Pacific

South Korea

South Korea's population of 49 million enjoys relatively good health. Life expectancy at birth is 79.1 years, exceeding the OECD average of 78.9 years. Korea's 27-year increase in longevity between 1960 and 2006 was the most rapid gain in life expectancy among OECD countries (OECD Health Data 2008). The three major causes of death are cardiovascular disease, cancer, and accidents. Korea's population is also rapidly aging, with the 65-or-older population expected to increase to more than 13 percent by 2020 (Kwon 2005).

Health spending absorbed 6.4 percent of Korea's GDP in 2006, and health spending per capita was $1,480 (calculated based on purchasing-power parity). Public spending accounts for 55 percent of Korea's total health spending. Out-of-pocket payments account for 37 percent of total health spending, more than in most OECD countries (OECD Health Data 2008).

Korea has had universal coverage since 1989, through national health insurance and a government-managed Medicaid program. In July 2000, the nation's many health insurance programs were merged into a single insurer system to address inequity. Health-care expenditure has continually increased due to the requirements of an aging population, poor physician incentives for cost-effective care, and increasing demands for health care (Kwon 2005). Payment for services is chiefly on a fee-for-service basis.

The private sector dominates health-care delivery in Korea (fewer than 7 percent of hospitals are public; Kwon 2005). As in many Asian countries, hospitals have large outpatient departments, most clinicians are trained as specialists, there is little or no primary care gatekeeping, and large tertiary hospitals are overcrowded while smaller clinics and hospitals (often physician-owned) have lower occupancy. The number of doctors per capita in Korea doubled between 1990 and 2005, the fastest growth rate in the OECD (OECD Health Data 2008). Like Japan, Korea has a high number of beds per capita, and its inpatient length of stay is longer than that of most other OECD countries.

Korea implemented controversial reforms in 2000 to separate prescribing and dispensing, both to help reduce pharmaceutical spending and to correct distorted incentives for overuse (Kwon and Reich 2005; Kim and Prah Ruger 2008; Soonman Kwon, chapter 1, this volume). These reform objectives have only been partially realized. Korea's drug spending in 2006 absorbed 25.8 percent of total health spending, compared to the OECD average of 17.6 percent. But when compared in terms of per capita purchasing power parity, Korea's drug spending remains below the OECD average and less than half of that in the United States (OECD Health Data 2008).

Japan

Japan's population of 128 million enjoys the longest life expectancy in the world, which stood at 82.4 years in 2006. Mortality rates for heart disease are the lowest in the OECD. But smoking rates among males remain high, at 41 percent (the highest among OECD countries after Turkey, South Korea, and Greece; OECD Health Data 2008). As Hyoung-Sun Jeong and Jeremy Hurst note, "Japanese health status is, in most respects, the highest observed among OECD countries, but it is not clear to what extent this is due to the health system and to what extent due to other factors such as the Japanese culture, diet, or social conditions" (2004:4).

Japan devoted 8.2 percent of its GDP to health spending in 2005, slightly less than the OECD average of 8.9 percent. Health spending per capita was

$2,474 (adjusted for purchasing power parity) and was growing slower than the OECD average. Public sources fund 82.7 percent of health spending, well above the OECD average of 73 percent (OECD Health Data 2008).

Japan achieves universal coverage through a social insurance system that includes separate funds for different population groups (employees of large firms and their dependents, retirees, the self-employed, residents of different regions, and so on). Insurance premiums are proportional to income.

The delivery system in Japan is pluralistic. Hospitals, mostly not-for-profit, include small, physician-owned facilities and large tertiary facilities that employ their own physicians. Recently, investor-owned hospitals have been permitted in specific localities. But they are not allowed to charge patients more than the regulated price and do not receive reimbursement from public health insurance (Ikegami and Campbell 2004). Japan has fewer physicians per capita than other OECD countries but the highest number of hospital beds and magnetic resonance imaging (MRI) units—40.1 units per million people, compared to an OECD average of 10.2 per million people in 2006 (OECD Health Data 2008).

The government regulates fees paid to health-care providers, and all citizens enjoy similar benefits (aside from some differences in the modest, capped copayments) regardless of their specific insurance plan or where they receive their care (Ikegami and Campbell, 1995 and 2004). A "free access" guarantee assures patients access to the hospital of their choice within their *iryo-ken*, a region that may encompass several municipalities but is smaller than a prefecture (Noguchi, Shimizutani, and Masuda 2008). Although reimbursement has traditionally been on a fee-for-service basis, payment for university hospitals, subacute care, and long-term care now features inclusive fees that are case-mix-adjusted but independent of actual interventions (Ikegami and Campbell 2004; Nomura and Nakayama 2005).

Relative economic stagnation and rapid population aging have put additional pressure on Japan's system. Public long-term-care insurance started in April 2000, with government subsidies financing about half of the long-term-care insurance benefits. Since October 2007 government subsidies, financed by general tax revenues, have paid for half of the health insurance benefits for those aged 75 and older (Ikegami and Campbell 2004). The introduction of a separate insurance program for this population has proved controversial.

Japan's health-care system has attracted international attention for its relative success in fostering good population health at modest cost. In the World Health Organization (WHO) ranking of health systems in 2000, Japan ranked tenth overall, with top-ten rankings in virtually all categories (level of health, responsiveness, fairness of financial contribution, spending, and so on). In many studies of high-income countries, such as the Health Care Quality Indicators Project focusing on twenty-three OECD countries, Japan is the only Asian country included. Japan is also the second-largest market for pharmaceuticals in the world, and therefore critical to that industry.

Thailand

Thailand is a middle-income country (per capita GDP of $8,440 in 2005) with a population of more than 65 million and relatively fast economic growth. The infant mortality rate decreased from 31 per 1,000 live births in 1990 to 18.2 in 2004, and life expectancy rose from 68 to 70.5 years. HIV/AIDS is the leading cause of death, especially among the working-age population, followed by traffic accidents (WHO 2007; Hanvoravongchai and Hsiao 2007).

Total health expenditure accounts for 3.5 percent of GDP, which is relatively low when compared to that of nations with similar per capita incomes. The national health budget increased from 5.8 percent of total government expenditure in 1993 to 7.6 percent in 2004 (WHO 2007). Public spending accounts for more than 60 percent of health expenditure (Hanvoravongchai and Hsiao 2007).

Thailand recently became one of the few developing countries to achieve universal health coverage. The system features multiple insurance plans. The Civil Service Medical Benefits Scheme covers government employees and their dependents (about six million people). It is financed by taxes, and pays for pharmaceuticals on a per item basis. Similar benefit packages are also available for the employees of public enterprises (i.e., industrial firms rather than government agencies). The Social Security Scheme covers private business employees—a category that comprises about eight million people—and is financed by contributions from employees, employers, and the government. Payment to contracted hospitals is made on a capitation basis (with additional payments based on utilization). Pharmaceuticals are included in the overall per person payment (Ratanawijitrasin 2005).

The 30 Baht Health Insurance Scheme is the largest insurance program in Thailand, covering approximately 48.4 million people, or 76.6 percent of the insured population. According to the National Health Security Act, anyone who is not covered under the other two public schemes is eligible under this one, which is funded by general taxes (Ratanawijitrasin 2005). The 30 Baht Scheme requires all beneficiaries to register with a local contracting unit for primary care, an innovative channeling of funds intended to promote primary care and fundamentally change how public hospitals are financed (Hughes and Leethongdee 2007). The scheme employs capitation and diagnostic-related groups (DRGs) as its main payment methods. Payment for drugs is included in the capitation and DRG rates (Ratanawijitrasin 2005).

In addition to these three schemes, private insurance companies offer a multitude of health insurance policies, covering approximately 1.5 million people and generally paying on a fee-for-service basis (Ratanawijitrasin 2005).

At present, these schemes cover services and pharmaceuticals given by hospitals—both private and government-owned—and government-owned health centers. A small number of privately owned clinics are eligible for payment under health insurance within pilot projects managed by public insurers. Drugstores and physician clinics are generally excluded from insurance payment, so their clients pay out of pocket (Ratanawijitrasin 2005). Many public doctors also work in the private sector for extra income (Hanvoravongchai and Hsiao 2007).

Taiwan

Taiwan, with a population of almost 23 million, enjoys comparatively high life expectancy (77.8 years). Like many middle- and high-income economies of the Asia-Pacific, Taiwan has experienced an epidemiological transition—with the burden of disease from infectious diseases declining and the burden attributable to noncommunicable diseases such as heart disease and cancer increasing over the past several decades—and now faces relatively rapid population aging.

Taiwan spends about 5.5 percent of GDP on health and since 1995 has had a compulsory universal health insurance scheme financed through premiums and taxes. Most services require a modest copayment, with an annual cap of 10 percent of average income; low-income households, veterans, and some other vulnerable groups are exempt from copayments (Cheng 2003).

Taiwan's health-care system includes both public and private hospitals, with the latter more numerous. The majority of physicians work in hospitals on a salary basis; the remainder practice fee-for-service primary care in their own clinics. Private clinic doctors do not have hospital admitting privileges, and there is no referral system. Patients can freely choose among providers.

The social insurance program traditionally paid providers on a fee-for-service basis at a uniform rate. More recently, to address growing financing pressures, Taiwan's authorities introduced bundled payments for some hospital services and global budgets for separate components of health spending, as well as increased premiums and some copayments (Cheng 2003; Chee-Ruey Hsieh, chapter 5, this volume). The health insurance system has enjoyed a high public satisfaction rate.

Providers in Taiwan traditionally earned a large share of their revenue from dispensing medications, but reforms since 1997 have sought to separate prescription from dispensation, with mixed results. Pharmaceutical regulation has also figured prominently in general cost-containment efforts (Hsieh, chapter 5).

Australia

Australia is a high-income, highly urban economy with a population of 20.6 million in 2006. Life expectancy is 78 years for men and 83 years for women. Leading causes of death are heart disease, stroke, and cancer. Morbidity and mortality rates are higher among people living in rural areas than in urban ones and especially among indigenous Australians. The population is aging, with 12.8 percent of the population aged 65 and over (Healy, Sharman, and Lokuge 2006).

Australia spends 9.7 percent of GDP on health, representing $3,652 per capita in terms of purchasing power parity, slightly above the OECD average. Since 1984, Australian Medicare has provided unlimited subsidized access to the doctor of choice for out-of-hospital care, subsidized prescription drugs, and free public hospital care. Financing (about 68 percent public) comes from general taxation, a small insurance levy, private insurance, and out-of-pocket payments. The Medicare levy is 1.5 percent of taxable income above a certain income threshold, with an additional 1 percent surcharge for high-income earners who choose not to buy private insurance (Healy, Sharman, and Lokuge 2006).

The private sector delivers most of the primary and specialist medical care and runs private hospitals. The public sector provides some primary health care and includes public hospitals and public health programs. The majority of doctors in Australia are engaged in private practice. Additionally, private health insurance funds are heavily subsidized by a tax rebate on premiums. Private hospitals are traditionally smaller than public ones, deal with a more limited range of cases, rarely offer emergency services, and undertake a substantial amount of elective surgery. More than two-thirds of all private hospital beds are owned by large for-profit chains and by the Catholic Church (Healy, Sharman, and Lokuge 2006).

Doctors can choose to "bulk-bill" Australia's Medicare program, charging no more than the Medicare rebate and receiving payment from Medicare directly; there is no out-of-pocket cost for the patient. Patients must pay the difference if the doctor charges more than the rebate. Free treatment under Medicare at a public hospital is provided by doctors nominated by the hospital. Treatment as a private patient allows a choice of doctor. For patients in private hospitals, Medicare pays 75 percent of the schedule fee for medical services. Private health insurance covers spending that is not covered by Medicare, such as treatment and accommodation as private patients in hospitals; the gap between the Medicare benefit and fees charged for inpatients; and charges for ancillary services. Primary medical care provided by doctors is not covered by private insurance (Healy, Sharman, and Lokuge 2006).

Australia's Pharmaceutical Benefits Scheme has aimed, since 1948, to provide "timely access to the medicines that Australians need, at a cost individuals and the community can afford." Patients make a copayment for drugs depending on income. The scheme is an international pioneer in adopting economic evaluation in benefit decisions (Healy, Sharman, and Lokuge 2006).

India

India is the second most populous country in the world, with 1.1 billion people diverse in ethnicity, religion, and language. Although a rapidly developing economy, poverty persists, and there are large regional variations in income. For example, residents of New Delhi—the richest city in India—have an average per capita income of $532, which is more than double that of the rest of the country (Das and Hammer 2007a and 2007b).

According to the WHO, communicable diseases account for 38 percent of India's disease burden. Maternal and child-health issues, such as malnutrition, are prevalent. Noncommunicable diseases have also become major health problems, accounting for 53 percent of all deaths in people between the ages of 30 and 59. There are significant differences in health outcomes between rich and poor. Many factors account for this difference, such as nutrition, education, hygiene, and quality of health care (Das and Hammer 2007a).

India spends about 5 percent of its GDP on health. Of this, the government contributes 18 percent, and 82 percent comes from out-of-pocket payments (WHO National Health Account, 2005). Public-sector services are financed through taxes and other revenue. India's public health-care expenditure is among the bottom 20 percent of countries (Peters et al. 2002).

India's health-care delivery system consists of private providers and public central, state, and local hospitals and first-responder primary health centers. Visits to private providers constitute 82 percent of all visits. There is no medical insurance scheme, except for the free service in the public health system; thus, families incur high out-of-pocket costs in the private system (Das and Hammer 2007a).

Despite India's low GDP per capita, Indian residents visit the doctor more frequently than Americans do (Banerjee et al. 2004), and the poor visit doctors more than the rich (Das and Hammer 2007a).

The World Bank has described the public health-care sector in India as underfunded and not large enough to meet current health needs (Peters et al. 2002). The system is overly centralized, bureaucratic, inflexible, and poorly managed. It is widely perceived to provide poor treatment and also suffers from high absentee rates among public-sector providers (Das and Hammer 2007b).

At the same time, many private providers are unlicensed (Deshpande et al.). There are also a large number of traditional health practitioners. Incentives in the public and private sectors do not promote high-quality care. For example, according to one study, providers ask patients only 22 percent of the questions that a qualified provider should ask to provide appropriate diagnosis and treatment for a specific disease—26 percent for tuberculosis and 18 percent for diarrhea (Das and Hammer 2007a and 2007b).

China

With over 1.3 billion people, China is the most populous country in the world. Life expectancy has increased to 73.2 years from 50 in the 1960s and 65 in the 1970s. Health improvements vary greatly by income and geographic location. Among those covered by the Maternal and Child Health Surveillance System in 2003, for example, maternal mortality was 73 per 10,000 live births among the poorest fifth, compared to 17 per 10,000 live births in the richest fifth (Wagstaff and Lindelow 2008).

China spends about 5.6 percent of GDP on health, comparable to economies of similar per capita GDP. But until recently, the majority of spending was made up of private out-of-pocket payments, and only 20 percent was spent in rural areas, where most of the population still lives (Evans and Xu 2008).

Before economic reform, universal affordable basic health care had been provided in rural areas by the Cooperative Medical System (CMS), a government insurance scheme for government employees and teachers. In urban areas, employees and their dependents received their health care through firm-based schemes. CMS covered 90 percent of the rural population in the late 1970s (Yip and Hsiao 2008). As a result of rural economic reform in 1979, CMS disappeared, and 90 percent of peasants became uninsured. In urban areas, a social health insurance scheme financed by employer and employee contributions replaced the previous government and worker schemes, but only formal employees, not their dependents or migrant workers, were eligible (Yip and Hsiao 2008; Eggleston 2008). In 2006 only 27 percent of urban residents received coverage under the scheme (Ministry of Labor and Social Security 2007).

Under this system, the average cost of a single inpatient episode represented 60 percent of annual household per capita consumption (Wagstaff and Lindelow 2008). The cost of health care led to the impoverishment of 5.2 percent of households, or 67.5 million people, disproportionately in rural areas (Evans and Xu 2008). Out-of-pocket payments have been common even for preventive public health services (Wagstaff and Lindelow 2008). Such access barriers have contributed to the problem of oversupply in China's health-care delivery system. Bed occupancy rates (60 percent) and the number of cases per bed per year are the second lowest of the OECD countries, behind Turkey and Japan, respectively (Wagstaff and Lindelow 2008).

Recently, under the Chinese government's broader goal of a "harmonious society," health has become a high priority. In 2003 a medical assistance safety net scheme was implemented to further assist specific vulnerable groups. Between 2006 and 2007, the central government's health budget rose 87 percent (Yip and Hsiao 2008). The government put in place social insurance programs designed to fill the gaps in coverage—the New CMS (NCMS) in rural areas and a pilot program for other urban residents—with a goal of achieving universal basic coverage by 2010 (Yiyong Yang, chapter 9, this volume). Over the next several years, in order to provide universal basic coverage, the Chinese government has committed to triple government funding for health care by 1 to 1.5 percent of GDP.

The NCMS aims to protect rural residents against catastrophic health expenses and impoverishment. Benefit packages vary by county, with copayments ranging from 30 to 80 percent of charges; counties cover different inpatient and outpatient services, but all programs must be voluntary and cover some expenses for catastrophic illness. The NCMS has increased health-care utilization but has apparently not reduced out-of-pocket spending (Evans and Xu 2008; Wagstaff and Lindelow 2008). And because the benefits coverage of the new insurance scheme for urban residents is limited, its effect on out-of-pocket payments has likewise been constrained. Providers are paid mostly on a fee-for-service basis according to a government-set fee schedule, with low fees for basic services and higher fees for high-tech diagnostic procedures and for dispensing pharmaceuticals. Hospitals and clinics derive substantial income from drug sales to their patients (Sun et al. 2008). A few localities have experimented with different forms of provider payment, including global budgets, diagnosis-related groups, and capitation payments.

In urban areas, consumers prefer large tertiary hospitals over primary care physicians, although the government has recently tried to promote community health centers. Reforms announced in April 2009 call for prescribing and dispensing of drugs to be separated, for an essential drug list to be established, and for drug production and distribution systems to be improved. Broader reforms are also in store, which will increase government financing, expand social insurance toward universal coverage, improve public health services, reform public hospitals, and encourage private investments in the health sector.

Overview of the Book

The first section of the book features analysis of the pharmaceutical policies of seven health-care systems of the Asia-Pacific. Chapter 1, by Soonman Kwon, provides an overview of pharmaceutical policy in South Korea, focusing on the contentious pharmaceutical reform of 2000. Previously, physicians and pharmacists both prescribed and dispensed drugs in Korea, but the reform mandated that the two tasks be separated. The goal was to change providers' economic incentives by eliminating their profit from dispensing drugs—up to that point a major source of their income. When the president and civic groups succeeded in quickly setting the reform agenda, the medical profession was unable to block it. But a series of nationwide physician strikes forced the government to modify critical elements of the reform package and to raise medical fees substantially. Kwon argues that the reform resulted in little behavioral change among physicians and smaller net social benefits than expected, primarily because it failed to provide physicians with a financial incentive to prescribe in a cost-effective manner. Recently, the Korean government has implemented several policy measures for pharmaceutical cost containment. These include price negotiation between the National Health Insurance Corporation and pharmaceutical manufacturers, and economic evaluation for positive listing of reimbursable drugs. Until it finds a way to change the prescribing behavior of physicians, however, Kwon concludes that the South Korean government will probably fail to contain rapidly increasing pharmaceutical expenditures.

Chapter 2, by Toshiaki Iizuka, focuses on the economics of pharmaceutical pricing and physician prescribing in Japan. The Japanese government regulates consumer prescription drug prices using a unique dynamic rule called Yakka Kijyun, which updates regulated retail prices based on the previous period's transaction prices. Other aspects of Japan's policies are not unique. For example, as in many regions of East Asia, Japan's separation of prescribing and dispensing has historically been weak. Indeed, at the end of 2007, 40 percent of all prescriptions were filled at hospital and clinic pharmacies.

Iizuka describes in detail recent empirical evidence of how physician prescribing is influenced by price-cost markups—the difference between the doctor's cost of purchasing a drug and the price at which he or she sells the drug to a patient. In particular, Iizuka discusses two of his recent studies that investigate the effect of pharmaceutical policy on physician prescribing. These studies provide compelling evidence that profit margins impact the prescribing behavior of Japanese physicians, in one case affecting the choice of hypertension drug and in the other influencing the choice between brand-name and generic drugs. At the same time, evidence suggests that Japanese doctors do care about the cost of the drug to the patient.

Iizuka's econometric estimates provide some of the first quantitative evidence on the extent to which the integration of prescribing and dispensing, common in many economies of the Asia-Pacific, distorts prescribing behavior. For example, he finds that the average doctor is willing to forgo one dollar of markup in exchange for a twenty-eight-cent reduction in patient cost. A counterfactual simulation suggests that expenditures on drugs are inflated by 10.6 percent due to overprescribing and by another 4.4 percent by the substitution of more expensive drugs that offer higher markups. Iizuka's chapter concludes with a brief discussion of recent changes in Japan's pharmaceutical policy, including a new prescription pad to promote generic substitution and new pricing rules to provide greater rewards for innovative or high-quality drugs.

In chapter 3, Naoko Tomita describes the political economy of separating prescribing from dispensing in Japan. She traces a long historical trajectory of efforts to separate the two tasks, from an 1874 Meiji government law through another law in the 1950s that generated strong protests from the Japan Medical Association to the manipulation of medical and pharmaceutical fee schedules since the mid-1970s. She describes the decision-making process behind health and pharmaceutical policy in Japan and discusses its relationship to the gradual separation of prescribing from dispensing and the continued growth of pharmaceutical expenditures despite strong attempts at cost containment.

The third economy covered is Thailand. In chapter 4, Sauwakon Ratanawijitrasin provides a comprehensive overview of the last three decades of Thai pharmaceutical policies, from now defunct budgeting rules to more recent procurement policies to the controversial issuing of compulsory licenses for seven pharmaceutical products. After briefly describing the Thai pharmaceutical sector, Ratanawijitrasin summarizes five key aspects of Thai government pharmaceutical policies: procurement, production, price, payment, and patents. She then analyzes the causes, contents, contexts, consequences, and controversies surrounding these policies. Arguing that Thailand enacted patent laws not for intellectual property protection but for international trade promotion, she notes that the government must strongly commit to investing in domestic industrial production if it is to benefit from its patent laws.

In chapter 5, Chee-Ruey Hsieh provides an overview of pharmaceutical policy in Taiwan, using drug policies to illustrate how policymakers in a rapidly growing economy with universal health insurance struggle to balance the short-run cost impacts and long-run health benefits of increasing health care. Hsieh first examines the evolution of pharmaceutical policy in Taiwan by focusing on three specific issues: reimbursement policy, the separation of prescribing and dispensing since 1997, and pharmaceutical innovation. Hsieh highlights the economic trade-offs associated with policies in each arena and the empirical evidence of their impacts. He then analyzes several options for reforming the pharmaceutical reimbursement policy in Taiwan and discusses the policy implications of his findings.

The fifth economy covered in the book—Australia—is actually a continent and a pioneer in pharmaceutical benefit coverage policies. Australia's government subsidizes more than 70 percent of all prescriptions through the Pharmaceutical Benefits Scheme (PBS). In chapter 6, Hans Löfgren describes the evolution of a half-century of pharmaceutical policy in Australia, identifying three phases: state dominance and decommodification (1951–1987), pluralist bargaining (1987–1996), and then the uneven advance of neoliberalism. Löfgren's account begins with the founding of the PBS and then covers the 1987–1999 Factor Scheme, which supported the expansion of drug production, exports, and R&D (the single largest program ever administered by the Australian Department of Industry). The chapter continues with a description of Australia's pioneering of cost-effectiveness analysis in pharmaceutical purchasing under the PBS, the systematic application of reference pricing, and the 1994–1995 adoption of the National Medicines Policy. It concludes with a discussion of the recent controversies surrounding pharmaceutical pricing within the Australia–United States Free Trade Agreement. Löfgren argues that although globalization and the reconfiguration of the international drug industry have made the pharmaceutical policy domain more fluid, regulatory issues are typically managed through cooperative exchange within relatively closed networks of core stakeholders in Australia. That subsidy arrangements were never devolved to regional government partly explains the PBS's capacity to effectively withstand lobbying against it.

Chapter 7, by Mark Johnston and Richard Zeckhauser, provides a conceptual framework for understanding how regulated insurance coverage, rather than direct drug price controls, can achieve regulators' equity and efficiency objectives while benefiting pharmaceutical firms and patients alike. Although Johnston and Zeckhauser focus on Australia's PBS as it operated in the 1980s, their analysis has broad relevance. Schemes with many similar features operate in several European countries as well as in Canada and New Zealand (Wright 2004), and developing and middle-income countries in the Asia-Pacific have shown interest in introducing elements of such a system.

The Johnston and Zeckhauser model draws on basic microeconomics and game theory to elucidate the interaction between regulators and pharmaceutical firms in what the writers term "an ingenious price-contingent subsidy scheme," which turns deadweight loss (due to pricing above marginal cost) into consumer surplus. In the stylized model, the government offers pharmaceutical companies a per unit subsidy for selling their products at marginal cost. The subsidy is calibrated to enable the companies to recover what they would otherwise receive in monopoly profits. When two or more firms possess market power for a particular therapeutic use, the subsidy scheme creates a game—in effect a race—to determine who joins first and reaps most of the benefits. Properly constructed, the game transfers significant oligopoly profits to consumers.

Several key insights from the Johnston and Zeckhauser analysis—such as the use of the PBS to make transfers to pharmaceutical firms in return for agreeing to be regulated, and the regulators' role in achieving greater consumer surplus for patients—hold true in more complicated models of Australia's system, such as the five-stage game developed by Wright (2004).[5] Although Australia no longer focuses exclusively on achieving low pharmaceutical prices, and has pioneered the use of cost-effectiveness analysis in benefits coverage since the early 1990s, the analytic framework developed in chapter 7 remains instructive for understanding the trade-offs facing government regulators in structuring pharmaceutical benefits for their citizens.

India is the sixth economy examined in this volume. In chapter 8, Chirantan Chatterjee discusses the evolution of India's patent regime and its implications for the development of India's pharmaceutical industry. Chatterjee traces the industry from its humble pre-1947 beginnings through the process patent period (between 1970 to 1995), when it rapidly developed, and into the era of strengthened intellectual property rights laws, during which India signed the WTO–TRIPs agreement and then implemented product patents in January 2005. He describes empirical studies of the impact that patent regime change had on firm innovation and concludes by comparing the development of India's thriving pharmaceutical industry with that of other countries, such as Japan, Italy, and South Korea.

In chapter 9, Yiyong Yang, director general of the Institute of Social Development Research in China's National Development and Reform Commission (NDRC), briefly summarizes the increasingly important role of the government in China's health sector. Public health subsidies will be increased significantly between 2009 and 2011 as China's reforms continue to unfold. New social insurance programs in rural and urban areas aim to achieve close to universal coverage within a few years, and the government recently announced a medical reform plan to restructure delivery and other aspects of the system in order to guarantee access to basic medical and health services for all Chinese by 2020. Yang describes how pharmaceutical reform fits in with this dynamic picture and argues that the reform should be open and transparent to be successful.

Chapter 10, by Mingzhi Li and Kai Reimers, presents an overview of the drug distribution and procurement process in China. The authors draw on an analytic framework and historical account that situate reforms within the broader debate

19

about how and why China chose to reform its health-care system the way it did during the transition from central planning to a market-based economy. As the authors note, critics of China's health sector reforms accuse the government of unleashing market forces in the absence of any effective regulatory framework, resulting in a chaotic and corrupt drug procurement process.

Each province (or province-level city) in China has discretion in implementing its own reforms, within the national guidelines. Li and Reimers present case studies of the centralized drug procurement processes in Beijing and Guangdong Province, paying specific attention to the stated goals and actual use of the e-commerce system. They find that although the centralized process is clearly technologically feasible and may have enhanced transactional efficiency, the e-commerce platforms are not used for their stated purpose: monitoring hospitals' compliance with drug procurement rules. Li and Reimers discuss how Oliver Williamson's model of transaction cost analysis applies to and illuminates the primary features of China's efforts to move drug procurement transactions into the e-commerce realm. They conclude that without significant and complementary reforms at both the macro- and micro- level of China's health sector, the centralized drug procurement process will likely continue to fall short of its intended goals.

In chapter 11, Qiang Sun and Qingyue Meng analyze key elements of China's pharmaceutical policy, especially the unintended (but predictable) consequences of physician incentives to prescribe according to profitability rather than clinical effectiveness. The authors also provide an overview of the domestic production and distribution sectors and describe how pharmaceutical policy reforms should be undertaken in conjunction with other reforms, especially those that pertain to hospital financing (to address the problematic system of medical care services supported by selling drugs). In addition to taking steps to remedy the perverse incentives of the current system, the government should, according to the authors, develop a monitoring and evaluation mechanism for pharmaceuticals, especially to monitor the availability of essential medicines in both rural and urban areas.

Yanfen Huang and Yiyong Yang analyze China's pharmaceutical price regulation policy in chapter 12. Citing NDRC documents, the authors describe the evolution of China's pharmaceutical pricing and current regulation policy. After assessing the effects of pharmaceutical price regulation and its associated problems, Huang and Yang offer policy suggestions for further reform. They recommend that China move away from pricing pharmaceuticals based on average social cost and instead consider economic evaluation and reference pricing. They also urge officials to establish an essential medicines system, which would strengthen the purchasing role of social insurance programs, and increase government fiscal support of the health sector.

Chapter 13, by Wei Wilson Zhang and Xue Liu, looks at China's pharmaceutical policy challenges from the perspective of the pharmaceutical industry. After a brief review of China's domestic industry structure and its regulatory context, Zhang and Liu draw on their recent study of drug policy in a large metropolitan area in China to describe challenges to quality, expenditure control, and access. They then analyze pharmaceutical industry incentives and behavior in light of current industrial and regulatory structures and discuss implications for regulatory reform. These authors suggest that China's authorities should impose direct and immediate supervision of corporate behaviors by tightening regulatory standards; approving only bioequivalent generics; enforcing compliance with existing standards of production, distribution, and marketing; and fixing policy loopholes that allow superficial differentiation of drug products. Long-term policy, they suggest, could then focus on changing the industry's structure and promoting innovative products and R&D capacity.

Michael A. Santoro and Caitlin M. Liu also examine the complexity and ineffectiveness of drug regulation in chapter 14, the final China-specific essay in the book. In particular, they address the problem of adulterated and misbranded drugs manufactured in China. After discussing recent reforms in drug regulatory structure and evaluating their likely impact, the authors conclude that both China's regulatory system and the current bilateral efforts between China and the United States to provide further regulation are inadequate to assure drug safety and quality. Santoro and Liu propose reforms to make the pharmaceutical supply chain more transparent, hold responsible parties accountable, and improve safety for global consumers.

The second section of the book highlights cross-cutting themes of prescribing cultures and access versus incentives for innovation. Chapter 15, by Maarten Bode, explores the marketing of traditional Ayurvedic medicines in India. Bode describes the dual rhetoric of modernity and tradition that advertisers invoke for Ayurvedic products, using a case study of the most successful such product, Chavanprash, to show how the marketing claims measure up against the scientific evidence regarding its effectiveness and that of its primary ingredient. His account covers Ayurvedic medicines and the knowledge tradition they embody; the "bypassing" of Ayurvedic physicians (*vaidyas*); and the rational use of Ayurvedic medicines, including considerations of quality, effectiveness, and the possible policy role of modern pharmacology.

Such analyses speak directly to the "prescribing cultures" evoked in the title of our book. Traditional herbal or humoral medical traditions established a set of norms for health, medical care, payment for services, and expectations regarding the role of medicines in health care. Such norms have shaped the evolution of modern health-care systems in India, China, and elsewhere in the Asia-Pacific. Incorporating these traditions into the modern regulatory and industrial market structures and subjecting them to effectiveness (and cost-effectiveness) analyses present many distinctive challenges. Understanding how each society chooses to address these challenges and assessing the relative strengths of a variety of policy approaches can provide important insights for other nations. Here, again, the benefit of comparative analysis seems apparent.

In chapter 16, Karen Eggleston and Bong-Min Yang examine the integration of prescribing and dispensing in comparative perspective, drawing in particular from the history of medicine and pharmacy in South Korea. To explain the institution of physician dispensing, the authors, both economists, use theories of vertical integration and game theory to sketch a conceptual framework that emphasizes shared beliefs and internalized norms. The persistence of physician dispensing illustrates how the incentive structures of current health-care systems are embedded in institutions shaped by culture and history.

In chapter 17, the last chapter to focus on prescribing cultures, Siaw-Teng Liaw describes the efforts to promote quality use of medicines in Australia, one of the four goals of the Australian National Medicines Policy. Liaw summarizes a wide body of literature on the topic, comparing regulation and practice in Australia with those of other Asia-Pacific health-care systems. He argues that prescribing patterns flow from a complex interplay of intrinsic and extrinsic factors, including public institutions, the pharmaceutical industry, the health profession, and consumers, and can be improved through well-implemented e-prescribing and decision-support systems. His analysis provides a natural segue into the final section of the book, on balancing appropriate access to medicines with incentives for innovation in new drug discovery.

In Chapter 18, Anita Wagner and Dennis Ross-Degnan describe the potential for insurance systems to increase access to and appropriate use of medicines. The chapter begins with an illustration of activities undertaken in the Philippines by the Medicines and Insurance Coverage (MedIC) initiative of the WHO's Collaborating Center in Pharmaceutical Policy. The authors argue that governments in the Asia-Pacific region can design pharmaceutical coverage policies within their broader health-care coverage systems to address many of the supply- and demand-side factors that contribute to patients failing to obtain the medicines they need in a timely manner and at an affordable price. The MedIC initiative seeks to support the development, implementation, and evaluation of evidence-based medicine coverage policies in the Asia-Pacific, which in turn can contribute to individual health, household economic security, health-care system efficiency, and economic productivity.

Both the discovery and the availability of pharmaceuticals are shaped by medicines coverage, patent protection, and other policies balancing access with incentives for innovation. Chapter 19 by John H. Barton and chapter 20 by Henry G. Grabowski, David B. Ridley, and Jeffrey L. Moe concentrate on the incentives for the discovery of new drugs. Barton proposes a bold compromise to address the global market failure in pharmaceuticals. The current system provides many pharmaceuticals for the wealthiest nations and few to meet the needs of the poorest, which often cannot afford the products that have been developed. This disparity has led to substantial debate. Barton suggests that the United States and other wealthy nations support a compromise "international orphan drug" approach. Developed-world governments would promise to pay an adequate price for pharmaceuticals—rather than forcing prices down to the level at which research is unprofitable—and to subsidize efforts to develop drugs for diseases found only in the developing world. All countries would cooperate to create an efficient generic market for drugs for the poorest nations, including for medicines that are still on-patent in the developed world. Developing countries would work with their higher-income counterparts to eliminate tax and customs barriers, strengthen controls on corruption and counterfeiting, and otherwise streamline the supply of drugs. Clearly, details of such a plan would need to be negotiated for it to be globally acceptable, and the nations of the Asia-Pacific would be critical to determining its fate.

As the largest pharmaceutical market in the world and the home to a considerable proportion of pharmaceutical industry R&D, the United States plays an extraordinarily important role in determining incentives for pharmaceutical innovation. In 2007, to stimulate research in diseases that affect the world's poorest citizens, the U.S. Congress created a novel program promoting "priority review vouchers." In chapter 20, the three Duke University professors upon whose proposal the legislation was based—Grabowski, Ridley, and Moe—discuss its evaluation and implementation. They estimate that the vouchers—which reward developers of drugs for neglected diseases with a voucher for priority FDA review of a different drug—could be worth hundreds of millions of dollars based on the time value of money associated with faster reviews, increases in effective patent life, and early-mover advantages vis-à-vis competitors. The vouchers could therefore be a powerful stimulant for developing new drugs for neglected diseases, complementing other mechanisms such as public-private partnerships and advanced market commitment incentive programs. As was true for the Orphan Drug Act, Europe and Japan could pass their own variants of the concept, further fueling innovation for neglected diseases.

In the conclusion, F. M. Scherer provides a critical overview of the contributions assembled in this book. As one indicator of industry dynamics and relative success in global terms, he presents data on economies' success in developing pharmaceutical manufacturing and in exporting to the United States. The forte of India (the sixteenth largest pharmaceutical importer to the United States) has been low-priced generic drugs. In Scherer's estimation, India's ethical drug producers are likely to continue making inroads into the U.S. market, despite the recent loss of generic sales advantages. Japan (the twelfth pharmaceutical importer to the United States) posted weak performance relative to its potential, possibly because of low standards for new drug product approval, fragmentation of innovative effort on minor local products, and reluctance to deal with FDA approval hurdles and establish extensive sales networks in the United States (also see Reich 1990).

Scherer comments on two overriding themes in the book: the dominant role that physicians play in dispensing medicines and the effect that various government price controls have on the pharmaceutical industry. He brings historical and comparative knowledge to bear in discussing many of the book's key themes: the distribution system and drug prices of China, drug price regulation in the Asia-Pacific region, global controversies over patent protection and compulsory licensing, and the challenges of regulating industries that have not developed scale economies. His conclusions suggest a broad agenda for future research and policy analysis, including how further study of pharmaceutical policies in the Asia-Pacific could make a significant contribution to U.S. policy deliberations.

Notes

[1] However, even in such systems, physicians can use renewing or adjusting prescriptions to stimulate additional patient visits, especially if paid on a fee-for-service basis. This is one reason why physician drug budgets have been used to considerable effect in some European economies (Danzon 1997:24).

[2] Indeed, in Wolinsky (1993), whether reputation and customer search function to discipline providers depends on search-cum-diagnosis costs. For example, specialization is more likely when search-cum-diagnosis costs are smaller. In other words, if many experts locate next door to one another and all offer "free" diagnosis, this allows both shopping for treatment and associated consumer demand discipline on providers' prices and recommendation strategies. (In this model, specialization does not have to do with investing in diagnosis skills; it is a way to deal with information asymmetry and commitment not to defraud—because providers specializing in low-cost treatments have to refer patients to other providers for the high-cost treatments.) Moreover, in Wolinsky's model, a reputational equilibrium can be sustained only if search-cum-diagnosis costs are not too low (p. 391).

[3] A whole range of pharmaceutical policies can be examined as case studies in difficult questions of ethics and distributional justice (Santoro and Gorrie 2005).

[4] For an excellent concise overview of the "global drug gap," see Reich 2000.

[5] Both Johnston and Zeckhauser (chapter 7, this volume) and Wright (2004) assume that pharmaceutical innovation is exogenous and pharmaceutical manufacturers are foreign firms. The observation that Australian regulators do take international prices into account when setting their own prices may indicate not an ignorance of the economic logic of the scheme as Wright suggests, but rather regulators' consideration of forces not included in the models (but discussed briefly in chapter 7), such as the credibility of property rights regimes and international relations with countries that are home to large research-based pharmaceutical firms.

References

Afendulis, Christopher C., and Daniel P. Kessler. 2007. Tradeoffs from integrating diagnosis and treatment in markets for health care. *American Economic Review* 97 (3): 1013–20.

Banerjee, A. V., A. Deaton, and E. Duflo. 2004. Wealth, health, and health services in rural Rajasthan. *American Economic Review* 94 (2): 326–30.

Cheng, Tsung-Mei. 2003. Taiwan's new national health insurance program: Genesis and experience so far. *Health Affairs* 22 (3): 61–76.

Danzon, P. M. 1997. *Pharmaceutical price regulation: National policies versus global interests.* Washington, D.C.: American Enterprise Institute Press.

Das, J., and J. Hammer. 2007a. Location, location, location: Residence, wealth, and the quality of medical care in Delhi, India. *Health Affairs* Web Exclusive, March 27. http://content.healthaffairs.org/cgi/content/abstract/26/3/w338.

———. 2007b. Money for nothing: The dire straits of medical practice in India. *Journal of Development Economics* 83 (1): 1–36.

Deshpande, K., Ravi Shankar, V. Diwan, K. Lonnroth, V. K. Mahadik, and R. K.Chandorkar. 2004. Spatial pattern of private health-care provision in Ujjain, India: A provider survey processed and analysed with a geographical information system. *Health Policy* 68: 211–22.

Eggleston, K. 2009. Kan Bing Nan, Kan Bing Gui: Challenges for China's health-care system thirty years into reform. In *Growing pains: Tension and opportunity in China's transformation*, ed. Jean C. Oi, Scott Rozelle, and Xueguang Zhou. Stanford, CA: Walter H. Shorenstein Asia-Pacific Research Center.

Evans, David B., and Ke Xu. 2008. Funding public health. In *Public finance in China: Reform and growth for a harmonious society*, ed. Jiwei Lou and Shuilin Wang, 255–64. Washington, D.C.: World Bank.

Gruber, Jonathan, and Maria Owings. 1996. Physician financial incentives and cesarean section delivery. *Rand Journal of Economics* 27 (1): 99–123.

Hanvoravongchai, Piya, and William C. Hsiao. 2007. Thailand: Achieving universal coverage with social insurance. In *Social health insurance for developing nations*, ed. Hsiao and Shaw, 133–54. Washington, D.C.: World Bank.

Healy, J., E. Sharman, and B. Lokuge. 2006. Australia: Health system review. *Health Systems in Transition* 8 (5): 1–158.

Hughes, David, and Leethongdee Songkramchai. 2007. Universal coverage in the land of smiles: Lessons from Thailand's 30 baht health reforms. *Health Affairs* 26 (4): 999–1008.

Iizuka, T. 2007. Experts' agency problems: Evidence from the prescription drug market in Japan. *RAND Journal of Economics* 38 (3): 844–62.

Ikegami, N., and J. C. Campbell. 1995. Medical care in Japan. *The New England Journal of Medicine* 333 (19): 1295–99.

———. 2004. Japan's health-care system: Containing costs and attempting reform. *Health Affairs* 23 (3): 26–36.

Jeong, H., and J. Hurst. 2001. An assessment of the performance of the Japanese health-care system. OECD *Labor Market and Social Policy Occasional Papers* 56, OECD Publishing. doi:10.1787/445332508603. http://econpapers.repec.org/paper/oecelsaaa/56-en.htm.

Johnston, M., and R. Zeckhauser. 1991. The Australian pharmaceutical subsidy gambit: Transmuting dead-weight loss and oligopoly rents to consumer surplus. National Bureau of Economic Research Working Paper 3783, http://www.nber.org/papers/w3783.pdf.

Kim, Hak-Ju, and Jennifer Prah Ruger. 2008. Pharmaceutical reform in South Korea and the lessons it provides. *Health Affairs* 27 (4): w260–w269. http://content.healthaffairs.org/cgi/content/abstract/hlthaff.27.4.w260.

Kwon, Soonman. 2005. Korea. In *Comparative health policy in the Asia-Pacific*, ed. Robin Gauld, chapter 3. New York: Open Univ. Press.

Kwon, S., and M. R. Reich. 2005. The changing process and politics of health policy in Korea. *Journal of Health Politics, Policy and Law* 30 (6): 1003–26.

Lou, J., and S. Wang. 2008. Public Finance in China: Reform and Growth for a Harmonious Society. Washington, D.C.: World Bank.

Ministry of Labor and Social Security (People's Republic of China). 2007. *The statistical report on the development of labor and social security in 2006.* http://www.molss.gov.cn/gb/news/2007-05/18/content_178167.htm.

Mossialos, Elias, Monique Mrazek, and Tom Walley. 2004. Regulating pharmaceuticals in Europe: Striving for efficiency, equity, and quality. New York: McGraw-Hill International.

Noguchi, H., S. Shimizutani, and Y. Masuda. 2008. Regional variations in medical expenditure and hospitalization days for heart attack patients in Japan: Evidence from the Tokai Acute Myocardial Study (TAMIS). *International Journal of Health Care Finance and Economics* 8 (2): 123–44.

Nomura, H., and T. Nakayama. 2005. The Japanese health-care system. *BMJ (Clinical Research Ed.)* 331(7518): 648–49.

Organisation of Economic Co-operation and Development. 2008a. *Health data 2008: How Does Japan Compare.* http://www.oecd.org/dataoecd/45/51/38979974.pdf.

———. 2008b. *Health Data 2008: How Does Korea Compare.* http://www.oecd.org/dataoecd/46/10/38979986.pdf.

Peters, D. H., Abdo S. Yazbeck, Adam Wagstaff, G. N. V. Ramana, Lant H. Pritchett, and Rashmi R. Sharma. 2002. *Better health systems for India's poor: Findings, analysis, and options.* Washington, D.C.: World Bank Publications.

Ratanawijitrasin, Sauwakon. 2005. *Health insurance: An in-depth guide.* Bangkok: Chulalongkorn Univ. Press.

Reich, M. R. 1990. Why the Japanese don't export more pharmaceuticals: Health policy as industrial policy. *Journal of Research in Pharmaceutical Economics* 2 (3): 57.

———. 2000. The global drug gap. *Science* 28 (5460): 1979.

Santoro, M. A., and T. M. Gorrie. 2005. *Ethics and the Pharmaceutical Industry.* Cambridge: Cambridge Univ. Press.

Sloan, Frank A., and Chee-Ruey Hsieh. 2007. *Pharmaceutical innovation: Incentives, competition, and cost-benefit analysis in international perspective.* New York: Cambridge Univ. Press.

Sun, Qiang, Michael A. Santoro, Qingyue Meng, Caitlin Liu, and Karen Eggleston. 2008. Pharmaceutical policy in China. *Health Affairs* 27 (4): 1042–50; 10.1377/hlthaff.27.4.1042.

Wagstaff, Adam, and Magnus Lindelow. 2008. Health reform in rural China: Challenges and options, chapter 13. In Lou and Wang 2008, 265–86.

Wolinsky, Asher. 1993. Competition in a market for informed experts' services. *RAND Journal of Economics* 24(3): 380–98. http://links.jstor.org/sici?sici=0741-261%28199323%2924%3A3%3C380%3ACIAMFI%3E2.0.CO%3B2-O.

WHO (World Health Organization). 2005. *National health accounts.* http://www.who.int/nha/en/.

———. 2007. *Country cooperation strategy: Thailand.* http://www.who.int/countryfocus/cooperation_strategy/ccs_tha_en.pdf.

WHO Western Pacific Region. 2007. *Statistical tables.* http://www.wpro.who.int/NR/rdonlyres/7BA135DF-394C-42A4-83A9-E020D65A61C2/0/StatisticalTables07.pdf.

Wright, D. J. 2004. The drug bargaining game: Pharmaceutical regulation in Australia. *Journal of Health Economics* 23 (4): 785–813.

Yip, Winnie, and William C. Hsiao. 2008. The Chinese health system at a crossroads. *Health Affairs* 27 (2): 460–68.

PHARMACEUTICAL POLICY IN SEVEN ASIA-PACIFIC HEALTH-CARE SYSTEMS

SOUTH KOREA

PHARMACEUTICAL POLICY IN SOUTH KOREA

Soonman Kwon

As patients age and financial barriers to use are removed, the resultant growth of drug consumption and spending can negatively impact the financial sustainability of a nation's health-care system (Davis 1997). South Korea (hereafter Korea) is facing these challenges and more. Before 2000, physicians and pharmacists were allowed to both prescribe and dispense drugs; driven by economic incentives, this resulted in drug overuse and overspending. But despite an urgent need, the strong opposition of physicians and pharmacists was a critical and longtime barrier to reform.

On July 1, 2000, the Korean government mandated the separation of drug prescription and dispensation. The reform aimed to fundamentally change the inefficient pattern of pharmaceutical provision and consumption, reduce the resultant overuse and misuse of drugs, and contain pharmaceutical expenditures. But the reform triggered severe physician strikes, since profits from drug prescriptions had been a major source of physicians' income. These strikes distorted the contents of the pharmaceutical reform and reduced the social benefits from the policy change, which in turn affected government plans for other health-care reforms.

In this chapter, I examine the pharmaceutical reform in Korea—including the separation of drug prescribing from dispensing—and evaluate its impacts. I analyze several aspects of the reform, including its context, contents, policy formulation, implementation, and evaluation. I also evaluate the impact of the pharmaceutical reform on physician behavior and the pharmaceutical market. In particular, I look at how the new policy affected vested economic interests and thus changed the pharmaceutical sector—and the entire health-care system—in Korea. I also address more recent changes to Korean pharmaceutical policy such as pharmaceutical pricing and economic evaluation.

The Pharmaceutical Reform: Context and Contents

Korea's national health insurance provides universal coverage of its population. Rapid expansion of population coverage was made at the expense of limited-benefit coverage with low contributions. Despite social insurance for health care, public financing accounts for less than 60 percent of total health-care expenditures in Korea.[1] Health-care providers are reimbursed on a fee-for-service basis. Since fees are strictly regulated, physicians have strong incentives to provide more profitable services and higher-margin products (that is, drugs)—in other words, those services and products for which the difference between the government reimbursement and actual cost is the greatest.

Profit-maximizing behavior is the norm among health-care providers because the private sector dominates health-care delivery in Korea. Hospitals have little to do with community-based financing or the nonprofit sector; in most cases, entrepreneurial physicians have expanded the scale of their clinics to form hospitals. The roles of physician clinics and hospitals are not differentiated, and outpatient clinics are a major source of profit for most hospitals. Membership in the medical and hospital associations overlap since physicians are also owners and managers of hospitals. The associations have long been strong allies against government health-care policy in general and reimbursement policy reforms in particular.

Physicians and pharmacists both prescribed and dispensed drugs until 2000. Pharmacists have long played the role of primary health-care providers, evident when comparing the number of pharmacies with that of physician clinics. The practice of Oriental medicine, in which the roles of physicians and pharmacists are not differentiated, is an important influence across East Asia; physicians traditionally both prescribed and dispensed drugs in China, Japan, Korea, and Taiwan. Traditional treatment in Korea depends a lot on medication, contributing to people's perception that the fees they pay are compensation for drugs rather than for physician labor (consultation).

The Need for Reform

Without the separation of drug prescribing and dispensing, physicians and pharmacists had financial incentives not necessarily in the best interests of their patients. Missing were the checks and balances between pharmacists and physicians prescribing drugs. Nor did patients have access to information on the type and amount of medication prescribed to them. By separating drug prescription from dispensation, reforms aimed to reduce the overuse and misuse of drugs, improve the quality of the prescription process, and address patients' right to know about their medications.

From the perspective of economic theory, separation is not necessarily superior to the integration of drug prescribing and dispensing (see the introduction and chapter 16, Eggleston and Yang, this volume). But in Korea, this separation had more important policy implications than a simple division of labor. Since the fees for medical services were strictly regulated, dispensing drugs was more profitable for physicians than providing their own services. The government set prices for insured drugs on the basis of data reported by pharmaceutical manufacturers and wholesalers. Physicians, however, purchased drugs at prices much lower than those that insurers reimbursed. This high profit margin induced physicians to prescribe and dispense more drugs. For internal medicine, almost 50 percent of the revenue of physician clinics came from pharmaceuticals. For family medicine, dermatology, urology, and pediatrics, the revenue from drugs accounted for more than 40 percent of total revenue

(Ministry of Health and Welfare, MOHW, 2000). In tertiary and general hospitals, drug revenue represented 43.7 percent and 45.4 percent, respectively, of total revenue. The mandatory separation of drug prescribing and dispensing thus promised to substantially reduce hospital profits.

To increase these profits, both physicians and pharmacists preferred whatever drugs were offered by pharmaceutical manufacturers and wholesalers at below the rates reimbursed by insurers. In other words, providers' selections of drugs did not necessarily depend on quality or cost-effectiveness—and physicians had a strong incentive to overprescribe. As a result, Koreans consumed more drugs than people in other developed countries. In the mid-1990s, pharmaceutical spending accounted for 31 percent of total health-care expenditures in Korea, whereas that in Organisation for Economic Co-operation and Development (OECD) countries was below 20 percent on average (OECD 1995). In 2004 pharmaceuticals still accounted for 27.4 percent of health expenditures in Korea (figure 1.1).

Figure 1.1 The Proportion of Pharmaceutical Spending in Health-care Expenditure in OECD countries, 2004 (%)

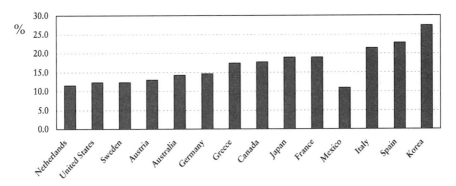

Source: Author's analysis.

While these problems were long recognized, reform seemed impossible due to the strong opposition of physicians and pharmacists. Physicians sought to retain their right to dispense drugs, since it was a major source of income. Pharmacists also favored the combined system because they wanted to keep the right to prescribe. Under the authoritarian regime, when bureaucrats played the major role in making health policy decisions, physicians and pharmacists could influence policymaking and effectively block change. But the new government and democratizated policy process of the late 1990s provided a window of opportunity for finally separating drug dispensation from prescription (Kwon and Reich 2005).

The Substance of the Reform[2]

Drug Classification

Physicians favored classifying more drugs as prescription drugs, whereas pharmacists wanted more to be classified as nonprescription drugs. An increase in nonprescription drugs would result in consumer savings, in terms of both time and money. When classification changes increase access to medication, the role of the pharmacist is likely to be strengthened. This in turn affects the boundaries between pharmacist and physician. As of 2000, 61.5 percent of drugs (17,187 items) were classified as prescription drugs and 38.5 percent (10,775 items) as nonprescription drugs (MOHW 2000). Physicians in Korea strongly maintained that convenience stores be allowed to sell some nonprescription drugs, believing this would reduce pharmacists' influence on drug consumption.

The Role of the Pharmacist

Physicians were concerned that their prescriptions would be revealed to pharmacists, who could then use this information to mixing nonprescription drugs in their own way (so-called quasi-prescribing). It is very hard to differentiate such quasi-prescribing from providing explanations and recommendations to consumers, both of which are basic functions of pharmacists. Physicians were worried that the greater the proportion of nonprescription drugs, the more likely that pharmacists would quasi-prescribe.

Brand-name Prescriptions

Under the mandatory separation policy in Korea, physicians can prescribe either brand-name or generic drugs. Pharmacists can substitute generic for brand-name drugs only when a generic substitute—verified by a bioequivalence test—is available. Patient consent is necessary, and the pharmacist should inform the physician of the substitution afterwards. When pharmacists have little scope to substitute generic drugs, physicians' strong influence over the selection of brand-name drugs can induce pharmaceutical manufacturers to continue unfair trade practices and to provide commissions to physicians. To promote cost-effective drugs in Korea, it is essential to increase the role of the bioequivalence test and expand the list of generic substitutes for brand-name drugs. Financial incentives for pharmacists—such as higher dispensing fees for generic drugs—may also be necessary to increase generic substitution.

Hospital Outpatient Pharmacies

The mandatory separation of drug prescribing and dispensing was applied to all outpatient care units, and hospital outpatient pharmacies were closed. They reasoned that if former patients of a hospital outpatient unit were given a choice between the hospital and local pharmacies, many would choose the former because of convenience. But this would aggravate the distortion in health-care delivery in Korea, as patients would rush to outpatient units of large hospitals and cause wasteful competition between physician clinics and hospitals. And it is doubtful that hospital-based pharmacists would check physicians from prescribing drugs that increase hospital profits. Because of these reasons, the Korean Medical Association (KMA) lobbied to eliminate the hospital outpatient pharmacy. This issue triggered a conflict between the medical and hospital associations, traditionally strong allies.

Injectable Drugs

Initially, injectable drugs—prevalent in Korea—were also subject to mandatory separation. It is ironic that physician clinics, which are likely to treat less severe illnesses, depend more on injectable drugs than hospitals do. In the 1990s, 62 percent of visits to physician clinics involved injections, compared with only 8 percent of hospital outpatient visits (MOHW 2000). Even when physicians' disproportionate use of injectable drugs could not be justified, physicians forced the government to exempt many such drugs from mandatory separation, citing patient inconvenience.

Reform Implementation

Interest groups are especially influential when public understanding of policy reforms is relatively undeveloped (Jacobs 1992). This trend held true in Korea. Under the authoritarian regime, the public was more concerned about citizens' rights and overall economic development than health policy. When the political environment changed and the policymaking process was democratized, civic groups moved to block the dominance of the medical profession and set the reform agenda for pharmaceutical policy. But, at the same time, interest groups influenced policy implementation by exercising veto power with less political cost than before (Kwon and Reich 2005). For example, strikes by professionals would have been hardly imaginable under the authoritarian regime. Even after parliament passed a reform law, important implementation decisions were subject to physician influence. And the general public had difficulty understanding the details and implications of the separation process.

Physicians' strikes became the major stumbling block to pharmaceutical reform. In addition to elitism and strong esprit de corps, the high turnover rate of hospital physicians might explain the nationwide strikes that united doctors of all kinds. Except at university or large general hospitals, physicians working in hospitals are usually at an early stage of their careers and tend to open their own practices later. With their future in mind, hospital-employed physicians thus share the economic interests of office-based physicians. There is little differentiation between specialists and general practitioners in Korea, and most office-based physicians are board-certified specialists.

The strikes by physicians in the private sector panicked the health-care system, in part because public hospitals account for only about 10 percent of the hospital system. After a series of nationwide strikes, physicians gained a much stronger voice in policy decisions. They pushed the government to change the original version of the pharmaceutical reform package. They protected their right to prescribe brand-name drugs, increased the ratio of prescription drugs to nonprescription drugs, and overturned the government plan of including injection drugs in the reform package. Most notably, physician strikes drove the government to raise the reimbursement fees for physician services by 44 percent[3] as compensation for income loss caused by the pharmaceutical reform. This in turn contributed to the 2001 fiscal crisis affecting national health insurance (Kwon 2007).

The pharmaceutical industry, on the other hand, played a minor role in pharmaceutical reform. Before the reform, physicians preferred drugs that provided them with higher margins, and high-quality drugs did not necessarily have larger market shares. Consequently, the domestic pharmaceutical industry was structured inefficiently. Of more than 450 manufacturers, two-thirds were small companies with fewer than 100 employees and little capacity for research and development. Because the pharmaceutical reform would lead physicians to prescribe high-quality drugs, many small firms would have to exit the market, and the market share of domestic pharmaceutical companies was expected to decline. Although the pharmaceutical reform was more of a threat than an opportunity for domestic pharmaceutical manufacturers, they were too fragmented and weak to oppose the government.

Physicians' strikes against the pharmaceutical reform gave doctors increased political bargaining power. Physicians succeeded in overturning the government's plan to extend the diagnosis-related group (DRG) payment system to all health-care institutions (for inpatients). The DRG-based payment system had undergone pilot programs with volunteer providers, showed positive outcomes in terms of cost and quality, and was scheduled to be extended to all health-care providers for selected diagnoses (Kwon 2003b).

Effects of the Pharmaceutical Reform

According to a report by the Korea Institute for Health and Social Affairs (KIHASA 2002a), physicians' prescribing behavior changed little after reform. The percentage of insurance claims (made by physician clinics) that included prescriptions was 95.15 percent before the new policy and declined slightly to 92.99 percent and 92.64 percent in 2001 and 2002, respectively (table 1.1).[4] Almost all visits to physician clinics still resulted in prescriptions. These high postreform prescription rates were partly due to the separate fee that physicians received for writing a prescription, which gave them an incentive to prescribe rather than only consult.[5] In fact, average prescription days (the average number of medication days per prescription) increased from 5.05 days to 7.54

days in two years. The average number of medicines per prescription was 6.18 before the reform and was still 5.58 as of January 2002. On the other hand, the percentage of prescriptions that contain antibiotics—57.72 percent before reform—decreased to 45.06 percent. Yet physicians still prescribed antibiotics in almost half of all cases. True, there was a huge drop in the use of antibiotics for upper respiratory diseases, but this is not the complete picture. Physicians substituted stronger, newer antibiotics for old ones—the use of cephalosporin increased by 30 percent, while that of tetracyclines dropped by as much as 80 percent.[6]

Table 1.1 Change in Prescription Behavior among Physicians

	January 2000	January 2001	January 2002
Percentage of claims with prescriptions	95.15%	92.99%	92.64%
Number of prescription days per claim	5.05 days	6.18 days	7.54 days
Number of medicines per prescription	6.18	5.70	5.58
Percentage of claims with antibiotic prescription	57.72%	51.47%	45.06%
Percentage of high-priced medicines*	29.80%	37.48%	38.54%

Source: Korea Institute for Health and Social Affairs (KIHASA), Evaluation of the Separation of Drug Prescribing and Dispensing, 2002.
Notes:
* Number of high-priced medicines/number of medicines (per prescription).
+ New pharmaceutical policy was implemented in August 2000.

In its current form, the new policy is not likely to significantly change physician behavior or decrease pharmaceutical spending. The current reform package—particularly the rules governing brand-name prescription and the large proportion of prescription drugs (62 percent) compared with nonprescription drugs—grants too much power to physicians and limits the role of generic drugs. More importantly, while the separation of drug prescribing and dispensing reduces the incentive to overprescribe, it does not encourage doctors to prescribe cost-effective drugs. After the pharmaceutical reform was implemented, physicians in Korea substituted more expensive brand-name drugs for generic and less costly ones. For example, the proportion of high-priced medicines[7] prescribed (defined as the number of high-priced medicines divided by the total number of medicines in a prescription) was 29.80 percent in January 2000, increasing to 37.48 percent in 2001 and 38.54 percent in January 2002 (table 1.1). As more prescription information is revealed to patients, physicians may think that prescribing expensive brand-name drugs signals quality of care.

Even in developed countries where drug prescription and dispensation are separate, physicians still play a pivotal role in selecting drugs and hence have a critical impact on pharmaceutical expenditures (Hellerstein 1998; Lundin 2000). The separation of drug prescribing and dispensing may be insufficient to contain pharmaceutical expenditures. But it is hoped that it is the first step toward effective government oversight of pharmaceuticals in Korea.

The new pharmaceutical policy may have difficulty affecting the entrenched prescribing habits of physicians. Traditional medicine is very popular in Korea. When patients visit physician clinics, they expect to get tangible results from the treatment process. For a long time, physicians have fulfilled this expectation, and a visit to a physician clinic almost always results in at least one prescription. It will take time for this culture to change.

Although the pharmaceutical reform had a large and sudden negative impact on physician income, it increased the relative bargaining power of physicians in clinical decisions. It is now unlawful for pharmacists to prescribe, and physicians monopolize prescription decisions. Now pharmacists tend to open pharmacies close to physician offices. There is likely to be collusion between physicians and pharmacies, with physicians channeling patients to a favored pharmacy. Such collusion undermines the benefits of the new pharmaceutical policy and will contribute to a further increase in pharmaceutical expenditures.

The separation of drug prescribing and dispensing seems to benefit international pharmaceutical manufacturers as well as physicians. As physicians prefer high-quality brand-name drugs, large firms and global manufacturers increased their market share. A survey of pharmaceutical companies (both multinational and domestic) showed that sales in the second half of 2001 increased by 118.7 percent, on average, compared with the second half of 1999 (KIHASA 2002b). Compared with this overall trend, multinational pharmaceutical manufacturers experienced a 172.8 percent increase in sales during the same period. Among the top ten medicines (in terms of sales value) that were prescribed and reimbursed by national health insurance in 2002, eight were produced by multinational firms (National Health Insurance Corporation, NHIC, 2003). As the role of physician prescribing becomes more critical, pharmaceutical firms' marketing efforts increasingly target physicians. Sixty-one percent of pharmaceutical firms reported that they increased marketing efforts targeting physician clinics, whereas the percentage of firms that increased efforts targeting pharmacists was only 31 percent. The larger the pharmaceutical firm, the greater the increase in postreform marketing expenses (KIHASA 2002b).

Recent Changes in Pharmaceutical Policy

Even after the pharmaceutical reform that separated prescribing from dispensing, pharmaceutical expenditures continued to increase rapidly (figure 1.2). In May 2006 the government introduced additional policy measures to contain pharmaceutical expenditures. Two major elements are price negotiation and positive listing.

Figure 1.2 Trends in Pharmaceutical Spending in Korea

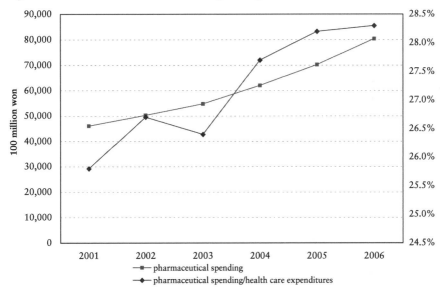

Source: NHIC 2007.

Pharmaceutical Pricing

Previously, the insurance-reimbursed price of a new drug was set as the average price across seven countries (United States of America, United Kingdom, Germany, France, Italy, Switzerland, and Japan). More specifically, the price of innovative new drugs was set as the average of manufacturing prices (65 percent of the list price) plus value-added tax (VAT) and the distributors' margin. For noninnovative drugs, the price was determined as the average of the relative prices of similar domestic medicines or the same/similar medicines in the seven countries. The previous pricing mechanism was criticized because it was difficult to differentiate between innovative versus noninnovative medicines (in terms of efficacy, cost, and so on). At the same time, the policy tended to result in high prices because it depended on the list price rather than the real (transaction) price in wealthy countries. Considering that Korea is a rather early adopter of new drugs, it was often the case that same/similar medicines

39

were listed in only a limited number of countries, where the price was very high. There has also been criticism that the NHIC has not played a prudent role in purchasing pharmaceuticals.

To contain pharmaceutical expenditures, the Korean government decided to change the pricing rules. Instead of formula-based pricing, the NHIC as purchaser now bargains with pharmaceutical manufacturers over prices. In the price negotiation, the NHIC considers the size of the market, drug substitutability, the impact on health insurance, and so on. Furthermore, the NHIC takes into account the quantity of drugs to be consumed (that is, the volume). At the time of listing, the pharmaceutical manufacturer submits the expected volume. If the actual sales volume is greater than expected, the drug's price can be cut. By formally adopting price negotiations, the role of the NHIC in pharmaceutical policy has been strengthened.

In the new pricing scheme, when a patent expires and a generic enters the market, the price of the original brand is reduced to 80 percent of the previous price. The price of the first generic is set at 85 percent of the price of the original brand (or 68 percent of the price of the original before the entrance of a generic). The price of the second to fifth generics are set at 85 percent of the price of the first generic.

Such price negotiations and price-volume considerations improve upon the old pricing scheme. It is hoped that the NHIC will use its bargaining power to reduce the price of pharmaceuticals. Because the price negotiations take into account the volume of pharmaceuticals sold, they can also affect the quantity of drugs consumed. The pharmaceutical industry has criticized the policy, arguing that price negotiations that account for volume can eventually cap the profits of pharmaceutical manufacturers, reducing research activities and the development of innovative drugs.

Positive Listing and Economic Evaluation

In the past, health insurance reimbursement of pharmaceuticals was based on negative listing, which resulted in too many drugs listed for reimbursement. As of January 2006, 21,740 were listed for reimbursement (5,411 molecules). To contain pharmaceutical expenditures, the government decided to introduce the positive listing of reimbursable drugs. Now the listing criteria includes economic evaluations, submitted by pharmaceutical manufacturers to the national health insurance.

The pharmaceutical industry has argued that positive listing can lead to the abuse of market power by a single purchaser (national health insurance). Some domestic pharmaceutical manufacturers are worried that those drugs not in the reimbursement list will have to exit the market, and the new policy will cut prices with the threat of delisting. Multinational pharmaceutical manufacturers maintain that positive listing based on economic evaluations will have a serious negative effect on the development and introduction of new innovative drugs because the policy will favor less effective but cheaper drugs. They request that an independent committee mediate conflicts.

Positive listing based on economic evaluations will initially be used for new drugs. But it should also be used to evaluate and reassess drugs already listed. The capacity of pharmaceutical manufacturers to conduct economic evaluations of their drugs is still limited, however, especially in the case of domestic firms. In addition, the small number of expert health economists who can work with insurers to evaluate the data submitted by pharmaceutical producers may slow the new policy's implementation.

Limitations

As previously stated, the new pharmaceutical policy has two key components: positive listing and price negotiation. The Health Insurance Review Agency (HIRA) is responsible for positive listing, based on economic evaluations, and the NHIC for price negotiations. Economic evaluation data can provide crucial information on the price range of drugs. Coordination between the NHIC and HIRA will be key to the success of the new policy. The NHIC also needs to strengthen its capacity to negotiate with manufacturers over pharmaceutical prices.

Pharmaceutical spending is driven not only by price but also by volume, and pricing policy alone has a limited effect. In Taiwan, for example, limiting pharmaceutical prices has not reduced overall pharmaceutical expenditures, suggesting that price is not the primary driver of spending on medicines (see chapter 5, Hsieh, this volume). The quantity of pharmaceuticals consumed is determined to a great extent by physicians. Without the regulation of physician prescribing or at least economic incentives to prescribe in a cost-effective way, pharmaceutical cost containment will fail. Revising the reimbursement system for physicians needs to be considered. In addition, financial incentives to increase the consumption of generics are essential. The government needs to consider increased pay for physicians who prescribe generics or discounted copayments for consumers who consume generics. Policymakers also need to reexamine the price gap between the original brand-name drugs and later generics, which is smaller in Korea than in other countries.

Lessons and Concluding Remarks

The pharmaceutical reform directly impacted physicians by eliminating an important source of their income. A change of government, democratized policy process, and a new president's keen interest in health and social policy provided favorable conditions for a big policy change and opened a window for the separation of drug prescribing from dispensing. It was possible for progressive civic groups to participate in the health policy process and play a pivotal role in the formation of health-care reform. In a suddenly expanded policy community, new members quickly set the reform agenda, and government bureaucrats and the medical profession failed to dominate the policy formulation process. The change in political environment also affected the role of interest groups (such as medical associations) in the policy process. Pharmaceutical reform was implemented but with greater social costs than expected, because physicians tried to veto the reform implementation through nationwide strikes.

The separation of drug prescribing and dispensing in Korea was a radical and comprehensive reform. The political feasibility of a comprehensive reform is often low, not only because it offends many established interests and adds costs and complexity but also because it departs from traditional ways. Because of the cultural and historical patterns of drug consumption related to traditional medicine, the pharmaceutical reform, in order to accomplish its goals, has to change not only formal rules and regulations but also popular attitudes toward drugs.

Japan and Taiwan adopted less comprehensive approaches to pharmaceutical reform than Korea, and it will be worthwhile to compare policy performance in these three countries over time. Japan adopted a voluntary scheme in which the patient has a choice between the pharmacy and the physician clinic for the dispensing of medicines (Rodwin and Okamoto 2000). By squeezing the profit margin on drugs and increasing the dispensing fees for doctors, policymakers have increased the separation rate to more than 50 percent (see chapter 2, Iizuka, this volume). In Taiwan, physicians can employ on-site pharmacists for dispensing, allowing them to maintain a financial interest in prescription (Chou et al. 2001; chapter 5, this volume).

As discussed in this chapter, the Korean government has recently implemented additional policy measures for pharmaceutical cost containment. It decided to empower the NHIC by introducing price negotiations between the NHIC and pharmaceutical manufacturers to set the price of drugs for health insurance reimbursement. The government also introduced the positive listing of reimbursable drugs. While it is too early to evaluate the impact of these policy changes, the government will probably fail to contain Korea's rapidly increasing pharmaceutical expenditures without changing physicians' prescribing behavior.

Notes

[1] See Kwon (2003c, 2005) for a detailed description of health-care financing and delivery in Korea.

[2] See Kwon (2003a) for a more detailed description, including key actors.

[3] It is not certain whether the sharp increase in physician fees overcompensates for the potential loss of physician income resulting from the new pharmaceutical regulation. But it was reported that after the pharmaceutical regulation was implemented, many hospital-based physicians rushed to open their own clinics, which to some extent signals the generosity of the fee increase. In a survey of 144 small and medium-sized hospitals (with less than 400 beds) by the Korean

Hospital Association, 34 percent of medical staff left hospitals in 2001 to open clinics (KHA 2001).

[4] Numbers in this paragraph are all from a report that, based on sample data from 20 percent of claims made by 1,654 physician clinics (9 percent of all physician clinics in Korea), compared the prescription pattern of physicians before the policy change (January 2000) and after (January 2001 and 2002). Although this type of comparison cannot control for the impact of a potential change in patient or disease factors, it gives us some crude measure of the effect of the new pharmaceutical regulations.

[5] Although the fee for writing a prescription was not high, it was still greater than the marginal cost. This fee was abolished in 2001.

[6] The use of tetracyclines declined sharply from 0.331 to 0.064 DDD (defined daily dose) per 1,000 persons per day. The use of beta-lactam antibacterials (penicillins) was reduced from 2.164 to 1.411 DDD/1,000 persons/day (by 35 percent). However, the use of 1st cephalosporins increased from 0.184 to 0.213 DDD/1,000 persons/day (by 16 percent). The use of 2nd cephalosporins increased by as much as 86 percent, from 0.039 to 0.073 DDD/1,000 persons/day.

[7] High-priced medicine is defined as the most expensive choice among medicines with the same ingredients, strength, and dosage.

References

Chou, Y., W. C. Yip, C-H. Lee, N. Huang, Y-P. Sun, and H-J. Chang. 2001. Impact of separating drug prescribing and dispensing on provider behavior: Taiwan's experience. *Health Policy and Planning* 18 (3): 316–29.

Davis, P. 1997. *Managing medicines: Public policy and therapeutic drugs.* Philadelphia: Open Univ. Press.

Hellerstein, J. 1998. The importance of the physician in the generic versus trade-name prescription decision. *Rand Journal of Economics* 29 (1): 108–36.

Jacobs, L. 1992. Institutions and culture: Health policy and public opinion in the U.S. and Britain. *World Politics* 44 (2): 179–209.

KIHASA. *See* Korea Institute for Health and Social Affairs.

Korean Hospital Association. 2001. Internal report [in Korean]. Seoul.

Korea Institute for Health and Social Affairs. 2002a. *Evaluation of the separation of drug prescribing and dispensing* [in Korean]. Seoul.

———. 2002b. *Symposium on the separation of drug prescribing and dispensing* [in Korean]. Seoul.

Korean Association of Pharmaceutical Manufacturers. 1998. *Pharmaceutical industry statistics* [in Korean]. Seoul.

Kwon, S. 2003a. Pharmaceutical reform and physician strikes in Korea: Separation of drug prescribing and dispensing. *Social Science and Medicine* 57 (3): 529–38.

———. 2003b. Payment system reform for health care providers in Korea. *Health Policy and Planning* 18 (1): 84–93.

———. 2003c. Quality of life associated with health and health care in Korea. *Social Indicators Research* 62/63: 171–86.

———. 2005. Health policy in South Korea. In *Comparative Health Policy in the Asia-Pacific*, ed. Robin Gauld, 48–68. Buckingham and Philadelphia: Open Univ. Press.

———. 2007. Fiscal crisis of the national health insurance in Korea: In search of a new paradigm. *Social Policy and Administration* 41 (2): 162–78.

Kwon, S., and M. Reich. 2005. The changing process and politics of health policy in Korea. *Journal of Health Politics, Policy and Law* 30 (6): 1003–26.

Lundin, D. 2000. Moral hazard in physician prescription behavior. *Journal of Health Economics* 19 (3): 639–62.

Ministry of Health and Welfare. 2000, 2001. Internal report [in Korean]. Seoul.

MOHW. *See* Ministry of Health and Welfare.

National Health Insurance Corporation. 1997. *Trend in health care provision in health insurance* [in Korean]. Seoul.

———. 2003. Health insurance statistics [in Korean]. Seoul.

NHIC. *See* National Health Insurance Corporation.

OECD. *See* Organisation for Economic Co-operation and Development.

Organisation for Economic Co-operation and Development. 2006. *Health data 2006.* Paris.

Rodwin, M., and E. Okamoto. 2000. Physicians' conflicts of interest in Japan and the United States: Lessons for the United States. *Journal of Health Politics, Policy and Law* 25 (2): 343–75.

Pharmaceutical Policy in Seven Asia-Pacific Health-care Systems

Japan

THE ECONOMICS OF PHARMACEUTICAL PRICING AND PHYSICIAN PRESCRIBING IN JAPAN

Toshiaki Iizuka

Most countries have unique pharmaceutical policies; Japan is no exception. Under its dynamic price-control rule, retail prices are updated based on the transaction prices of the period immediately previous. Meanwhile, doctors have been allowed to both purchase and sell drugs to their patients and thus pocket the price-cost markup. These factors appear to have affected prescription practices. I analyze them in more detail before turning to two studies I recently conducted to empirically investigate their impact on physician prescription practices. Ongoing changes in pharmaceutical policy and their expected impacts are also discussed.

The Regulatory Environment

Under Japan's universal health coverage system, the entire population is covered by some level of public health insurance. Most medical services (including prescription drugs) are provided on a fee-for-service basis, and the government sets these fees. All physicians get the same reimbursement for the same treatment, and they have to charge the same price to all patients. Patients pay 10 to 30 percent of doctors' fees (including for prescription drugs), depending on their eligibility category.

Two aspects of Japanese pharmaceutical policy are worth noting. First, the separation of prescribing and describing has been historically weak, and it is not uncommon for doctors to both prescribe and dispense drugs to patients through in-house pharmacies. Receiving medicine directly from the doctor is a tradition of Oriental medicine.[1] After WWII, the government implemented various policies to separate the two functions. But, as figure 2.1 shows, 45 percent of all prescriptions were still filled at in-house pharmacies as of 2005. Please see chapter 3 of this book for further historical background.

Second, the government regulates prescription drug prices, using a dynamic pricing rule. The pricing rule sets (1) the initial entry price and (2) the updated price after entry. Upon entry, the government sets the initial retail price in reference to the closest substitute drug on the market. For example, if the new drug exhibits substantially higher efficacy and/or safety than the comparison drug, the new drug's price will be set up to 100 percent higher than that of the comparison drug. This policy is designed to encourage innovation. If no close substitutes exist, the government sets the price based on industry-average costs and profits. For generic drugs, the government sets the initial retail price at 70 percent of the price of the comparable brand-name drug.

Figure 2.1 Percentage of Prescriptions Filled at Pharmacies

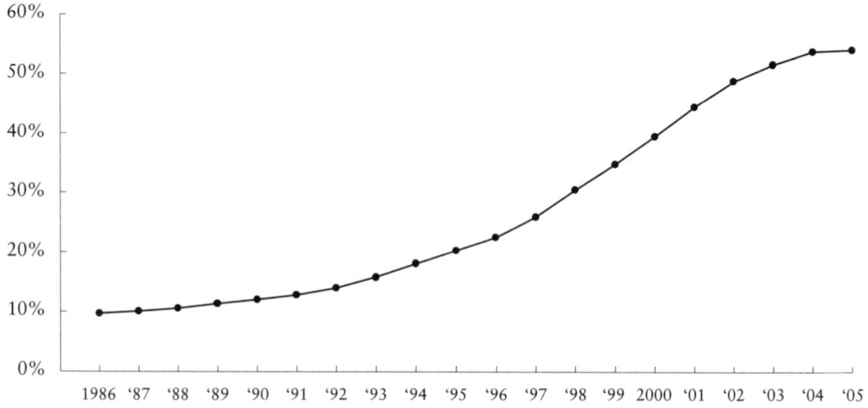

Source: Drug Magazine 2007.

After entry, the government updates the price of each drug in April of every other year. The updated price is based on the previous year's retail price and the average transaction price of the drug. Specifically, the government uses the following dynamic pricing rule:

$$P^R_t = P^W_{t-1} + R_t * P^R_{t-1} \quad (1)$$

where P^R and P^W denote the retail price and the average wholesale price, respectively, and R_t is the weight that the government places on the previous year's retail price (see also figure 2.2). In principle, the government doesn't allow the retail price to rise over time. So, if the computed new retail price, P^R_t, exceeds the previous one, P^R_{t-1}, the retail price in the next year will be set equal to P^R_{t-1}.

R_t is called the "reasonable zone" (R-zone) and was designed to cover technical fees and inventory costs. The government learns the average wholesale price, P^W_{t-1}, based on extensive data-collection efforts that involve a number of wholesalers and medical providers. The dynamic pricing rule was introduced in 1992, and the R-zone was initially set at 0.15. But it was gradually reduced to 0.02 in the hope of reducing the difference between the retail price and wholesale price. In 2000, while the government continued using equation (1) to update the retail price, R_t was no longer called the R-zone. Thereafter, R_t has been set at 0.02.

48

Figure 2.2 The Dynamic Pricing Rule

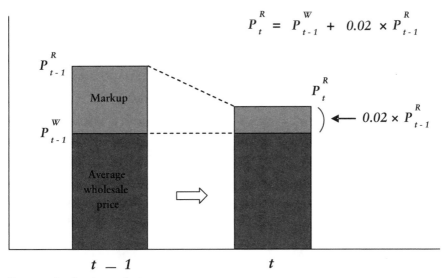

$$P_t^R = P_{t-1}^W + 0.02 \times P_{t-1}^R$$

Source: Author's analysis.

An important aspect of the pricing rule is that the government regulates only the retail price, and the wholesale price is set freely by market participants. This means that, combined with the weak separation of prescribing and dispensing, the doctor can obtain the price-cost markup if he can purchase the drug below the regulated retail price. This is in fact the case, as figure 2.3 shows. Although the average price-cost markup has declined over time, it has been continuously positive and was still above 6 percent in recent years.

These pharmaceutical policies are likely to have various effects on the Japanese pharmaceutical market. In the following sections, I discuss their impact on (1) physician prescribing practices and (2) prescription drug prices.

Japan's Pharmaceutical Policy: Impacts

The fact that doctors can profit from the price-cost markup raises concerns that their prescription choices may be distorted. In an extreme case, the doctor may choose a drug not because of efficacy, safety, or cost-effectiveness but rather the markup earned. Overprescribing may result, since a doctor can increase his profits by dispensing more. This implies that some patients are taking suboptimal drugs for their health conditions or are taking drugs when none are necessary. Such an agency problem, if it exists, may not only affect patients' welfare—drugs have side effects and high-profit-margin drugs are also usually more expensive for patients—but also significantly increase overall medical expenditures since prescription drugs are commonly covered by insurance in Japan.

Figure 2.3 Estimated Price-Cost Markup (Industry Average Weighted)

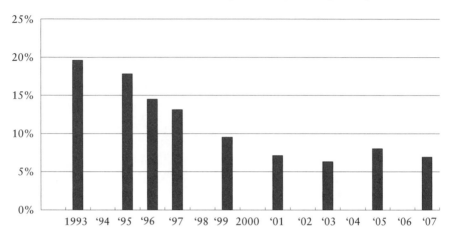

Source: Central Social Insurance Medical Council, Drug Price Expert Committee.

These concerns are not unrealistic. Most patients are not well informed about drug efficacy and safety and thus find it difficult to verify that a doctors' choice is appropriate. Moreover, it is not likely that a patient knows which drugs provide higher profit margins for the physician. In fact, the patient has little incentive to detect and monitor doctors' prescribing behavior since insurance coverage leaves the patient paying only 10 to 30 percent of the retail price of a prescription drug.

While the patient may not have a strong incentive to monitor and discipline the doctor, the insurer might. This is, for example, the role of health maintenance organizations (HMOs) in the United States. In Japan, however, the insurer may not have a strong incentive to contain costs—or the means to do so. For example, the patient has open access to any doctor and to any drug, and thus the insurer cannot shift demand to specific medical providers and/or to particular drugs (such as generic drugs). Also, there is a moral hazard on the side of the insurer, since the government usually bails out insurers in the case of bankruptcy. Since neither the patient nor the insurer has a strong incentive or the necessary discretion to discipline the physician, the agency problem can be substantial in this market.

Pharmaceutical Retail Prices

We now turn our attention to the impact of the pharmaceutical policy on retail prices. Figure 2.4 shows changes in the retail prices of major drugs in the statin class, used to treat patients with high cholesterol. These are the per-day prices of brand-name drugs (generic drugs do not exist except for Pravastatin and Simvastatin, whose generics entered in 2003). The figure shows that retail prices for brand-name drugs have continuously declined throughout the period. For example, the nominal price for Pravastatin sodium declined by 46 percent between 1992 and 2006. This trend also applies to the entire market; figure 2.5 shows the change in the average retail price (weighted by volume) every year the government revised the retail price. This figure confirms that retail prices have continuously declined and the resulting reduction has been substantial.

Figure 2.4 Retail Prices for Major Statin Drugs (Nominal Prices)

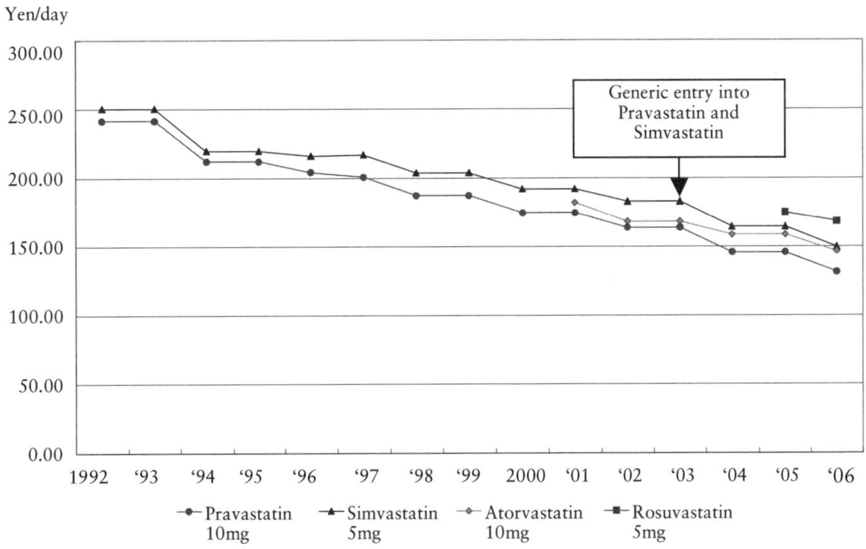

Yen/day

Generic entry into Pravastatin and Simvastatin

- Pravastatin 10mg
- Simvastatin 5mg
- Atorvastatin 10mg
- Rosuvastatin 5mg

Source: Jiho Inc., 1992–2006.

It should be noted that although the government doesn't allow retail prices to rise, the dynamic pricing rule does not necessarily mean that retail prices have to decline. If we take a look at the pricing rule once again, it is clear that the retail price declines if and only if the price-cost markup $(=P^R_{t-1} - P^W_{t-1})$ is higher than $R_t * P^R_{t-1}$. In fact, if the doctor does not respond to the markup when choosing a prescription drug, then the sellers may have no reason to lower the wholesale price below the retail price. In this case, the retail price may stay flat. The fact that retail prices have continuously declined indicates

Figure 2.5 Annual Change in Retail Price (Industry Average Weighted)

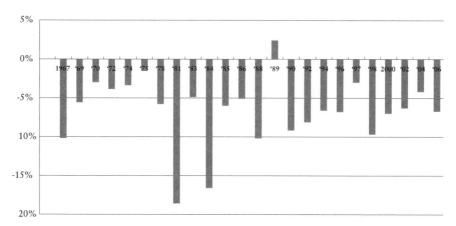

Source: Central Social Insurance Medical Council, Drug Price Expert Committee.

that demand for prescription drugs is sensitive to the price-cost markup. In other words, doctors' sensitivity to the markup is likely to drive prescription drug prices down in Japan. One interesting question is whether prescription drug prices will continue to decline in the future. As we saw in figure 2.1, the vertical separation of prescribing and dispensing has progressed, and as figure 2.3 indicates, the fall of retail prices seems to be slowing. The relationship between the two trends might be an interesting topic for future research.

Empirical Evidence on Physician Prescribing

This section reviews two recent studies I conducted to empirically investigate the impact of pharmaceutical policy on physician prescribing. Although both of these studies look at the Japanese market, they differ in terms of their scope and data. My first study (Iizuka 2007) examines whether and to what extent the physician markup affects prescription choice among different hypertension drugs. This study uses aggregated market-level data for 1991 to 1997. In contrast, my second study (Iizuka 2008) looks at the determinants of generic substitution using prescription-level microdata for 2003–2005 and follows the prescription history of a patient over time. While the approaches differ, both studies indicate that the price-cost markup affects physician prescribing. This indicates the existence of the agency problem in physician prescribing.

Do Physician Markups Affect Physician Choice of Brand-name Drugs?

The aim of my first study (2007) was to empirically investigate the degree of the agency problem in the Japanese prescription drug market. As noted, the physician who both prescribes and dispenses drugs in Japan can pocket the price-cost markup, and this may create an agency problem. A natural concern is that the markup may distort a physician's prescription choices. I attempted to answer this question by examining the factors that affect prescription choice.

The study took the following approach: first, using the data for hypertension drugs between 1991 and 1997, I estimated the factors that affect pharmaceutical demand. Whether the physician markup affects prescription choice was the central interest of the study.[2] In my model, the physician is allowed to choose a drug from more than forty alternatives, taking into account both patient welfare and the profits he earns from each drug. Whether the doctor is a good agent was inferred from the weight he places on these two variables. I estimated a utility-based random coefficient discrete choice model à la Berry, Levinsohn, and Pakes (1995), taking into account the endogeneity of price and markup. After estimating the demand model, I conducted counterfactual experiments using the estimated parameter values. In particular, I simulated a hypothetical case in which prescribing and dispensing are vertically separated. By comparing this hypothetical case with the actual one, I quantified the impact of physician financial incentive on pharmaceutical demand and on medical expenditures.

One difficulty that I faced in the study was that although the regulated retail price is publicly announced, the markup that the physician earns is difficult to observe. I overcame this difficulty by exploiting the dynamic pricing rule of the government. Recall that the government updates the retail price for each drug using information on the previous year's prices: $P^R_t = P^W_{t-1} + R_t * P^R_{t-1}$. Note that although we don't know P^W_{t-1}, we know P^R_t, P^R_{t-1}, and R_t. Thus, it is easy to back up P^W_{t-1} by using only publicly available data. Then we can compute the average markup by $M_{t-1} = P^R_{t-1} - P^W_{t-1}$.[3]

The estimation results of the study show that, first, the price-cost markup significantly affects doctors' decisions, as one might have expected. Interestingly, however, doctors also care about patient out-of-pocket costs. In fact, the estimated parameter values indicate that the physician is more responsive to patient costs than to his own profits from the markup: the doctor is willing to forego one dollar of markup in exchange for a 28-cent reduction in patient costs. This may be because the patient can limit the extent of the agency problem through referrals or repeat visits. Alternatively, the physician may be altruistic in his concern for patient welfare. I conclude (see Iizuka 2007) that the agency problem exists, but the degree of the agency problem may be viewed as modest.

A counterfactual simulation indicated that if the physician markup were eliminated, demand for hypertension drugs would decrease by 10.6 percent, and medical expenditures would decline by 15 percent, holding all other factors (including prices) constant. This suggests that expenditures on these drugs are inflated by 10.6 percent due to overprescribing and by 4.4 percent due to the substitution of more expensive drugs that offer higher markups. Thus, the economic impact of the physician markup does not appear to be trivial. This finding raises concerns about integrating prescribing and dispensing from both the perspectives of population health and public finance.

What Factors Affect the Choice between Generic and Brand-name Drugs?

In my second study (Iizuka 2008), I analyze the factors that affect generic substitution in the Japanese market.[4] In contrast to my first study (Iizuka 2007), this working paper utilizes detailed patient-level microdata and follows patient prescription history over time. This is an advantage, because the prescription process often exhibits state dependence: once the generic versions are chosen, this choice is likely to persist. Also, the rich data set makes it possible to control for both observed and unobserved patient and doctor characteristics, while controlling for state dependence. This extends the findings of previous studies that have analyzed the conditions of generic substitution (Hellerstein 1998; Lundin 2000).

Another unique aspect of the study is how it examines whether and to what extent the financial incentive to dispense generic drugs affects generic substitution. This is done by taking advantage of Japanese data on the average price-cost markup that dispensing agents receive. Studies of the U.S. prescription drug market, including those of Grabowski and Vernon (1996) and the Congressional Budget Office (2005), have recognized that newer generic drugs tend to offer higher markups to pharmacies than do brand-name drugs, and this appears to have encouraged generic substitution. But because obtaining data on these markups is difficult, existing studies such as those of Hellerstein (1998) and Ching (2004, 2005) do not examine their impacts. This is unfortunate since generic substitution is prevalent in U.S. pharmacies.

To understand when generic substitution occurs, I chose to analyze the forty most frequently prescribed drugs whose generic versions entered the market for the first time after 1998. The data analyzed contain approximately 360,000 observations from August 2003 through December 2005. My basic approach was to explain the factors that affect the choice of generic versus brand-name drugs by estimating a probit model that incorporate the previous choice made in any one doctor-patient-drug scenario. The entire analysis is conditional on an active ingredient (or molecule), and I don't address the choice among alternative active ingredients.

Similar to my first study mentioned (Iizuka 2007), the doctor is assumed to act as an agent for the patient. The doctor chooses the generic or branded drug, taking into account the pros and cons for both the patient and the doctor. In addition to the choice made at the patient's previous visit, the estimation includes the markup and price differential as well as observed doctor and patient attributes. In my second study (Iizuka 2008), I also attempt to control for unobserved doctor and patient attributes.

Descriptive statistics show that generic use substantially differs by hospital size and by whether prescribing and dispensing are separated. Small clinics (with

0 beds) are most active in using generic drugs (36.1 percent of the drugs they prescribe), and generic use declines as hospital size (measured by number of beds) increases. The largest hospitals (with 500+ beds) are least active in using generic drugs (1.7 percent of prescriptions). Note that the data contain only the drugs that have generic counterparts; thus, even if larger hospitals tend to use newer drugs, this difference will not explain the trend discussed above. If we further split the sample by vertical integration status, it becomes clear that vertically integrated clinics—in which generic-drug-use rates reach as high as 50.1 percent—are driving generic substitution in this market. In contrast, when prescribing and dispensing are separated, small clinics prescribe generic drugs only 18.5 percent of the time.

In this second study, I argue that the differential financial incentives faced by medical providers may explain these differences. It is easy to understand that vertically integrated providers prefer generic drugs, because generic drugs tend to offer higher price-cost markups soon after entry, and only the vertically integrated providers can take advantage of such markups. The reason why larger hospitals tend to use fewer generic drugs is less clear. One possibility is that—in contrast to small clinics, typically owned and operated by one doctor—doctors in larger hospitals are less likely to personally gain by prescribing generic drugs. This may explain why small clinics prescribe generics more often than larger hospitals.

The results of formal regression models support these conjectures. First, small clinics where doctors both prescribe and dispense drugs are more likely to dispense generic drugs. Moreover, doctors' prescription choices are responsive to the markup differential between brand-name and generic drugs. These findings suggest that financial incentives affect generic substitution. Second, in small clinics we find that when the doctor both prescribes and dispenses a drug, he is sensitive to both the price-cost markup he pockets and to the patient's out-of-pocket expense. But the doctor is no longer sensitive to either when he prescribes a drug but does not dispense it. Thus, while financial incentives do affect generic substitution, lowering retail drug prices alone does not appear to effectively promote generic substitution. Third, the choice between generic versus brand-name drugs exhibited strong state dependence: a generic prescription given in the previous visit increases the probability of getting the same generic in the next visit by up to 75 percent. This indicates that the government and firms who wish to affect generic substitution would be better off employing policy instruments (such as pricing, markup, advertising, and promotion) that affect the choice early, because these instruments tend to have a cumulative impact on demand.

Recent Changes in Japanese Pharmaceutical Policy

In this last section, I briefly review two recent policy changes that might have a large impact on the Japanese pharmaceutical market. First, a new prescription pad was introduced in April 2008, which may boost the use of generic drugs. Second, the pricing rule for new drugs has been changed.

A New Prescription Pad

The use of generic drugs in Japan is low relative to that of other countries (see figure 2.6). Since 2002 the government has implemented various policies aimed at increasing the use of generic drugs, but generics still only accounted for 16 percent of the market in quantity as of 2005. In April 2006 a new prescription pad was introduced that allowed generic substitution at the pharmacy for the first time. If, on the new pad, a doctor signed the column stating "generic substitution is allowed," a generic drug could be dispensed at the pharmacy. Prior to this change, generic substitution was not allowed at the pharmacy, and the pharmacist could dispense a generic drug if and only if the doctor wrote down the *exact* proprietary name of the generic drug. Since there are numerous generic drugs on the market, this regulation created an obstacle for generic substitution.

Figure 2.6 Market Share of Generic Drugs, 2006

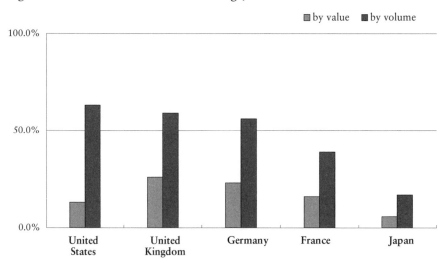

Source: Japan Generic Pharmaceutical Manufacturers Association.

After just two years, the government introduced another new prescription pad in April 2008. The government viewed the 2006 prescription pad as unsuccessful, since only 17 percent of all prescriptions permitted generic substitution. The new 2008 prescription pad instead has a column that indicates "*no* generic substitution allowed." Unless the doctor denies substitution by signing this, generic substitution is permitted at the pharmacy. In addition to changing the pad, the government devised additional incentives for pharmacies: dispensing fees paid to pharmacies are differentiated by whether the share of generic prescriptions exceeds 30 percent or not.

Will these changes increase the use of generic drugs? According to a survey conducted by the Japanese Medical Association (JMA), about 30 percent of doctors are against the new prescription pad. While it is expected that the number of prescriptions that permit generic substitution will certainly increase, it is not clear if the new policy provides sufficient incentives to pharmacies. One concern is that although generic drugs provide higher price-cost markups after entry, this advantage tends to quickly dissipate. A higher markup induces a lower retail price the following year, which prevents a generic drug firm from continuously providing a high price-cost markup. It may be necessary to review the pricing rule for generic drugs if the government wishes to substantially increase the use of generic drugs.

Pricing Rule for New Drugs

The second policy change is to the pricing rule for new drugs. As noted before, the government sets the price of a new drug by comparing its efficacy and safety to those of existing drugs.[5] If a comparable drug exists and the quality of the new drug exceeds it, the government sets the new drug price up to 100 percent higher than the comparison drug. The first change implemented in April 2008 was to increase this markup to a maximum of 120 percent. This change was motivated by the government's recognition that prescription drug prices are now *low* in Japan and that the prices of high-quality drugs should be valued more appropriately.[6]

The pricing rule for new pharmaceuticals with no comparison drugs was also changed. Note that many of these may be breakthrough drugs that treat previously untreatable diseases. In the past, the government set their prices by looking at industry-average costs and profits. By only providing industry average profits, the pricing rule might have discouraged innovation and/or product introduction into the Japanese market. The change sets the profit markup up to 50 percent above the industry average if a new drug exhibits higher efficacy and safety relative to other drugs that treat the same disease. Although this is consistent with the government objective of encouraging pharmaceutical innovation, we will have to wait to see whether these changes speed up the entry and development of new drugs in the Japanese market.

Notes

[1] China, South Korea, Taiwan, and Thailand share the same tradition. As noted by Kwon in chapter 1, South Korea forced the vertical separation of prescribing and dispensing in the early 2000s.

[2] In addition, the estimate takes into account drug safety and efficacy. The results indicate that doctors prefer to prescribe higher-quality drugs, all other factors (including price and markup) constant.

[3] The reader may note that wholesale prices can vary depending on the bargaining power of medical institutions vis-à-vis sellers. Unfortunately, no available systematic data show the extent of heterogeneity in wholesale prices. Available information indicates, however, that the difference in the price-cost markup may not be large across different types of hospitals.

[4] In contrast, in Iizuka 2009, I look at the supply side and examine the factors that affect generic entry. I show that pharmaceutical policies and their consequences—such as the weak separation of prescribing and dispensing and physicians' financial incentives—also affect the extent of generic entry.

[5] The government finds a comparison drug based on similarity in (1) efficacy and effectiveness, (2) pharmacological action, (3) composition and chemical structural form, and (4) administration and dosage form.

[6] Central Social Insurance Medical Council, Drug Price Expert Committee (2008).

References

Berry, Steven, James Levinsohn, and Ariel Pakes. 1995. Automobile prices in market equilibrium. *Econometrica* 63 (4): 841–90.

Central Social Insurance Medical Council, Drug Price Expert Committee. 2007a. Yakka Santei Rule Kanren Siryo. May 30.

———. 2007b. Heisei 20 Nendo Yakka Seido Kaikaku no Kossi. December 5.

———. 2008. Heisei 20 Nendono Yakka Santei Kijyun-tou no Minaoshi ni Tsuite. January 30.

Central Social Insurance Medical Council, General Assembly. 2007. Iyakuhin Kakaku Chosa no Sokuhou-chi ni Tsuite. November 28.

Ching, Andrew. 2004. A dynamic oligopoly structural model for the prescription drug market after patent expiration. Mimeo, University of Toronto.

———. 2005. Consumer learning and heterogeneity: dynamics of demand for prescription drugs after patent expiration. Mimeo, University of Toronto.

Congressional Budget Office. 2005. Payments for prescription drugs under Medicaid. CBO testimony, Washington, D.C.

Drug Magazine. 2007. All data and ranking, special edition. Drug Magazine Publishing.

Grabowski, Henry G., and John Vernon. 1996. Longer patents for increased generic competition in the U.S.: The Waxman-Hatch Acts after one decade. *Pharmacoeconomics* 10 (suppl. 2): 110–23.

Hellerstein, J. 1998. The importance of the physician in the generic versus trade-name prescription decision. *RAND Journal of Economics* 29 (1): 108–36.

Iizuka, T. 2007. Experts' agency problems: Evidence from the prescription drug market in Japan. *RAND Journal of Economics*, 38 (3): 844–62.

————. 2008. Financial incentives, agency problems, and the choice of generic pharmaceuticals. Working paper, Aoyama Gakuin University.

————. 2009. Generic entry in a regulated pharmaceutical market. *Japanese Economic Review*, 60(1): 63–81.

Japan Generic Pharmaceutical Manufacturers Association. 2007. *On generic pharmaceuticals*.

Jiho Incorporated. 1992–2006. Yakugyou kenkyuu kai, Hokenyakujiten edition.

Lundin, D. 2000. Moral hazard in physician prescription behavior. *Journal of Health Economics* 19: 639–62.

THE POLITICAL ECONOMY OF
INCREMENTALLY SEPARATING PRESCRIPTION
FROM DISPENSATION IN JAPAN

Naoko Tomita

In recent years, pharmaceutical affairs have been the focus of health policy in many countries. In Japan, where pharmaceutical expenditures have been growing since the early 1980s, the economic aspects of pharmaceutical policy are increasingly in the limelight. The Japanese government is now addressing issues such as the overprescribing and overconsumption of drugs.[1]

In health care, incremental change is more common than radical change because of the necessity for compromise among stakeholders (Reich 2002). Medical associations tend to have political power and significant leverage over the implementation of new health policies—and Japan is no exception.

In pursuit of cost containment, the Japanese government designed various health policy reforms, including separating responsibility for drug dispensation from that for prescription. The separation has been incrementally achieved through the manipulation of medical and pharmaceutical fee schedules from the mid-1970s. As of December 2007, 59.7 percent of prescriptions in Japan were dispensed at pharmacies rather than by physician prescribers (a so-called "ratio of separation" of 59.7 percent; Japan Pharmaceutical Association, JPA).[2]

This chapter examines how and why Japan adopted a policy of separating responsibility for dispensing from that for prescribing. It also explores the reasons for implementing this policy incrementally and the challenges that the separation reforms posed.

Need for Cost Containment of Pharmaceutical Expenditures

As gross domestic product (GDP) per capita rises, the share of total health expenditure as a percentage of GDP tends to rise (O'Connell 1996; Pfaff 1990). Indeed, after the two world wars, health care in Japan expanded along with economic growth, and increases in health spending were perceived as increasingly problematic (figure 3.1). Economic turmoil triggered by the first oil shock in 1973 ushered in an era of low economic growth. Along with dwindling tax revenues, the surge in social security payments emerged as a pivotal political issue.

At the same time, pharmaceutical expenditures in Japan grew because of advances in technology, changes in disease structure, and expanding health insurance coverage. Thus, economic aspects of pharmaceuticals, such as cost-effectiveness, gradually attracted more attention. But it was difficult for the government to control pharmaceutical expenditures as physicians had historically dispensed medicines and exerted significant influence over pharmaceutical policy.

Figure 3.1 Total Health Expenditure, 1955–2005

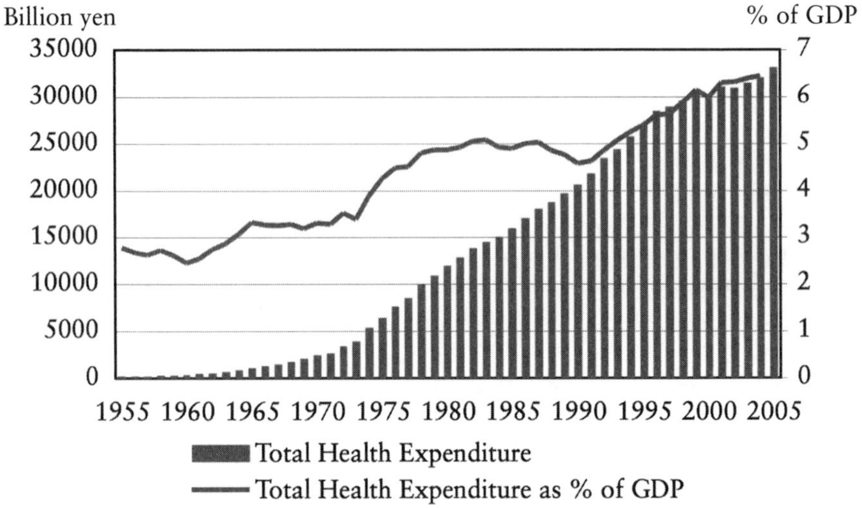

Billion yen   % of GDP

Legend: Total Health Expenditure
Total Health Expenditure as % of GDP

Source: MHLW 2007; National Accounts, Cabinet Office 2000, 2005, 2008.

Institutional Problems Surrounding Pharmaceutical Policy in Japan

Doctors Dispensing Medicine

As described in chapter 16 of this book (Eggleston and Yang), the traditions of Oriental medicine are deeply rooted in many Asian countries, including Japan. Until the late nineteenth century, medicine meant Oriental medicine and doctor meant herb doctor in Japan (Kosaka 1997). The main work of the doctor was to compound Oriental medicines based on consultations.[3] In other words, physician profits were based on selling medicine directly to patients, without prescriptions. This custom—and the conventional view that remuneration is more for medication than counsel—has continued despite the dissemination of Western medicine and treatments. Bolstered by fee-for-service payments, largely private delivery, and a government reimbursement policy,[4] doctors have relied on dispensing medications for a large part of their revenue. Such a system provides the incentive to overprescribe drugs and dispense higher-margin over cost-effective products.

Health Care in Japan

As described in the introduction to this book (Eggleston), in Japan, universal health services are provided under a social health insurance scheme. Medical services are mainly provided by private clinics and hospitals[5] whose administrators are required by law to be physicians. This means that many physicians in clinics are not only medical providers but also business managers.

Patients have almost free and unlimited access to any clinic or hospital. Unlike countries such as the United Kingdom where health care is primarily delivered by one's registered general practitioner, it is difficult to constrain the health-care utilization of Japanese patients. For example, the elderly usually visit more than two physicians and may receive duplicate medications.[6] Patients pay copayments to medical providers for each visit and the rest of the expenses are reimbursed by a third party.[7] Thus, the end consumer, selector of medicine (and treatment provider), and insurer each face different financial incentives. This institutional reality decreases the price elasticity of drug demand. In addition, private medical institutions compete for patients, with an incentive to indulge patients' moral hazard (tendency to overuse services when someone else is paying) as well as to generate revenues from profitable services and pharmaceuticals. These incentives exacerbate drug overprescription and overconsumption, which the government has limited power to regulate.

To remunerate health-care providers, Japan stipulates central fee schedules for all insurance plans. The central fee schedule sets down which treatments, pharmaceuticals, and medical supplies are reimbursed and by how much, and consists of two parts: the medical fee schedule and the pharmaceutical fee schedule. Medical fees are set low since, in the practice of traditional medicine, patients paid for drugs rather than consultation. This means that a disproportionate emphasis has been placed on pharmaceuticals rather than the medical advice and treatment of health professionals.[8] Together with physician self-dispensing, these incentives encourage drug price markups or margins—the price differential between the pharmaceutical fee reimbursed by the insurer and the wholesale purchase price—to compensate for low technical fees. Under these fee-for-service incentives, physicians are motivated to overprescribe high-margin medicines.

Separating Prescription from Dispensation

Past Attempts

In 1874 the Meiji government implemented a law prohibiting doctors from dispensing medications. The law stipulated the separation of dispensing from prescribing in the Isei (the foundational manifesto on medical matters), which is the origin of the current (Westernized) medical practitioners' law and medical administration system. But the number of pharmacies and pharmacists was limited[9] and it was impossible to attain this separation in reality; besides, the Isei was not legally binding. After the enactment of Yakuhin Eigyo Narabi Yakuhin Toriatsukai Kisoku (Regulation of sales and handling of pharmaceuticals) on March 15, 1889, prescribing became legally optional.

Under the occupation of the Allied Forces from 1945 to 1952, several fundamental reforms were carried out to democratize and liberalize Japan, the main aims of the General Headquarters of the Allied Forces (GHQ). One law stipulated the separation of medicine dispensing from prescribing, the so-called Iyaku Bungyo Law of 1951 (enforced on April 1, 1956). This law obliged doctors to prescribe and pharmacies to accept prescriptions. Crawford F. Sams, chief of the Public Health and Welfare Section of the GHQ, strongly believed that separation would improve health-care quality (Sams 1986). During the planning and implementation process, however, the law generated protests from the Japan Medical Association (JMA).[10] Meanwhile, its many loopholes allowed physicians to continue dispensing (Arioka 1997; Mizuno 2003; Takemi 1983). Despite the efforts of the GHQ and the Ministry of Health and Welfare (MHW), the JMA succeeded in watering down the separation reform and preserving doctors' vested interests.

Triggers for Separation

The oil shock and subsequent economic ills introduced two important factors to Japan in the 1980s: neoliberalism and financial woes. Neoliberalism raised public awareness of welfare and the importance of reasonable pricing, although the demand for services continued. Financial difficulties created a consensus that welfare expenditures had reached their limit. Crisis seemed imminent at the Bank of Japan, which had attached high value to balancing the budget since Japan had suffered from post–WWII inflation (Yamaguchi 1989). Two major economic groups, the Federation of Economic Associations and the Federation of Employer Associations, also strongly desired to reduce corporate contributions to pensions, health insurance, and employee taxes.

Against this background, the ruling Liberal Democratic Party (LDP) and the MHW unveiled the slogans "Japanese-style welfare" and "Health expenditure ruins Japan," respectively. The first argued that Western-style welfare caused nothing but "welfare disease," hence Japan should have its own welfare system emphasizing the role of family. The second expressed concern over the potential bankruptcy of health finances as Japanese society aged. The second Ad Hoc Commission on Administrative Reform, set up by the government to deal with the mounting government bond deficit, employed the slogan "Reconstruction of public finances without tax increases" (Nishio and Muramatsu 1994).[11] As a result, by the end of the 1980s there was a shared awareness of the need to cap future welfare expenditures.

Foreign pressures

Meanwhile, Japan, currently the second-largest pharmaceutical market in the world, has been under external pressure since 1986 to liberalize pharmaceutical and medical device markets. The General Agreement on Trade and Tariffs (GATT), subsequently taken over by the World Trade Organization (WTO), negotiated lower trade barriers for health-care products. In addition, Japan and the United States have continued bilateral discussions to improve access and transparency in Japan's health-care market through the U.S.-Japan Enhanced Initiative on Deregulation and Competition Policy following market-oriented selective sector talks in 1986. These foreign pressures helped increase the MHW's efforts to decrease drug price margins.

Separation through Manipulation of Medical and Pharmaceutical Fee Schedules

Learning from Past Attempts

The previous two attempts to enforce separation have left policymakers some lessons. First, the MHW realized how difficult it was to implement comprehensive reform in an area that impacted medical culture and strong economic interests; gradual separation seemed preferable. Second, as the aftermath of the 1951 separation law showed, mandatory separation would provoke strong protests from the JMA. Third, promoting separation on a voluntary basis would require giving physicians alternative financial incentives to counteract the heavy economic costs imposed by separation. Without compensation for dispensing profits, doctors would continue to dispense.

Decision-making in Health and Pharmaceutical Policy

In Japan, most health policy reforms start with a request from the Ministry of Health, Labour, and Welfare (MHLW) to affiliated consultative councils.[12] Legislative committees of the Diet do not involve themselves in the process of reform discussion before the submission of a final report, though subcommittee members of the Policy Affairs Research Council (PARC) of the LDP conduct regular study sessions and occasional public hearings. Thus, decision-making in health policy usually centers on the MHLW and its associated consultative bodies and discussion groups.

Above all is the Central Social Insurance Medical Council, which deliberates on fee schedules (usually reviewed biannually) within the budget allocated by the Ministry of Finance for health-care goods, services, and pharmaceuticals.[13] The council comprises representatives of medical service providers, insurance societies, and public interests. The JMA recommends most of the medical representatives, and the MHLW appoints the representatives of public interests, usually from academia.[14] The council does not include representatives of either domestic or international pharmaceutical companies, who now generally favor separation because it seems to promise greater profit by decreasing competitive price cuts.

Under ordinary circumstances, it is not the council or discussion group members but the council staff, namely bureaucrats, who draft proposals and revise them to reflect members' concerns. Bureaucrats choose the council chairperson, and usually seek to appoint someone they can "lead by the nose" (anonymous interview 2005). Once the council agrees on a fee schedule change, the council reports it directly to the MHLW to be stipulated without any further legislative review. This institutional decision-making process has enabled frequent and detailed policy changes—including manipulation of the fee schedules to promote separation—without implementing or amending the law. The process lacks accountability and transparency.

Manipulation of Medical and Pharmaceutical Fee Schedules for Separation

By manipulating fee schedules, the MHLW aimed to influence provider behavior and control costs. To promote separation, the prescription-issuing fee (*syohosen ryo*, a service fee for physicians)[15] was dramatically raised from 100 yen (about $1) to 500 yen (about $5) in 1974. Despite this substantial increase, the separation rate remained very low in the 1970s (3.5 percent in 1979), arguably because of high price margins.

Together with the slogans concerning welfare disease and the bankruptcy of health finances, the policy of manipulating fees to contain overall health expenditures—particularly pharmaceutical expenditures—has been reinforced since the 1980s. In fact, it was 1980 when the MHW addressed the issue of separation in a report entitled "Survey of National Medical Care Insurance Services." Policymakers continued to increase the prescription-issuing fee from 550 yen in 1981 to 640 yen in 1989 (figure 3.2). In addition, changes rectifying the imbalance between fees for pharmaceuticals and medical advice and treatment, by increasing the latter, contributed to gradual decreases in drug price margins. Steps toward separation were being taken.

To squeeze drug price margins even further, the MHW reduced prices on the pharmaceutical fee schedule throughout the decade. To do so, it biannually conducted a wholesale price survey called the Survey on Pharmaceutical Prices.[16] Based on collected data, the MHLW estimated the difference between the market price and the reimbursement price and then revised the pharmaceutical fee schedule accordingly.[17]

Figure 3.2 Prescription-issuing Fee and Consumer Price Index, 1974–2008

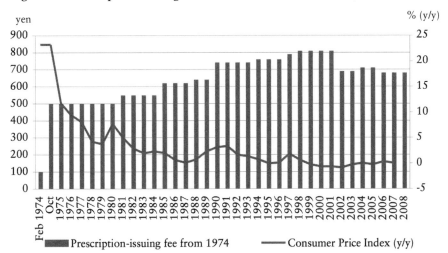

Source: Medical Fee Schedule, various years; Ministry of Internal Affairs and Communications 2008.

Note: For data before 1994, the prescription-issuing fees are for the Otsu class, chosen mainly by private hospitals and clinics. After the introduction of a reduced prescription-issuing fee for more types of drugs (starting with ten, now seven), this figure uses the unreduced prescription-issuing fee.

Before 1982 the 90 percent bulk line (BL) calculation method, which takes the 90th percentile from the lowest-priced drug in the Survey on Pharmaceutical Prices, was used to decide new prices in the pharmaceutical fee schedule. In 1982, 81 percent BL was introduced; later, 81 percent BL for greater variation and 90 percent BL for smaller variation were used according to price fluctuations. From 1987, though these methods were still used, a weighted average was introduced for drugs with greater price dispersion. With a series of drug price reductions in the 1980s, the government expected to decrease pharmaceutical expenditures and drug price margins. The increasing volume of pharmaceutical consumption, however, kept pharmaceutical expenditures growing, and drug price margins did not decrease as much as expected. Despite drastic reductions in drug reimbursement prices throughout the decade, drug price margins remained high and progress toward separation slow (figures 3.3 and 3.4).

Figure 3.3 Estimated Drug Price Margin and Rate of Overall Drug Price Reduction on the Pharmaceutical Fee Schedule, 1981–2008

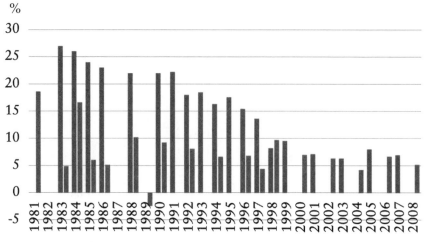

■ Estimated Drug Price Margin

■ Rate of Overall Drug Price Reduction in Pharmaceutical Expenditure

Source: Drug Price Expert Committee, Central Social Insurance Medical Council 2000, 2005, 2007; MHLW 2007.

Note: With the introduction of the consumption tax, drug prices on the pharmaceutical fee schedule were increased in 1989.

In the 1990s the annual increase in total health-care expenditure slowed (figure 3.1).[18] To further squeeze drug price margins, policymakers introduced a new calculation method in 1992, the so-called R-zone (see chapter 2 of this book, Iizuka, for details). As a result, drug price margins were substantially narrowed during that decade. At the same time, the prescription-issuing fee continued to increase slightly, from 740 yen in 1990 to 810 yen in 1998 (figure 3.2). With this combination of factors, progress toward separation accelerated during the 1990s (figure 3.4).[19]

It is worth noting that, though retaining substantial power, the JMA gradually lost its organizational strength and influence to an important stakeholder, the LDP (Noto 1999). But the JMA still clamored against any change that reduced physician income or restricted professional freedom, usually asserting that its objections were for the sake of the public. In this way the JMA managed to win small concessions.

Figure 3.4 Ratio of Achieved Separation, 1970–2007

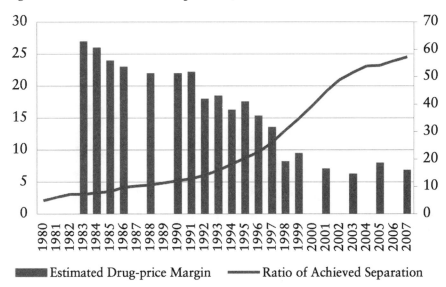

Estimated Drug-price Margin ——**Ratio of Achieved Separation**

Source: JPA 2008; Drug Price Expert Committee, Central Social Insurance Medical Council 2000, 2005; MHLW 2007.

The Challenges of Separation

Pharmaceutical Expenditures

Policymakers expected that expenditures might increase after introducing separation policies, at least in the short run, because of the introduction of the pharmacists' prescribing fee. But since separation was achieved mainly by reducing provider markups, or profit margins from dispensing drugs, the government expected cost containment in pharmaceuticals. In fact, considerable decreases in drug price margins in the 1990s were arguably based on measures taken in the 1980s. Pharmaceutical expenditures as a percentage of total health expenditures were curtailed, but pharmaceutical expenditures continued to increase at a gradual rate (figure 3.5).

Progress toward Separation Is Slow

As figure 3.4 shows, the rate of achieved separation has been flattening out. Furthermore, regional disparity is substantial. Fukui Prefecture had the lowest separation ratio at 25.1 percent and Akita Prefecture the highest at 72.9 percent as of September 2007 (figure 3.6). The achieved separation ratio also differs across specialties, with obstetrics and gynecology having the lowest at 20.7 percent and otorhinolaryngology the highest at 60.9 percent (figure 3.7). These differences may stem from variations in specialties, patient mix (aging versus young), and the proportion of clinics, hospitals, and pharmacies across regions; more empirical analysis is needed to determine the key factors and their influence.

Figure 3.5 Trends in Pharmaceutical Expenditure

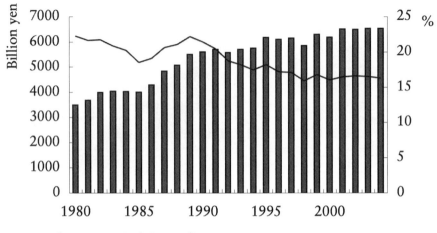

■■■ Pharmaceutical Expenditure

—— Pharmaceutical Expenditure as % of Total Health Expenditure

Source: OECD Health Data 2007.

Note: Since 2003, when the diagnosis procedure combination system—which is similar to the diagnostic-related group/prospective payment system (DRG/PPS) in the United States but reimbursed per diem—was introduced, pharmaceutical expenditure has been underestimated.

Collusive Relationships of Clinics, Hospitals, and Pharmacies

In Japan, if one's spouse or one's relative within the third degree of kinship is affiliated with a neighborhood clinic or hospital, one cannot open a pharmacy or join its board. Also, pharmacies are not supposed to be located on the same premises as a clinic or hospital, unless both rent their offices from a third party. Despite these regulations, gateway pharmacies (*monzen yakkyoku*) have emerged in order to get around separation policies. Gateway pharmacies are usually located near (often in front of or next to) clinics or hospitals and collude with them to increase profits.

Changes in Prescription Patterns

Before separation became popular, physicians preferred generic to brand-name drugs because the former usually brought in higher profits (see chapter 2 of this book).[20] As efforts toward separation have progressed, however, brand-name drug sales have increased, although many other factors have contributed to this trend. For example, in July 2006, 48.6 percent of prescriptions from dispensing doctors included at least one generic, whereas only 41.4 percent of prescriptions from nondispensing physicians did so. Prescribing doctors choose generics less frequently than dispensing doctors in proportions that have remained steady over five years (Survey of National Medical Care Insurance Services, MHLW 2006).

Figure 3.6 Separation Ratio by Prefecture, September 2007

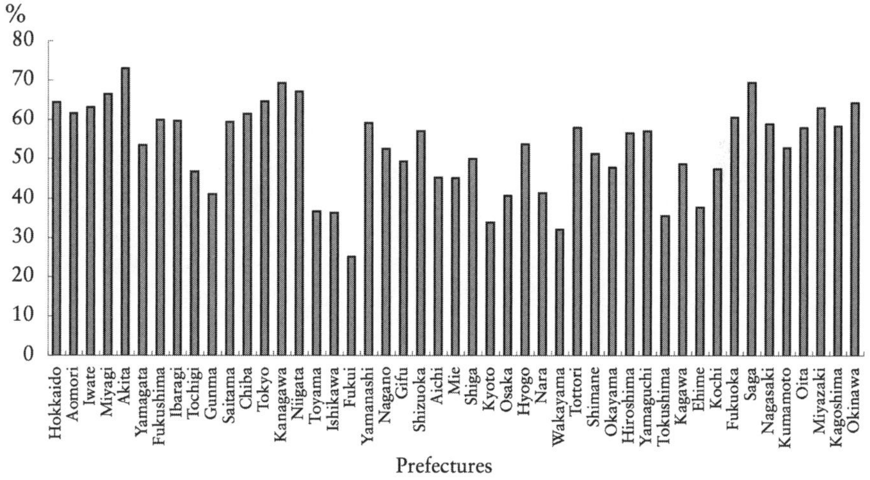

Source: JPA 2008.

Implications and Concluding Remarks

Confronted with rising pharmaceutical expenditures and low economic growth, health policymakers in Japan have worked to promote the separation of medical practice from drug dispensing since 1980. Yet despite implementing relevant laws, the government could not achieve separation for many years because of the opposition of vested interests, especially those of physicians. Learning from previous unsuccessful attempts, the MHW chose to incrementally introduce separation by giving financial incentives to physicians through the manipulation of the medical and pharmaceutical fee schedules. Mainly as a result of efforts to diminish drug price margins, the number of prescriptions dispensed by pharmacies rather than doctors grew rapidly throughout the 1990s.

This incremental approach, however, encountered obstacles such as collusive relations between providers and pharmacies, a shift toward prescribing brand-name drugs, and (perhaps as a result) the continuing increase of pharmaceutical expenditures. The MHLW's primary response to these challenges has been to promote generic substitution since 2002, but further action is needed.

Figure 3.7 Separation Ratio by Specialty

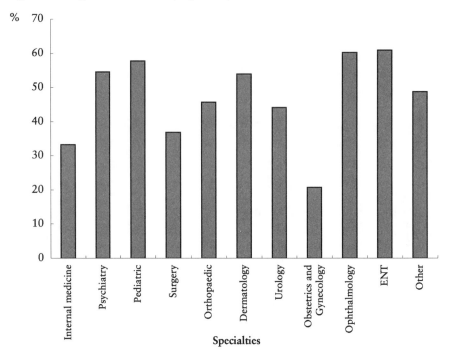

Source: MHLW 2002.
Note: Hospital outpatient service is excluded. ENT = ear, nose, and throat.

A fundamental but unaddressed issue is the recent leveling off of progress toward separation. This stagnation may be attributable to incremental reform and suggests that full separation is unlikely if nothing further is done. The MHLW has done little more than manipulate fee schedules; its interest in promoting separation seems to have flagged outside its recent enthusiasm for promoting generic substitution.

As described by Kwon and Hsieh in chapters 1 and 5 of this book, respectively, both South Korea and Taiwan have also made efforts to separate prescribing from dispensing—but using strategies different from those of Japan. South Korea implemented mandatory separation in August 2000; Taiwan implemented separation over four years, region by region. Comparing Japan's case with that of Taiwan (which allowed hospitals to keep pharmacy departments and clinics to hire pharmacists to dispense) would be mutually beneficial for considering the advantages and disadvantages of specific strategies to promote separation. Comparing Japan with South Korea offers insights into how to carry out the comprehensive reform of pharmaceutical and health policies. Instructive aspects of Korea's reforms include the role of civic groups led by academics, whose strategies to encourage separation include problem definition and policy framing (which Japan lacks partly due to its institutional decision-making process in the health arena). To further progress toward separation and move beyond incremental policy changes in the pharmaceutical area, Japan should perhaps take cues from South Korea and Taiwan.

Notes

[1] This chapter uses the official English names of surveys, departments, and agencies from the *Japanese-English Dictionary for Health and Labour Administration* compiled by the National Institute of Population and Social Security Research (http://www.ipss.go.jp/site-ad/yougo/gyousei.html). If no official name is included in the dictionary, the author uses names consistent with chapter 2 of this book.

[2] There are two kinds of data available on separation. One is from the MHLW, called *ingai shohouritsu* (rate of separation), and another is from the JPA, called *syohousen uketoriritsu* (ratio of received prescriptions). The former is only available for June every year, whereas the latter is available for each month and for each prefecture. Therefore, the ratio of received prescriptions is used throughout this chapter as the ratio of achieved separation. The numerator of this ratio is the number of prescriptions received at pharmacies. The denominator is an approximation of the total number of prescriptions issued (calculated as the total number of outpatients times the dispensing rate, plus the total number of dental patients times the dispensing rate). The dispensing rate is calculated yearly based on the most recent three years' Survey of National Medical Care Insurance Services (MHLW) after FY1999. For the dispensing rate from FY 1986 to FY1998, the survey in 1992 is used.

[3] Since medical practice was considered a humanitarian service, it was thought that doctors should not charge a consultation fee. As a result, the consultation fee was included in the charge for medication (Ikegami and Campbell 1996: 46).

[4] The government had let doctors make a profit on drugs in return for low consultation and treatment fees.

[5] In 2006, 82.1 percent of hospitals and 94.8 percent of clinics were operated privately (Survey of Medical Care Institutions, MHLW 2006).

[6] Above all, vitamins, poultices, and other antiphlogistic analgetics for external use appear to be overused.

[7] The amount of copayment or coinsurance depends on the type of medical insurance; except the elderly, most patients pay 30 percent of their medical treatment and pharmaceutical costs.

[8] The main income of clinics and hospitals is from health insurance reimbursements. Clinics and hospitals basically have to pay their operating

costs, fixed costs, and plant and equipment investments from the insurance reimbursement of medical fees.

[9] According to a survey conducted by the Ministry of Interior in 1877, there were 5,993 druggists in Japan (except Kagoshima Prefecture), of which only 23 had passed the exam laid down by Isei (Aoyagi 1996).

[10] Pharmaceutical companies kept silent about this because they thought that separation was a disadvantage to them. The JPA welcomed this but failed to let the law be implemented.

[11] Initially the government tried to respond to this by introducing a consumption tax. This was changed it to retrench finances in the wake of the general election in 1979.

[12] The MHW was reshaped into the MHLW as part of the reorganization of cabinet-level ministries and agencies in January 2001.

[13] Meanwhile, the Central Pharmaceutical Affairs Council oversees changes to the Pharmaceutical Affairs Law and the licensing of new drugs and medical devices.

[14] In March 2007 the number of committees from public interest increased from four to six. Accordingly, numbers of both representatives of medical service providers and insurance societies decreased from eight to seven.

[15] As of April 2008, the prescription-issuing fee was 400 yen if more than 7 kinds of oral medicines were prescribed and 680 yen otherwise. In addition, outpatient services, clinics, and hospitals with fewer than 200 beds could receive an additional 180 yen twice a month at maximum. If the prescription period exceeded 28 days, 450 yen could be claimed instead of the above-mentioned additional 180 yen (that is, the 450 yen and the 180 yen additions could not be claimed simultaneously). Dispensing physicians could not claim the prescription-issuing fee; they instead received a service fee for their prescription instructions (*shoho ryo*) and a dispensing fee (*chozai ryo*). Prescribing and dispensing fees for physicians are different from those for pharmacies that receive prescriptions and vary depending on type of drug and medical institution.

[16] The most recent Survey on Pharmaceutical Prices was carried out in October 2007. About 4,000 wholesalers, 900 hospitals, 1,000 clinics, and 1,600 pharmacies were surveyed on the numbers and purchasing/selling prices of drugs in September 2007. This data is not public.

[17] Before 1982 the pharmaceutical fee schedule was reviewed once every two or three years.

[18] Fee schedule prices have a strong correlation (0.78) to national health expenditures (Ikegami 2006:18).

[19] In some years, estimated drug price margins rose slightly from previous years while ratios of achieved separation increased. This is partly because of the administration costs of self-dispensing. As pharmaceutical expenditures and

total health expenditures are contained, some physicians who own their own clinics or hospitals prefer ending self-dispensing to having dead stocks of drugs and paying the labor costs involved.

[20] Under such circumstances, domestic pharmaceutical companies have competed by lowering prices rather than by developing new, innovative drugs. As a result, the pharmaceutical market in Japan is dominated by relatively small and medium-size domestic pharmaceutical manufacturers.

References

Aoyagi, S. 1996. *History of remuneration for medical services* [in Japanese]. Kyoto: Shibunkaku.

Arioka, J. 1997. *Fifty years of health care after the Second World War* [in Japanese]. Tokyo: Nihon iji shinpo.

Drug Price Expert Committee, Central Social Insurance Medical Council. 2000, 2005, 2007.

Hokkaido, Iho. 2005. The 112th JMA Regular Board of Representatives [in Japanese]. *Hokkaido iho* 1040: 6–13.

Ikegami, N. 2006. The mechanism of health care system and major issues for reform [in Japanese]. *Shakai hoken junpo* 2266: 12–19.

Ikegami, N., and J. C. Campbell. 1996. *The art of balance in health policy—maintaining Japan's low cost, egalitarian system* [in Japanese]. Tokyo: Chuo kouron.

Japan Pharmaceutical Association. 2008.

JPA. *See* Japan Pharmaceutical Association.

Kosaka, H. 1997. *The era of separation of dispensary from medical practice* [in Japanese]. Tokyo: Keiso.

Medical Fee Schedule. Various years.

MHLW. *See* Ministry of Health, Labour, and Welfare.

Ministry of Health, Labour, and Welfare. 2002, 2006, 2007. Survey of National Medical Care Insurance Services.

Ministry of Internal Affairs and Communications. 2008.

Mizuno, H. 2003. *Untold Japan medical association* [in Japanese]. Tokyo: Soushi sha.

National Accounts, Cabinet Office. 2000, 2005, 2008.

Nishio, M., and M. Muramatsu. 1994. *Welfare state and public administration* [in Japanese]. Kouza Gyoseigaku 1. Tokyo: Yuhikaku, 35–72.

Noto, Y. 1999. *American Medical Association (AMA) and its membership strategy and possible applications for the Japan Medical Association (JMA).* Boston, MA: Takemi Program in International Health, Harvard School of Public Health.

O'Connell, J. M. 1996. The relationship between health expenditures and the age structure of the population in OECD countries. *Health Economy 5* (6): 573–78.

OECD. *See* Organisation for Economic Co-operation and Development.

Organisation for Economic Co-operation and Development. 2007. Health data.

Pfaff, M. 1990. Differences in health care spending across the countries: statistical evidence. *J. Health Politics, Policy Law* 15 (1): 1–67.

Reich, M. R. 2002. The politics of reforming health policies. *Promotion & Education* 9 (4): 138–42.

Sams, C. F. 1986. *DDT revolution* [in Japanese]. Tokyo: Iwanami.

Takemi, T. 1983. *Factual story of Japan Medical Association* [in Japanese]. Tokyo: Asahi.

Yamaguchi, J. 1989. *Collapse of single-party regime* [in Japanese]. Tokyo: Iwanami.

Pharmaceutical Policy in Seven Asia-Pacific Health-care Systems

Thailand

PHARMACEUTICAL POLICY IN THAILAND: A REVIEW OF THREE DECADES OF GOVERNMENT INTERVENTIONS

Sauwakon Ratanawijitrasin[1]

The announcement that Thailand's Ministry of Public Health (MOPH) had issued compulsory licenses for three pharmaceutical products in November 2007 and January 2008 intensified global debates on the protection of intellectual property rights (IPRs) versus the provision of greater access to medicine. It also triggered some developing countries to follow suit.

The Thai government's action is but one in a long stream of public policies targeting pharmaceuticals. In recent years, the government has adopted a series of policy interventions with broad impact on the Thai health sector and pharmaceuticals in particular. Such policies have sought to regulate pharmaceutical procurement, production, pricing, payment, and patents.

In this chapter, I trace key pharmaceutical policies, assess their consequences, and examine them in relation to the country's specific context. I emphasize current policies of broad interest; those that do not involve concrete policy mechanisms such as laws, rules, or mandates are not included. I first provide a brief background to the country's pharmaceutical sector. This is followed by a review of the core content of key pharmaceutical policies implemented over the past three decades. I conclude by analyzing the causes, contents, contexts, consequences, and controversies surrounding these government measures.

Please note that this chapter focuses only on markets and policies related to Western medicine, or the category called "modern medicine for human use" under Thai law; it does not address traditional medicine (which has a consumption value of about 3 percent of modern medicine).

Pharmaceutical Sector Overview

The Market

Both locally manufactured and imported pharmaceutical products compete in the Thai market. In 2006 the total value of pharmaceutical production and imports amounted to $2.5 million (75,429 million Thai baht at a rate of 30 baht per dollar). Finished products manufactured locally accounted for over $1 million, or 41 percent of the market. These included both generics—mostly manufactured by locally owned firms—and brand-name drugs either produced by subsidiaries of multinational companies (MNCs) or local firms manufacturing under license.

Figure 4.1 shows the local production and import values of modern finished pharmaceutical products for human use over the past two decades. In the 1980s the value of products manufactured in the country were significantly higher than imports. The proportion of imports rose in the early and mid-1990s, a period of high economic growth. The value of both locally manufactured and imported pharmaceutical products dropped in 1998, the year following the economic crisis. The market picked up again in 1999 and has continued to grow since. In 2005 the value of imported pharmaceutical products, rising at an accelerated rate, surpassed the value of locally manufactured products for the first time.

According to the Office of Industrial Economics, over 40 percent of imported medicines come from the United States, France, Germany, Switzerland, and Great Britain. Exports constitute a small proportion of the overall volume, approximately 11 percent of domestic pharmaceutical production in 2005.[2] The main export market is within the Association of Southeast Asian Nations (ASEAN) region. About 60 percent of pharmaceutical exports, mostly generic drugs, go to Vietnam, Myanmar, Cambodia, Malaysia, and Hong Kong (Office of Industrial Economics 2007). The 2007 value of pharmaceutical exports was approximately 0.14 percent of the country's total exports (Department of Export Promotion 2008).

The Industry

Similar to the majority of its ASEAN neighbors, Thailand's pharmaceutical industry is in a formulation stage. It relies on the import of raw materials—especially active pharmaceutical ingredients—to manufacture finished products, which are mostly consumed domestically.

With the exception of manufacturing facilities under the Government Pharmaceutical Organization (GPO), the Military Pharmaceutical Organization, and very small-scale production in some government hospitals, the majority of pharmaceutical production is done by the private sector, including both multinational subsidiaries and local companies. There are 168 manufacturers and 635 importers of modern medicines in the country, all of which are small and medium-size enterprises (SMEs) (table 4.1). Over 86 percent of local manufacturers are small companies with investments of less than $2 million (Amprai et al. 2000).

Thailand depends on the research, development, and supply of pharmaceuticals from other countries. Not only are almost all raw materials imported, but new drugs are almost all introduced into the market by MNCs. The revealed comparative advantage index of pharmaceuticals ranges only between 0.1 and 0.24, indicating that this sector is not competitive in the global market (Supakanjakanti et al. 2001).

Thailand manufactures only a few raw materials for pharmaceuticals. There are some ten manufacturers of pharmaceutical raw materials, of which the GPO is a key player (Thai Drug System Study Project Committee 2002).

Raw materials produced locally include both active ingredients and additives. But all the active ingredients made locally are low-priced drugs that have been on the market for decades.

Although the actual research and development (R&D) tasks performed and the extent of investment allocated to R&D are not known, it is generally agreed that pharmaceutical companies in Thailand invest little in R&D. These small investments, where available, are mainly used to develop product formulations rather than research new drugs. Unsurprisingly, then, Thailand does not possess adequate capability for new drug discovery (Janjaroen et al. 1999).

Figure 4.1 Trends in the Local Production and Import of Pharmaceutical Products, 1987–2005

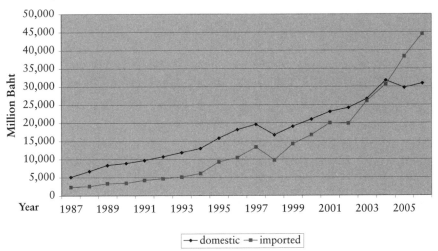

Source: Data from the Thai FDA Web site, http://wwwapp1.fda.moph.go.th/drug/zone_search/files/sea001_001.asp.
Note: Values in Thai currency (baht).

Market Competition

The Drug Act, which currently governs pharmaceutical sector activities, allows the lifelong registration of pharmaceutical products. That is, once a product is registered, there is no need to renew the license. According to the Thai Food and Drug Administration (FDA) Web site, as of November 2007, 33,743 modern pharmaceutical products were registered for human use. Among them, 25,297 were locally manufactured and 8,446 were imported.[3] Products under the same brand name but with more than one color or dosage form are required to have a different registration license for each color and form.

Table 4.1 Number of Manufacturers, Importers, and Drugstores (2007)

License type	Bangkok	Other provinces	Total
Manufacturer of modern drugs	102	66	168
Manufacturer of traditional drugs	293	702	995
Importer of modern drugs	547	88	635
Importer of traditional drugs	161	22	183
Modern drugstore (class A)	3,765	5,186	8,951
Modern drugstore (class B)	462	4,031	4,493
Traditional drugstore	418	1,696	2,114

Source: Thai Food and Drug Administration Web site, http://wwwapp1.fda. moph.go.th/drug/zone_search/files/sea001_003.asp.

Widely used generic products are manufactured by a large number of companies, creating a competitive environment. But because the advantages of research or claims of superior quality are almost absent in the generic market, most generic suppliers compete mainly on price.

Tables 4.2 and 4.3 list the hospital purchase and sale prices of selected drugs with high and low degrees of price competition, respectively. Note that in table 4.2, among the 36 brands of diclofenac 25 mg tablets/capsules purchased by 526 hospitals, the highest price is 182 times the lowest price. For the 10 brands of ranitidine 150 mg tablets/capsules purchased by 400 hospitals, the price differential is 112 times; and for the 23 brands of glibenclamide, it is 39 times. By contrast, products with fewer suppliers differ less in price, as shown in table 4.3. Price differentials occur not only between different brands of the same drug (with the same generic name) but also when the same product is sold to different hospitals (Ratanawijitrasin et al. 2003).

Distribution

Pharmaceutical products are distributed to consumers through different channels, as depicted in figure 4.2. The majority, in terms of value, go through government health facilities—hospitals and health centers. Together with private hospitals, which make up 14 percent of the total, the hospital sector is the largest channel, distributing approximately 58 percent of the total value of medicine reaching end users. With the introduction of the 30 Baht Health Insurance Scheme, which pays for visits to hospitals but not to private clinics and drugstores, the percentage of medicines distributed through hospitals is expected to increase.

Table 4.2 Prices of Selected Pharmaceuticals with High Degree of Market Competition Bought and Sold by Hospitals (prices in baht)

Generic	No. brands	Sale price				Purchase price			
		No. hosp.	Lowest	Highest	Diff.	No. hosp.	Lowest	Highest	Diff.
Diclofenac 25 mg.	36	578	0.06	15.00	250.0	526	0.04	7.29	182.3
Ranitidine 150 mg.	10	425	0.25	43.25	173.0	400	0.13	14.61	112.4
Glibenclamide 5 mg.	23	594	0.10	12.00	120.0	547	0.07	2.74	39.1

Source: Ratanawijitrasin et al. 2003, p. 16.

Table 4.3 Prices of Selected Pharmaceuticals with Low Degree of Market Competition Bought and Sold by Hospitals (prices in baht)

Generic	No. brands	Sale price				Purchase price			
		No. hosp.	Lowest	Highest	Diff.	No. hosp.	Lowest	Highest	Diff.
Atrovastatin 10 mg	1	95	37.98	85.00	2.2	73	26.59	61.50	2.3
Celecoxib 200 mg	1	109	22.44	50.00	2.2	76	22.36	24.61	1.1
Hepatitis B vaccine 20 mg/ml	4	126	200.00	675.00	3.4	152	140	428.00	3.1
Methrotrexate 2.5 mg	5	142	4.80	35.00	7.3	113	2.85	15.47	5.4
Sulbutamol 100 mcg/dose	2	33	182.33	585.00	3.2	50	150	508.25	3.4

Source: Ratanawijitrasin et al. 2003, p. 18.

Figure 4.2 Distribution of Pharmaceutical Products through Various Channels with Percentage in Values

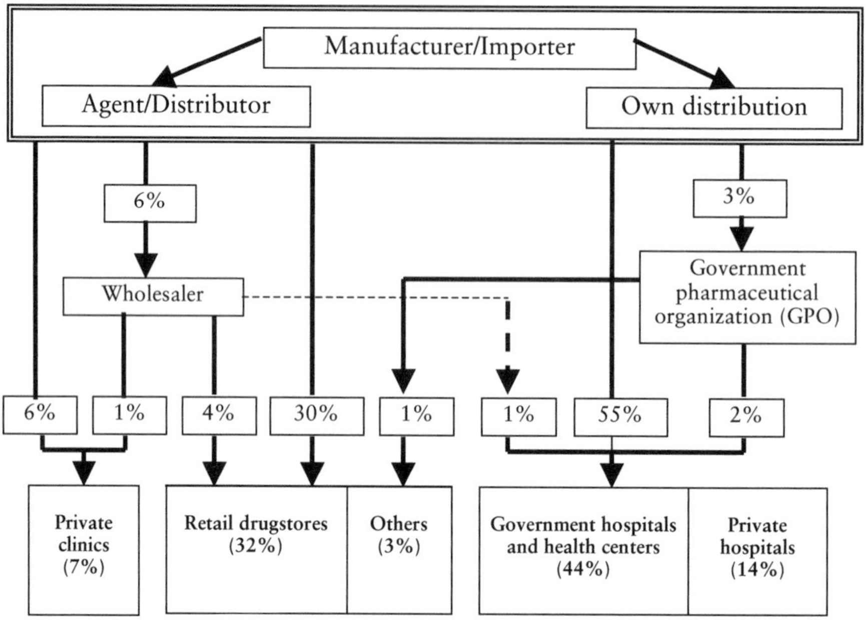

Source: Adapted from Thai Drug System Study Project Committee 2002, p. 92.

Three Decades of Pharmaceutical Policy Interventions

Thai government interventions in the pharmaceutical sector have historically been limited to regulating certain aspects of pharmaceutical manufacturing and sale, with a focus on the safety and efficacy of pharmaceutical products and business enterprises involved in the pharmaceutical trade. The Drug Act of 1967 (Buddhist Era, B.E., 2510), which is currently in use, sets basic requirements for drug registration; product quality; labeling; advertising; and licensing of drug manufacturers, importers, distributors, and sellers. The Drug Act has been amended several times since but without significant changes in its scope and focus. A new Drug Bill has been drafted and debated for several years now, yet controversies persist. One of the main issues keeping the bill in limbo is the proposed separation of prescribing from dispensing, a longstanding policy in Western countries more recently implemented in several Asian countries (as described further in this book).

An attempt by the government to exert broader influence over the pharmaceutical sector came in the early 1980s. Responding to drug policy initiatives put forth by the World Health Organization (WHO) in 1975, Thailand formulated a National Drug Policy (NDP) put into effect in 1981. The NDP was revised in 1993, with minor changes. The NDP states broad goals to be achieved. These include: (1) ensuring that effective, safe, good-quality, and reasonably priced pharmaceuticals are distributed throughout the country; (2) achieving rational use of medicine and reducing waste in utilization; (3) helping the local pharmaceutical industry achieve self-sufficiency; (4) supporting the production of raw pharmaceutical materials; (5) encouraging research in traditional medicines; and (6) enforcing the use of the National Essential Drug List (NEDL) in both public and private sectors (National Drug Committee 1993). The first concrete policy measures to directly follow the NDP were the development of the NEDL and directives on using the list for pharmaceutical procurement. These directives aimed to control pharmaceutical spending within government health facilities.

Since enacting the NDP in 1981, the Thai government has initiated a number of other policies and programs that either directly regulate or impact the pharmaceutical sector. Some of these claim a link to the goals set in the NDP, such as programs targeting the rational use of drugs in hospitals, support of the local pharmaceutical industry, and updates of the NEDL. Other policies, however, are not contained in the NDP or envisioned by it, such as laws covering product patent, adopting ASEAN-harmonized standards of product registration, and use of the NEDL as the reimbursement list for civil service medical benefits. After decades of implementation, it is unclear to what extent the NDP has played a role in shaping the Thai pharmaceutical sector.

Five areas in the pharmaceutical sector have been the main targets of policy interventions in the past three decades: procurement, production, pricing, payment, and patents. I will discuss these five areas in turn.

Pharmaceutical Procurement: Cost Containment of Public-sector Health Services

Most hospitals in Thailand are government owned. To save money, the government exerts control over drug procurement and inventory management in its health facilities. The two policies described in this subsection are the main instruments used by the government to achieve this aim.

Procurement Rules for Government Agencies

Immediately following the introduction of the NDP, the MOPH instituted a central procurement system for the purchase of drugs within the health facilities under its jurisdiction. It required that only items listed in the NEDL be purchased using government-allocated drug budgets. The GPO was assigned the responsibility of serving as a central purchaser agency.

As the system was being implemented in the five years that followed, many complained of inefficiency, especially long delays in purchase order delivery. A study found that, after filing a purchase order, the average hospital waited 52 days to receive medicines—about three times longer than when ordering from pharmaceutical companies. Nonetheless, the prices of most items purchased using the centralized procurement system were lower than those purchased directly from pharmaceutical companies (Ratanawijitrasin 1987).

In 1986 the MOPH procurement regulations were replaced by new rules established by the Office of the Prime Minister. These applied to all government agencies and to all categories of government procurement and included a special section on pharmaceutical procurement. They expanded the scope of drug procurement regulation to all government health facilities, added new requirements, and substituted a decentralized system for the centralized one.

The Office of the Prime Minister's rules on government procurement, in the 1992 version currently in use, consist of the following key mandates:

- *Drug list to be tied to budget.* MOPH health facilities must use no less than 80 percent and other government health facilities no less than 60 percent of their allocated drug budgets to purchase drugs listed under the NEDL.
- *Price ceiling.* the price of essential drugs purchased must not exceed that listed on the median price list established by the government.
- *GPO privilege.* if the GPO manufactures any items on the NEDL, government health facilities are required to buy these from only the GPO unless the GPO price exceeds the median price by 3 percent.

In actuality, however, hospitals have not strictly followed the budgetary limits set for the procurement of essential drugs. This is especially true in secondary and tertiary care settings. In addition, because the restriction on what percentage of the budget can be used to purchase essential drugs only applies to the government-allocated budget, providers are free to use extrabudgetary funds (for example, revolving funds and donations) to purchase what they want. In large hospitals, drug purchases using these additional sources may significantly exceed those using the government-allocated drug budget. Furthermore, the median price list is not updated regularly enough to keep pace with market changes. Since the generics market is highly competitive, hospitals are generally able to purchase generics on the NEDL for prices lower than those specified on the median price list. By contrast, essential drug items that have only a single supplier or a small number of suppliers often cost more than the median price listed, making it infeasible to purchase at the regulated price.

After the introduction of the 30 Baht Health Insurance Scheme in 2002, the government began allocating hospital budgets as fixed sums calculated on a per registered person basis. There is not yet any clear statement reconciling the procurement rules of the government drug budget with the current capitation payment rules.

Of the three key mandates set by the government procurement rules, the budget proportion and the median price requirements are confusing in practice and have proved ineffective in bringing down costs. By late 2007 a new set of government procurement rules—without the clause granting GPO privilege—was drafted and in the process for adoption.

The "Good Health at Low Cost" Initiative

Because Thailand is dependent on pharmaceutical imports, when the Thai baht crumbled during the 1997 economic crisis, medicine prices soared. In response, in early 1998, the MOPH announced a set of new measures for pharmaceutical procurement and inventories dubbed the "Good Health at Low Cost" initiative. This policy aimed to control costs by limiting the number of drugs that hospitals were allowed to stock and by setting minimum percentages of essential drugs. It also called for all health facilities to prescribe generic drugs and to increase the number of items that hospitals would purchase through a pooled procurement system.

Studies on the implementation of this policy found that while the number of pharmaceuticals purchased through the pooled procurement system increased, compliance with other components of the policy package varied. Although the percentages of items listed in the NEDL and stocked by the hospitals grew somewhat, it was unclear if this was a result of the policy or the new version of the NEDL, which significantly expanded the number of drug items (Thai Drug System Study Project Committee 2002).

Pharmaceutical Production: Attempts to Ensure Quality Manufacturing

The MOPH introduced good manufacturing practice (GMP) standards to the pharmaceutical manufacturing processes in 1984. The policy started as a voluntary measure that firms were encouraged to follow. The Thai FDA organized training courses to support local industry in meeting the standards. GMP certificates were awarded to companies that met the GMP standards based on manufacturing category (that is, for tablets, injectables, and so on).

After twenty years as a voluntary program, the GMP standards were made mandatory for local manufacturers in 2003. At that time, only about three-fourths of pharmaceutical producers met the standards in at least one manufacturing category. Four years into implementation, the Thai FDA Web site (as of December 2007) showed that 92 percent of pharmaceutical producers were GMP-certified (table 4.4), while the rest were classified as "in the process of improvement," with their businesses still in operation.

Table 4.4 Number of Manufacturers that are GMP-certified Compared with Total

Year	Manufacturers of modern medicines	
	Total	GMP-certified
2000	174	127
2001	172	131
2002	174	134
2003	174	133
2004	171	141
2005	166	151
2006	162	153
2007	166	153

Source: Thai Food and Drug Association Web site, http://wwwapp1.fda.moph. go.th/drug/zone_search/files/sea001_008.asp.
Note: The number of manufacturers for 2007 shown here is different from that shown in table 4.1 (two manufacturers short), also from the Thai FDA Web site. GMP = good manufacturing practice.

Pharmaceutical Prices: Regulating What Consumers Pay

Thai law allows direct control of consumer prices for goods considered essential. As pharmaceuticals are one of the key commodities affecting cost of living, they are subject to price control.

The Price Regulation Act of 1979 (B.E. 2522) provided the legal basis for price control of commodities, including pharmaceuticals, until the Goods and Services Price Act and the Trade Competition Act replaced it in 1999. The Department of Internal Trade in the Ministry of Commerce has the authority to carry out this consumer price control function.

In practice, price regulation of pharmaceuticals is relatively limited. It normally targets manufacturers' and importers' price increases and retail prices. To raise a price, pharmaceutical companies are required to request approval. But the said price applies to companies' listed price rather than to the actual cost to health-care providers. The decision to grant a price increase is generally a procedural matter. Only twice in recent history have pharmaceutical price increases been limited. The first was when the government reformed the country's sales tax system, adopting a new 7 percent value-added tax (VAT) in January 1992. When the VAT was introduced, pharmaceutical prices rose disproportionate to the tax increase. Consequently, the Ministry of Commerce requested pharmaceutical companies to hold their prices at October 1991 levels. The ministry later allowed a price increase of no greater than 10 percent for individual items submitted and approved by the ministry.

The second time such limits were set was in 1997–1998, the aftermath of the economic crisis, when the Ministry of Commerce placed percentage caps on allowable price increases for both imported and locally manufactured pharmaceutical products.

Traditionally, the Ministry of Commerce oversaw prices of pharmaceutical products sold by drugstores but not those sold by hospitals. Hospital prices for the same products were often higher than drugstore prices. Only recently did the Ministry of Commerce take a more active role in the oversight of hospitals. When drug prices attracted media attention during the debates surrounding compulsory licensing, the ministry demanded cooperation from private hospitals to present their medicine price list upon patient request, reduce prices by 5 to 15 percent on selected drugs, and to not increase prices for at least six months (Matichon 2008).

Payment Incentives: Altering Pharmaceutical Prices and Utilization

Health Insurance

Public policies governing health insurance generally address issues related to coverage, benefits, and financing. And, often, they have significant implications for the utilization of pharmaceuticals.

In the past three to four decades, the Thai government has launched a number of health security policies, beginning with offering coverage for specific population groups, then moving to provide universal coverage. In the 1970s the government introduced a program to provide free care to low-income families and individuals, elderly people, children, and people with disabilities. In the 1980s, it initiated a subsidized health insurance system for rural communities. With the introduction of the Social Security Act in 1990 (B.E. 2533), Thailand instituted a major social health insurance system for the first time. This scheme covers employees of private businesses in the formal sector. Substantial movements in health-sector reform aimed at introducing universal health insurance coverage started in the mid-1990s. The reform efforts culminated in 2001 with the launch of the 30 Baht Health Insurance Scheme, which brought universal coverage to the population. This was followed by the enactment of the National Health Security Act in 2002 (B.E. 2545), which provided a legal basis for universal health insurance.

This new insurance program consolidated several previous government welfare and small-scale health insurance programs, including the low-income and rural-focused programs described above. The program name derives from the 30 baht ($1) copayment initially charged for each visit. Although the 30 baht copayment was abolished in late 2006, making it a "0 baht" scheme, "30 baht" remains the most popular way to refer to this program. At present it operates alongside two other major public schemes—the Social Security Scheme (SSS) and Civil Service Medical Benefits Scheme (CSMBS)—as well as private health insurance (Ratanawijitrasin 2005). Together, these programs covered approximately 63.24

million people (96.3 percent of the population) in 2007, with the majority under the 30 Baht Scheme (National Statistics Bureau 2007).

Finance and provider payments for outpatient and inpatient services are summarized in table 4.5; methods of pharmaceuticals payment are presented in a separate column. Note that this table indicates only major payment mechanisms; there are minor variations in payment method (for example, additional payment for outlier cases) not presented here.

Because of its sheer size, the introduction of the 30 Baht Scheme significantly shifted the landscape of the country's health-care financing and delivery systems. The capitation payment, as used by the 30 Baht Scheme and the SSS, placed the financial risk of service provision on health-care providers as never before. Hospitals have now become active players in cost containment, complementing the efforts of the MOPH, which has traditionally taken the key role in cost control. But closer examination reveals that hospitals play only a selective role in cost control. Clearly, the different methods of pharmaceutical payment employed by the various health insurance schemes have introduced different financial pressures and incentives for health-service providers. This has led to several phenomena in the utilization of pharmaceuticals:

Originator-generic discrepancy. Prescribing patterns differ for originator drugs and generic drugs among the different groups of health insurance beneficiaries. Empirical data show that a higher percentage of patients whose health insurance pays on a per-item basis receive originator (brand-name) products than those whose health insurance pays on a capitation basis (figure 4.3).

High-low technology discrepancy. Similarly, higher percentages of self-pay patients and patients whose health insurance pays on a per-item basis received new or expensive medicines than those whose health insurance pays on a capitation basis (figures 4.4 through 4.6). Many hospitals providing services to patients from different health insurance schemes have multiple formularies, each of which lists medicines allowed for prescribing to beneficiaries of a specific health insurance scheme.

Inpatient-outpatient shift. With the CSMBS adopting diagnosis-related groups (DRGs) as the payment method to control inpatient spending while retaining fee-for-service payment for outpatient services, there is strong incentive to shift services from an inpatient to an outpatient setting. Utilization shifts are consistent with this incentive. But it is unclear what part of this trend is attributable to the payment incentives and what to the development of medical technologies that allow treatments previously performed on an inpatient basis to become outpatient services.

Table 4.5 Main Features of Financing and Payment for Thai Health Insurance Schemes

Health insurance scheme	Finance source	Main provider/Payment method		
		Outpatient	Inpatient	Drugs
30 Baht	Taxes	Capitation	DRG	Capitation (included)
Social Security Services	Tri-partite contributions	Capitation (all inclusive)		
Civil Service Medical Benefits	Taxes	FFS	DRG	Per item
Private	Premiums	FFS	FFS	Per item

Source: Translated from Ratanawijitrasin 2005, p. 6.
Note: DRG = diagnostic-related group payment; FFS = fee-for-service payment.

Figure 4.3 Percentages of Prescriptions with Originator versus Locally Manufactured Epoetin among Patients Covered under Different Health Insurance Schemes

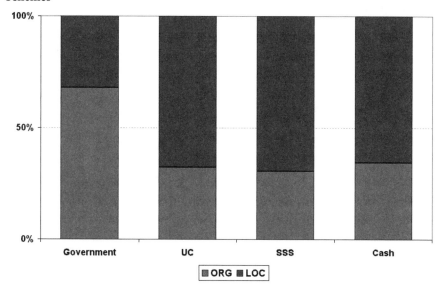

Source: Pharmaceutical System Research and Intelligence Center (PSyRIC) hospital drug utilization database.
Note: FY 2006 data from nine government hospitals. Self-pay patients include those who get reimbursed afterwards.
SSS = Social Security Scheme; CSMBS = Civil Service Medical Benefits Scheme; ORG = originator; LOC = local.

Figure 4.4 Percentage of Patients Prescribed Epoetin, Classified by Insurance Scheme

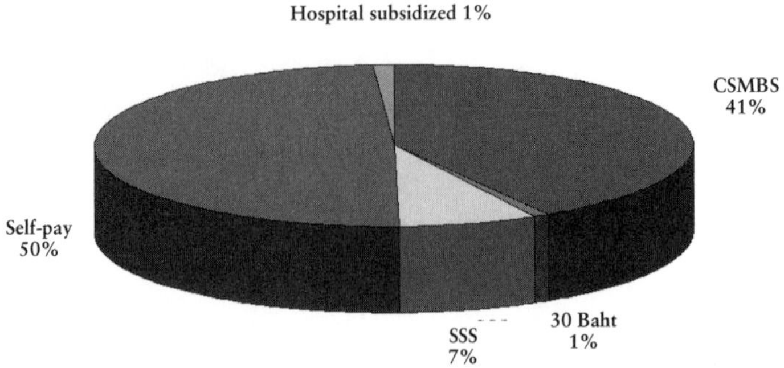

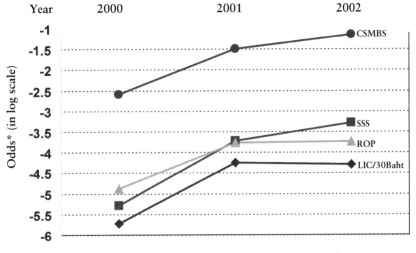

Hospital subsidized 1%
CSMBS
41%
Self-pay
50%
SSS
7%
30 Baht
1%

Source: Pharmaceutical System Research and Intelligence Center (PSyRIC) hospital drug-utilization database.
Note: FY 2006 data from nine government hospitals. SSS = Social Security Scheme; CSMBS = Civil Service Medical Benefits Scheme; 30 Baht = 30 Baht Health Insurance Scheme.

Figure 4.5 Odds of Receiving COX2 Inhibitors among Patients Covered by Different Insurance Schemes

Year
2000
2001
2002
-1
-1.5
-2
-2.5
-3
-3.5
-4
-4.5
-5
-5.5
-6
Odds* (in log scale)
CSMBS
SSS
ROP
LIC/30Baht
Odds* = exp(constant+bAge+bGender+bScheme+bYear+bSchemexYear+bHosp)

Source: Limwattananon et al. 2004.
Note: Analysis of data from eighteen provincial hospitals indicates that patients covered by the Civil Servant Medical Benefit Scheme (CSMBS) were 9.7–13.2 and 15.6–23.1 times ($P<0.001$)) more likely to receive COX2 inhibitors in a year than Social Security Scheme (SSS), low-income card/30 Baht Scheme beneficiaries and the rest of population, respectively. The analysis is from prescription data, no adjustments made for possible factors affecting utilization.

Figure 4.6 Time-series Data Showing Proportion of Diabetic Patient Visits with Thiazolidinediones Prescribed

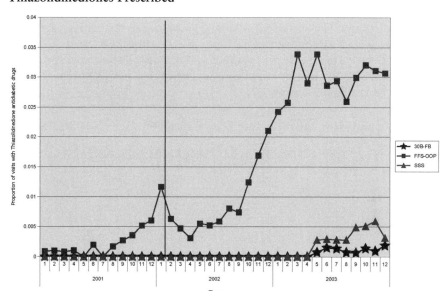

Source: Kanchanaphibool 2005.
Note: Time-series data from four government hospitals. The 30 Baht Health Insurance Scheme was introduced in January 2002.

It appears that insurance payment methods exert a strong influence on prescribing choices and pharmaceutical utilization. Discrepancies in the use of medicines among beneficiaries covered by different insurance schemes raise concerns regarding access to new medicines, quality of care, and equity among beneficiaries of different health insurance systems. More in-depth studies on these issues, with adjustments for relevant factors (such as age, diagnosis mix, and so on) should provide a clearer picture of the drug-utilization patterns under the various health insurance schemes.

The NEDL: From Procurement List to Insurance Payment List

The NEDL was first introduced in 1981 as a procurement list to control costs in government health facilities. After the economic crisis, the Cabinet decided to use it as a reimbursement list for the CSMBS as well as a cost-containment measure in 1998. This led to a major revision of the NEDL, which resulted in a greatly expanded list in 1999. According to this Cabinet resolution, CSMBS beneficiaries have to pay out of pocket for drugs not contained on the NEDL. Nevertheless, prescription of nonlisted drugs can be authorized for reimbursement if signed by hospital drug committee members, who thus confirm the appropriateness of prescribing such drugs.

This policy met with the same fate as the government rules over procurement of essential drugs. The stipulated reimbursement requirements have generally not been followed. Prescriptions for "nonessential" drugs are regularly signed, endorsing them for reimbursement without actual review. The overall expenditure figures of the CSMBS do not provide any evidence that this particular Cabinet resolution was effective (figure 4.7).

Figure 4.7 Outpatient, Inpatient, and Total Expenditure Trends of the CSMBS

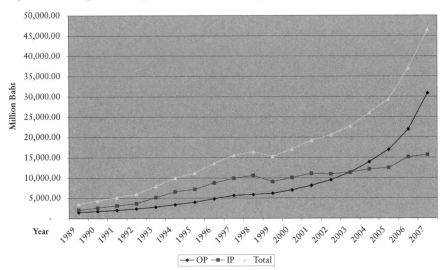

Source: Charted using data from the Department of the Comptroller General, Ministry of Finance.

Note: CSMBS = Civil Service Medical Benefits Scheme; IPD = inpatient department; OPD = outpatient department.

Pharmaceutical Patents: Dispute over IPR Protection, Public Health, and Trade

The Patent Act

Thailand adopted its first patent law in 1979, exempting pharmaceutical products from patent protection. Considering the lack of domestic capacity to conduct R&D, the 1979 legislation only allowed for pharmaceutical process patents, not product patents. Under this legal environment, the Thai pharmaceutical industry, which had started as a formulation industry, grew further by supplying more generic versions of originator products to the local market. Domestic pharmaceutical firms registered generic drugs, imported raw materials, and produced generic preparations to compete in the domestic market based on lower prices. Local companies generally did not invest in R&D and the government did not systematically promote a research-based domestic pharmaceutical industry.

In the late 1980s, pressure from foreign chambers of commerce and governments of countries with major pharmaceutical businesses resulted in a quid pro quo in trade and legal structure on IPR protection. The Thai government revised its patent law. The Patent Act of 1992 (B.E. 2535) provided for IPR protection of pharmaceutical products and production processes but included a provision intended to protect consumers from the impact of high prices. The law called for a Committee on Pharmaceutical Patents to monitor drug prices and to propose corrective actions for inappropriate price behavior. During the six years after the 1992 act came into effect, this mechanism did not function in practice. When the patent law was revised again and a third law was enacted in 1999, the special provision for pharmaceutical patents was taken out.

Although patent protection is a key policy to promote innovation and help developing countries accelerate technology transfer and foreign investment, such potential benefits have not materialized for Thailand. A 1999 study found no evidence of any positive trend in pharmaceutical R&D or other developments that would lead to innovation. Nor did it find increased foreign direct investment (FDI) and technology transfer in the Thai pharmaceutical industry since 1992 (Supakanjakanti et al. 2001).

Compulsory Licensing

The military coup in September 2006 led to an appointment of a nonelected government. The majority of the cabinet members at that time were retired high-level technocrats. A former ministry permanent secretary became minister of the MOPH. In his second month in office, on November 29, 2006, the minister announced that a compulsory license of Efavirenz had been issued and would be valid until 2011. The need to provide greater access to such medicines for beneficiaries of the three government health insurance schemes was cited as the reason for the licensing. A royalty fee of 0.5 percent of the GPO total sales value was to be paid to the patent holder (MOPH 2006). The MOPH chose to import these generics as finished products from India rather than supporting the local pharmaceutical manufacturers to supply them. The GPO was tasked with importation and sales.

Table 4.6 List of Compulsory Licenses Issued

Generic name	Brand name	Date	Signatory
Efavirenz	Stocrin	November 29, 2006	Director general, Department of Disease Control
Clopidogrel	Plavix	January 25, 2007	Permanent secretary of public health
Lopinavir+ Ritonavir	Kaletra	January 29, 2007	Director general, Department of Disease Control
Docetaxel	Taxotere	January 4, 2008	Minister of public health
Letrozole	Femara	January 4, 2008	Minister of public health
Erlotinib	Taroova	January 4, 2008	Minister of public health
Imatinib	Glivec	January 25, 2008	Minister of public health

Source: Compiled from Ministry of Public Health 2006, 2007a, 2007b, 2008a, 2008b, 2008c, 2008d.

On January 25 and 29, 2007, two more compulsory licenses on the AIDS drug Kaletra (lopinavir + ritonavir) (MOPH 2007) and the heart-disease drug Plavix (Clopidogrel bisulfate) were announced. The royalty fees and other arrangements were similar to those specified in the first decree.

These announcements were immediately followed, on the one side, by loud cheers from organized patient groups—especially people with HIV and a number of nongovernmental organizations (NGOs) both in and outside Thailand—and on the other side, strong protests from multinational pharmaceutical companies, their trade associations, and government trade representatives of some developed countries. After the United States put Thailand on its Priority Watch List in 2007, Thai exporters and the Ministry of Commerce joined in to voice their concerns regarding the impact on trade.

In January 2008, four more compulsory licenses were authorized. This time the decrees were signed by the minister himself, during his last days in office. This was followed by a dramatic shift in tone, if not actual policy, immediately after the new cabinet was sworn in. The new minister of public health announced, on the very first day he took office, that he would review the compulsory licenses issued. Subsequently and amid NGO protests, representatives from three ministries—public health, commerce, and foreign affairs—met to consider the next steps to be taken. They agreed not to reverse the course on the decrees already issued. Meanwhile, some NGOs moved to collect 20,000 signatures to submit to the Senate to impeach the health minister (Sarnsamak 2008).

The major government policy interventions on modern pharmaceuticals of the past three decades are summarized in table 4.7.

Issues Surrounding Pharmaceutical Policies in Thailand

The past three decades have witnessed the introduction of a host of new public policies affecting the pharmaceutical sector. The scope of these policies extends beyond traditional regulatory oversight of pharmaceutical manufacturing and sales. This section looks at the causes, content, context, consequences, and controversies surrounding these policies.

Multiple Policies, One Aim

Persistent concern over costs has led the Thai government, especially the MOPH, to adopt a series of policies aimed at cost containment. The focus has been on reducing costs in government health facilities and government-managed health insurance schemes. Government procurement rules, the "Good Health at Low Cost" initiative, the NEDL, the use of capitation payment, and the issuance of compulsory licenses are all policy tools formulated to serve such a purpose. Capitation payment also motivated health service providers to become active players in cost containment, at least for services provided to beneficiaries insured by programs paying on capitation basis.

Government policies have used several means of control:

- *Type restrictions*. Procurement rules that require government health facilities to spend 60 to 80 percent of their drug budgets on items from the NEDL and limit CSMBS reimbursement only to items on the NEDL.
- *Restrictions on number of drugs*. Setting a maximum allowable number of pharmaceutical items for hospital drug lists under the "Good Health at Low Cost" initiative.
- *Price ceilings*. Using the median price as the maximum price for procurement.
- *Breaking monopoly prices* through actions such as compulsory licensing.
- *Insurance payment incentives*. Paying health providers fixed, per person, amounts for services.

All these efforts directed toward the health service sector have taregted pharmaceuticals first for cost control. At the macrolevel, among all the policy attempts to contain costs, pharmaceuticals have been the target of most. At the microlevel, hospitals have responded to cost pressure by squeezing expenses on pharmaceuticals.

Table 4.7 Major Pharmaceutical Policies on   in Thailand

Year	Policy measure	Key content
1936	Drug Sale Control Act	Regulate the sale of medicines
1950 [revised 1955, 1956, 1957]	Drug Sale Act	Regulate the sale of medicines
1967 [revised 1975, 1979, 1984, 1987, 1992]	Drug Act	A set of comprehensive regulations of the registration, licensing, manufacturing, import, sale, quality control, and advertising of pharmaceutical products and businesses
1979	Price Regulation Act	Control of retail sales prices of key commodities, including pharmaceuticals
1979	Patent Act I	Allow process patents for pharmaceuticals
1981 [revised 1993]	National Drug Policy	Broad policy directions containing multiple components
1981	Essential drug list and government central procurement	Centralized pharmaceutical procurement in health facilities under the jurisdiction of the Ministry of Public Health
1986	Office of Prime Minister Rules on Government Procurement (later replaced by the 1992 rules and amendments)	Decentralized pharmaceutical procurement in government health facilities (expansion of and changes to the 1981 rules to cover all government health facilities with price ceilings and other policies)
1990	Social Security Act	Mandatory health insurance for employees of private businesses
1992	Patent Act II	Provision on product patents for pharmaceuticals, with special provisions aiming to reduce the impact of high prices
1993	Safety Monitoring Program (SMP)	Conditional product registration granting originator exclusive rights on sales and requiring clinical studies of products

Table 4.7 continued

1994 [repealed 1996]	Generic labeling and advertising rules	Mandate display of generic name in Thai language of "non-dangerous finished-packaged drugs" (OTC) on package labels, inserts, and advertisements, according to specified standards. Later repealed on grounds that the MOPH Executive Order misquoted the Drug Act, and hence, has no legal basis.
1998	NEDL for Civil Service Medical Benefits Scheme reimbursement	Restricts pharmaceutical benefits of the Civil Service Medical Benefits Scheme to drugs listed on the NEDL only
1998	"Good Health at Low Cost" initiative	Limits the number of pharmaceutical items allowed in each hospital
1999	Patent Act III	Omission of special provisions for pharmaceutical patents
1999	Goods and Services Price Act and Trade Competition Act	New laws to replace Price Regulation Act
2001–2002	30 Baht Health Insurance Scheme and National Health Security Act	Introduction of the largest health insurance scheme and establishment of the National Health Security Office
2003	Good Manufacturing Practice (GMP)	Making it compulsory for pharmaceutical manufacturers to abide by GMP standards
2004	ASEAN-harmonized format accepted for pharmaceutical registration	Pharmaceutical companies can choose to register a product using the traditional format or a new ASEAN-harmonized format
2006	Compulsory license for Efavirenz	Allow imports of cheaper drugs to be used in government health insurance schemes
2007	Compulsory licenses for Lopinavir+Ritonavir and Docetaxel	Allow imports of cheaper drugs to be used in government health insurance schemes
2008	Compulsory licenses for Letrozole, Erlotinib, Imatinib	Allow imports of cheaper drugs to be used in government health insurance schemes

Source: Adapted from Ratanawijitrasin 2003, with new information added.

Old Policy, New Environment

Some drug policies have been in place for a long time. While the policy environment has changed, the policies themselves have not. When changes in a policy context shake the very foundations upon which that policy was formulated, its relevance is called into question.

Government procurement regulations are a case in point. The key policy requirements are based on the percentage of the government-allocated budget for medicine. The policy came into effect when the government directly allocated annual budgets to hospitals. Today, hospitals are financed by contract-based payments from the SSS and the 30 Baht Scheme. Under this new arrangement, the financial relationship between the government and public hospitals changed from budget allocation to contracting. In a contractual mode with lump-sum financing, hospitals must decide how to allocate their resources to provide services for insurance beneficiaries. Keeping government mandates for hospitals to use a specified percentage of budgets to purchase drugs listed on the NEDL does not fit the contractual health insurance management. The basis for the budget requirements on procurement is no longer valid. Yet the policy still remains in effect.

Ambitious Policy, Ambiguous Results

What results have these pharmaceutical policies produced? Few systematic evaluations exist. Without rigorous analysis to guide the evaluation of policy impacts, one has to look for other available statistics and information sources to get a glimpse of policy consequences, with the awareness that there can be confounding factors.

Although statistics in the past several years show that an increasing proportion of local manufacturers are meeting the GMP standards, some that do not are still in operation. The level of progress made in the past twenty-five years to institute GMP in the pharmaceutical industry begs serious reexamination of the political will and the policy mechanisms employed.

Has the patent law been successful in stimulating innovation in pharmaceuticals? Thailand's pharmaceutical industry remains a formulation industry without adequate capacity for new drug discovery. The highly price-competitive environment has led the industry to focus more on cost cutting than investing in R&D.

Spending on pharmaceuticals in the public sector continues to grow despite the many policies aimed at containing costs. For the CSMBS, although it is not known how much is actually spent on pharmaceuticals, the overall expenditures for outpatient services—which compose a large percentage of pharmaceutical expenses—have accelerated after the use of the NEDL to control reimbursement (figure 4.7). Does the seeming futility of efforts to control costs reflect a problem in policy design or implementation? What are the impacts of cost-containment policies on other aspects of the health system (such as quality of care and equity) and on other sectors of the economy? Unfortunately, we lack sufficient evidence to answer these questions. There is a serious need for the development of systematic policy monitoring and evaluation mechanisms and a process for evidence-based policymaking.

Same Policy, Different Purposes

That protection of IPRs serves to encourage innovation is the conceptual basis of patent laws. But how effective patents are in the promotion of innovation depends on context and circumstance. As the WHO Commission on Intellectual Property, Innovation, and Public Health (CIPIH) delineated in its report, many developing countries lack the required capital and innovative capacity to allow patent protection laws to perform their incentive function in stimulating innovation (CIPIH 2006). Yet countries with these limitations have proceeded to enact patent laws as demanded by the Agreement on Trade-Related Aspects of Intellectual Property Rights (TRIPS). Do these countries adopt legal structures for IPRs similar to those of developed countries to promote innovation or for a different reason?

With the current structure and capability of the country's formulation-based pharmaceutical industry, Thai policymakers understand that adopting a policy to protect IPRs in medicine does not serve to enhance the innovative developments that lead to the discovery of new pharmaceuticals. The structure of Thailand's pharmaceutical industry, coupled with its reliance on exports as the engine of economic growth, dictate that the issue of IPR protection is linked not to innovation but to international trade. The laws allowing pharmaceutical product patents were enacted with the purpose of promoting exports, not pharmaceutical innovation.

Current disagreements between policymakers and interest groups over compulsory licenses do not consider how such licenses will deter innovation but how they will deter trade, and how they will make medicines affordable. Amid disagreement over policy interventions, there remains a general agreement in Thai society that the high prices of patented medicines are prohibitive. The debate then centers on whether the government should cut the prices of these medicines with compulsory licensing or boost exports so that more taxes can be collected to pay for them.

Thailand and many other middle-income developing countries face trade-offs between public health and international trade as they seek to formulate policies that serve their national interests.

Domestic Policy, Global Impact

The compulsory licensing policy puts Thailand at the forefront of international policy debates and stimulates interest among other countries in adopting TRIPS flexibilities.

On the one hand, international agreements such as TRIPS are instruments of globalization that help foster the adoption of policies made outside national borders. On the other hand, processes of global exchange in the modes and means of policy help spread domestic initiatives—like compulsory licensing—beyond the boundary of a country. Public policies become contagious when countries facing common constraints learn from each other and follow examples pioneered by one another. Thus, what begins as a domestic policy can have an impact on a global scale.

Shift in Policy Landscape, Shift in Policy Mindset

The complexity of today's policy problems demands deep understanding of the interrelated factors underlying the formulation of public policy. Two policy perspectives are worth rethinking.

Piecemeal versus systems thinking

Thailand, like many middle-income developing countries, faces a host of pressures and constraints related to its pharmaceutical policies. Among them are increasing demand to provide health care for the entire population, high prices of patented medicines due to TRIPS agreement obligations, and a pharmaceutical industry that, although viable, lacks the capacity to innovate.

With its largest health insurance system designed to be financed entirely from general taxes, the Thai government has a huge public program with intrinsic cost pressure. Reforming the financing structure by drawing from more sources of finance, in addition to general taxes, to make public health insurance more sustainable has not received serious consideration. Health policymakers have primarily focused on curbing costs and trying to push prices down. The recent policy move to issue compulsory licenses is such an effort.

Compulsory licensing brings immediate benefits to the health sector by making available generics with lower prices. But the relationship between lower price and actual access to these selected medicines in the current health insurance environment is not a direct one. It is important that policymakers understand the nature of multistage causal relationships in public policy (Ratanawijitrasin, Soumerai, and Weerasuriya 2001). Under the capitation system, it is not the patient who buys the medicines but the hospital. And hospitals have to manage a multitude of unmet demands as well as financial pressures. Prescribing more of these medicines is one among many demands. But how much compulsory licenses increase access to medicine remains to be seen.

Furthermore, questions can be raised regarding the long-term and broader consequences of such a policy. A point already put forth in the public debate by the Ministry of Commerce and exporters is that policy impacts international trade. The scope and scale of the impact are currently unknown. Another legitimate policy question is how (and if) the compulsory licensing of a few medicines (seven so far) improves overall access to medicine in the Thai health-care system. How many drugs are relatively inaccessible? Is this number of licenses adequate? How many compulsory licenses should be issued and on which medicines in order to significantly improve access?

The enactment of a public policy is indicative of government intentions. As the MOPH cited in its decrees, medicines were to be selected for compulsory licensing on the basis of their effectiveness, safety, and importance to public health. Does this mean that a company that is successful in its R&D, bringing patients good medicines of public health significance, is more likely to face compulsory licensing than one that is less successful, or one that develops so-called lifestyle medicines? What signal does this government action send to the scientific community?

That prices of patented medicines are extremely high is indisputable. But there is more than one policy mechanism to affect drug prices. Experiences from other countries, such as the United Kingdom, France, and Australia, may be relevant for Thailand. Policies that systematically address relevant causes and exercise fairness will yield longer-term and broader benefits than ones that single out good medicines for policy pressure. More importantly, any attempts to reduce medicine prices should not blind policymakers to the necessity of real financing reform to introduce multiple sources of finance for the long-term sustainability of the health insurance system.

Pairing IPR protection with industry capability promotion

The fact that countries without adequate capacity for pharmaceutical innovation make concessions on patents for trade exposes a major problem facing the world today: the current IPR-protection regime fails to induce new drug development in all countries adopting it. As such, patent laws simply become an instrument to globalize trade rather than to stimulate new drug discovery.

As there is a perennial need for new medicines, so there is a need for policy mechanisms to encourage R&D. It is a global challenge to find ways to realign the system of IPR protection, as well as to redirect pharmaceutical industry development in developing countries. This will help fulfill the dual needs of not only making new drugs available globally but also making them affordable to the world's poor.

For countries that, like Thailand, have a viable pharmaceutical industry but inadequate R&D capacity, a key policy question is whether to move up the ladder of innovation. Instead of simply accepting patents for trade, a better alternative would be to develop industry capability with the ultimate aim of new drug discovery, which could lead to the better utilization of patent laws already in place.

The past policy experiences in Thailand's pharmaceutical industry are not encouraging. The NDP goals of helping the local pharmaceutical industry achieve self-sufficiency and supporting the production of raw pharmaceutical materials are far from realized. Sporadic government efforts to promote the local industry have had little impact.

103

For the pharmaceutical industry to make real progress, there is need for a comprehensive policy with a clear plan and strong commitment to invest sufficiently in R&D capabilities. One first step could be building the industry up as a reliable supplier of quality generics with the ability to fill global demand. The next step would be to build on such initial strength and focus efforts in areas with potential and resources, such as indigenous medicines and medicines for tropical diseases.

Without an adequate innovative capacity, the difficult trade-off between public health and international trade will be a recurrent problem in public policy decisions. This is a key challenge for Thailand and other middle-income developing countries.

Conclusion

Over the past three decades, government intervention in the pharmaceutical sector in Thailand focused on procurement, production, prices, payment methods, and patent rights. The majority of these policies aimed at cost containment. But with the continuing rise in pharmaceutical spending, the results of such policies seem to be less than satisfactory. Most recently, compulsory licenses on seven drugs were issued in an effort to acquire lower-priced drugs. This new government activism not only triggered a serious debate between the country's health and trade sectors but prompted global controversies related to innovation promotion and access to medicine.

Because of the capacity constraints in its local pharmaceutical industry, Thailand enacted patent laws not for IPR protection but for international trade promotion. To be able to benefit from its patent laws, the government must make a strong commitment to invest in building industry capacity.

Notes

[1] This work was initiated by Dr. Karen Eggleston. I would like to express my sincere appreciation of her insightful comments on this chapter, as well as her efforts to coordinate the entire process of producing this book. Thanks also to Dr. Wei Wilson Zhang and other colleagues for their valuable suggestions and ideas generated during the authors meeting. I would also like to thank Dr. Puree Anantachoti, whose thoughtful analysis of hospital drug data has revealed many interesting utilization patterns.

[2] Calculated from Thai FDA data presented at http://wwwapp1.fda.moph. go.th/drug/zone_search/files/sea001_009.asp and http://wwwapp1.fda.moph. go.th/drug/zone_search/files/sea001_001.asp.

[3] From http://wwwapp1.fda.moph.go.th/drug/zone_search/files/sea001_003. asp.

References

Amprai, Kraisi, Vithapol Johjitt, Chalermporn Kaoian, and Janist Arpornrat. 2000. Analysis of Thai pharmaceutical industrial structure and its export potential to the ASEAN region. *Chulalongkorn Review* 13 (49): 60–76.

CIPIH. *See* Commission on Intellectual Property Rights, Innovation, and Public Health.

Commission on Intellectual Property Rights, Innovation, and Public Health. 2006. *Public health, innovation and intellectual property rights: Report of the commission on intellectual property rights, innovation and public health.* Geneva: World Health Organization (WHO).

Department of Export Promotion, Ministry of Commerce. 2008. *Thailand trading report.* http://www2.ops2.moc.go.th/export.

Janjaroen, Wattana S., Chitr Sitti-Amorn, Siripen Supakankunti, Sauwakon Ratanawijitrasin, Kammalin Pinitpuwadon, Sathirakorn Pongpanich, and Ratana Somrongthong. 1999. *Preliminary study of the impacts of free trade and service policy on the Thai society and health care system.* Bangkok, Thailand: College of Public Health, Chulalongkorn Univ.

Kanchanaphibool, Inthira. 2005. Health insurance schemes and patterns of drug use and care in diabetic outpatients. PhD dissertation, Chulalongkorn University.

Limwattananon S., C. Limwattananon, and S. Pannarunothai. 2004. Rapid penetration of cox2 inhibitors in the non-steroidal anti-inflammatory drug market: An implication for hospital cost containment policies. Poster presented at the 2nd International Conference for Improving Use of Medicines, Chiang Mai, Thailand, March 30–April 2.

Matichon Newspaper. 2008. Private hospitals agree to cut drug prices. March 1.

Ministry of Public Health. 2006. *Decree of the department of disease control, Ministry of Public Health, regarding exploitation of patent on drugs and medical supplies by the government on Effavirenz.*

———. 2007a. *Decree of the department of disease control, Ministry of Public Health, regarding exploitation of patent on drugs and medical supplies by the government on Clopidogrel.*

———. 2007b. *Decree of the department of disease control, Ministry of Public Health, regarding exploitation of patent on drugs and medical supplies by the government on Lopinavir and Ritonavir combination drug.*

———. 2008a. *Decree of the department of disease control, Ministry of Public Health, regarding exploitation of patent on drugs and medical supplies by the government on Docetaxel.*

———. 2008b. *Decree of the department of disease control, Ministry of Public Health, regarding exploitation of patent on drugs and medical supplies by the government on Letrozole.*

———. 2008c. *Decree of the department of disease control, Ministry of Public Health, regarding exploitation of patent on drugs and medical supplies by the government on Erlotinib.*

————. 2008d. *Decree of the department of disease control, Ministry of Public Health, regarding exploitation of patent on drugs and medical supplies by the government on Imatinib.*

MOPH. *See* Ministry of Public Health.

National Drug Committee. 1993. *National drug policy 1993.* Nonthaburi: Thai Food and Drug Administration, MOPH.

National Statistics Bureau. 2007. *Health and welfare survey: Summary of preliminary results.* http://www.nso.go.th.

Office of Industrial Economics, Ministry of Industry. 2007. *Annual report on conditions of manufacturing industries.* http://www.oie.go.th/industrystatus2/454.zip.

Office of the Prime Minister. 1998. Rules for government procurement B.E. 2535 and amendments B.E. 2538, B.E. 2539, B.E. 2541.

Pharmaceutical System Research and Intelligence Center hospital drug-utilization database. http://www.phared.org.

Ratanawijitrasin, Sauwakon. 1987. Essential drug policy: Implementation and evaluation. Masters Thesis, Thammasat University.

————. 2004. System of pharmacy services. Proceedings at the Conference on Health Insurance Systems in Thailand, Health System Research Institute, Bangkok, Thailand. February 19–20.

————. 2005. *Health insurance: An in-depth guide.* Bangkok, Thailand: Chulalongkorn University Press.

Ratanawijitrasin, Sauwakon, Puree Anantachote, Inthira Kanchanaphibool, Arthorn Riewpaiboon, and Siripa Udomugsorn. 2003. *Pharmaceutical price study.* Bangkok, Thailand: Health System Research Institute/Department of the Comptroller General, Ministry of Finance.

Ratanawijitrasin, Sauwakon, Stephen Soumerai, and Krisantha Weerasuriya. 2001. Do national drug policies and essential drug programs improve drug use? A review of experiences in developing countries. *Social Science and Medicine* 53 (7): 831–44.

Sarnsamak, Pongphon. 2008. Protest starts to oust Chaiya: Health activists launch campaign to collect 20,000 signatures for petition. *The Nation*, March 7. http://www.nationmultimedia.com/2008/03/07/politics/politics_30067428.php.

Thai Drug System Study Project Committee. 2002. *Thai drug system.* Nonthaburi, Thailand: Health System Research Institute.

Pharmaceutical Policy in Seven Asia-Pacific Health-care Systems

Taiwan

PHARMACEUTICAL POLICY IN TAIWAN

Chee-Ruey Hsieh

Technological advances in medicine have been a major cause of rising health expenditures in many countries (Newhouse 1992; Fuchs 1996), and a growing body of empirical evidence shows that such advances have substantially prolonged and improved life for many patients (Cutler and McClellan 2001; Murphy and Topel 2006). How, then, can countries provide access to new medical technologies while at the same time controlling their health-care budgets?

Following the paradigm in the literature on economic growth, researchers have traditionally treated technological change in medicine as an exogenous factor and as such have neglected to examine why and how this change takes place. But in fact, technological change in medicine—like technological change in the economy as a whole—is endogenous, or generated by factors within the health-care system. Researchers who have recognized this have produced several important studies in recent years. Finkelstein (2007) demonstrates that the introduction of a social insurance program, such as Medicare in the United States, is a driving force behind advances in medical technologies. Hall and Jones (2007) suggest that the rise in per capita income, together with an increased willingness to pay for health care, explains the rising share of gross domestic product (GDP) spent on health care. These studies align with a pattern seen around the world: that countries with rapid economic growth and universal health insurance face a persistent and dynamic challenge in striking a balance between controlling health-care costs and pursuing population health.

This chapter examines how policymakers in Taiwan—a country with rapid economic growth and universal health insurance—handle the conflict between the short-run costs and long-run health benefits of increased health care. I focus specifically on pharmaceutical policy because pharmaceutical innovations are among the most important new health-care products. Not only have many studies shown that new prescription drugs contribute significantly to increased longevity (Cutler 2004; Lichtenberg 2005), but in Taiwan, as in many other Asian countries, pharmaceuticals account for more than one-fourth of health expenditures, making them a frequent target of cost containment.

In the next section, I examine the evolution and impact of pharmaceutical policy in Taiwan. I begin by focusing on three specific issues: (1) the pharmaceutical reimbursement policy, (2) the policy of separating drug prescription and dispensation, and (3) the effects of policy on pharmaceutical innovation. I then analyze several options for reforming the pharmaceutical reimbursement policy in Taiwan. Finally, I summarize the research findings and discuss their public policy implications.

Pharmaceutical Reimbursement Policy

National Health Insurance Formulary

The national health insurance (NHI) program in Taiwan provides comprehensive coverage for prescription drugs on its national formulary, a list that includes all pharmaceuticals subject to reimbursement. At the inauguration of universal coverage in 1995, the NHI program adopted the formulary from two old social insurance programs—namely, labor insurance and government employee insurance. This practice allows almost all drugs that receive market approval by the regulatory agency to be listed as insurance-reimbursed drugs.

Since the establishment of universal health insurance, many new pharmaceutical products have been introduced. In addition to requiring that firms obtain authorization to market a new drug, Taiwan, like other countries with direct price controls on pharmaceutical products, requires that the manufacturer obtain approval for insurance coverage and a price for reimbursement by the Bureau of National Health Insurance (BNHI), a single public payer in Taiwan. As a result, many new prescription drugs are added to the NHI formulary each year, including new molecular entities, formulations, combinations, and indications. Table 5.1 shows the number of new drugs included in the NHI formulary between 1996 and 2006. (A new drug is defined here as one that was added to the formulary after 1996.) During this period, a total of 556 new drugs were added to the NHI formulary, with 13 to 75 included each year.

Comprising more than 21,000 drugs, Taiwan's NHI formulary is huge compared with those of many other countries (Hsieh and Sloan 2008). The government imposes direct price controls on pharmaceuticals by fixing the price product by product, and an extraordinarily large number of drugs are included. Taiwan's large formulary is similar to that of South Korea, but it stands in stark contrast to those of many Organisation for Economic Co-operation and Development (OECD) countries, which typically include only 3,000–8,000 drugs in their insurance formularies (Yang, Bae, and Kim 2008).

Taiwanese providers offer only a select number of drugs from the national formulary to their patients, however. For example, a large hospital with more than a thousand beds, such as an academic medical center, typically includes only about a thousand drugs in its formulary, or about one in twenty that are available. This practice gives hospitals significant power in the pharmaceutical market. As I explain below, although the government regulates the reimbursement price for drugs on its formulary, there is price competition in the wholesale market.[1] With a long list of many substitutable drugs in a given therapeutic group, the pharmaceutical manufacturers are forced to compete by cutting wholesale (acquisition) prices. The resulting price competition has driven many products from the wholesale market. As reported in Hsieh and Sloan (2008), there are more than 5,000 products in the NHI formulary that do not have any sales in a given year.[2] About 3,700 drugs, or 17 percent of the products listed in the NHI formulary, account for about 97 percent of expenditures on pharmaceuticals. This suggests that only about 3,700 drugs are actively sold on the market—the result of competition in the wholesale market.[3]

Pricing

To control the cost of public insurance, the Taiwanese government regulates the price its health insurance plan pays for drugs—hereafter referred to as the reimbursement price. This section analyzes the reimbursement of (1) old drugs and (2) new drugs.

Taiwan introduced universal health insurance in 1995 by integrating the three existing programs into a single system.[4] The pricing of old (then extant) drugs follows the rule adopted by the former insurance programs. This rule sets the reimbursement price product by product on the basis of brand instead of ingredients. In other words, drugs with the same ingredients but produced by different manufacturers are treated as different products. Because there are a large number of drugs on the reimbursement list, it is difficult to set the reimbursement prices for drugs in a consistent way. As a result, some of the reimbursement prices, especially for generic products, may be higher than their values in a competitive market due to outdated pricing information and insufficient international price comparison. In addition, there are significant price differences among products with multiple sources (Huang and Chiang 2003). This provides room for pharmaceutical manufacturers to cut the acquisition price in the wholesale market in order to be selected for inclusion in the provider's formulary.[5]

Since 1996 the public payer (BNHI) has adopted two major policies to mitigate the problems of overpricing and inconsistent pricing of drugs that were already on the market at the time national health insurance was introduced. The first approach uses generic grouping as the basis for pricing to reduce the differences in prices among multiple-source products. This approach classifies off-patent products with the same ingredients, dosage, and format as a group and uses the weighted average price (WAP) of the same group as the benchmark to adjust the reimbursement price for each drug. The reimbursement price remains unchanged if the price of the drug is less than the WAP. The new reimbursement price is set equal to the WAP if the price of the specific drug is greater than the WAP (Huang and Chiang 2003).

The second approach uses a market survey of prices and sales as the basis for updating the reimbursement price. Since the government regulates only the reimbursement price (the retail price) and not the wholesale price by which the provider purchases drugs from pharmaceutical manufacturers, the difference between the reimbursement price and the wholesale price becomes the provider's profit margin. Thus, the payer conducts market surveys regularly to collect information on the actual wholesale price of a drug and then adjusts the reimbursement price level accordingly. During the period 1996–2006, the BNHI updated the reimbursement price eight times after it estimated the average wholesale price based on extensive surveys.

To determine the reimbursement price of new drugs, Taiwan does not employ formal economic evaluation. Rather, the BNHI has adopted a mix of strategies to determine the price, including comparing each drug to existing products and to international equivalents and assessing its therapeutic value.

To sum up, the BNHI uses the median price of international comparisons to set the cap on regulated prices of branded drugs still on patent. For off-patent branded drugs, the price cap is 85 percent of international median prices. For generic drugs, the price cap is the mean price of the branded price in the same therapeutic group if the drug has passed a bioequivalence test—and 80 percent of the mean price of the branded drugs in the same therapeutic group if a bioequivalence test has not been conducted (Hsieh and Sloan 2008). The BNHI selects ten countries as the reference group for international comparison: Australia, Belgium, Canada, France, Germany, Japan, Sweden, Switzerland, the United Kingdom, and the United States.

NHI Drug Spending

Table 5.1 shows the real NHI pharmaceutical expenditures (in 2006 NT$) between 1996 and 2006. In 1996 the NHI program spent NT$67.4 billion, or about 28 percent of total NHI health expenditures, on pharmaceuticals. This figure increased to NT$114.1 billion in 2006, a 69 percent rise over the eleven-year period. This implies that the mean annual growth rate of NHI drug spending was 5.4 percent, which was slightly higher than the mean annual growth rate of total NHI spending (5.1 percent).

Compared to the annual growth rates of pharmaceutical expenditures in other countries, such as South Korea and the United States, the real growth rate of drug spending in Taiwan has been moderate. This suggests that some of the cost-containment policies mentioned above have been effective. But with drug spending continuing to rise in Taiwan, it is important to further explore what is driving this trend.

As shown in table 5.1, the introduction of new products into the NHI formulary has contributed to the increase in pharmaceutical expenditure. As mentioned above, during the 1996–2006 period, the public payer (BNHI) introduced 565 new products into the formulary. In 2006 the spending on these 565 new products amounted to NT$26.82 billion, accounting for about 24 percent of total NHI drug spending. But these 565 products represent only 15 percent of the 3,700 products that are actively sold in the market. This suggests that pharmaceutical innovation is the major driver of increased spending.

Table 5.1 National Health Insurance (NHI) Spending on Pharmaceuticals and the Number of New Drugs Included in the NHI Formulary, 1996–2006

Year	Real NHI drug spending (in 2006 NT$ billion)	Real total NHI spending (in 2006 NT$ billion)	Drug spending as % of total NHI spending	Number of new drugs added to the NHI formulary[a]	Real total spending on the stock of new drugs (in 2006 NT$ billion)[b,c]	Spending on new drugs as percentage of total NHI drug spending
1996	67.4	243.5	27.68	13	–	–
1997	68.7	262.8	26.14	54	0.50	0.73
1998	76.3	288.3	26.47	75	2.04	2.67
1999	84.7	307.8	27.52	42	4.28	5.05
2000	86.3	310.3	27.57	36	6.37	7.38
2001	88.4	334.5	26.42	73	8.79	9.93
2002	94.4	353.5	26.70	56	13.41	14.21
2003	98.8	369.9	26.72	50	17.45	17.66
2004	112.5	381.8	29.46	82	22.46	19.97
2005	112.7	390.5	28.88	37	24.04	21.32
2006	114.1	403.8	28.26	38	26.82	23.51

Source: Bureau of National Health Insurance, Taipei, Taiwan.
Note:
[a] The definition of new drugs includes (1) new molecular entities, (2) new formulations, (3) new combinations, and (4) new indications.
[b] New drugs refer to those included in the NHI formulary after 1996.
[c] The spending on new drugs does not include that of physician clinics claimed by the flat payment system.

Hsieh and Sloan (2008) provide additional quantitative evidence to support this argument. They use NHI claims data from 1997 to 2001 to break down the growth of pharmaceutical expenditures into three components: (1) the treatment expansion effect, (2) the treatment substitution effect, and (3) the price effect. The treatment expansion effect indicates that the introduction of new drugs into the formulary leads to an increase in the number of people being treated for the diseases the drugs are designed to address. The treatment substitution effect describes the tendency of physicians to substitute new drugs for older ones when treating established patients. Hsieh and Sloan find that from 1997 to 2001, NHI nominal expenditures on pharmaceuticals grew by 57 percent. The decomposition reveals that prices declined by 18 percent but that the indexes measuring treatment expansion and substitution increased by 20 percent and 59 percent, respectively. Given that both treatment expansion and substitution are made possible only through the introduction of new drugs into the formulary, it stands to reason that these new drugs are the main driver of increased spending on pharmaceuticals.

Separating Drug Prescribing from Dispensing

Taiwan's health-care system, like those of many Asian countries, allows physicians to both prescribe and dispense drugs. This practice, in combination with direct government price controls, enables physicians and hospitals to profit from the sale of prescription drugs. Beginning in March 1997, the government adopted a series of reforms mandating the separation of drug prescribing from dispensing. But as a result of concessions to providers, the reform is incomplete: hospitals are still allowed to house outpatient pharmacies, and physicians practicing in clinics can still hire pharmacists to dispense drugs on site. In other words, the reform has defined a division of labor between physicians and pharmacists, but it has not broken the conflict of interest arising from the link between profits from the sales of pharmaceuticals and physicians' prescribing behavior.

Chou et al. (2003) have attempted to evaluate the impact of the separation policy on provider behavior. Their study indicates that almost no physician clinic hired on-site pharmacists before the separation policy was implemented, and 60 percent did so after implementation. The probability of hiring on-site pharmacists increases with patient volume, suggesting that it has a fixed cost.

The separation policy was implemented in different cities at different times, making it easier to evaluate the policy's impact. Based on a difference-in-difference (DID) analysis, Chou et al. (2003) found that both drug expenditures and prescriptions decreased slightly after policy implementation—among patients of physician clinics without on-site pharmacists. But both variables remained virtually unchanged for patients of physician clinics with on-site pharmacists. These results suggest that the policy's intended effects are completely offset if physicians are allowed to hire on-site pharmacists, which further indicates that delinking physician income from drug dispensing is key to changing physicians' prescribing behavior.

When it realized that by allowing physicians to hire on-site pharmacists it was dooming its separation policy to fail, the Taiwanese government adopted another pharmaceutical payment reform in 2002. This reduced the flat payment rate for pharmaceuticals in physician clinics from NT$35 to NT$25 per day but kept the rate for pharmacies constant (at NT$30 per day). The purpose of this payment adjustment, in combination with the design of a prescription release fee (NT$25 per visit) to physicians, was to provide financial incentives for physicians to release their prescriptions to community pharmacies. But the incentive has not worked as expected. To the contrary, many physicians quickly learned that they could take advantage of this payment reform if they opened gateway pharmacies (Lee, Huang, and Huang 2007). A physician-owned gateway pharmacy is typically located in the neighborhood of the physician clinic and dispenses the drugs that the physician-owner prescribes. Under this arrangement, physicians can earn extra income from three sources: (1) the prescription release fee (NT$25); (2) a higher flat payment to pharmacies than to clinics (NT$5 per day); and (3) pharmacy dispensing fees (NT$11). These extra payments account for 13 percent of the average revenue that physicians receive from each patient visit.

Lee, Huang, and Huang (2007) define a physician-owned gateway pharmacy as one in which more than 70 percent of the prescriptions filled come from the same clinic. Their study finds that the proportion of gateway pharmacies increased from 1.44 percent in 1997 to 33.86 percent in 2003. Although gateway pharmacies only account for about one-third of the total number of pharmacies in Taiwan, they fill about 80 percent of all prescriptions. An important implication of this study is that most physicians in Taiwan still earn profit by linking drug prescribing and dispensing a decade after the reform to separate the two.

Given the evidence, what are the major consequences for the health-care sector if physicians continue to earn profit from both drug prescribing and dispensing? Tan, Hong, and Hsieh (2007) investigate this issue. They argue that the existence of profit margins for pharmaceuticals gives rise to three distortions in relative prices in the health sector, which in turn lead to a loss of efficiency in resource allocation.

The first distortion is of the price of prescription drugs relative to health-care services. Compared to prescription drugs, health-care services such as providing diagnostic information and surgical treatment are very labor intensive. In contrast to physical products, there is no wholesale market for services, and hence no profit margin between reimbursement and acquisition prices. In view of the margin on prescription drugs, providers have a financial incentive to substitute prescription drugs for other inputs, which in turn leads to overprescribing.

Iizuka (2007) provides direct evidence to support this theoretical prediction. Based on a panel of aggregate sales data, he calculates the profit margins that Japanese physicians earn from more than forty anti-hypertension drugs. He then estimates the effect of the profit margins on physicians' prescription decisions. His findings indicate that physicians' prescription choices are significantly influenced by profit margins. Based on the estimated results, he further simulates the impact of the hypothetical separation policy on pharmaceutical demand by removing the profit margin from the physician's objective function. The simulation shows that the demand for prescription drugs decreases by 10.6 percent if physicians do not earn a profit margin, suggesting that overprescribing is due to the link between physician income and prescribing.[6]

The second distortion attributable to physician dispensing is between the prices of brand-name and generic drugs. Profit margins induce physicians to choose drugs based on the size of the margin instead of efficacy, safety, or cost. Using data obtained from Taiwan and focusing on diabetic patients, Liu, Yang, and Hsieh (2009) find evidence that physicians' choice of brand-name or generic drugs is influenced by profit margins.

As I will discuss in the next section, the generic-to-brand-name-price ratio is relatively high in Taiwan compared with other countries that have strong generic competition, such as the United States.[7] In Taiwan, many generic firms offer high discounts to providers in order to be included in their formularies. As a result, physicians may be more likely to prescribe generic products to their patients because they earn higher profits from generic than from brand-name drugs. Liu, Yang, and Hsieh (2009) find that private providers, including physicians practicing in clinics and private hospitals, are more likely to prescribe generic drugs to their patients than their counterparts in public hospitals. As noted by Duggan (2000), private providers are more responsive to financial incentives. These findings are yet more evidence that profit margins significantly influence physicians' choice between brand-name and generic drugs.

The third distortion is of competition between large and small hospitals (measured by outpatient flow). Large hospitals are often targeted by pharmaceutical firms seeking to penetrate the market. Thus, they possess significant market power and are likely to obtain larger discounts, even for brand-name drugs. Such profit margins are a significant revenue source for all providers, but large hospitals are likely to have a financial advantage over their counterparts—and to use this advantage to further expand their operations, which further sharpens their competitive edge. As a result, large hospitals are likely to grow more rapidly and force smaller hospitals out of the market.

Table 5.2 indicates a trend over time in the connection between the share of the market for outpatient drugs and provider size. In Taiwan, the regulatory agency classifies hospitals into three accreditation levels: (1) local community hospitals, (2) metropolitan hospitals, and (3) academic medical centers. These levels correlate to hospital size. In 2006 the average number of hospital beds in academic medical centers was about 1,300. By contrast, the average size of metropolitan hospitals and local community hospitals was 650 beds and 120 beds, respectively. In 1997 academic medical centers accounted for about 25 percent of the market for outpatient drugs. This share increased to about 35 percent in 2002. By contrast, the market share of small community hospitals declined from 18 percent in 1997 to 13 percent in 2004. In addition, clinics' market share of outpatient drugs declined by nearly 50 percent over the same period. These results further bolster the argument that the greater profit margins enjoyed by large hospitals prescribing drugs is an important determinant of the increasing size of hospitals in Taiwan.[8] As a result, the market for outpatient drugs is increasingly concentrated on large hospitals.

Table 5.2 Market Share of Outpatient Drugs and Share of Generic Prescriptions in Total Prescriptions Based on the Provider's Accreditation Level

	1997	2000	2002	2004
Market share (%)				
Academic medical centers	24.67	29.07	34.28	31.19
Metropolitan hospitals	18.27	21.15	24.12	23.54
Local community hospitals	18.05	15.81	13.71	12.57
Clinics	37.98	30.67	21.38	22.19
Share of generic prescriptions (%)				
Academic medical centers	0.36	0.40	0.38	0.43
Metropolitan hospitals	0.46	0.48	0.45	0.47
Local community hospitals	0.55	0.61	0.57	0.57
Clinics	0.63	0.71	0.71	0.72

Sources: Data on the market shares of outpatient drugs are from the Bureau of National Health Insurance, Taipei, Taiwan. Data on the share of generic prescription drugs in total prescription are calculated from the regression results reported in Liu, Yang, and Hsieh 2009.

Liu, Yang, and Hsieh (2009) provide further evidence that large hospitals have more market power than smaller hospitals and clinics. And because of the greater discounts they receive, they are more likely to prescribe brand-name drugs to their patients. By contrast, small hospitals and clinics do not possess significant bargaining power. They are less likely to get good discounts from brand-name firms, and so are forced to turn to generic firms to earn their profit margins. As shown in table 5.2, the mean probability that physicians will prescribe generic drugs to diabetic patients is about 40 percent in academic medical centers, after controlling for other factors. This probability increases as provider size decreases. In physician clinics, more than 70 percent of diabetic patients receive generic drugs for their treatments.[9]

The Impact of Policy on Pharmaceutical Innovation

The regulation of prices combined with the failure of the separation policy has had two important consequences for pharmaceutical innovation.[10] First, price regulation leads to a higher generic-to-brand price ratio, which in turn provides a disincentive for innovation. Second, the public payer concentrates on cutting the reimbursement price as the strategy for cost containment, which provides another disincentive for innovation. In this section, I analyze these two effects in detail.

The current regulatory approach serves as price protection for generic drugs and hence undermines competition in the generic market (Danzon and Chao 2000; Ekelund and Persson 2003). Because there is no competitive pressure to reduce the reimbursement price of generic drugs as more generic drugs enter the market, the price difference between brand-name and generic drugs is small. This in turn leads to a persistently high generic-to-brand-name-price ratio. By contrast, in a market in which pharmaceutical manufacturers are price makers, the real price of branded drugs may rise over time and the price of generic drugs may decline sharply as more generic drugs enter the market (Lu and Comanor 1998; Grabowski 2007). Thus, in a free market, the price difference between brand-name and generic drugs tends to be substantial and to only increase over time, in contrast with the regulated market. For example, in the United States, the average generic-to-brand-name-price ratio generally declines to about 0.3 three years after first generic entry (Saha et al. 2006). But in a regulated market such as Taiwan and South Korea, the average ratio is in the range of 0.7 to 0.8 (Yang 2005; Liu, Yang, and Hsieh 2009).

This high regulation-induced ratio not only reduces the reward for innovation but also affects the physician's choice between brand-name and generic drugs. In a free market in which pharmaceutical manufacturers are price makers, market competition drives down the average generic-to-brand-name-price ratio to a relatively low level. Thus, using generic drugs as a substitute for brand-name drugs becomes an effective policy tool for controlling health-care expenditures. But when generic prices are regulated, as in Taiwan, then generic substitution cannot be an effective cost-containment strategy.

Even when generic substitution does not lower costs, physicians may prescribe generic drugs for other reasons. As mentioned earlier, pharmaceutical manufacturers in Taiwan compete in the wholesale market by cutting the acquisition price. Compared to manufacturers of brand-name drugs, manufacturers of generic drugs do not invest large amounts in research and development (R&D) before bringing their products to market. Thus, the fixed cost of generic drugs is much lower than that of brand-name drugs. This fact, combined with the higher generic-to-brand-name-price ratio, suggests that generic firms are more likely to offer providers a favorable price discount (bringing the acquisition price below the reimbursement price) so that their drugs will be included in the prescribing formulary. As a result, branded firms may be at a competitive disadvantage and lose market share. Liu, Yang, and Hsieh (2009) provide evidence that branded firms do in fact have a significantly smaller market share in clinics and small hospitals than in large hospitals (table 5.2).[11]

As already mentioned, the single public payer (BNHI) in Taiwan has frequently cut the reimbursement price over the last decade. The payer has had two justifications for such a policy: (1) to offset the increase in spending as new drugs are added to its formulary, and (2) to reduce the profit margins earned by providers. But this policy has not achieved both goals. Although consistently lowering the reimbursement rate has reduced the rise in drug price, it has not reduced the overall expenditure on pharmaceuticals, as shown in table 5.1. This suggests that price is not the primary driver of increased pharmaceutical spending.

Even with cuts to the reimbursement rate, physicians in Taiwan are still earning profit margins from their prescribing behavior. This suggests that the level of reimbursement is not the reason for the profit margin. Rather, the margin is unavoidable in a system that allows physicians to both prescribe and dispense drugs. When pricing policy aims to "squeeze" the profit margin, Liu, Yang, and Hsieh (2009) find that providers use generic substitution to offset the policy's impact. In addition, cutting prices and increasing the ratio of generic to brand-name prescriptions have hurt pharmaceutical innovation.

Future Reform of Pharmaceutical Reimbursement

As in many countries, the government in Taiwan is seeking to introduce a series of reforms to achieve a better balance between cost containment and access to innovative products. There are currently two policy options on the reform agenda: economic evaluation and reference pricing. In this section, I provide a brief review of these two policies and their potential effects.

Economic evaluation compares the costs and consequences of alternative health-care treatments, such as the use of specific prescription drugs or programs. Since Australia led the way in 1993, economic evaluation has been adopted in more than ten countries as a tool for resource allocation in health care, especially for reimbursement decisions in pharmaceuticals (Drummond 2007).

As mentioned above, Taiwan does not employ economic evaluation as a formal component of reimbursement decisions but instead as a mechanism for providing information in the planning stage. The health authority in Taiwan has established a semipublic and not-for-profit agency, the Center for Drug Evaluation (CDE), to conduct economic evaluation relevant to the planning of future reform. But CDE's research findings only serve as reference information for the public payer and are not formally binding upon reimbursement rates for new drugs. This treats the information obtained from economic evaluation as a public good. The CDE serves to disseminate information on the cost-effectiveness of new drugs, similar to the model proposed by Reinhardt (2004). The government might eventually adopt economic evaluation as a component of reimbursement decision-making if all stakeholders are satisfied with its function in the planning process.

In contrast to the conservative policy adopted in Taiwan, South Korea—which has a very similar development path and faces many of the same challenges—has publicly announced a reform plan to formally adopt economic evaluation in the process of setting prices for new drugs (Yang, Bae, and Kim 2008). South Korea's experience in establishing such a system will provide Taiwan with useful insights.

One of the potential benefits of employing economic evaluation in this area is a shift in policy focus from cost containment to increasing product value. During the past decade, health policymakers in Taiwan have persistently focused on controlling costs. Policies such as capping the prices of new pharmaceuticals and reducing reimbursement rates for old products limit consumer access to new drugs and discourage innovation. But as Cutler (2004) argues, cost containment is not in itself a health-care goal; rather, it is an appropriate social objective in that it increases the value derived from scarce resources. A key goal of health policy should be to decrease *wasteful* spending—that is, spending that yields minor or no benefits—and not spending overall. To achieve this goal, Cutler suggests that "the right step is to move toward a system that improves our health, spending less as appropriate but more if need be" (p. 123). Adopting economic evaluation in the pharmaceutical reimbursement decision-making process is an important first step toward this goal.

With regard to reference pricing, a specific reform proposal has been agreed upon by the health authority but is yet to clear the legislative process. Since reference pricing has been widely adopted in many European countries, the potential policy effects are well known. On the efficiency side, this policy has the potential to solve the problem of overpricing and inconsistent pricing of the many pharmaceuticals on the NHI formulary. But the policy raises concerns over the equity of health-care financing, since out-of-pocket payments may increase following its implementation.

There are several other ways Taiwan might increase the value of its pharmaceutical sector. First, the nation's high generic-to-brand-name-price ratio needs to be addressed. As pointed out by Sloan and Hsieh (2008), this ratio is an important market signal affecting innovation. As compared to the prices of innovative products, the high prices of generic products discourage innovation. To strike a better balance between controlling health-care budgets and maintaining innovation, the government might want to integrate the use of reference pricing and economic evaluation.

Second, the failure of Taiwan's separation policy suggests that it is important to seek other approaches to break the link between profit margins and the prescribing behavior of physicians. During the past decade, other countries such as Japan and South Korea have adopted similar reforms but using different strategies. Japan's policy allows physicians to keep their profit margins but makes them transparent and within a reasonable range (Iizuka 2007). Also, the reform in Japan was incremental; it took more than three decades to increase the percentage of prescriptions filled at pharmacies from less than 10 percent in the 1970s to 54 percent in 2005 (chapter 2, Iizuka, and chapter 3, Tomita, in this volume). Meanwhile, South Korea has banned hospital outpatient pharmacies but compensates the provider by increasing fees for other health-care services (Kwon 2003; chapter 1, Kwon, in this volume). The experiences of Japan and South Korea provide useful insights for future reform.

Conclusion

This chapter provides a comprehensive review of the evolution of the pharmaceutical policy in Taiwan and its impact on various aspects of the health-care market. I find that over the past decade, pharmaceutical policy in Taiwan has primarily focused on cost containment. As a result of direct price regulation, the mean annual growth rate of pharmaceutical expenditure has stayed within a moderate range, suggesting that price regulation achieved its goal of controlling the health-care budget. But this has come at the expense of discouraging pharmaceutical innovation and distorting prices in the health-care market.

In addition, I find that the separation policy has not achieved its expected goal. Several unexpected policy effects have emerged and physicians are still in a position to earn profit directly from pharmaceutical sales. Specifically, the separation policy has induced physicians practicing in clinics to establish on-site or gateway pharmacies that allow them to maintain profits from both pharmaceutical sales and drug prescribing. This in turn gives rise to price distortion and inefficient allocation of health-care resources, including overprescribing, overpricing of generic drugs, and increases in the market share of large hospitals.

As a result of the policy failure to separate drug prescribing from dispensing, the public payer (BNHI) in Taiwan has attempted to use price-cutting as a strategy to squeeze profit margins. But this has been ineffective because the profit margin depends not only on the rate of reimbursement but also on the balance of market power. The policy is doomed to failure if it does not change the relative bargaining power between providers and pharmaceutical manufacturers. The wrong policy tools not only fail to reduce profit margins but also give rise to adverse side effects such as discouraging innovation and increasing the prescription share of generic drugs. Although generic substitution has the potential to reduce costs, the associated savings mainly go to providers via higher profit margins. By contrast, the public payer (BNHI) and consumers receive little benefit from generic substitution because the price difference between brand-name and generic drugs is small.

The findings of this study have important policy implications. Specifically, they suggest that price regulation is not an effective approach for controlling pharmaceutical expenditures. Although the empirical evidence shows that the direct regulation of reimbursement rates has effectively slowed the rise of pharmaceutical prices, it has not reduced overall pharmaceutical expenditure. Side effects include delays in the launch of new drugs and disincentives for innovation. Furthermore, when providers profit directly from prescribing drugs, containing costs by cutting regulated prices often alters profit margins. This in turn creates incentives to select drugs with higher profit margins. From a clinical point of view, the unjustified substitution of one drug for another may adversely affect the quality of health care. But this does not imply that all regulation should be eliminated, leaving it to the market. Rather, the analysis in this chapter suggests the need to redesign regulatory policy to reduce distortions created by physician prescribing behavior.

In conclusion, focusing exclusively on cost containment is not a wise strategy. Rather, as noted by Cutler (2004), the goal of pharmaceutical policy should be to increase the value of the overall health-care system. To achieve this goal, the key policy challenge is to improve the health of the population while controlling the health-care budget. As noted earlier, over ten countries in the world have formally adopted economic evaluation as an important input in reimbursement decisions. By contrast, Taiwan has not yet formally implemented this approach. Such evaluation promises to further boost the value of public spending.

Notes

[1] In the wholesale market, providers are buyers and pharmaceutical manufacturers are suppliers. The government only acts as a regulator for the reimbursement price and plays no role as supplier or buyer of pharmaceutical products since almost all pharmaceutical manufacturers are private firms. Further, providers have the freedom to select (i.e., purchase) drugs for their patients.

[2] This suggests that there is no actual market transaction for these products; that is, that no clinic or hospital purchases these products, even though they are part of the NHI formulary.

[3] The NHI formulary is defined as the list of drugs that are covered and reimbursed by the public payer. Each clinic and hospital establishes its own drug formulary by selecting a subset of drugs from the NHI formulary. As a result, the wholesale market indicates the point of transaction at which providers purchase drugs that are included in their formularies from the pharmaceutical manufacturers.

[4] Prior to NHI, there were three public insurance programs in Taiwan: (1) government employee insurance (GEI); (2) labor insurance (LI); and (3) farmer health insurance (FHI). FHI was administered by the Bureau of Labor Insurance and had almost the same insurance coverage and reimbursement policy as LI.

[5] For a detailed model to explain this price-cutting behavior, see Liu, Yang and Hsieh (2009).

[6] See chapter 2 of this book for a more detailed description of this study and its policy implications.

[7] The generic-to-brand-name price ratio is defined by P_g / P_b where P_g and P_b are the reimbursement price for generic and brand-name drugs, respectively.

[8] Other determinants of the increased size of hospitals in Taiwan include the cost advantage of not-for-profit hospitals arising from tax exemption and the design of the NHI payment policy, which correlates payment amount to accreditation level (Lu and Hsieh 2003).

[9] In Taiwan, as the result of the integration of prescribing and dispensing, physicians practicing in hospitals do not have complete freedom to prescribe the drugs that they prefer. Rather, their prescription choices are restricted by the list of the hospital formulary, which tends to be significantly influenced by the profit margins that hospitals receive. Therefore, the prescription patterns of hospital physicians are also influenced by the profit margin, although their income does not depend on it.

[10] The discussion of innovation in this section refers to both domestic and multinational firms.

[11] Taking the 2004 data as an example, table 5.2 shows that the share of generic prescriptions in clinics is 0.29 (0.72-0.43) higher than that in medical centers. Clinics account for 22 percent of outpatient-drug sales in Taiwan. This indicates that brand-name drugs lose more than 6 percent (0.29×0.22) of their market share in the clinic's outpatient-drug market as the result of size effect. Following the same reasoning, table 5.2 suggests that brand-name drugs lose about 2 percent of their market share in local community hospitals.

References

Chou, Y. J., W. C. Yip, C. H. Lee, N. Huang, Y. P. Sun, and H. J. Chang. 2003. Impact of separating drug prescribing and dispensing on provider behaviour: Taiwan's experience. *Health Policy and Planning* 18: 316–29.

Cutler, D. M. 2004. *Your money or your life: Strong medicine for America's health care system.* New York: Oxford Univ. Press.

Cutler, D. M., and M. McClellan. 2001. Is technological change in medicine worth it? *Health Affairs* 20 (5): 11–28.

Danzon, P. M., and L. W. Chao. 2000. Does regulation drive out competition in pharmaceutical markets? *Journal of Law and Economics* 42: 311–57.

Drummond, M. 2007. Using economic evaluation in reimbursement decisions for health technologies: Lessons from international experience. In *Pharmaceutical innovation: incentives, competition, and cost-benefit analysis in international perspective*, ed. F. A. Sloan and C. R. Hsieh, 215–25. New York: Cambridge Univ. Press.

Duggan, M. G. 2000. Hospital ownership and public medical spending. *Quarterly Journal of Economics* 115: 1343–73.

Ekelund, M., and B. Persson. 2003. Pharmaceutical pricing in a regulated market. *Review of Economics & Statistics* 85: 298–306.

Finkelstein, A. 2007. The aggregate effects of health insurance: Evidence from the introduction of Medicare. *Quarterly Journal of Economics* 122: 1–37.

Fuchs, V. R. 1996. Economics, values, and health care reform. *American Economic Review* 86 (1): 1–24.

Grabowski, H. G. 2007. Competition between generic and branded drugs. In Sloan and Hsieh, 153–73.

Hall, R. E., and C. I. Jones. 2007. The value of life and the rise in health spending. *Quarterly Journal of Economics* 122 (1): 39–72.

Hsieh, C. R., and F. A. Sloan. 2008. Adoption of pharmaceutical innovation and the growth of drug expenditure in Taiwan: Is it cost effective? *Value in Health* 11 (2): 334–44.

Huang, W. F., and H. C. Chiang. 2003. Pharmaceutical benefit scheme and cost containment in Taiwan's national health insurance. *Journal of Pharmaceutical Finance, Economics, and Policy* 12: 133–49.

Iizuka, T. 2007. Experts' agency problems: Evidence from the prescription drug market in Japan. *Rand Journal of Economics* 38: 844–62.

Kwon, S. 2003. Pharmaceutical reform and physician strikes in Korea: Separation of drug prescribing and dispensing. *Social Science & Medicine* 57: 529–38.

Lee, Y. C., K. H. Huang, and Y. T. Huang. 2007. Adverse pharmaceutical payment incentives and providers' behaviour: The emergence of GP-owned gateway pharmacies in Taiwan. *Health Policy and Planning* 22: 427–35.

Lichtenberg, F. R. 2005. The impact of new drug launches on longevity: Evidence from longitudinal, disease-level data from 52 countries, 1982–2001. *International Journal of Health Care Finance and Economics* 5: 47–73.

Liu, Y. M., Y. H. K. Yang, and C. R. Hsieh. 2009. Financial incentives and physicians' prescription decisions on the choice between brand-name and generic drugs: Evidence from Taiwan. *Journal of Health Economics* 28 (2): 341–49.

Lu, J. F., and C. R. Hsieh. 2003. An analysis of the market structure and development of Taiwan's hospital industry [in Chinese]. *Taiwan Economic Review* 31: 107–53.

Lu, Z. J., and W. S. Comanor. 1998. Strategic pricing of new pharmaceuticals. *Review of Economics and Statistics* 80: 108–18.

Murphy, K. M., and R. H. Topel. 2006. The value of health and longevity. *Journal of Political Economy* 114 (5): 871–904.

Newhouse, J. P. 1992. Medical care costs: How much welfare loss? *Journal of Economic Perspectives* 6: 3–21.

Reinhardt, U. E. 2004. An information infrastructure for the pharmaceutical market. *Health Affairs* 23: 107–12.

Saha, A., H. Grabowski, H. Birnbaum, P. Greenberg, and O. Bizan. 2006. Generic competition in the U.S. pharmaceutical industry. *International Journal of the Economics of Business* 13: 15–38.

Sloan, F. A., and C. R. Hsieh. 2008. Effects of incentives on pharmaceutical innovation. In *Incentives and choice in health care*, ed. F. A. Sloan and H. Kasper, pp. 227–62. Cambridge, MA: MIT Press.

Tan, L. T., Y. C. Hong, and C. R. Hsieh. 2007. On the pharmaceutical price gap [in Chinese]. *Taiwan Economic Review* 35: 451–76.

Yang, B. M. 2005. Pharmaceutical pricing and reimbursement in South Korea: Facing a new initiative. Paper presented at International Conference on Pharmaceutical Innovation, Taipei, May 25–26.

Yang, B. M., E. Y. Bae, and J. Kim. 2008. Economic evaluation and pharmaceutical reimbursement reform in South Korea's national health insurance. *Health Affairs* 27 (1): 179–87.

PHARMACEUTICAL POLICY IN SEVEN ASIA-PACIFIC HEALTH-CARE SYSTEMS

AUSTRALIA

REGULATION AND THE POLITICS OF PHARMACEUTICALS IN AUSTRALIA

Hans Löfgren

Pharmaceutical policy in Australia, as elsewhere, involves a bewildering range of actors, including firms and business associations, regulatory agencies, wholesalers and retailers, research establishments, medical and other professional groups, and, increasingly, consumer and patient advocacy organizations. Issues of affordability and access occasionally give rise to political conflict but, typically, regulatory issues are managed through cooperative exchange within relatively closed networks of core stakeholders (Löfgren and de Boer 2004). As in many other countries, there have long been regulatory arrangements to ensure drug safety and efficacy; achieve health and social policy objectives; and promote investment in pharmaceutical research and development (R&D), production, and exports. In Australia, pharmaceutical regulation is, to all intents and purposes, the responsibility of the national government in Canberra. The Therapeutic Goods Administration (TGA), an agency under the Department of Health and Ageing (DOHA), has responsibilities similar to those of the U.S Food and Drug Administration (U.S FDA). (The present name of the department is used throughout this chapter though its precise designation has differed over the years.) TGA approval is required for domestic marketing or exports of prescription and over-the-counter (OTC) medicines, medical devices, and related products. The government subsidizes more than 70 percent of all prescriptions through a second program within DOHA, the Pharmaceutical Benefits Scheme (PBS), which works to ensure timely and affordable access to a wide range of approved prescription medicines (Sweeny 2007; DOHA 2007). That subsidy arrangements were never devolved to state (regional) governments (as in Canada) partly explains the capacity of the PBS to effectively withstand, over the decades, lobbying by the drug industry and other sectional interests.

This chapter provides a broad perspective on the regulation and politics of pharmaceuticals in Australia since the 1950s. Three policy phases are identified: state dominance and decommodification (1951–1987), pluralist bargaining (1987–1996), and (since 1996) the uneven inroad of neoliberalism. The purpose is not to assign great importance to these dates but to render visible key dynamics and significant policy shifts. In essence, until Australia's break with protectionism in the 1980s, health and social policy objectives prevailed over economic considerations. In the decades after WWII and before globalization, the PBS provided the government with a mechanism for sourcing medicines at low prices, effectively reining in the pricing and profit aspirations of the drug industry (Johnston 1986). Trade barriers made it necessary for foreign companies to engage in small-scale manufacturing for the local market, but R&D and exports were negligible. Government-industry relations were infused by mutual distrust—a pattern that began to change only in 1987, when a Labor government initiated regulatory reform to promote the pharmaceutical industry, triggered by fears that the economy relied too much on low-tech resources. From this time forth, pharmaceuticals and biotechnology have been viewed by Canberra and several of the states (notably Victoria and Queensland) as quintessential "knowledge economy" sectors, and programs have been implemented to draw "big pharma" into Australia's national innovation system (Löfgren and Benner 2003). But this newfound emphasis on industry development was tempered by the introduction of cost-effectiveness analyses into the PBS listing process and the systematic application of reference pricing. Indeed, Australia was the first country to make assessing cost-effectiveness mandatory before listing on a public reimbursement formulary. All the same, drug industry perspectives have gained increasing salience in policy and regulation, a shift captured in the National Medicines Policy, which identifies "a viable industry" as one of its four "arms" (Sansom 1999). What gives policy in the past decade a neoliberal flavor is the withering of 1990s efforts to catalyze structural change in the drug industry and the tacit adoption of the premise that there can be no basic disparities between public and business interests in a modern globalized economy. Step-by-step adjustments to the TGA and the PBS have made regulation more industry friendly, and drug firms, through Medicines Australia, have become increasingly influential interlocutors with both agencies (Löfgren and de Boer 2004; Morgan et al. 2008). Nevertheless, the social and political sensitivity of health policy and medicine impose limits on neoliberal orthodoxy in this domain. Many policy actors remain wedded to the ethos of the welfare state, and the DOHA continues to pursue a "value for money" approach to PBS listings. The National Medicines Policy and a plethora of deliberative and collaborative arrangements provide frameworks for debates and compromises, but complex conflicts of interest inevitably endure. These tensions revolve around the PBS, one of the enduring legacies of the post-1945 welfare state.

State Dominance and Decommodification (1951–1987)

The PBS was designed in the late 1940s under Labor but implemented in 1950 by a conservative government after years of opposition by the medical profession to pharmaceutical benefits. The scheme was progressively expanded into a universal welfare program that met most therapeutic needs, irrespective of ability to pay. Prescription drugs were de facto decommodified as far as consumers and prescribers were concerned; that is, prescribing and consumer behavior ceased to be influenced by price signals. In the 1950s, PBS items were supplied at no direct cost to consumers, but pensioners and their dependants had access to a more extensive range of drugs than general consumers. In 1960 a single list of entitlements was created and the number of generally available subsidized drugs greatly increased. At the same time, a copayment was introduced for general consumers, later extended (at a lower rate) to the concessional consumer category (Sloan 1995). Over several decades, effective policy control by the DOHA was achieved through bargaining over PBS arrangements with associations representing suppliers, pharmacists, the medical profession, consumers, and other interests.

Until the early 1960s, drugs were recommended for PBS listing on medical grounds alone. By then drugs formed the largest single item of government expenditure under national health benefits, and costs became a political concern (Hunter 1963). A Cabinet report in 1963 affirmed that drug prices in Australia were significantly higher than prices for the same products in the United Kingdom. The government responded that same year by establishing the Pharmaceutical Benefits Pricing Bureau (PBPB) to examine and confirm prices emerging from negotiations between suppliers and the DOHA. The new arrangements helped reduce many prices in 1963–1964, with consequent budgetary savings (Industries Assistance Commission 1986:28). Over subsequent years, the department became increasingly adept at achieving relatively low drug prices for the Australian government through effective use of its purchasing power. Suppliers were generally dependent on PBS listing for commercially viable sales and had little option but to accept prices that the government deemed reasonable. The private prescription market—comprising prescription products approved for marketing by the TGA but not included on the PBS and paid for in full by the patient—was and remains marginal. From the mid-1960s to the late 1980s, the PBS served to maximize the value of taxpayers' money while maintaining the availability of a comprehensive range of drugs. In 1978 the DOHA defined the role of the PBS as follows:

> The Government [through the PBS] aims at having a comprehensive range of drugs and medicinal preparations available on a subsidised basis to all persons being treated by a medical practitioner in Australia . . . The Department's main process for achieving the maximum value for Government expenditure under the Scheme is its price negotiation system. (Commonwealth Department of Health 1978)

Thirty years later, this statement remains broadly accurate—with the important qualification that the introduction of cost-effectiveness assessments and the extension of reference pricing in the 1990s gave the "value for money" approach a somewhat different context, as will be explained. The basic arrangement remains that products are listed on the PBS following a positive recommendation by the Pharmaceutical Benefits Advisory Committee (PBAC), established in 1954 as an independent statutory body under the National Health Act of 1953. Committee members are appointed by the minister for health and ageing, and include medical practitioners, pharmacists, a health economist, and a consumer representative. Over many years the DOHA sought to insulate the scientific and medical experts and departmental officials participating in the listing process from lobbyists promoting industry and other interest groups. Until 1970 even the composition of the PBAC was not made public, but over the years the process has been made more transparent (Sloan 1995; Sweeny 2007).

Friction between the government and the drug industry is intrinsic to the PBS. Plainly, the industry aim of maximizing sales and profits was inconsistent with the pre-1990s approach of paying the lowest possible prices for reliable supply. This clash continues, along with contention over cost-effectiveness and the appropriate use of medicine. Tension of this kind is of course inherent in all public insurance schemes. In the United States, similar pressures for cost-effectiveness are exercised by managed care and pharmaceutical benefit management companies. Since the 1990s, instruments derived from pharmacoeconomics have been extended across many of the countries of the Organisation for Economic Co-operation and Development (OECD) in the form of reference pricing schemes and techniques for comparing the value of new medicines against existing drugs and therapies (Walley, Haycox, and Boland 2004; Lopez-Casanovas and Puig-Junoy 2000). In addition, Wagner and Ross-Degnan (chapter 18 of this volume) and Hsieh (chapter 5) examine a trend toward insurance systems premised on the application of purchasing power and economic analysis in developing countries and emerging economies such as Taiwan. In this context, the Australian experience of value-for-money assessments under a national drug insurance scheme can serve as exemplary in at least some respects.

Until 1987 the National Health Act did not specify the factors to be considered by the PBAC when making listing recommendations. An amendment to the act in that year established that the PBAC had to take account of cost and comparative effectiveness. This not only gave legal authority to the cost-containment approach already applied for many years but also pointed to a more sophisticated pricing system incorporating economic analysis. The cost-effectiveness requirements were phased in over the following years, and in 1993 Australia became the first country to make mandatory the inclusion of "an assessment of comparative effectiveness and comparative cost-effectiveness against existing therapies" with applications for government subsidies (Roughead, Lopert, and Sansom 2007:515; see also Drummond 1992). This shift, which represented the end of cost containment as the singular objective of the PBS pricing (subject to reliable supply) was accompanied by several measures to attract drug industry investments, including the so-called Factor (f) Scheme (which channelled substantial funding to participating firms in exchange for expanded investment in production, R&D, and exports) and an overhaul of the TGA to make the approval process more industry friendly.

Pluralist Bargaining (1987–1996)

The turn to economic analysis in PBS pricing and other reform initiatives in the early 1990s occurred within an emerging framework of pluralist bargaining, which gave the pharmaceutical industry and (to a lesser extent) consumer organizations a voice in the policy process. The newfound emphasis on deliberation and compromise was framed by the Labor government's objective of making Australia an attractive location for industry activities. Building partnerships with key stakeholders was part of a concerted effort to achieve structural change. The government's capacity to exercise control, however, began to decline as the dismantling of trade barriers and changes in the global industry augmented the bargaining power of international drug companies vis-à-vis Australian regulators.

The early introduction of mandatory economic analysis for PBS listing cemented Australia's international reputation for innovative drug policy. It may seem curious that cost-effectiveness assessments were pioneered at a time of growing industry allegations that the PBS was free-riding on global R&D. The conceptually straightforward model of applying purchasing power to ensure the lowest possible costs subject to reliable supply was under severe strain by the late 1980s. Only then was the drug industry recognized as a potentially important high-tech sector; meanwhile, the DOHA—wedded to health and welfare policy objectives—remained the dominant actor in the policy process. But the government was keen to make the regulatory environment more industry friendly and to move beyond the long-standing conflict over PBS pricing. To continue the cost-minimization model of the previous twenty years threatened the viability of local industry activities; the disinvestments of the 1980s signalled that supplying drugs at prices significantly lower than offered by comparable countries was no longer acceptable to international companies (Parry and Thwaites 1988). In submissions to an inquiry in 1986, drug firms claimed that low prices resulted in the closure of manufacturing plants. Unless policies changed, Merck threatened, it would withdraw entirely or "at least substantially reduce" its presence in the country (Löfgren 1997a:178). In this context, economic analysis offered a different pricing rationale, underpinned by the strong public policy theory developed in a burgeoning health economics literature (for example, Drummond, Stoddart, and Torrance 1987). The industry hoped that cost-effectiveness assessments would raise the prices of truly innovative products, and so this "approach to subsidy listing was initially well accepted by the industry" (Birkett, Mitchell, and McManus 2001:113). Indeed, over subsequent years, innovative products came to be priced at levels similar to those in comparable countries (Roughead, Lopert, and Sansom 2007; Productivity Commission 2001). The Factor (f) Scheme and other initiatives of this period—framed by the new partnership rhetoric—further diluted industry opposition to the integration of economic analysis into the PBS listing process.

Until the 1990s, drug manufacturing was protected behind high tariffs, as was Australian manufacturing in general (Bell 1993). Consistent with this pattern, most of the international drug companies set up small-scale Australian plants in the 1950s and 1960s for the formulation and packaging of imported active ingredients; R&D was largely confined to the adaptation of imported drugs to local requirements. The size and growth of the market, sustained by the PBS, largely compensated for its price-depressing effects and made local manufacturing viable, at least until the 1980s (Industry Commission 1995a). The Hawke and Keating Labor governments (1983–1996) dismantled protectionism to open up the Australian economy. Privatization, deregulation initiatives, and the liberalization of financial markets were combined with interventionist measures to restructure key industries and promote high-tech sectors such as pharmaceuticals. The concern was that Australia's export dependence on resources and agriculture (coal, iron ore, wheat, wool, and so on) could not sustain a high-wage, advanced economy (Jones 1995).

This was the context for a wave of industry-friendly regulatory reform, including the 1987 replacement of the PBPB (which had been part of the DOHA) with a more independent body, the Pharmaceutical Benefits Pricing Authority (PBPA); an extension, in the same year, of the patent term to twenty years; and a shake-up of the TGA and the marketing approval system, triggered by an inquiry initiated in 1991 (Baume 1991). The implementation of the recommendations of the Baume Review delivered a significant reduction of review times, and a new management team from 1992 made good relations with drug companies a key TGA priority. Relations had previously been characterized by mutual distrust; indeed, the major industry association claimed that:

[M]ost senior TGA officers have a strongly negative attitude towards the industry and this philosophy has permeated relatively low levels of the agency. The role of TGA officers has been emphasised as being the protectors of the public's safety rather than its health and welfare. Sponsor companies are seen as adversaries rather than organisations which share many of the TGA's goals and with considerable expertise to offer. (Australian Pharmaceutical Manufacturers Association 1991:10)

A turnaround in organizational culture was achieved in the next few years. The agency sought to involve the industry in ongoing dialogue, and notions of partnership, transparency, accountability, and accessibility figured centrally in policy documents. Responsiveness to the agency's clients and customers—increasingly understood as the drug industry rather than the general community—was made imperative by the TGA's growing reliance on revenue raising, including annual licensing, good manufacturing practice inspections, and evaluation fees (first introduced in 1991). In 1997–1998 the government moved further in this direction with the mandating of 75 percent cost recovery, then full cost recovery from 1998–1999. According to a leading industry figure:

[T]he accessibility and attitude of people at the TGA is light years ahead of where it was pre-Baume [the 1991 inquiry], just in being able to see people, talk to them and have a dialogue . . . the personnel changes that have taken place in the TGA are greatly facilitative of discussions on many of these points . . . (Industry Commission 1995b:43)

The other major government initiative in this period was, as already mentioned, the Factor (f) Scheme, the largest program ever administered by the Department of Industry at a total cost of around A$1 billion. In operation between 1987 and 1999, the scheme notionally "compensated" eligible companies for relatively low PBS prices, in exchange for the expansion of production, exports, and R&D (Löfgren 1997b). Programs based on similar principles as Factor (f) have continued up to the present, though on a lesser scale. Between 1999 and 2004 the Pharmaceutical Industry Investment Program (PIIP) channelled around A$300 million to the industry, and the Pharmaceuticals Partnerships Progam (P3) was valued at around A$150 million in the period 2004–2009 (Department of Innovation Industry Science and Research 2007; Productivity Commission 2003).

In a decade characterized here as one of pluralist bargaining, Labor governments reinvigorated long-standing collaborative and consultative arrangements and introduced new ones. Two new advisory committees were established in 1991: the Australian Pharmaceutical Advisory Committee (APAC) and the Pharmaceutical Health and Rational Use of Medicines (PHARM) Working Party (later upgraded to committee status). The APAC was established as a consultative body that included the formal representation of professional, industry, and consumer organizations, reporting directly to the minister for health. An Industry Government Consultative Forum was established in 1992—with secretariat services provided by the Department of Industry—to facilitate cooperative exchange between industry and government and to develop a national strategy for the pharmaceutical industry. Also in this period, the consumer health movement—at the peak level represented by the Consumers' Health Forum (CHF)—gained entry into the drug policy process and increased its presence on a range of government, industry, and provider group committees.

The CHF was an important driver of the process that resulted in the de facto adoption of Australia's National Medicines Policy in 1994–1995. This set of policy objectives encompasses four "arms": (1) timely access to the medicines that Australians need, at a cost that individuals and the community can afford (provided through the PBS); (2) medicines that meet appropriate standards of quality, safety, and efficacy (the role of the TGA); (3) quality use of medicines (the role of PHARM and, from 1998, the National Prescribing Service, as explained by Liaw in chapter 17 of this volume); and (4) maintenance of a responsible and viable medicine industry (programs administered by the Department of Industry) (DOHA 2000). The concept of a National Medicines Policy had its genesis in World Health Assembly resolutions and the activities of the World Health Organization (WHO); in the 1990s, Australia arguably led the world in this area (Sansom 1999). But the precise status of the National Medicines Policy is somewhat unclear. The closest thing to an authoritative pronouncement is a DOHA brochure that loosely refers to an agreement in 1996 between the Commonwealth and the states on health and community services delivery (DOHA 2000). The APAC had a role in its development and coordination, and the National Medicines Policy continues to provide a de facto framework for deliberations within the policy network and a reference point for lobbying by various stakeholders.

After 1996: The Uneven Inroad of Neoliberalism

Pharmaceutical firms operate in an increasingly complex environment that includes pricing pressures from the application of pharmacoeconomic assessments by public and private insurance providers, growing competition from generics, a paucity of new breakthrough drugs, and the expectation that companies be responsive to the calamitous health conditions in the developing world. Big pharmaceutical companies have consolidated into ever larger entities and made innovation and production systems yet more international, not least through outsourcing and other external collaborations (Mittra 2007).

Policy and regulation in Australia is characterized by stable institutional arrangements; it remains an "axiom in Australian medicines policy that everyone loves the PBS" (Henry 2007). But international companies have persistently, if quietly, criticized PBS pricing arrangements. One example is a 2007 Medicines Australia document that presents the results of a survey in which firms "cited the pricing policies and constraints operating under [the PBS] as the most negative factors of the industry's future development in Australia" (Medicines Australia 2008:6). The PBS listing process has now become more open to industry scrutiny. Changes to pricing arrangements introduced in legislation adopted in 2007 further protected innovative products from generic competition, while ensuring a greater market share for generics at prices significantly lower than before (Faunce and Löfgren 2007). The TGA is now more responsive to its fee-paying industry clients, and its activities are increasingly shaped by international standards (including those set through the International Conference on Harmonization). In 2003 the TGA was embarrassed by serious quality problems in Pan Pharmaceuticals, a major complementary medicines manufacturing company, but it has since reestablished its reputation for stringent regulatory controls. The influence of neoliberalism in incremental changes across different areas of drug regulation is also apparent in the demise of strategic policy measures to integrate the drug industry into Australia's national innovation system.

The Howard government relabeled the programs administered by the Department of Industry as "Action Agendas" promoting a range of different industries. In May 2001 the Pharmaceuticals Industry Action Agenda was launched as a framework for existing (mostly small-scale) programs and initiatives in this sector. The declared aim was to double Australia's share of the global drug industry by 2012 through facilitating interaction between multinational corporations, local firms, and research organizations—drawing on Australia's strength in such areas as basic scientific research and capacity to undertake cost-effective clinical trials (Hill, Kirchner, and Holmes 2001). The pharmaceutical industry was designated "the most innovative, knowledge-based industry in Australia" (Pharmaceutical Industry Action Agenda 2002:1). Medicines Australia claimed credit for persuading the government to initiate the agenda process, bringing together multinational research-based firms, the generics industry, the biotechnology and medical research sectors, and state agencies in a multitude of working groups and committees, with the stated aim of enabling dialogue and building trust (Australian Pharmaceutical Manufacturers Association 2001:6). Action Agenda issues were kept separate from the PBS, which was to be accepted "as a given, recognising that the PBS is the cornerstone of equitable access . . . and use of an evidence-based approach to listing will continue on into the foreseeable future in its present form" (Pharmaceutical Industry Action Agenda 2001).

The pharmaceutical sector had from 1987 been the central focus of Labor's effort to compensate for economic liberalization with strategic industry policy. The rhetoric of the knowledge-based economy, high-tech industry clusters, government-business partnerships, and technology and innovation policy continued within the Action Agendas, but the enthusiasm for strategic industry policy waned and the programs succeeding the Factor (f) Scheme were smaller. A departmental evaluation in 2005 found that the Pharmaceutical Action Agenda "had been a very useful program for all stakeholders," but the aim of doubling Australia's share of the global drug industry by 2012 would clearly not be achieved (Department of Industry Tourism and Resources 2005). The vision of Australia as a significant drug manufacturing location has lost credibility, and activities within the Action Agenda framework have dwindled in recent years. The volume of R&D (predominantly clinical trials) undertaken in Australia has expanded, but drug production is "conducted in relatively smaller plants used for the later stages of the manufacturing process," an account which echoes the industry inquiries of the 1970s and 1980s (Medicines Australia 2008:6; see, for example, Pharmaceutical Manufacturing Industry Inquiry 1979). A 2005 inquiry identified only fourteen secondary drug manufacturing plants (including contract manufacturing); only ten firms reported active ingredients production (Economist Intelligence Unit 2005:19). Australia's role in global biopharma production and innovation is today no less marginal than a few decades ago, and even much-hyped "biotechnology clusters and networks appear precarious. . . [and] a long way from providing the basis for a robust industry" (Gilding 2007:35). Moreover, the resources boom in the years leading up to the economic crisis, which commenced in Australia in late 2008, made promoting high-tech

137

industries seem less urgent. The aim of steering the pharmaceutical industry toward participation in the national innovation system has been progressively downplayed, and the expectation that Australia would attract significant investments as a drug-manufacturing center abandoned. In the recent period of neoliberal predominance, emphasis has been on the provision of a broadly accommodating business environment. Among the policy elite, the prevalent view is that high-tech industries are no more important than other economic activities, particularly as Australia, at least until late 2008, benefited from high world market prices for coal, iron ore, natural gas, copper, uranium, gold, wheat, and so on.

With the winding back of industry policy, debate in the drug sector has again come to focus squarely on the PBS and—as far as major industry groups are concerned—its purported lack of reward for innovation. The central issue in negotiations leading up to the Australia–United States Free Trade Agreement (AUSFTA), when the U.S. trade representative pushed for greater recognition of innovation, was its implications for the PBS. U.S. negotiators sought to achieve "the elimination of government measures such as price controls and reference pricing which deny full market access for United States products" (Trade Promotion Authority Act 2002, cited in Roughead, Lopert, and Sansom 2007). For this purpose, they "propose[d] changes that would improve transparency and the regulatory procedures for listing new drugs in Australia," and many of the provisions of the AUSFTA (which came into effect in January 2005) directly or indirectly relate to medicine regulation in Australia (deputy U.S. trade representative cited in Faunce et al. 2005). The PBS weathered this onslaught relatively unscathed, and some positive changes were associated with the AUSFTA commitments, including greater transparency through the issuing of public summary documents of PBS drug-listing decisions. But the introduction of a new independent review mechanism—available after a PBAC rejection of an application for the PBS listing or the extended listing of an already listed drug—caused concern among PBS advocates (Australian Government 2008). Also, a Medicines Working Group was established, comprising high-level officials of both countries, "to promote discussion and mutual understanding of issues related to the importance of innovation and pharmaceutical R&D to continued improvement of healthcare outcomes in both countries" (U.S. Department of Health and Human Services 2007). At the very least these changes have put added pressure on the Australian government to balance the rigorous application of "value-for-money" assessments with recognition of the value of innovation, as understood by the industry (Searles 2009). In the context of the PBS, innovation refers to therapeutic advancements; the scheme "operates as a therapeutic-value-based pricing system: it may be thought of as 'purchasing outcomes' rather than drugs" (Lopert and Rosenbaum 2007:645). In contrast, from an industry perspective, all new patented products are innovative by definition, irrespective of therapeutic value-added.

In 2007 complex and significant changes to drug-pricing arrangements were set to be phased in over several years (Buckmaster and Spooner 2007). These were not only intended to rein in the interrelated problems of unnecessarily high PBS prices for generics and the large discounts provided to pharmacists by generics suppliers, but also to protect the prices of patented products irrespective of their therapeutic benefits. For pricing purposes, the PBS was separated into two formularies: F1, which mostly contains single-brand medicines under patent; and F2, which mostly contains multiple-brand, mainly generic, medicines. Historically, the prices of generics in Australia have approximated those of the originator brands, and so, until recently, generics held an insignificant market share; in 2007, only 28 percent of all prescriptions were dispensed with a generic (Generic Medicines Industry Association 2007). As the number of major drugs facing patent expiry multiplied, pressures for lower generic prices became increasingly compelling (Löfgren 2007). The effect of the F1/F2 bifurcation, however, undermined the principle of cost-effectiveness; high-priced single-brand (patented) F1 drugs were insulated from price cuts that would follow from the reference pricing applied under previous PBS arrangements (de Boer 2009).

Evidence that market signals are becoming important to consumers can be found in the marked increase of the PBS copayments; for the first time since the introduction of the scheme, costs are impeding some consumers from access to necessary medicines (Searles et al. 2007). Between 1997 and 2007, copayments increased by about 50 percent and safety-net thresholds by about 70 percent (Sweeny 2009). The copayment for general users in 2009 was as high as A$32.90, meaning that many products are now priced below the level at which the government subsidy takes effect (for nonconcessional consumers). With the expansion of low-cost generics and annual indexed adjustments to copayments and safety-net thresholds, the range of nonsubsidized drugs will likely increase further in the next few years. In 2002 the Labor party in the Senate blocked legislation enabling large increases in copayments, but two years later Labor allowed the increases to proceed. Thus, there is bipartisan support for a slow but steady increase in the cost burden for prescription drugs carried by consumers. Another contentious issue is the introduction of full cost recovery for the PBS listings, announced in the 2005–2006 budget, which was opposed by Medicines Australia, the Australian Medical Association, PBS advocates (who saw reliance on industry funding as undermining the independence of the PBAC) and by Labor in opposition. In government after the November 2007 election, however, Labor sought to introduce the same arrangements for PBS cost recovery. At the time of this writing, the necessary legislation was yet to be passed by parliament, despite being referred twice to a Senate committee (de Boer 2009).

Cost issues tend to be central to discussions about the PBS. In June 2007 there were 680 individual drugs (or molecules) listed. These were available in 1,600 different forms and marketed as 2,900 differently branded items. The PBS's annual cost to taxpayers is determined by prices paid for listed drugs, changes to these prices, the number of dispensed prescriptions for each drug, copayment and safety-net threshold levels, and the number and cost of newly listed drugs. In recent years, increases in government expenditure have declined to well below the approximately 10 percent annual increase in the decade up to 2004–2005, as a consequence of copayments, generic competition, and other factors. In 2006–2007, total government PBS expenditure increased by 4.3 percent to A$6.4 billion while the volume of prescriptions increased by only 0.1 percent to 168.5 million, or 8.1 prescriptions per capita (Pharmaceutical Policy and Analysis Branch 2007). This compares with a 2.7 percent increase in the previous year (when there was a 1.1 percent decrease in the volume of prescriptions; DOHA 2007). In addition, around 33 million PBS prescriptions did not appear in the official statistics because they were priced below the general copayment level and paid for entirely by the consumer. Private prescriptions, that is, approved drugs not listed on the PBS, were also not included in the available statistics (DOHA 2007).

Conclusion

Australia has a tradition of effective and at times innovative pharmaceutical regulation and sophisticated policy analysis and debate. The TGA is internationally regarded as an effective regulator that ensures the safety and high quality of medicines and medical devices. The PBS has for almost sixty years provided timely and affordable access to a wide range of TGA-approved prescription medicines. For most of this period, the terms of pharmaceutical policy were set by the government: suppliers, pharmacists, and other stakeholders were and remain highly dependent on regulatory arrangements administered directly or indirectly by the DOHA. Globalization and the reconfiguring of the international drug industry have made the pharmaceutical policy domain more fluid. For its part, the pharmaceutical industry has long argued that incentives for innovation and local R&D are inadequate, and it was a central aim of the United States to bring about major changes to the PBS through the AUSFTA negotiations. The step-by-step changes made to the TGA and the PBS in the past decade point toward the growing influence of neoliberal policy prescriptions and a weakening of the authority of the government in the drug sector. But this is an uneven process with countervailing tendencies. The industry's growing voice is consistent with the ostensible mandate that governments provide favorable conditions for local R&D organizations and firms to link into global production and innovation networks. Yet Australia remains as marginal a contributor to the global drug industry as it was several decades ago. Economic, regulatory, and social policy outcomes in this sector remain indeterminate, and the Australian government—irrespective of party and political composition—must take into account the widely held belief that all citizens should continue to enjoy affordable access to a comprehensive range of high-quality medicines.

References

APMA. *See* Australian Pharmaceutical Manufacturers Association.

Australian Government. 2008. *Independent review (PBS)*. http://www. independentreviewpbs.gov.au/internet/independentreviewpbs/publishing. nsf/Content/home-1.

Australian Pharmaceutical Manufacturers Association. 1991. *Submission by the Australian Pharmaceutical Manufacturers Association to the Bureau of Industry Economics Review of the Pharmaceutical Industry Development Program—Factor F*. Unpublished submission.

———. 2001. *Annual report 2001*. Sydney: APMA.

Baume, Peter. 1991. *A question of balance: Report on the future of drug evaluation in Australia*. Canberra: Australian Government Publishing Service (AGPS).

Bell, Stephen. 1993. *Australian manufacturing and the state*. Cambridge: Cambridge Univ. Press.

Birkett, Donald J., Andrew S. Mitchell, and Peter McManus. 2001. A cost-effectiveness approach to drug subsidy and pricing in Australia. *Health Affairs* 20 (3): 104–14.

Buckmaster, Luke, and Diane Spooner. 2007. *National Health (Pharmaceutical Benefits Scheme) Bill 2007*. Parliamentary Library, May 31.

Commonwealth Department of Health. 1978. *Submission to pharmaceutical manufacturing industry inquiry* [Ralph report]. Canberra, p. 1.

de Boer, Rebecca. 2009. PBS reform: A missed opportunity? *Australian Health Review* 33 (2): 176–85.

Department of Health and Ageing. 2000. *National medicines policy*. Australian Government. http://www.health.gov.au/internet/wcms/publishing.nsf/ Content/nmp-objectives-policy.htm.

———. 2007. *Submission by the Australian government Department of Health and Ageing*. Canberra: Senate Community Affairs Committee: Inquiry into National Health Amendment (Pharmaceutical Benefits Scheme) Bill 2007.

Department of Industry Tourism and Resources. 2005. *Pharmaceutical industry action agenda: Executive summary of the evaluation report*. Canberra: Department of Industry Tourism and Resources.

Department of Innovation Industry Science and Research. 2007. *Pharmaceuticals partnerships program (P3)—Fact sheet*.

DOHA. *See* Department of Health and Ageing.

Drummond, Michael F. 1992. Basing prescription drug payment on economic analysis: The case of Australia. *Health Affairs* 11 (4): 191–96.

Drummond, Michael F., Greg L. Stoddart, and George W. Torrance. 1987. *Methods for the economic evaluation of health care programmes*. Oxford: Oxford Univ. Press.

Economist Intelligence Unit. 2005. *Benchmarking study of the characteristics of the Australian and international pharmaceuticals industries*. Canberra: A study undertaken for the Australian Government Department of Industry,

Tourism and Resources, Invest Australia, and the Victorian Government Department of Innovation, Industry and Regional Development.

Faunce, Thomas, and Hans Löfgren. 2007. Drug price reforms: The new F1-F2 bifurcation [editorial]. *Australian Prescriber* 30 (6): 138–40.

Faunce, Tom, Evan Doran, David Henry, Peter Drahos, Brita Pekarsky, Warwick Neville, and Andrew Searles. 2005. Assessing the impact of the Australia-United States free trade agreement on Australian and global medicines policy. *Globalization and Health* (1) 15. October 6.

Generic Medicines Industry Association. 2007. *Submission to Senate inquiry: National Health Amendment (Pharmaceutical Benefits Scheme) Bill 2007.*

Gilding, Michael. 2007. Biotechnology clusters and networks in Australia: Patterns of national collaboration and international inter-organisational collaboration. In *Human biotechnology & public trust: Trends, perceptions and regulation*, ed. M. Stranger. Hobart: Centre for Law and Genetics.

Henry, David. 2007. Patients the losers and makers of the winners in PBS tinkering. *The Weekend Australian*, June 9–10, Health section, p. 19.

Hill, Justin, Adrian Kirchner, and Anne Holmes. 2001. *Pharmaceutical industry action agenda: Discussion paper*. Canberra: Pharmaceuticals Section, Department of Industry, Science and Resources.

Hunter, Thelma. 1963. Some thoughts on the pharmaceutical benefits scheme. *Australian Journal of Social Issues* 1 (4): 32–40.

Industries Assistance Commission. 1986. *Pharmaceutical products*. Canberra: AGPS, p. 28.

Industry Commission. 1995a. *The pharmaceutical industry: Draft report*. Canberra: Industry Commission.

———. 1995b. *Transcript of proceedings from round table discussion on prescription products in Sydney, 16 August*. Unpublished.

Johnston, Mark. 1986. *Australia's pharmaceutical pricing strategy*. Cambridge: Harvard Univ. Press.

Jones, Barry. 1995. *Sleepers, wake! Technology & the future of work*. Melbourne: Oxford Univ. Press.

Löfgren, Hans. 1997a. Globalisation of the pharmaceutical industry and the Australian state: The transformation of a policy network. PhD Dissertation, Department of Political Science, Univ. of Melbourne, Melbourne.

———. 1997b. Industry policy to set the market free: Drug pricing and the Factor (f) program. *Labour & Industry* (2): 67–84.

———. 2007. Reshaping Australian drug pricing: The dilemmas of generics medicines policy [editorial]. *Australia New Zealand Health Policy* 4: 11.

———. 2009. The economic crisis, the Pharmaceutical Benefits Scheme, and the dilemmas of medicines policy. Special issue, *Australian Health Review* 33 (2): 171–75.

Löfgren, Hans, and Mats Benner. 2003. Biotechnology and governance in Australia and Sweden: Path dependency or institutional convergence. *Australian Journal of Political Science* 38 (1): 25–43.

Löfgren, Hans, and Rebecca de Boer. 2004. Pharmaceuticals in Australia: Developments in regulation and governance. *Social Science and Medicine* 58 (12): 2397–407.

Lopert, Ruth, and Sara Rosenbaum. 2007. What is fair? Choice, fairness and transparency in access to prescription drugs in the United States and Australia. *Journal of Law, Medicine and Ethics* 35 (4): 643–56.

Lopez-Casanovas, Guillem, and Jaume Puig-Junoy. 2000. Review of the literature on reference pricing. *Health Policy* 54: 87–123.

Medicines Australia. 2008. *Australian pharmaceutical industry at a crossroad? Report of the 2007 Medicines Australia member economic survey*. Canberra: Medicines Australia.

Mittra, James. 2007. Life science innovation and the restructuring of the pharmaceutical industry: Mergers, acquisitions and strategic alliance behaviour of large firms. *Technology Analysis & Strategic Management* 19(3): 279–301.

Morgan, Steve, Meghan McMahon, and Devon Greyson. 2008. Balancing health and industrial policy objectives in the pharmaceutical sector: Lessons from Australia. *Health Policy* 87 (2): 133–45.

Parry, Thomas G., and Robert M. A. Thwaites. 1988. *The pharmaceutical industry in Australia: A benchmark study*. Sydney: APMA.

Pharmaceutical Industry Action Agenda. 2001. Action agenda terms of reference. In *Bulletin no. 1*, Canberra: Department of Industry Science and Resources.

———. 2002. *Local priority: Global partner*. Canberra: Department of Industry Science and Resources.

Pharmaceutical Manufacturing Industry Inquiry. 1979. *Pharmaceutical manufacturing industry inquiry [Ralph report]*. Canberra: AGPS.

Pharmaceutical Policy and Analysis Branch. *Expenditure and prescriptions twelve months to 30 June 2007*. Department of Health and Ageing 2007. http://www.health.gov.au/internet/main/publishing.nsf/Content/pbs-stats-pbexp-jun07.

Productivity Commission. 2001. *International pharmaceutical price differences: Research report*. Canberra: AusInfo.

———. 2003. *Evaluation of the pharmaceutical industry investment program: Research report*. Canberra: AusInfo.

Roughead, Elizabeth E., Ruth Lopert, and Lloyd Norman Sansom. 2007. Prices for innovative pharmaceutical products that provide health gain: A comparison between Australia and the United States. *Value in Health* 10(6): 514–20.

Sansom, Lloyd. 1999. The Australian national medicinal drug policy. *Journal of Quality in Clinical Practice* 1 (1): 31–35.

Searles, Andrew. 2009. The PBS in a globalised world: Free trade and reference pricing. *Australian Health Review* 33 (2): 186–91.

Searles, Andrew, Susannah Jefferys, Evan Doran, and David A. Henry. 2007. Reference pricing, generic drugs and proposed changes to the pharmaceutical benefits scheme. *Medical Journal of Australia Rapid Online Publication.* http://www.mja.com.au/public/issues/187_04_200807/contents_200807.html.

Sloan, Clyde. 1995. *A history of the Pharmaceutical Benefits Scheme 1947–1992.* Canberra: AGPS.

Sweeny, Kim 2009. The impact of copayments and safety nets on PBS expenditure. *Australian Health Review* 33 (2): 215–30.

———. 2007. Key aspects of the Australian pharmaceutical benefits scheme. In working paper #35, Pharmaceutical Industry Project. Melbourne: Centre for Strategic Economic Studies, Victoria Univ. of Technology.

U.S. Department of Health and Human Services. 2007. *Australia-U.S. Medicines working group holds first meeting.* HHS.gov. http://www.globalhealth.gov/news/news/011406.html.

Walley, Tom, Alan Haycox, and Angela Boland, eds. 2004. *Pharmacoeconomics.* Edinburgh: Churchill Livingstone.

The Australian Pharmaceutical Subsidy Gambit: Transmuting Deadweight Loss and Oligopoly Rents to Consumer Surplus

Mark Johnston and Richard Zeckhauser[1]

Australia has long managed to pay pharmaceutical manufacturers substantially less for their products than other developed nations. Figure 7.1, based on data from the late 1970s, shows Australia paying prices substantially lower than those of ten comparison countries.[2] The average U.S. payment was 225 percent of the Australian average. In 1986–1987, the average global price of the eighty largest-selling drugs was 82 percent higher than that paid in Australia.[3] This pattern was remarkably consistent across drugs: about 90 percent had world average prices greater than the Australian price. Today, in most instances, Australian prices for patented medicines continue to be low relative to those of other Organisation for Economic Co-operation and Development (OECD) countries.[4]

Unlike most other developed countries, Australia does not regulate its drug prices directly. Any drug that meets Australian safety and efficacy standards can be marketed, and standards are administered without attention to the price of the drug.[5] Indeed, the prevailing legal view is that the Australian federal government lacks the constitutional power to regulate prices directly.

Australia's success does not depend on substantial purchases; the country represents only a small share of the world pharmaceutical market. How then has Australia managed to pay such low prices for its drugs?[6]

Australia's Price-contingent Subsidy Program

Australia's secret lies in a price-contingent subsidy program. Its government pays a per-unit subsidy to the drug producer—but only if the manufacturer and the government reach an agreement on the price. The program is a large one relative to Australia's gross domestic product (GDP).[7]

The essence of the Australian scheme is simple, and we have developed a model that captures its fundamentals. In the model's one-producer form, a monopolist is offered a per-unit subsidy if it will set the consumer price equal to the marginal cost. Sales increase substantially, and the subsidy allows the monopolist to earn slightly more than it would receive under monopoly pricing.

Figure 7.1 Manufacturers' Prescription Drug Prices, December 1977

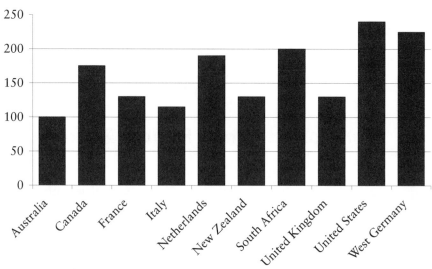

Note: Australia = 100.

The deadweight loss of monopoly pricing is thus eliminated—transmuted into consumer surplus (save a smidgen for the manufacturer). In practice, Australia's arrangement is somewhat more complex, for three reasons: (1) it serves distributional goals beyond reducing the average price that Australians pay for drugs, (2) the government does not have full information about costs, and (3) its specific form reflects the tug-of-war inherent in the political process.

A subsidy scheme can provide a still more impressive feat of alchemy when more than one manufacturer is competing for a market—say, for statins. The government can play off one oligopolist against another, inducing a race to join the subsidy scheme. If Company A has joined the scheme and is therefore charging marginal cost, profits for Company B, at any price, will be much lower than at the initial oligopoly equilibrium—hence its incentive to join the scheme immediately. If both producers join the scheme, each is offered less than initial oligopoly profits.

Variants of this subsidy arrangement could be employed in any market where, because of market power, price significantly exceeds marginal cost. The subsidy scheme is particularly effective when producers are foreign, and the government's concern for their welfare is solely strategic (for example, it just wants them to remain in the market); their profits receive zero weight as a welfare consideration. To remove as much clutter as possible, we consider only the goal of increasing consumer surplus. We recognize that most subsidy schemes, including the Australian pharmaceutical subsidy arrangement, serve additional purposes. To simplify, we shall assume away any externality, distributional, or merit-good arguments for consumption of the subsidized good.

The Australian government is engaged in an unusual form of a two-level game. By choosing an appropriate strategy in its domestic market, it substantially increases the benefits of its dealings with foreign producers. Domestic politics have frequently been manipulated (or misrepresented) to improve outcomes in international arenas.[8] Here that stratagem is extended to the microeconomic arena.

In considering consumer surplus we take research and development (R&D) expenditures by the manufacturer as a given. Schumpeter has launched a lively argument about the economics of invention, with some analyses (for example, Schumpeter 1975; Arrow 1962; Mansfield et al. 1977), emphasizing that invention is a collective good, while others (for example, Hirshleifer 1971; Loury 1979; Mortensen 1982) point to factors that encourage private firms to spend more on R&D than is socially optimal. For present purposes, however, we need not enter that debate since Australia comprises such a small proportion of the international pharmaceuticals market that its expenditure has a negligible impact on the level of international R&D. In contrast to most of the literature on technical innovation, we take an unashamedly single-country perspective.

There are good theoretical reasons for the success of the Australian scheme. Underpinnings for the case of the monopolist are reviewed in this chapter. We then show that, applied to an oligopoly, the subsidy scheme proves to be an ingenious real-world application of game theory. We then return to the Australian scheme and conclude.

Transmuting Deadweight Loss

We shall refer to the government as A and the producer as B. A wishes to subsidize B's production in order to garner additional consumer surplus. But of course A must consider the cost of the subsidy. For the process of subsidization to be worthwhile, the gain in consumer surplus must exceed the cost of the subsidy. In deciding whether to undertake subsidies, therefore, the government needs to look at the net consumer surplus—what we shall call the *citizens' surplus*.

The Monopolist's Decision

Consider a monopolist, B, with no fixed costs and marginal cost (c), selling in a separable market offering the downward sloping demand curve DD, as shown in figure 7.2. The monopolist maximizes profits by setting marginal revenues equal to marginal cost at q^*, with resulting price p^*. The deadweight loss is the triangle ABE; profits are $ABCp^*$.

The knowledgeable government, A, looking out for all of its consumers, notices the divergence between price and marginal cost. Given prohibitions on tariffs or price controls, it may try to remedy the situation by shifting out the demand curve. If the government adds some demand at relatively low prices, shifting the demand curve to DD', the marginal revenue curve shifts to MR' once the new portion of the demand curve becomes relevant. Now marginal revenue and marginal cost are equated in two places. To choose between them, B will see which offers higher profits. In figure 7.2, B selects the lower-priced intersection and sets price at p^{**}, reaping the rectangle $FGCp^{**}$ as profit—an amount slightly greater than $ABCp^*$. Consumer surplus increases by the trapezoid under the original demand curve, bounded on top by p^* and on bottom by p^{**}.

Figure 7.2 Adding Demand to Lower the Price

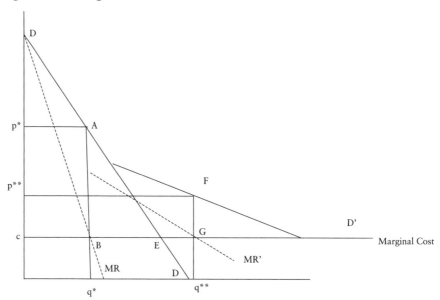

The scheme just outlined has one major disadvantage: the government ends up purchasing a considerable amount of the good. Presumably it can be resold, perhaps overseas, but not without financial loss and transactions costs. This problem can be avoided if A instead chooses to subsidize its own consumers as a mechanism for lowering price—it is their welfare, after all, that is to be maximized.

A straightforward, per-unit subsidy is likely to be most unattractive; it is both expensive and gives most of the subsidy to the producer. In figure 7.2, for example, the subsidy would have to raise the demand curve sufficiently to have the MR curve cut the cost curve at E. For this, a per-unit subsidy significantly greater than p^* would be required. Not only would this require a substantial government outlay, but the producer would capture the vast preponderance of the benefits.

To resculpt the firm's marginal revenue curve, shifting it out at low prices—but not at high prices—is a much more attractive option. Indeed, outward shifts at high prices are counterproductive. The simple way to accomplish the appropriate reshaping is to make the subsidy contingent on price, as is shown in figure 7.3.

Figure 7.3 The Subsidy that Maximizes Consumer Surplus

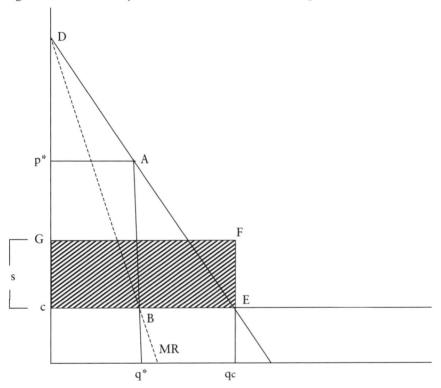

The government tells the manufacturer: "charge consumers marginal cost, and I shall pay you a per-unit subsidy equal to s." The diagram is drawn so that the subsidy offers just a smidgen more profit, the cross-hatched area, than B would reap by charging the original monopoly price. The net gain to the citizens equals the increase in consumer surplus ($AECp^*$), less the cost of the subsidy ($FECG$). Given that the subsidy offered to the producer is just a little more than the profit it could earn outside the subsidy scheme, the increase in citizens' surplus (the net gain in consumer surplus after paying the subsidy) will almost equal the original deadweight loss triangle. Deadweight loss has been transmuted to consumer surplus.[9]

If the government seeks to maximize citizens' surplus, the optimal price to charge consumers is the marginal cost of the good, whether marginal cost is constant or increasing. (In effect, the government is paying a lump-sum amount and then purchasing at marginal cost.) This assumes that no deadweight loss is associated with raising the funds to pay the subsidy. If there is such loss, the optimal price to consumers will be somewhat above the marginal cost (see Johnston and Zeckhauser 1991:9–11).

Transmuting Oligopoly Rents

Frequent rents are earned not by a monopolist but by an oligopoly that is able to exercise some market power. Under oligopolies, subsidy schemes cannot merely transmute the deadweight loss into consumer surplus but can also extract some of the rents, which can then be turned over to consumers. We consider a two-player oligopoly selling two differentiated products: each firm enjoys some degree of market power but each one finds demand influenced by the other firm's price as well as its own. For the sake of simplicity, we deal with two firms. They are engaged in Bertrand (price) competition, which captures our real-world situation much better than Cournot (quantity) competition. We shall assume Nash-equilibrium behavior, in which each player takes the other's behavior as fixed, rather than more collusive but more speculative equilibrium concepts.

The Duopolist's Decision

If we assume linear demand functions, the demand for firm i can be expressed:

$$q_i = a - bp_i + dp_j \quad (1)$$

where $0<b<d$ and p_j is the price charged by the other firm. Assume the firms have the same costs (a constant marginal cost of c) and demand. In the absence of collusion and with neither product subsidized, the firms could be expected to charge a price somewhere between the monopoly price and the competitive price— namely, the marginal cost. Though they compete, they have differentiated products. It is straightforward to derive the reaction function for each firm, assuming that it takes the other firm's price as given. The resulting Nash-equilibrium price for both firms:

$$p_e = p_i = p_j = [a + bc]/[2b - d] \quad (2)$$

To illustrate, set $a_1 = a_2 = 10$ million, $b_1 = b_2 = 1$ million, and $d_1 = d_2 = 0.25$ million, with marginal cost assumed to be 2. The unsubsidized equilibrium p_1, p_2 pair has both prices set at \$6.86 (currency throughout is in Australian dollars). The optimization process for either firm, with its fellow duopolist's price at \$6.86, is shown in figure 7.4. Profits are equivalent to the shaded area in figure 7.4.

Subsidizing One Firm

Now let the government subsidize one of the firms, say Firm 1. Assume that the other firm does not react and that the price paid by consumers is set at the marginal cost of 2. To ensure that Firm 1's profit just exceeds its initial level would require a subsidy of a little over $2.43 per unit. If Firm 1 were subsidized, of course, the other firm would lower its price in response, which in turn would reduce the profits of the subsidized firm.

Figure 7.4 A Duopolist's Outcome, Absent Subsidy

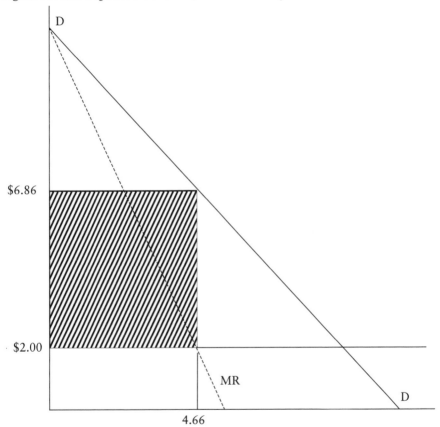

If the government decided in advance (and was committed) to subsidizing Firm 1 but not Firm 2, presumably the potentially subsidized firm would notice this chain of events looming and would demand a larger initial subsidy as a condition to participate in the scheme. The government must therefore offer Firm 1 a subsidy that is sufficient to offer profits at the new Nash equilibrium that just exceeds its Nash-equilibrium profits in the previously unsubsidized scheme.

151

We know the subsidized firm will be charging customers $2 for its product. The other firm, optimizing against this price of $2, will reduce its price by 61 cents to $6.25. If the first firm is to regain its presubsidy profits, it must be given a slightly larger subsidy of $2.47 for each of the units it sells.

Note that Firm 1 receives roughly the same profits as it did without the subsidy scheme. Firm 2, however, is now competing with a lower-priced firm and will sell less at any price; hence, Firm 2's profits will fall. Except in pathological cases, we would expect its optimal price to be somewhat lower than it was initially. In the example here, Nash-equilibrium profits for Firm 2 fall by 23 percent to $18.1 million.

Consumers gain in two ways. First, the reduction in the consumer price of the subsidized drug directly increases consumer surplus (in our example producing a net gain of $35.4 million). Second, the consequent reduction in demand for the second unsubsidized drug induces a voluntary price reduction (from $6.86 to $6.25 in our example). The resulting increase in consumers' surplus comes to $2.4 million in our example. The cost of the subsidy is $23.6 million, the old initial profits. The net result (after taking account of the direct cost of the subsidy) is therefore an increase in citizens' surplus of $14.2 million.[10]

The Subsidy Game

Selecting one firm to subsidize may not be optimal from the standpoint of the government or its citizens. Instead, the government can place the firms in a competitive situation, where each has the temptation to bolt the no-subsidy arrangement, though their joint profits will fall as soon as either bolts.

The interesting question then is what the first firm must be offered to participate, given the possibility that the government will entice Firm 2 into the subsidy scheme. In fact, as long as the firms are unable to collude, the government does not have to guarantee Firm 1 the full amount that it could earn were the scheme not implemented, because there is the risk that Firm 2 will participate and leave Firm 1 out in the cold.

Various structures might be considered for the subsidy offer. Consider five options:

(1) Subsidize only one firm to slightly increase its profit relative to the Nash-equilibrium profit when neither firm is subsidized.

(2) Offer to slightly increase the profit of any firm that bolts and takes the subsidy (again relative to the Nash-equilibrium profit).

(3) Subsidize, at the Nash-equilibrium level, any firm that bolts in the first round. Then subsidize the follower at a lower level that just exceeds the profits it could earn without a subsidy.

(4) Offer to subsidize either firm at the Nash-equilibrium level if it is the first to bolt, with the follower subsidized at a lower level just sufficient to induce it to opt in. If both bolt in the first round, subsidize only

slightly above the level of profits each could earn without a subsidy, assuming the other were subsidized.

(5) Proceed as with 4, but offer the first bolter more than it would receive in the initial Nash equilibrium as a form of temptation.

Clearly, Option 1 would never be optimal for the government, given that citizens' surplus can always be increased by subsidizing the second product once the first is in the scheme.

Option 2 maximizes the sum of citizens' and producers' surpluses (given our initial assumption that direct price controls are not feasible). It does not reduce producers' profits and thus represents a Pareto improvement on the no-scheme situation. Such a scheme could be implemented with the full consent of the industry participants.

If the government wants only to maximize citizens' welfare or places greater weight on citizens than producers, it is better to drive a harder bargain with producers and pay a lower subsidy to a firm that does not participate immediately, giving it an incentive to join later. option 3 is designed on this basis.

Option 4 creates a "prisoner's dilemma" by offering the first bolter a tiny amount (ε) more than it would receive without the scheme. If both firms bolt simultaneously, each receives ε more than it would by not participating in the scheme, assuming the other *does* participate. Both firms have a dominant strategy to bolt at the outset.

It is by no means certain that option 4 will succeed in enticing the firms to bolt, especially if the game is expected to go on for some time. The firms may build up a trust relationship that enables them to resist the small, government-offered ε temptation to defect from the nonsubsidized equilibrium. But the government could inhibit the development of trust by how it structures the subsidy scheme, in particular negotiations with manufacturers.

Alternatively, the government might consider Option 5, which raises the payoff to the first bolter, which would then earn considerably more than it does at the initial equilibrium. When the reward for joining up first is large enough, the temptation to bolt or the fear that the other firm will is likely to lead both firms to bolt at the outset.

We have argued that a government seeking to maximize its citizens' surplus should capitalize on the subsidy game. Because each firm fears that the other might jump to embrace the scheme, both jump and each receives less than it did at the outset. Once one firm joins the scheme, the other will be given a small incentive to do so, though receiving slightly more than it would outside the scheme. All deadweight loss is eliminated. Equally important to a government that does not value firm welfare over citizen well-being, oligopoly profits are transmuted into consumer surplus.

The Scheme in Practice: Australian Pharmaceuticals

Our analysis has been concerned with a hypothetical market, hypothetical competitors, demand curves, and so on. We have shown how subsidies might be used to transmute deadweight loss and oligopoly profits to citizens' surplus. But economics is replete with optimal tax and subsidy schemes that will probably never be employed. Our interest in this scheme relates to its potential application in the real world in contexts where goods are priced considerably above the marginal production cost. We are encouraged by Australia's use of a fundamentally similar arrangement in an important policy context.

The extent to which a price-contingent subsidy can increase net consumer surplus depends on own- and cross-price elasticities of demand in a slightly complex fashion. Low own-elasticities imply that profits are high but deadweight loss is low. High cross-price elasticities boost the potential for playing firms against one another.

Historically, Australia chose an indirect approach to pharmaceutical price controls because its federal government was barred from direct price regulation. But its experience highlights some strong reasons for using a price-contingent subsidy even if direct price control is an option.

One consideration is the credibility of the government's threat not to subsidize a drug if the firm does not agree to the offered price. In general, the effectiveness of a threat depends not only on the penalty, but also on the probability that the threat will be carried out (Schelling 1960). The Australian government can afford to take a tougher stance in price negotiations because the manufacturer knows that even if it does not accept the government's price, the drug will still be marketed in the country through the private (unsubsidized) market and through state hospitals (where pensioners and low-income individuals, who might not be able to afford to purchase in the private market, have limited access). This possibility reduces both the manufacturer's and the government's losses if agreement is not reached. It also improves the government's bargaining position. For example, supplying only 10 percent of the potential market provides the firm with less than 10 percent of its potential profits (given start-up costs within Australia), but because the demand curve is falling, patients obtain substantially more than 10 percent of the potential consumer surplus.[11]

By contrast, in most other developed countries, drug prices are directly regulated and marketing approval is conditional upon agreement on price. The officials of such governments are in a much weaker position when negotiating the prices of new breakthrough drugs—a major concern for any policymaker. Officials must agree to the price before the drug can be made available to anyone in the country, and the manufacturers know this.

The effectiveness of Australia's indirect approach to regulating prices, in which marketing is not dependent on pricing agreement, hinges on:

- *The heterogeneity of patients.* The benefits of new drugs vary considerably across patients, with a relatively small proportion benefiting much more than the others (in economic terms, a steep demand curve).
- *The fixed costs that manufacturers face in marketing a new drug.* These include the costs imposed by national regulatory requirements and the higher costs associated with small production runs. The firms earn little, if any, profit if a new drug attracts only a small proportion of its potential market (in economic terms, a falling marginal cost curve—even for small quantities).
- *Limitations on the supply of unsubsidized drugs.* Typically only those who most need a drug will obtain it through state hospitals or the private prescription market. Inhibiting factors include the inconvenience and other indirect costs of obtaining the drug through a hospital, explicit rationing by the hospital, and the high price demanded for private prescriptions (including a higher retail markup).
- *An environment that discourages collusion.* Along with antitrust laws and the structure of the pharmaceutical industry, specific features of the subsidy arrangements make it unlikely that pharmaceutical manufacturers would collude to avoid a "prisoner's dilemma." (There is no evidence they have colluded in Australia.) The detailed procedures for approving new drugs for subsidy, including the discrete timing of approvals and confidentiality of applications, would undermine any cartel. A firm that chooses to renege on the agreement could easily get a big jump on a competitor. Most manufacturers have just one or a few big sellers, making the situation more like a one-play game. Promises of future reciprocity are unlikely to bind good behavior.

Because citizens with particularly pressing medical needs can obtain a drug even if its manufacturer refuses to reduce its price, the government is better able to weather any political storm that develops if a drug remains unsubsidized.[12] Otherwise, negotiators who refuse to subsidize a drug would risk very concentrated criticism and lobbying. As Olson (1968) points out, such concentrated interests often prevail over the diffuse interests of smaller players even though the latter's total stakes may be greater. Sales outside the subsidy arrangement thus serve as a safety valve.

A second advantage of the subsidy approach is reducing the adverse impact that price constraints might have on other sectors of the economy. Because Australia has always depended heavily on trade with the rest of the world, on foreign investment, and on technology imports, its government has been keen to maintain a reputation for stability and for respect of property rights. Australia is not a country where an investor's property is likely to be appropriated through nationalization or, more indirectly, through such policy measures as price controls. The government is also eager to maintain its reputation with domestic investors, consumers, and voters.

By working through a subsidy program that is not billed as a price-control mechanism and by focusing on other program objectives—especially pensioner and low-income family access to needed medication—successive Australian governments have achieved powerful price leverage in the pharmaceutical market without causing unwarranted fear in other markets.

Conclusion

Like alchemy, the use of subsidies to increase economic efficiency is out of fashion. But we have demonstrated here how a price-contingent subsidy can be used to transmute deadweight loss (due to pricing above marginal cost) into consumer surplus. When more than one firm possesses market power, the subsidy can be used not only to boost efficiency but also to generate involuntary transfers. Oligopoly profits are turned into net consumer surplus. This transmutation is particularly beneficial if the subsidizer's only concern with producer profits is strategic. We believe that the subsidy arrangements discussed are worthwhile. And they may help to break down the solidarity of cartels.

In the 1970s and 1980s, Australia used a variant of this alchemy scheme to reap benefits equal to about 15 percent of its drug expenditures.[13] Though additional elements have been introduced, the central elements of that mechanism remain in use today. Australia (1) offers subsidies to provide firms with greater sales in exchange for lower prices and (2) allows sales of drugs outside the subsidized scheme as a "safety valve."[14]

In part, Australia's success may be due to the small size of its market and its geographical distance from most developed countries. Its transmutation of pharmaceutical profits to consumer surplus has had a negligible effect on global drug development, allowing Australia to meet the needs of its citizens with relatively little criticism.

Notes

[1] This research was supported in part by the Decision, Risk, and Management Science Division of the National Science Foundation and the Australian Public Service Board. Karen Eggleston, Dani Rodrik, Barry Nalebuff, and participants in seminars at Harvard, Duke, and Yale universities made helpful comments.

[2] The figure is based on data in Ralph et al. (1979), using prices of twenty-five branded products and sales weights in each country. The comparisons in the figure are consistent with figures published by the Australian Pharmaceutical Manufacturers Association (1978), which also showed prices in Belgium and Sweden to be 92 percent and 64 percent higher, respectively, than in Australia.

[3] From Parry and Thwaites (1988). The world average was based on developed countries for which data were readily available: Austria, Belgium, Canada, Finland, France, Italy, Japan, New Zealand, Spain, the United Kingdom, the United States, and West Germany. Although the eighty drugs were selected on the basis of Australian sales, the averages were calculated using local weights so that the world average reflects the relative use of those drugs overseas and the relative size of each national market. Prices are those paid to manufacturers. In these calculations, and throughout this chapter, the term *drug* refers to a specific chemical compound that may be marketed under more than one brand name.

[4] See Healy, Sharman, and Lokuge (2006), who draw on the Productivity Commission (2001) report. This is particularly true for "me-too" pharmaceuticals and generics, for which Australian prices are substantially below those of the United States, Canada, United Kingdom, and France—albeit similar to those of Spain and New Zealand (Duckett 2004, figure 7.2, p. 61, based on Productivity Commission 2001). We thank Karen Eggleston for guiding us to information on recent developments.

[5] Safety and efficacy standards are administered by a government agency that is quite distinct from the pricing agency (see chapter 6, Löfgren, in this volume). Perhaps more important, when decisions are based on marketing approval, the safety regulators are usually unaware of the prices that the manufacturers will seek.

[6] This is based on Johnston and Zeckhauser (1991) and data has not been updated. See that paper for further details of the economic theory underlying this presentation and for significant elaboration of its game-theory presentation.

[7] See chapter 6, Löfgren, in this volume.

[8] See Putnam (1988) for a discussion of how domestic politics influence international negotiations.

[9] In the pure monopoly case, B might hold out for a greater subsidy, especially if A did not have full information about B's costs and the demand curve. In other words, B might demand a share of the gain in the consumer surplus. In the more realistic case of the oligopoly, however, the firm will be fearful of its competitors being subsidized and hence less likely to quibble.

[10] That is $14.2 = 35.4 + 2.4 - 23.6$—an uncompensated increase. Since prices are lower in the subsidized world, the value of the dollar is higher, which implies that the consumer surplus gains have been underestimated. On the other hand, no allowance has been made for the excess burden of taxation to be paid for the subsidy.

[11] Of course, if these sources comprised a major share of the market, the whole price-restraint mechanism would be undermined since manufacturers would have little incentive to participate in the scheme. But in fact, hospital and private market sales of unlisted drugs are only a small proportion of the market that can be achieved through the subsidy scheme.

[12] That the government's negotiators hold out and gamble on lower prices—offering the additional benefit of setting an example for other manufacturers—might be in the interest of other patients, but these benefits are diffused among many people, each of whom has little incentive to push the issue politically.

[13] See Johnston (1990).

[14] A major new element since the early 1990s is the use of cost-effectiveness in the pricing process. High prices are paid for innovative products, relatively low prices for less innovative products. A recent study by Roughead, Lopert, and Sansom (2007) finds that "Australian prices for medicines representing significant advances in therapy are similar to those paid under key U.S. programs" (p. 514).

References

APMA. *See* Australian Pharmaceutical Manufacturers Association.

Arrow, Kenneth. 1962. Economic welfare and the allocation of resources to invention. In *The rate and direction of inventive activity*, ed. R. Nelson. Princeton: Princeton Univ. Press.

Australian Pharmaceutical Manufacturers Association. November 1978. *Submission to the pharmaceutical manufacturing industry inquiry.* Sydney: APMA.

Duckett, S. J. 2004. Drug policy down under: Australia's pharmaceutical benefits scheme. *Health Care Financing Review* 25 (3): 55–67.

Healy, J., E. Sharman, and B. Lokuge. 2006. Australia: Health system review. *Health Systems in Transition* 8 (5): 1–158. http://www.euro.who.int/Document/E89731.pdf.

Hirshleifer, J. 1971. The private and social value of information and the reward to inventive activity. *American Economic Review* 61 (September): 561–74.

Johnston, Mark A. 1990. Australia's pharmaceutical pricing strategy. Doctoral dissertation, Harvard Univ.

Johnston, Mark A., and R. Zeckhauser. 1991. The Australian pharmaceutical subsidy gambit: Transmuting deadweight loss and oligopoly rents to consumer surplus. National Bureau of Economic Research (NBER) working paper 3783, Cambridge, MA.

Loury, Glenn C. 1979. Market structure and innovation. *Quarterly Journal of Economics* 93 (August): 395–410.

Mansfield, Edwin, J. Rapoport, A. Romeo, S. Wagner, and G. Beardsley. 1977. Social and private rates of return from industrial innovation. *Quarterly Journal of Economics* 91 (May): 221–40.

Mortensen, Dale. 1982. Property rights and efficiency in mating, racing and related games. *American Economic Review* 72: 968–79.

Olson, Mancur Jr. 1968. *The logic of collective action: Public goods and theory of groups.* Cambridge, MA: Harvard Univ. Press.

Parry, Thomas G., and Robert M. A. Thwaites. 1988. *The pharmaceutical industry in Australia: A benchmark study.* North Sydney: APMA.

Productivity Commission. 2001. *International pharmaceutical price differences: Research report.* Canberra: Ausinfo. http://129.3.20.41/eps/othr/papers/0107/0107004.pdf.

Putnam, Robert D. 1988. Diplomacy and domestic politics: The logic of two-level games. *International Organization* 42: 427–60.

Ralph, J. T., C. W. Conron, and A. H. Luchin. 1979. *Pharmaceutical manufacturing industry inquiry report.* Canberra: Australian Government Publishing Service.

Roughead, Elizabeth E., Ruth Lopert, and Lloyd Sansom. 2007. Prices for innovative pharmaceutical products that provide health gain: A comparison between Australia and the United States. *Value in Health* 10 (6): 514–20.

Schelling, Thomas C. 1960. *The strategy of conflict.* Cambridge, MA: Harvard Univ. Press.

Schumpeter, Joseph A. 1975. *Capitalism, socialism, and democracy.* New York: Harper.

Pharmaceutical Policy in Seven Asia-Pacific Health-care Systems

India

THE EVOLUTION OF MODERN INDIAN PHARMACEUTICALS

Chirantan Chatterjee[1]

A ntiretroviral therapy is a relatively new treatment intended to slow the growth of the human immunodeficiency virus (HIV). In 2000–2001 the Acceleration Access Initiative was started in response to Africa's acquired immune deficiency syndrome (AIDS) epidemic. The United Nations (UN) and the World Health Organization (WHO) came together with global pharmaceutical firms such as Abbott Laboratories, Boehringer Ingelheim, Bristol-Myers Squibb, GlaxoSmithKline, F. Hoffman–La Roche Ltd., and Merck to bring to the global market the world's most common combination of antiretroviral drugs: stavudine, lamivudine, and nevirapine. In late 2000 the combination package for all three drugs was exorbitantly priced at $10,439 and the market for this combination had one monopoly producer, F. Hoffman–La Roche. Doctors and policy experts dealing with Africa's AIDS epidemic were not satisfied with this price, given poverty levels on the continent. A few firms from India took up the challenge of reducing prices. In 2002 the Indian pharmaceutical firm Cipla Ltd. entered the antiretroviral market with a generic version of the F. Hoffman–La Roche combination, priced at $350. Two other pharmaceutical firms from India, Hetero Drugs Ltd. and Aurobindo Pharma, followed suit and the price of generic antiretroviral drugs was reduced to $152. This represented a 98.5 percent reduction in price over a span of only five years. By 2004 F. Hoffman–La Roche had also reduced its price by about 95 percent, possibly because it had no alternative (see figure 8.1). This story illustrates the potential impact of the Indian pharmaceutical industry on global drug markets.

But this influence was not quickly achieved. From 1972 Indian firms worked to develop process engineering capabilities. Then, in 1995, India signed a World Trade Organization (WTO) treaty on trade-related aspects of intellectual property rights (TRIPS). When India implemented product patents conforming to the treaty in 2005, it had long been preparing for the transition.

Scholars debate the consumer benefits of strong patents, whether for global or domestic markets. In a recent paper, Chaudhuri, Goldberg, and Jia (2007) argue that the change in the Indian patent regime is likely to have adverse welfare effects for consumers as well as for the industry. For example, they argue that withdrawing the systemic antibacterial medication fluoroquinolones from domestic markets, due to stronger patents, would cause a total annual welfare loss of $305 million. About 80 percent of this would be due to a loss of consumer surplus, with domestic producers losing some $50 million and

163

foreign producers gaining $20 million in profits. The other side of the argument is represented by Arora, Branstetter, and Chatterjee (2007), who acknowledge the adverse welfare effects of stronger patents but argue that benefits will flow from increasing incentives for research and development (R&D), especially among technologically progressive Indian drug firms.

The differing viewpoints on the value of stronger patents to the post-TRIPS Indian pharmaceutical industry will take some time to be reconciled (Lanjouw 2006; Dutta 2006; Sakakibara and Branstetter 2001). Yet one cannot ignore the effects of the period 1972–2005, when a process-leaning patent regime gave Indian pharmaceutical firms incentive to build complementary assets and process capabilities that led them to develop antiretroviral variants at low prices. The industrial history of Indian pharmaceuticals is thus critical to understanding the welfare implications of cheaper drugs, on the one hand, and rising drug prices (due to stronger patents), on the other.

In this chapter, I attempt to summarize this history. First, I look at the evolution of the industry through each of four important periods. I then examine innovation and trends in R&D in post-TRIPS Indian pharmaceuticals. I also outline policies other than those governing intellectual property rights (IPRs), namely foreign firm ownership rules and drug price controls, and their impact on India's industry. I then discuss the meaning of stronger IPRs for Indian pharmaceuticals in the context of recent industry dynamics. I conclude with a forward-looking view and compare India's adaptation to stronger patents with that of other economies.

Historical Development

Indian Pharmaceuticals before 1947

The history of modern Indian pharmaceuticals dates back to the early twentieth century, when increased Indian nationalism gave rise to greater interest in science, including pharmaceuticals. India has a rich history of traditional Hindu medicine. British, Dutch, French, and Portuguese scientists and pharmacists brought modern biomedicine to India. The creation of two firms, which are still in existence today, marks the start of the modern pharmaceutical industry. One is Bengal Chemical and Pharmaceutical Works (BCPW) Ltd., set up in Kolkata (formerly Calcutta), in eastern India, by nationalist scientist Acharya P. C. Ray. The other is Alembic Chemical Works Co. Ltd., in the modern-day city of Vadodara, in the western state of Gujarat. Both companies began an important shift from traditional methods to a more scientific approach to the discovery, development, and manufacture of pharmaceuticals. This period, 1904–1907, also saw the establishment of four research institutes—the Haffkine Institute in Mumbai (Bombay), Central Research Institute in Kasauli, Kings Institute in Chennai (Madras), and Pasteur Institute in Coonoor—for work on sera and vaccines. Meanwhile, the modern pharmaceutical industries of other countries was moving toward establishing more formal laboratories for isolating new

Figure 8.1 A Short History of Antiretroviral Drug Prices

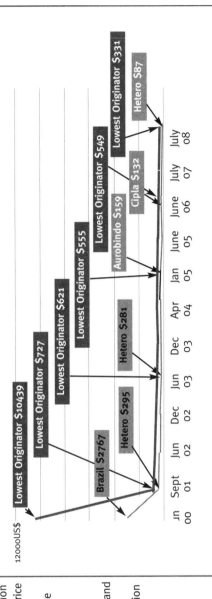

Graph 1: Competition as a catalyst for price reductions.
The fall in the price of first-line combination of stavudine (d4T), lamivudine (3TC), and nevirapine (NVP), since the first edition of Untangling the Web of Price Reductions.

12000US$

Lowest Originator $10439

Lowest Originator $727

Lowest Originator $621

Lowest Originator $555

Lowest Originator $549

Lowest Originator $331

Hetero $87

Cipla $132

Aurobindo $159

Hetero $281

Hetero $295

Brazil $2767

Hetero $87

Jn 00 Sept 01 Jun 02 Dec 02 Jun 03 Dec 03 Apr 04 Jan 05 June 05 June 06 July 07 July 08

Source: Courtesy Médecins sans Frontières, 2008.

chemicals and studying their biological effects. Chemical firms in Western Europe and the United States led this effort. At that early stage of pharmaceutical development, Indian pharmaceutical firms still relied heavily on Western firms for their intermediate requirements, and traditional remedies were prevalent among the larger populace.

Indian Pharmaceuticals from 1947 to 1970

Indian independence marked the beginning of a new era for Indian pharmaceuticals. India had adopted the British Patents and Design Act of 1911, which granted product patents for a period of fourteen years. A provision of the act allowed a product or each process in drug manufacturing to be patented. This regime inhibited the growth of the domestic pharmaceutical industry. Global pharmaceutical firms set themselves up in the Indian domestic market with preestablished global patents on drugs and manufacturing processes (Chaudhuri 2005a). In addition, drug prices were high in India, and most consumers were forced to rely on traditional medicine.

India's war with China in 1964 changed the situation. The war led the government of India to consider policy interventions in the domestic pharmaceutical industry. The urgent need to reduce the price of antibiotics and vaccines manufactured locally resulted in the Drug Price Display Order, which was enacted under the Defence of India Act. Following the war, the desire to keep prices at 1963 levels persuaded the Indian government to take a keen interest in pharmaceutical policymaking. Many policy changes were introduced from the mid-1960s through the early 1970s.

The 1970s and pre-TRIPS Indian Pharmaceuticals

One of the key policy changes was the implementation of the Indian Patents Act (1970) in 1972. Through this legislation, the government abolished the product patent regime inherited in the form of the British Patents Act of 1911. The Patent Act of 1972 ensured that a firm could now patent only a single method or process for any particular drug. The patent life was reduced to either five years from the date of sealing or seven years from the date of filing complete specifications, whichever was shorter. The act was restrictive in other ways as well (Fink 2000).

Thereafter, the Indian pharmaceutical industry focused on so-called reverse engineering. Essentially, this means that firms' competencies in imitative research, development, and manufacturing enabled them to manufacture knockoff drugs from molecules patented by global firms. Indian variants of key drug products were introduced within a few years of their global discovery and launch. Between 1970 (the act actually passed in 1972) and 2005, India became a hotbed of firms that, like Cipla Ltd., focused their capabilities on developing cheap processes for globally patented drugs. They used Indian patent law to their advantage to compete against global pharmaceutical companies in domestic markets and in global markets that were unregulated or had weak patent laws.

Changes in U.S. drug markets also had an effect on Indian markets. By the middle of the century, U.S. policymakers realized the importance of ensuring the safety and efficacy of generic drugs. In 1962 the National Research Council (NRC) of the National Academy of Sciences (NAS) formed the Drug Efficacy Study Implementation (DESI) program to review more than 3,000 generic drugs. This program and the Drug Price Competition and Patent Restoration Act of 1984 ultimately allowed manufacturers of generic drugs to file for approval to manufacture products ruled effective by the program—without the need to conduct biological studies. This opened the floodgates for generic competition in the pharmaceutical industry. Since 1984 the generic industry in the United States has grown to more than $16 billion in annual sales. By 2004 generic pharmaceuticals accounted for more than 53 percent of all U.S. prescriptions.[2]

The growth of the market for generic pharmaceuticals in the United States provided an opportunity for Indian manufacturers of generic drugs. "It helped that the Indian pharmaceutical industry had built its generic capabilities by then and could be the first mover in the U.S. market," noted D. G. Shah, secretary general of the Indian Pharmaceutical Alliance.[3] Between 1980 and 2001, exports of Indian pharmaceuticals increased from $96 million to $1.9 billion (Chaudhuri 2005a). Indian firms took little time to introduce cheaper, generic versions of globally introduced drugs. Global approval of Indian drug manufacturing standards grew. In 1999, 193 manufacturing plants in India complied with U.S. Food and Drug Administration (U.S. FDA) regulations. These plants represented 41 percent of all complying plants in Japan, Taiwan, Korea, and India. In 2006 the U.S. FDA contemplated establishing an office in New Delhi. All these developments also meant that, by 2004, Indian firms enjoyed a 77 percent share in the domestic market compared to the 23 percent share of global drug firms. The situation had been completely reversed from the early 1970s, when global drug firms had enjoyed close to 80 percent market share.

After 1995: Post-TRIPS Indian Pharmaceuticals

Indian pharmaceutical manufacturing underwent a period of transitional development from 1970 until the early 1990s. Meanwhile, Western countries were increasingly keen to reverse India's patent regime, even as Indian negotiators voiced concerns about the welfare effects of the higher domestic drug prices caused by stronger patents. But India eventually acquiesced to pressure from the developed world; by signing the WTO-TRIPS agreement in late 1994, India made a commitment to implement a globally consistent product patent regime by 2000. Changes to India's laws included a twenty-year patent term. Because of concerns and debates within the country, an extension of the 2000 deadline was granted, and eventually India implemented the new law, effective January 1, 2005.

The 2005 Patent Act was framed to maintain the competitiveness of Indian firms in the global generic pharmaceutical industry while ensuring consistency with the requirements of TRIPS. Provisions, such as not providing for patent-term restoration, were included to ensure Indian product patents would be likely to expire a few years before their counterparts in the global generics markets—allowing Indian firms to more quickly exploit expired patents.

The post-TRIPS period has seen considerable debate over where India's pharmaceutical industry is heading under the new patent system. A recent article in an Indian newspaper[4] reports that for cancer drugs alone, there were 413 product patent applications at the Indian Patent Office, 350 of them filed by multinational drug firms. There is a possibility that by invoking Section 3(d) and the "incremental innovation" criterion of the 2005 Patent Act, Indian patent courts could reject quite a few of these multinational drug patents.[5] The transition to the new system could thus lead to a patent war (which may have already begun), with multinational drug firms being granted product patents domestically and domestic firms managing to get staying orders that allow them to continue marketing their competitors' products.

Trends in Innovation, 1995 to 2005

The magnitude of the effect of stronger patent laws on India's pharmaceutical innovation remains unclear. Foreseeing the advent of product patents in India, the industry has increased investment in R&D. A few large firms have already made important deals related to R&D. Arora, Branstetter, and Chatterjee (2007) document these trends and also emphasizes the incentives to increase R&D activities. They report that in 1990, expenditures on R&D were negligible. By 2005 such expenditures had increased to some 8 percent of the value of sales. While this is still low by global standards, the R&D efforts of a few Indian firms are very advanced. Arora, Branstetter, and Chatterjee (2007) also note the increase in patents and other regulatory filings made by Indian pharmaceutical companies. In 2007 a total of 63 U.S. patents, 689 Indian patents, and 72 Abbreviated New Drug Applications (from the U.S. FDA) were approved for Indian pharmaceutical firms; a much greater number of patent applications were filed. While these numbers are still not comparable to the number of patents applications filed by large Western firms such as Merck or Pfizer, the authors also report a rising return on R&D, which could encourage an increase in pharmaceutical firms, patent applications, and expenditure on R&D in this sector.

Arora, Branstetter, and Chatterjee (2007) evaluate the return on pharmaceutical R&D expenditure by measuring the market value of the R&D stock of pharmaceutical firms engaged in R&D. The authors follow a framework pioneered by Griliches (1981) in the United States, in which the market value of a firm's assets is measured as a function of its tangible and intangible assets. In

Table 8.1 Intellectual Property Right (IPR) Laws and Indian Pharmaceuticals

Year	IPR events in India	Implications
Pre-1972 and post-1972	British Patents and Design Act, 1911; Patents Act 1970	• Pre-1972: A product and process patent regime; life of drug patents 14 years; firms can patent all processes for drug manufacturing. • Post-1972: Product patent regime abolished; patent only a method or a process; life reduced to 5–7 years; only one method or process patentable per drug.
1994–1995	Signing of the WTO TRIPS treaty by India following the 1986–1994 Uruguay round of negotiations	• December 31, 1994: The Patents (Amendment) Ordinance allows filing and handling of product patent applications for pharmaceutical and agricultural chemical products, as well as the granting of exclusive marketing rights on those products. The ordinance becomes effective on January 1, 1995. • The Patents Amendment Bill 1995 is introduced.
1996–1999	Transition period	• Indian Patent office keeps receiving product patent applications. • Meanwhile, disputes with the U.S. and EU at WTO over violation of product patents. • WTO asks government of India to complete institutional reform on new IPR laws by April 1999.
2000–2001	India signs and ratifies Paris convention and Patent Cooperation Treaty (PCT)	• WTO reviews the TRIPS terms and grants an extension to India beyond 2000, setting January 1, 2005, as the new deadline to implement product patents.
December 2004–January 1, 2005	Amendments to Patents Act before deadline January 1, 2005, as set by WTO	• Product patent regime in place. From January 1, 2005, a firm can file for and be granted a product patent within India.

Source: Author analysis, industry reports, and Chaudhuri 2005b.

this case, the value of the stock of R&D in pharmaceutical firms is the intangible asset, whereas Tobin's Q (Tobin 1969) gives a measure of the market value of the firms. The authors conducted an econometric analysis of a panel of 320 Indian pharmaceutical firms during the period 1990 to 2005. The dependent variable was Tobin's Q for firm i at time t. The independent variable was the value of the stock of R&D of firm i at time t, expressed as a proportion of the total assets of the firm. The ordinary least squares (OLS) regression coefficients were estimated after controlling for unobserved heterogeneity, the effect of year, and the effect of firm size. The results gave a sense of how returns on R&D expenditure changed during the period. From the pre-TRIPS period, 1990–1994, to the period 2000–2005, returns on R&D expenditure increased. The increase was greatest among technologically progressive firms. Interestingly, for nonprogressive firms, the returns on R&D expenditures declined during the same period. Many of these firms went out of business or were acquired by more progressive firms.

Figure 8.2 Rising Innovative Output in Indian Pharmaceutical Firms

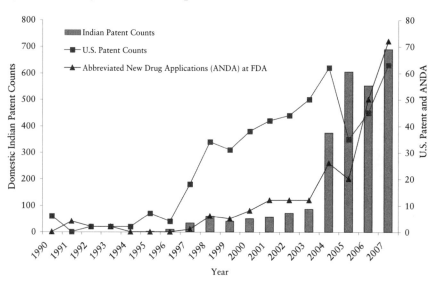

The study of Arora, Branstetter, and Chatterjee (2007) has several important implications. First, returns on R&D expenditure increased in India during the same period that more restrictive patent laws were enacted. This conclusion contradicts previous evidence on local industry responses to stronger patents as seen in other economies. Second, the study raises an important question regarding the magnitude of the effects of restrictive patent laws in the context of an emerging economy. Last, the study notes that the increase in returns on

R&D expenditure, at least among elite pharmaceutical firms, suggests that the Indian pharmaceutical industry has reached a high degree of sophistication and therefore requires more careful study in order to understand the dynamics of how firms are evolving, upgrading their capabilities, and fitting into the global pharmaceutical value chain.

Beyond IPRs in Indian Pharmaceuticals

Beyond IPR laws, India's pharmaceutical policy environment is affected by several other factors. Regulations related to foreign ownership of firms and drug price controls have played key roles in the evolution of the industry. The Foreign Exchange Regulation Act of 1973 (FERA 1973) was one of the key policies that came into effect along with the new patent regime in the early 1970s. FERA 1973 aimed to regulate foreign capital in India. Section 29 of FERA distinguished FERA companies (those with foreign equity of more than 40 percent) from others. FERA companies were required to request permission to operate in India. Additionally, a 74 percent limit was placed on foreign equity in all companies.

At around the same time, the government announced the New Drug Policy of 1978 (NDP 1978) based on the recommendations of the Committee on Drugs and Pharmaceutical Industries. NDP 1978 was critical of the activities of multinational companies (MNCs) in domestic markets and attempted to strengthen the domestic economy by strictly limiting MNC actions. The drug policy of NDP 1986 made licensing requirements for foreign firms more restrictive. Taken together, NDP 1978, NDP 1986, and FERA 1973 reduced the importance of foreign firms in the domestic drug market. The share of MNCs in the Indian pharmaceutical sector thus started declining from 1980.

Their response to the increased restrictions varied. Some MNCs, such as Bristol-Myers Squibb, did not enter the market at all. Others, such as the Winthrop Company, sold off shares. Smaller companies reduced their foreign equity participation. Only thirteen corporations retained greater than 40 percent foreign equity. In the mid-1990s, restrictions on foreign corporations were abandoned.

In addition to FERA 1973, NDP 1978, and NDP 1986, price controls played a key role in the development of the Indian pharmaceutical industry. Such controls were issued by the National Pharmaceutical Policy Authority through what is known as Drug Price Control Orders, issued in 1970, 1979, 1987, 1995, and 2007. The purpose of the early control orders was to ensure that drugs were sold at reasonable prices and to create incentives to encourage domestic producers to invest in original research for new drugs. The later price control orders drastically reduced drug prices.

Thus, government policies affecting the pharmaceutical industry in India have changed over time. In the 1970s the government controlled the industry; more recently, the industry has been left free to contend with market forces.

In sum, the combined impact of price controls and the regulation of foreign ownership in the Indian pharmaceutical industry has been quite substantial, perhaps as great as the impact of the IPR laws.

The Future of Indian Pharmaceuticals

Despite opening the industry to market forces, the government of India continues to take a keen interest in pharmaceutical policy. For example, clinical trials conducted in India are exempt from service taxes. In addition, a weighted deduction benefit of 150 percent on in-house R&D expenditures has been extended to 2012. This is not surprising given the importance of the pharmaceutical industry. It seems plausible that the government hopes to replicate the success of India's software industry. The promise of pharmaceuticals can be gauged by the entrepreneurial wealth in the sector. In 2007 Forbes published its list of the forty richest Indians. For the first time in two decades, India has replaced Japan as the Asian country with the largest number of very wealthy people. Notably, the sector of the economy that was best represented among the wealthiest Indians was not software or information technology (IT) but pharmaceuticals. Even more importantly, of those who became wealthy in the pharmaceutical industry, each was a first-generation entrepreneur. In some cases, they were scientists who had become entrepreneurs, or individuals who had left their parent organization and started firms of their own.

The list of India's wealthiest people suggests a bright future for the pharmaceutical industry in India not only in terms of innovation but also in terms of entrepreneurial behavior and shifting firm strategies. Students of innovation (for example, Aghion and Tirole 1994; Teece 1986) have long argued over whether R&D ought to be performed as a part of the vertically integrated structure of a firm or as a specialized endeavor. Others have emphasized the importance of appropriability or the impact of IPRs on the formation of independent research firms (Arora and Merges 2004). Strengthening IPR laws seems unlikely to increase the competitive advantage of firms that specialize in R&D. Two recent examples from India, Dr. Reddy's Laboratories Ltd. and Sun Pharmaceuticals, are particularly relevant in understanding firm responses in this context. In 2005 Dr. Reddy's Laboratories used venture capital and self-funding to form Perlecan Pharma, India's first integrated drug development company focused solely on R&D of new chemical entities. Similarly, Sun Pharmaceuticals formed Sun Pharma Advanced Research Company Ltd. in 2007. Thus, an optimal strategy for a pharmaceutical firm, given stronger IPRs in the post-TRIPS Indian industry, appears to be to retain its line of generic products while spinning off its R&D division. But the number of pharmaceutical firms capable of successfully executing this strategy remains unknown. It is also unclear how smaller pharmaceutical firms and multinational drug firms might adapt to an environment in which R&D programs are advantageous.[6]

Conclusion

In this chapter, I have examined some public policy effects on the development of the Indian pharmaceutical industry. This industry was established during a period of weak IPR laws, tight pharmaceutical price controls, and restricted foreign ownership. The industry continued to develop as government intervention in pharmaceutical markets lessened and the influence of market forces increased. A small number of technologically advanced firms have begun to make substantial investments in R&D in an effort to move beyond the manufacture of generic pharmaceuticals.

An interesting parallel is the development of the Japanese pharmaceutical industry. In Japan, product patents were introduced in 1976. After this, Japan's IPR regime was characterized by narrow scope and compulsory licensing through what the Japanese termed the *dependent patent arbitration* provided by the new regime. In contrast, India's post-TRIPS patent regime has focused on the criteria of patenting over scope. The narrow patents adopted in Japan provide weaker protection to patentees but also encourage incremental innovation. In the case of India, the opposite focus aims at allowing entry to its domestic generic firms once shorter exclusivity periods expire. How the patenting criteria will be interpreted—and its effects on the scope of patents—is not clear. While it might be beneficial in the short run, long-term innovation will only thrive with the encouragement of innovators. In India public policy that relates to the pharmaceutical industry could follow the Japanese model and maintain narrow patent scope, adequate patents, and cross-licensing provisions. Then the Indian pharmaceutical industry might have increased incentive to innovate and fewer adverse welfare effects caused by rising drug prices.

Pharmaceutical policymakers in India should also think of Italy's experience. Italy introduced drug product patents in 1978, overturning the old patent regime that banned patents for drugs from the early 1930s. In contrast to the rising returns on R&D described in the Indian case, the strategy of Italian firms related to R&D did not change as product patents were enacted. "Drug R&D expenditure growth did not accelerate after the patent regime transition, neither did the number or character of new product launches," note Scherer and Weisburst (1995:1023). These authors contend that strict governmental control of Italian drug prices might have discouraged Italian pharmaceutical firms from investing in R&D and launching new products. But the effects of drug price controls on R&D investment cannot be clearly distinguished from the effects of stricter patents. In light of the Italian experience, Indian pharmaceutical policymakers would do well to weigh the benefits of India's own system of price regulations vis-à-vis the new patent regime. This is particularly important for consistency between patent-granting verdicts and price regulatory agencies in India, especially in the post-TRIPS pharmaceutical industry.

Finally, based on the Korean experience of stimulating pharmaceutical R&D, the role of government is critical. From 1961 South Korea had a weak patent regime in place. South Korea did not implement product patents until 1986 but, to encourage domestic innovation, the government subsidized pharmaceutical firms. From 1995 to 2001, the South Korean government used about one-third of its total expenditure on drug R&D to directly subsidize pharmaceutical firms. Another third of the total expenditure was used to support research in universities. The remainder was invested in research in other types of institutes that indirectly strengthened the infrastructure of the South Korean pharmaceutical industry (Choi 2007). The Indian government appears to be following a similar course. In the budget of 2007–2008, it introduced a weighted deduction benefit that amounted to 150 percent for in-house expenditure on R&D.

In conclusion, stronger patents and their implementation in an emerging economy like India's will never be easy given the inheritance of a complex policy environment. But the Indian pharmaceutical industry has shown it is able to adapt to changes in market environments and looks forward to a future in which it could be very influential in global pharmaceutical markets.

Notes

[1] This chapter was written for the Shorenstein APARC conference "Pharmaceuticals in the Asia-Pacific: Prescribing Cultures, Industry Dynamics, and Health Policy," organized by Karen Eggleston in May 2008. I was originally directed to this interesting event by Prof. F. M. Scherer of Harvard University. To both of them I owe my sincere thanks. The chapter is also a product of my ongoing doctoral work on Indian pharmaceuticals at the Heinz College, Carnegie Mellon University. I owe deep gratitude for an evolving understanding of the industry to numerous discussions with professors Ashish Arora and Lee Branstetter, my faculty advisers and committee members here at Carnegie Mellon. Without their constant criticism this chapter would not have taken its current shape. In addition, industry experts from India have been kind enough to provide me with anecdotes. I am solely responsible for all errors in this chapter.

[2] The information on the generics industry comes from the old Web site of Barr Pharmaceuticals (now Teva Pharmaceuticals), which provides a concise description of the industry's evolution.

[3] Mr. Shah said this in an interview with the author in 2008 and agreed to be quoted accordingly.

[4] Interested readers are referred to the Business Standard India's Web site at http://www.business-standard.com and may search the site's archives using the keyword term *cancer patents*. A spate of articles will appear that have been published from January to March 2008.

[5] To focus on patent litigations and granting, the government of India has constituted the Intellectual Property Appellate Board in 2003, with headquarters in Chennai, India, and offices in key cities around the country. More details at http://www.ipab.tn.nic.in.

[6] During the writing of this chapter, the industry saw a landmark development. On June 11, 2008, Japanese drug discovery major Daiichi Sankyo acquired a majority stake in Indian pharmaceutical major Ranbaxy Laboratories Ltd. for a transaction value close to $3.4 billion–$4.6 billion. Such acquisitions of Indian drug firms are increasingly likely in the future, as innovation-focused global drug companies branch out and set up generics offshoots to strengthen their business. Indian generic makers will surely be among their prime targets.

References

Achilladelis, B., and K. Antonakis. 2001. The dynamics of technological innovation: The case of the pharmaceutical industry. *Research Policy* 30: 535–88.

Aghion, P., and J. Tirole. 1994. The management of innovation. *Quarterly Journal of Economics* 109 (4): 1185–209.

Aoki, Reiko, Kensuke Kobe, and Hiroko Yamane. 2006. Indian patent policy and public health: Implications from the Japanese experience. Economic working papers, University of Auckland.

Arora, Ashish, and R. P. Merges. 2004. Specialized supply firms, property rights, and firm boundaries. *Industrial and Corporate Change* 13 (3): 451–75.

Arora, Ashish, Lee Branstetter, and Chirantan Chatterjee. 2007. Strong medicine: Patent reform and the emergence of a research driven pharmaceutical industry in India. Heinz School working paper, Carnegie Mellon University and National Bureau of Economic Research (NBER) conference paper 2008. http://www.nber.org/~confer/2008/LBA/program.html.

Chaudhuri, S. 2005a. *The WTO and India's pharmaceuticals industry*. New Delhi, India: Oxford Univ. Press.

———. 2005b. Oxford analyst reports. Thomson Scientific online.

Chaudhuri, S., Pinelopi K. Goldberg, and Panle Jia. 2006. Estimating the effects of global patent protection in pharmaceuticals: A case study of quinolones in India. *American Economic Review* 96: 1477–1514.

Choi, Hwan Joon. 2007. Evaluation of government R&D subsidy: Does subsidy affect the size, composition, and productivity of private R&D of Korean pharmaceutical firms? Working paper, School of Social and Decision Sciences, Carnegie Mellon University, Pittsburgh.

Dutta, Antara. 2006. Intellectual property rights, market structure, and social welfare: Three essays in industrial organization. Massachusetts Institute of Technology (MIT) dissertation thesis.

Fink, C. 2000. How stronger patent protection in India might affect the behavior of transnational pharmaceutical industries. Working paper 2352, World Bank, Washington, D.C.

Griliches, Z. 1981. Market value, R&D and patents. *Economics Letters* 7: 183–87.

Lanjouw, O. J. 1998. The introduction of product patents in India: Heartless exploitation of the poor and suffering? Growth center discussion paper, Yale University; NBER working paper 6366.

Médecins sans Frontières. 2008. *Untangling the web of antiretroviral price reductions*, 11th edn. July. http://www.msfaccess.org/fileadmin/user_upload/diseases/hiv-aids/Untangling_the_Web/Untanglingtheweb_July2008_English.pdf.

Sakakibara, Mariko, and Lee Branstetter. 2001. Do stronger patents induce more innovation? Evidence from the 1988 Japanese patent law reforms. *The Rand Journal of Economics* 32: 77–100.

Scherer, F.M. and S. Weisburst. 1995. Economic effects of strengthening pharmaceutical patent protection in Italy. *International Review of Industrial Property and Copyright Law* 6: 1009–24.

Teece, J. D. 1986. Profiting from technological innovations. *Research Policy* 15: 285–306.

Tobin, J. 1969. A general equilibrium approach to monetary theory. *Journal of Money Credit and Banking* 1: 15–29.

Pharmaceutical Policy in Seven Asia-Pacific Health-care Systems

China

PHARMACEUTICAL POLICY
AND HEALTH REFORM IN CHINA

Yiyong Yang

At the end of 2007, the Chinese government announced plans to double the budget of the New Type of Rural Cooperative Medical Care System and the Basic Medical Insurance System for Urban Residents over two years. These schemes, which aim to help farmers and the urban unemployed, respectively, provide their recipients at least 50 yuan ($6.80) per year for medical costs. This figure is composed of 20 yuan from the central government, at least 20 yuan from the local government, and a 10 yuan copayment. In 2008 the government increased the combined contribution of central and local governments to 80 yuan.

Back in 2002, China launched a pilot phase of the New Type of Rural Cooperative Medical Care System to help farmers tackle rising health costs. The program was initiated in three provinces. By the end of 2007, more than 730 million farmers, residing in about 86 percent of China's counties, were involved. Authorities said the scheme would cover the entire rural population by 2009, one year earlier than previously planned. A total of 814 million people, accounting for 91.5 percent of the rural population, now benefit from the New Type of Rural Cooperative Medical Care System.

Similarly, the Basic Medical Insurance System for Urban Residents (for nonworking urban residents) was piloted in eighty-eight cities in 2007. It was scheduled to cover half of the country's cities by the end of 2008, 80 percent by 2009, and all the urban nonworking population by 2010. The number of selected cities participating in trials of the system increased to 317 in 2008, and the number of participating individuals grew by 73.59 million in 2007 and 117 million in 2008. The previously established Basic Medical Insurance for Urban Workers covered 180 million participants by the end of 2007. Although coverage almost doubled from 2002 to 2007, even then it reached only 62 percent of urban employed workers, or 23 percent of China's total labor force.

Reform Aims to Provide Equal Health Care for All

The new medical reform plan, announced in early 2009, aims to provide safe, effective, convenient, and low-cost public medical and health-care services to all rural and urban residents. Given its potential impact, the reform will certainly be in the limelight from its inception. If policymakers want to seize the opportunity to overhaul the country's health-care systems rife with problems—such as the mismatch between what it can provide and what people need, the imbalance between urban and rural medical services, the inadequacy of public health expenditure, and the rocketing price of medical and health-care services—they should solicit public opinion on the reform as soon as possible.

The reform plan is right to suggest that the government lead the provision of medical and public health services. Because of insufficient government funding, public medical institutions have become dependant on profits from medical services and drug prescriptions. This not only imposes a heavy burden on patients but also erodes professional ethics. For example, under pressure to increase profits, some doctors overprescribe to their patients.

As public criticism of soaring medical fees, lack of access, poor doctor-patient relations, and low system coverage intensified in recent years, a complete overhaul of the country's health-care system seemed imminent.

For years, government funding accounted for only about 17 percent of national health expenditures. Surely this figure had to be increased, especially as national revenue rocketed—from 2 trillion yuan ($272 billion) in 2003 to more than 5 trillion yuan in 2007.

The government knows it must address the problem of underfunded health care. In the first eleven months of 2007, central and local government health spending reached 142 billion yuan—up 40.6 percent from the previous year. The health sector is one of the few to witness such an increase in public spending.

Yet, to make fair and efficient use of this increase, it is necessary to align the medical system with the interests of the people. Public opinion—even when it differs from that of experts—is indispensable for any successful reform.

As emphasized by Secretary General Hu Jintao in a report to the Seventeenth National Congress of the Communist Party of China given on October 15, 2007: "Everyone will have access to basic medical and health services." This stipulation is also included in the "New Requirements for Attaining the Goal of Building a Moderately Prosperous Society in All Respects" in the same report. The government will do its best to ensure that all Chinese people enjoy their right to medical care by 2020.

Pharmaceutical Policy Must Be Transparent

Every phase of the reform should be open and transparent. Though the new health-care plan is not yet launched as of this writing, many supporting policies have been published. The Department of Price under the National Development and Reform Commission (NDRC) is responsible for regulating medical prices. It is known that a corrupt distribution chain is the root cause of medical devices' exorbitant prices. Despite this, the NDRC has focused on limiting the markup to the end user instead of regulating the distribution chain.

The State Food and Drug Administration announced ten designated pharmaceutical companies to produce safe and low-cost drugs for urban communities and rural areas, and the retail prices for eighteen categories of prescription drugs at the end of 2007. The selection of the ten companies has aroused much public controversy.

The country's medical system has been reformed time and again, but the results remain unsatisfactory. An important reason for this is that the decision-making process is not transparent. Lessons of the past should be incorporated in the next round of reform. Every step should be open and transparent in an effort to avoid corruption. But, thus far, the situation does not look good. Take the selection of the pharmaceutical companies, for example. Why were these companies selected? What are their standards? Will there be any changes in the list of these companies in the future? The public needs to know.

Their selection affects not only the interests of thousands of drug manufacturers but also the common people. The current selection process can easily lead to problems such as unfair competition and high drug prices. The authorities might squeeze out competition; even now, the designated companies as a whole are forming a monopoly power. Though the authorities can set prices to avoid exorbitant profits for now, this will be difficult as demand increases. That such a nontransparent step was made in the initial stage of the medical reform is worrisome. Once such a move is accepted, it will be difficult to stay on course. Therefore, all phases of the medical reform should be open, transparent, and democratic. This will ensure the reform's success.

STREAMLINING CHINA'S PHARMACEUTICAL DISTRIBUTION CHANNELS

Mingzhi Li and Kai Reimers[1]

The Chinese government started to centralize medicine procurement in 2000. Several years later, evidence shows that overall drug prices have fallen significantly—and that controversies are on the rise. Some insiders say that none of the three industry stakeholders (drug manufacturers, drug distributors, and hospitals) are satisfied, and that even consumers are not reaping the benefits of lower health-care spending (of which drug payments are a significant proportion). To make matters worse, adverse selection is increasingly apparent. Since the government centralized procurement, several effective but low-priced drugs have disappeared from the market because there is no incentive for manufacturers to produce, distributors to deliver, or hospitals to order them.

In this chapter, we analyze the Chinese government's efforts to centralize medicine procurement from the 1970s to the present. In particular, we look at how it sought to leverage technological innovations and institutional change to overcome old problems. Although technologically feasible, the practical difficulties of implementing centralized drug procurement suggest the importance of aligning the macrolevel institutional environment *and* microlevel individual behaviors with the new mechanism governing transactions. Based on experiences in Beijing and Guangdong Province, our analysis suggests that, as an important segment of the overall health-care industry, drug distribution channels cannot be successfully reformed without a substantial change of the overarching regulatory framework. This might include the elimination of cross-subsidies between drug prices and medical services, which in turn depends on broadening the overall sector reform.

The Evolution of China's Pharmaceutical Distribution System

A brief historical background will help us understand recent developments. China's pharmaceutical distribution system has undergone three stages since 1949. Amid difficulties facing the overall health-care industry, a chaotic pharmaceutical distribution chain triggered government interest in centralizing drug procurement in the late 1990s. In fact, today's fragmented drug market can be traced back to policy loopholes left open in past years. In a broader context, many researchers and industry analysts now ascribe the overall chaos of China's health-care sector to the government's rapid opening of the industry to market forces without the establishment of sufficient and enforceable regulations. Corruption and irregularities in drug distribution are often cited to support this argument.

The Three-Tier System of Drug Distribution in the Planned Economy Era

Before China's economic reforms of the 1980s, drug prices were tightly controlled in a three-tier distribution system. All medicines were dispersed through a few government-controlled regional (first-tier) wholesalers to provincial (second-tier) wholesalers, who would then distribute the medicines to city or county (third-tier) local drug wholesalers. Retailers—including hospitals, clinics, and pharmacies—ordered medicines from the third tier.

Figure 10.1 The Three-Tier Structure of Drug Distribution in China's Planned Economy

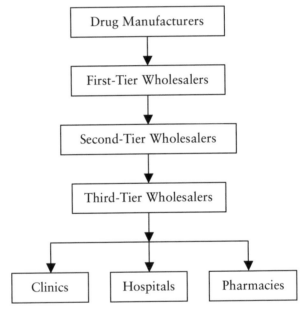

Deregulating Drug Distribution (mid-1980s to 1999)

The three-tier distribution system was inefficient and characterized by multiple intermediaries. In the mid-1980s, the government allowed private firms to enter the industry and began to gradually phase out its rigid distribution system. By the end of the 1990s, drug distribution was highly fragmented across more than sixteen thousand firms of various sizes. As the markets opened up and pricing was deregulated, pharmaceutical prices increased dramatically, which caused great public dissatisfaction. Ironically, despite rising drug prices, the average profitability rate was lower than 0.7 percent. The major reason behind such low profitability were high costs resulting from multiple levels of distribution and the strong bargaining power of hospitals, which provided about 80 percent of all revenue from drug sales. The profit margin on hospital drug sales (including "official" kickbacks) was between 20 and 50 percent; secret kickbacks to doctors and other relevant personnel were an additional 10 to 30 percent. These two items alone accounted for 30–80 percent of drug prices. The distribution sector's markups accounted for 3–10 percent and prices paid to drug manufacturers accounted for about 10–50 percent of retail prices. In general, drug manufacturers' sales income was divided into 3–5 percent on R&D expenditure, 10–30 percent on production costs, 30–70 percent on sales expenditure, and 10–20 percent on profit margins (Zhu 2007).

As previously stated, much of the chaos in the current market is due to past loopholes in the government's drug approval process. China's pharmacies and hospitals have long been plagued by low-quality and fake medicines made by local drug companies. In recent years, several publicized cases saw patients poisoned or even killed by such drugs. While blame always falls on small drug manufacturers—who the government accuses of skirting laws to earn a profit—the government's role in allowing shoddy medicine and corruption to thrive was exposed in an investigation conducted by China's State Food and Drug Administration (State FDA) in 2005. The fear is that lax government oversight is allowing drug companies to cut corners and circumvent safety procedures. While drug prices are subject to government price controls in China, drug approval can be used to boost profits. Drug companies sometimes modify a drug slightly by adding a new ingredient or changing the dosage. They then register the modified drug as a new medication that can command a higher price. In 2005 the State FDA licensed 1,113 new drugs; the United States approved only 81 in the same period (*Wall Street Journal* 2007).[2]

Government Efforts to Centralize Distribution (after 2000)

In 2000 the State Planning Committee issued a document on reforming the management of drug prices, which laid the foundation for the government's pricing regulations. Together with other legal rules (the Price Law, the Drug Regulation Law, Rules for Regulating Drug Prices), a set of government regulations was put in place. Meanwhile, the government decided to tighten its control over distribution and to implement centralized drug procurement. Although the Ministry of Health (MOH) had set procurement guidelines, different regions had different practices. In the next section we describe the experiences of Beijing and the province of Guangdong.

Implementing Centralized Medicine Procurement: Beijing and Guangdong Province[3]

The Process and Its Impact in Beijing

In Beijing, the capital city of China, three centralized, e-commerce-based procurement systems for drugs were implemented in 2004. The way had been paved by institutional reforms dating back to 2000, when the Beijing Bidding Center was set up by nine government agencies involved in regulating drug distribution to hospitals. These agencies included the Beijing Health Bureau (which has a role similar to that of the national MOH, albeit on a provincial level), the Beijing Price Bureau, and the Beijing Traditional Chinese Medicine Bureau. Based on experience with similar systems in other provinces, a process for auction-based drug procurement was established; while the core elements of this process were similar across the country, some elements were distinct from those implemented in other provinces. In general, drug distribution is still a localized business; therefore, distributors who are fierce competitors in one province can be business partners in another.

The bidding center usually initiates a bidding process once every year. The process steps are depicted in figure 10.2. The first is to evaluate competing bids by manufacturers of individual pharmaceutical agents (chemical substances) according to multiple criteria, including price and the service quality of distributors (who must be assigned by manufacturers in advance and who often take over the paperwork associated with the bidding process). Manufacturers can bid on a list of about fifteen thousand items. A group of experts evaluates bids for each of Beijing's six hospital groups, which have been categorized according to their varying demand for drugs. Once bids have been selected, hospitals are required to place purchase orders for drugs only among the winning bids. The main purpose of this process is to control price and to ensure that hospitals use high-quality drugs.

The bidding process is facilitated by a number of intermediaries certified for that purpose. While seven intermediaries have received such certificates, only three are active. Each hospital group selects one to help it with the bidding process. The requirements, according to the certification process, also include the need to own and operate an e-commerce system. The intermediary collects all the documents accompanying the bid and submits them electronically. The intermediaries then pass these data—after some data cleaning and formatting—on to the bidding center. Once the winning bids have been selected, the results are published on the e-commerce systems.

The e-commerce systems play an even more important role in the ordering process. According to the stipulations of the Beijing Health Bureau, hospitals are required to submit orders through them. For that purpose, hospitals log on using a Web interface and enter their orders directly. Distributors then download the order data—also using a Web interface—and hospitals are automatically informed. But distributors cannot confirm or change purchase orders.

Figure 10.2 The Bidding Process in Beijing

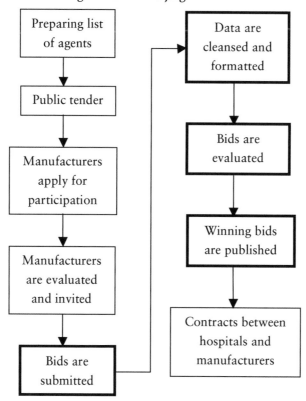

Note: Bold boxes indicate steps supported by the e-commerce systems.

The express purpose of using these e-commerce systems is to monitor compliance with the bidding process rules. The bidding center is specifically charged with the task of monitoring hospital purchasing activity in order to ensure that hospitals only buy from the list provided (that is, that they do not circumvent the drugs selected in the evaluation process).

The percentage of drugs sold or procured through these systems has increased continuously since their inception in 2004 and was estimated at close to 100 percent in 2006. Their use is also credited for a significant drop in the number of distributors in Beijing (from around 200 in 2004 to about 120 at the beginning of 2007).

Before the e-commerce systems, distributors took drug orders from hospitals by telephone (orders from distributors to manufacturers are still placed by phone or fax). The services of intermediaries complement the e-commerce functionality, mostly by offering a "screening service"; if a distributor does not respond to an order, an intermediary will help the hospital procure the drugs through other channels. The intermediaries also improve the efficiency of the ordering process by harmonizing data. For example, hospitals often use internal codes to identify drugs. These codes are matched to standards defined by the State FDA so that distributors need not cope with the multiple proprietary codes used by hospitals.

While some data used for the ordering and bidding processes are identical, the systems (including the databases) are separate because they are regulated by different government agencies. For the bidding process, the operational efficiency of the e-commerce systems is minor as compared to the ordering process. The main benefits are the ease of selecting and evaluating drugs, which facilitate the work of selecting bids. Again, this process requires that intermediaries harmonize data supplied by manufacturers (or distributors acting on behalf of manufacturers).

The original vision was that e-commerce would provide a comprehensive platform for managing the drug supply chain from manufacturers to hospitals. But currently only the ordering process is supported by the systems and even this support is rather limited (evident in the lack of order confirmation or change functions). For example, the systems were intended to enable zero inventories in hospital pharmacies, but hospitals are not interested in such a capability because they do not have to pay manufacturers for unsold inventories.

While the functional scope of the three e-commerce systems is rather narrow, they do improve the operational efficiency of the ordering process. Back in 2004, an association of drug wholesalers and pharmacies—with broad support from its constituency—submitted a government petition opposing the introduction of the e-commerce systems. Such opposition is waning as large distributors (wholesalers) discover the systems' operational benefits for a consolidating industry.

In the centralized e-commerce systems, hospitals have to contract with the intermediary as well as with manufacturers. Each hospital group selects one intermediary, which charges fees to the manufacturers as stipulated by the Beijing Health Bureau. The licenses of intermediaries need to be renewed each year, but the relationship between a hospital group and an intermediary tends to be stable and long term. Upon conclusion of the bidding process, hospitals have to contract with the winning manufacturers. Occasionally, hospitals also negotiate with manufacturers before placing orders on the e-commerce system, in order to receive discounts. In the evaluation process, it is also possible that the bidding center negotiates with manufacturers who have participated in the bidding process. This occurs when only one bid has been submitted for a specific chemical substance. In addition, manufacturers use sales agents and other wholesalers to market their drugs to hospitals. But these agents, who may receive the drugs at a discounted price, still have to use the licensed distributors for delivering the drugs to hospitals.

The specific governance structure used for operating e-commerce systems through intermediaries is justified by two rationales. First, the main benefit of the system is the ease of monitoring compliance with the bidding rules. This is considered crucial, since hospitals have very strong incentives to circumvent these rules in order to increase their income through the sale of brand-name and therefore high-margin drugs. Second, some experts argue that e-commerce in China is only viable if facilitated by third parties. In Shanghai some wholesalers have tried to build e-commerce systems to directly connect with hospitals, but these efforts have failed because of the fragmented market structure (hospitals typically deal with around thirty different distributors), fierce competition among distributors (forestalling cooperation), and low trust among all the parties involved.

In reality, however, the e-commerce systems are not being used to monitor compliance. Specifically, the bidding center does not make any use of its ability to log onto the systems in order to check hospitals' compliance with the bidding rules (as reflected in their ordering behavior). While the bidding center claims that intermediaries report 50 to 60 percent of all purchasing transactions, it turns out that this feedback is based on aggregated data provided infrequently (usually only once per year) on paper and only upon request. The intermediaries presume the bidding center lacks the technical skills required to make sense of the data provided by the systems directly. The bidding center itself indicates that its ability to sanction hospitals (through exposing noncompliance) is rather limited because it is difficult to differentiate rule violations from "market behavior." Frequently, hospitals often have sufficient market power to resist any sanctioning efforts. Another reason for the bidding center's failure to monitor hospital purchasing behavior via the e-commerce systems is that data is not standardized (apart from the product codes mentioned above) and so cannot be easily analyzed. Moreover, some hospitals ask intermediaries to provide them with so-called "soft systems" for their data input (which are tweaked), making it even more difficult to monitor their purchasing behavior.

Guangdong Province's Sunshine Drug Procurement Project

In comparison with the centralized drug procurement procedures in Beijing, Guangdong Province's Sunshine Drug Procurement Project has received much more attention—much of it controversial. The following case study draws upon information published in the news media.

The Process and Its Impact in Guangdong

After ten rounds of revision, the government's Guidelines for Guangdong Province Medical Institutions' Sunshine Drug Procurement Project: Online Bidding and Price Controlling were passed in October 2006, and the project was formally implemented in 2007. The main difference between this project and the one in Beijing is that in Guangdong, only drug manufacturers are eligible to participate in the bidding process. The winning manufacturers need to assign a distributor who will be responsible for delivering the medicines to the hospitals.

189

The process of completing an online contract between a drug manufacturer and a hospital includes the following stages: (1) manufacturers quote prices for their targeted drugs based on a list prepared by an expert group, (2) the bidding process includes three rounds on three consecutive days, (3) experts and manufacturers negotiate online, and (4) the experts and manufacturers negotiate face to face (figure 10.3).

Figure 10.3 The Bidding Process in Guangdong Province

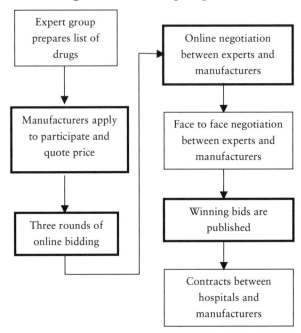

Note: Bold boxes indicate steps supported by the e-commerce systems.

After the bidding process in the second stage, no more than three manufacturers remain for each drug and the selection among these manufacturers is based only on the prices offered. This practice of combining online and face-to-face negotiations appears to be a Guangdong innovation. It facilitates communications between medical institutions and manufacturers, helps all parties understand underlying costs, and reduces price variations and patients' drug-spending burden.

The targets of face-to-face negotiations are drugs with price quotes twice or more than twice as high as those of other drugs in the same bidding group. During the 2007 bidding process, 271 drugs and 235 manufacturers belonged to this group—of which 137 manufacturers participated in negotiations and 98 withdrew in the process.

Statistics show that out of the 170 drugs entering the face-to-face negotiation stage, 121 were selected, 26 were designated as drugs "to be closely monitored" with "procurement quantity to be controlled," and 23 were excluded from further participation in the process. Compared with the initial prices quoted by drug firms, most of the negotiated prices were significantly lower.

By the end of March 2007, the online drug-bidding process came to an end after forty-three thousand types of drugs had applied and nearly ten thousand had been eliminated (because of high prices or other reasons) and therefore could not be sold in Guangdong. The drugs selected included all types listed in the catalog of medical insurance. Preliminary data showed that through this online procurement process, the prices of selected drugs were reduced by about 40 percent and some by almost 100 percent.

In addition to lowering drug prices, using e-commerce systems can help regulators monitor the circulation of drugs and enhance drug safety. When tragedy hit in 2006 and one drug company's fake medicine killed thirteen people in one hospital, investigators needed to know if other hospitals had purchased the same medicine. In the past, after such an incident, the Bureau of Health and the State FDA would issue a notice to their affiliated subunits to investigate. Through these agencies' investigations and the reports from hospitals, regulators could find out the whereabouts of problematic medicines—but only after a long wait. A government official in the Guangdong Province Center for Drug Procurement Service pointed out that now, with the electronic government monitoring platform in the Sunshine Drug Procurement Project, "through a click of a mouse, such information as names of hospitals, types and amounts of drugs, whether the orders have been confirmed by distributors etc. can be found out in one minute." In addition to government investigators, this platform allows hospitals above the county level to easily trace the whereabouts of fake medicines.

In practice, many pharmaceutical manufacturers find price a nonnegotiable barrier to entry. While the objective of the Sunshine Drug Procurement Project is to lower prices, other important factors are neglected, including brand and manufacturer reputation and firms' research and development (R&D) capability. As a result, many drugs belonging to select categories (such as "government protected Chinese traditional medicines," "exclusive types," "high quality and high priced types," "well-known brands of Guangdong Province," "patented brands," and "original types") were eliminated based on their high prices compared to competing drugs, even though their elimination could threaten drug safety. Some manufacturers argue that even for the same category of drugs, differences in formulation, ingredients, and production processes can influence the effects of drugs; in order to develop a more effective drug than those belonging to the same category, significantly higher amounts of R&D expenditure and production costs are incurred and, therefore, quoted prices are necessarily higher than those of the competitors.

Some drug manufacturers also believe that even if their products win a bid, this should be confirmed by the hospitals. But there is no guideline stating whether the hospitals must buy the drug in question, in what amount, and by what time—and this seen as unfair to drug manufacturers.

In order to win a bid, some drug manufacturers lower their price quotes but then do not supply the drugs to the hospitals when they receive orders. According to information available from the Province Medicine Procurement Service Center, by the end of July 2007, among the 30,000 types of drugs that won bids, 1,718 were never confirmed online or were cancelled by the distributors (284 distributors never confirmed online orders). One company that received 21 orders from 15 hospitals for about 558,322 yuan never supplied any product; another simply ignored or denied orders from 10 hospitals.

According to the Guangdong Province Rule on Sunshine Drug Procurement, drug distributors are assigned by manufacturers. Once a hospital sends a purchase order through the e-commerce systems, the distributor must confirm the order online within 48 hours. But according to the observation of one reporter, by July 31, 2007, there were 284 distributors with 0 confirmed orders.

The government can decide to investigate the manufacturers and distributors according to the information provided on the e-commerce systems, such as invoice amounts and the circumstances of denied orders. If a distributor does not have the capacity to (1) supply the drugs, (2) supply the drugs in the amount requested, or (3) supply on time, it will be put on an online warning list once the case is proved. If hospitals complain about a given distributor more than three times and the distributor is also found to have been involved in hostile bidding or is unable to supply drugs according to the contract, it will be put on a blacklist of "dishonest transaction firms" before being excluded from participating in Guangdong Province's drug procurement process in the future.

During price negotiations, some manufacturers compete fiercely to win the bid. Subsequent low prices and thin profit margins can lead to problems in drug supply because of increased raw material prices, shortages of raw materials, or manufacturers finding alternative sales opportunities.

Case Analysis: Are IT-enabled Electronic Transaction Platforms the Solution?

Transaction cost economics takes the transaction as its unit of analysis and is therefore well suited to studying the technological change affecting interaction among economic agents. Williamson (1993) has used a three-layer model to locate and motivate the analytic strategy of transaction cost economics. The focal layer concerns the governance of transactional relationships, which is influenced by both macro and micro factors. On the macro level, institutions such as contract law, property rights, and norms and customs affect the comparative costs of governance. Changes in this layer may therefore lead to policy adjustments as some forms of governance become relatively more cost advantageous while others become more costly. On the micro level, behavioral traits of individuals influence governance forms. Prominent among them—in Williamson's analysis—are opportunism and bounded rationality. For example, governance forms need to prevent economic agents from exploiting one another should the possibility for such behavior arise due to unanticipated changes in the economic environment.

Williamson (1993) is concerned with the governance mode of bilateral transactions at the firm level, including three basic types: market, hierarchy, and hybrid. The Chinese government's efforts to centralize the drug procurement process can be viewed as shifting industry transactions from reliance on markets to a more vertically integrated mode. While centralized, electronic-platform-based bidding and transactions are feasible from a purely technical perspective, the complex institutional environment at the macro and the micro levels makes the future of the practice uncertain and limits its ability to lower transaction costs and inefficiency in drug distribution (figure 10.4).

Figure 10.4 Technological Change in a Williamsonian Framework

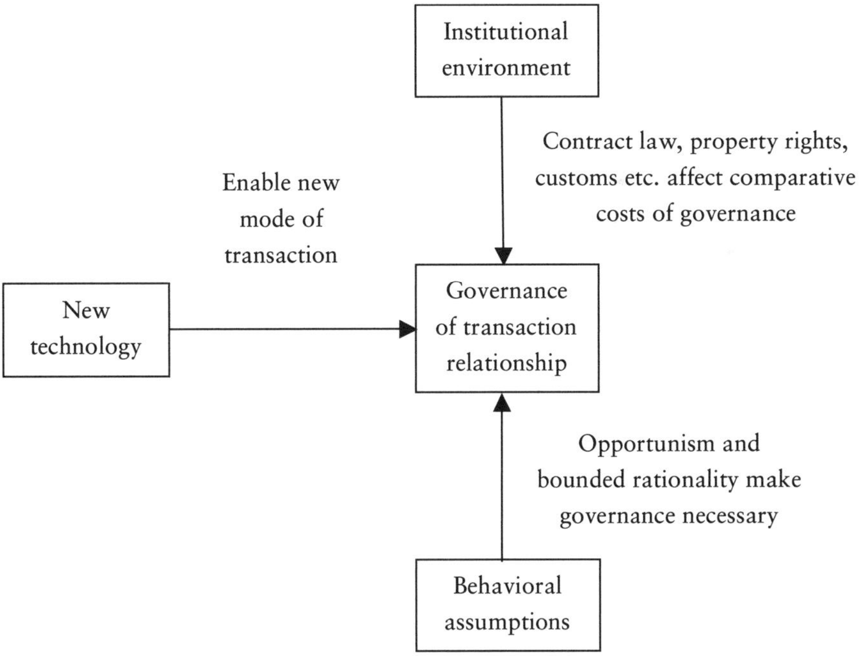

Source: Modified from Williamson 1993.

The e-commerce systems described in this chapter were implemented to facilitate institutional change by reducing the costs of monitoring hospital drug-purchasing behavior. Though these systems are not being used for their intended purpose, the main actors in the industry continue to offer it as a rationale for using the systems. The new institutional bidding process was not enabled by a reduction of transaction costs (in this case, monitoring costs) through the use of the e-commerce systems; continued existence of the new institutional arrangement can only be explained by government use of sanctions and administrative force. In addition, government agencies tolerated significant violation of the bidding process rules, reducing resistance to the new institutional order.

The governance structure underlying the e-commerce systems is likely to have actually increased overall transaction costs in the distribution of drugs. But operational efficiencies in the ordering process could (partly) compensate for these increased transaction costs, as is evidenced by a reduction in the number of drug distributors. As operational efficiencies became clearer, resistance to using the e-commerce systems waned. This change might also have come as the main players recognized that the systems were not being used to monitor their market behavior.

One of the presumed advantages of implementing the centralized drug procurement procedure is to eliminate the secret "kickbacks" allegedly behind unjustified fluctuations in drug prices. But the government is severely restricted in enforcing its policies for two reasons. First, it depends upon the services of hospitals, a fact that came to light during the severe acute respiratory syndrome (SARS) epidemic in 2003. Therefore, the government cannot afford to let a large number of hospitals go out of business. Second, the government is not a unified force but internally fragmented along vertical and horizontal lines. In 2002 regulatory and administrative powers over the health-care sector were distributed across nine governmental agencies and ministries (Dou 2003), some of which were later merged. Vertically, government power—inspecting and certifying drug manufacturers, for example—is spread across central and provincial governments.

The centralized drug procurement projects in both Beijing and Guangdong Province have experienced great resistance. Beijing has stopped its yearly bidding process and transactions are still based on the bidding results of 2005. It is speculated that the city government is waiting for a forthcoming health-care reform before taking any new steps in drug procurement. Guangdong Province is leading the nation in its implementation of the centralized procurement policy. Its experience will allow all parties to observe the impact of the new and highly controversial system.

Conclusion

The centralized drug procurement process implemented by the Chinese government has leveraged new technologies in the hope of overcoming old problems. Technological solutions that make sense from an economic perspective may not survive the constraints imposed by the institutional environment or human opportunism—both of which are difficult to change. Reforms in almost every country's health-care sector have experienced tremendous difficulties in one way or another. In 2000 South Korea implemented a reform mandating the separation of drug prescribing and dispensing that aimed to change providers' economic incentives by eliminating the profit from dispensing drugs—previously a major source of income. When South Korea's president and civic groups succeeded in quickly setting the reform agenda, the medical profession was unable to block the adoption of the reform. But a series of national physician strikes forced the government to modify some critical elements of the reform package and to raise medical fees substantially to compensate for the income loss to physicians. As a result, the reform has resulted in little behavioral change among physicians and smaller net social benefits than expected (see chapter 1, Kwon, in this volume).

As described in the other chapters in this book, China's health-care sector and pharmaceutical industry requires thorough reform of almost all relevant aspects: regulatory regime, pricing policy, R&D policy, drug safety issues, and so on. The future of the Chinese government's centralized drug procurement will hinge on the success of overall health-care sector reforms; the impact of such reforms on the drug distribution system and vice versa is an interesting topic left for future research.

Notes

[1] Mingzhi Li acknowledges support by the National Natural Science Foundation of China (NSFC) (grant numbers #70621061, #70672007 and #70890082) and the China Ministry of Education (MOE) Project of the Key Research Institute of Humanity and Social Sciences at Universities (#06JJD630014 and #08JJD630001). Kai Reimers acknowledges support by the Deutsche Forschungsgemeinschaft (grant number 1328/2-2).

[2] In late January 2007, the State FDA announced that the production licenses for 170,000 medicines would be reviewed.

[3] The case of Beijing is based on our interviews with manufacturers, wholesalers, bidding platform providers, and government agencies.

References

1718 drugs won the sunshine drug procurement contest but didn't supply the drugs [in Chinese]. 2007. http://www.sinopharm.com. August 24.

Dou, W. 2003. The Chinese pharmaceutical and biotechnology market guide 2003. *SCRIP Report No. BS1210* (March 28). Richmond/Surrey: PJB Publications.

Reimers, K. 1995. Normungsprozesse—Eine Transaktionskostentheoretische Analyse [in German]. Gabler Verlag, Neue betriebswirtschaftliche Forschung Bd. 146, Wiesbaden.

Williamson, O. E. 1993. Transaction cost economics and organization theory. *Industrial and Corporate Change* 2 (2): 107–56.

Wall Street Journal. 2007. Chinese government cited in medicine probe. February 9, p. A4.

Zhu, Hengpeng. 2007. Abuses in the health-care system and distortion in pharmaceutical pricing [in Chinese]. *China Social Sciences* 4: 89–103.

PHARMACEUTICAL POLICY AND THE APPROPRIATE USE OF MEDICINES IN CHINA

Qiang Sun and Qingyue Meng

China's government is working to develop and implement a new round of reforms meant to provide health-care access to all citizens by 2020. These efforts seek to address the problems of the current system, such as the high patient cost burden (out-of-pocket payments increased from 20.43 percent of total health expenditures in 1978 to 53.46 percent in 2004) (Zhao, Chen, and Wan 2006). The key strategies proposed include expanding the population coverage and benefit packages of social health insurance schemes, controlling the escalation of medical costs, strengthening the capacity of human resources for health, and increasing sector regulation. The reform agenda also includes establishing an essential medicines system, which aims to increase the use of cost-effective pharmaceuticals and assure safe drug utilization.

Pharmaceutical policy is a focus of the health-sector reforms for several reasons. First, overall cost containment will be largely determined by the effective control of drug spending. China's National Health Accounts for 2005 show that it spent 4.7 percent of its gross domestic product (GDP) on health care—and a full 44 percent of that was on pharmaceuticals (Ministry of Health 2006). Reducing drug prices is one way to contain overall costs. Provider payment reforms initiated by social insurance programs in urban and rural areas mainly target drug expenditures. Second, irrational drug use damages patients' health and wastes health-care resources. The essential medicine lists (EMLs) of social insurance programs aim to correct distortions in drug prescribing behavior and improve drug utilization. Standard treatment protocols—to be overseen by both central and local governments—are another such effort. Third, drug pricing policy must be reformed; warped prices have been blamed for improper utilization and escalating costs. The National Development and Reform Commission (NDRC) is developing new mechanisms for reforming the current pricing policy (see chapter 12, Huang and Yang, in this volume). Finally, an essential medicines system is being considered for regulating the production, distribution, and utilization of essential drugs.

This chapter analyzes the impact of China's drug regulations on cost, access, and use. After a brief background to China's pharmaceutical sector, we discuss some drug policy challenges and evidence of inappropriate utilization. This is followed by recommendations for reform.

The Chinese Pharmaceutical Industry: An Overview

China's pharmaceutical manufacturing firms number more than 5,000, most of them small producers of generic drugs.[1] The sales revenue of the top ten Chinese drug manufacturers accounts for only about 10 percent of China's total pharmaceutical market, and the top hundred firms account for only 33 percent of the market (as measured by total sales). In contrast, the top ten global pharmaceutical firms account for about 42 percent of pharmaceutical sales worldwide (China's State Food and Drug Administration, State FDA, 2007).

China's drug firms tend to compete on price rather than quality, and this has implications for appropriate drug use.[2] On average, research and development (R&D) spending accounts for only 2 percent of sales revenue, which is far lower than the 14 to 18 percent typical of leading global pharmaceutical companies. From 1986 to 2006, only forty kinds of chemical medicines (such as artemisinin, bicyclol, and butylphthalide) were independently researched and developed by domestic pharmaceuticals producers, but most of them were not patented. Recent government initiatives aim to improve innovative capacity and quality through the promotion of good manufacturing practices (GMPs) (Jiang and Zhang 2006). But the quality and safety of Chinese-manufactured pharmaceuticals remain problematic (see chapter 14, Santoro and Liu, in this volume).

China's pharmaceutical distribution system is also not very concentrated. In 2005 the market share of the top three Chinese pharmaceutical distributors amounted to about 25 percent of the industry's total sales revenue. In contrast, the top three drug distributors in the United States had 96 percent market share and the top three Japanese drug distributors had 67 percent market share (State FDA 2007). In China, however, despite the apparent competitiveness of the distribution market, some wholesalers dominate specific local markets (Zhang 2005), and the more than 19,000 pharmacies owned by hospitals exert considerable market power, dispensing about 80 percent of retail drug sales directly to their patients (Wang 2006).

The State FDA established fifty interprovincial pharmaceutical retail chain enterprises in 2000. But concerns about high retail prices due to multiple middlemen persist. There are usually six to nine supply-chain links from production to final sale to patients; manufacturers receive only 10 to 20 percent of the final retail price (Liang 2005).

Pharmaceutical Pricing Policies

Generally, government control of pharmaceutical prices has continued after economic reform (1) due to market failure (because of information asymmetry and monopoly power) and (2) to assure affordability for all Chinese patients.

As described in more detail in chapter 12 of this volume (Huang and Yang), from 1992 to 1996 the Chinese government tried to loosen control of the pharmaceutical industry and let the market set drug prices. Market-oriented medicine pricing policies greatly improved the development of the domestic pharmaceutical industry but also contributed to drug price increases, duplicative production facilities, low drug quality, and severe corruption and kickbacks caused by irregular competition in drug distribution (Wang and Qiu 2006).

In 1997 many medicine prices came to be government controlled again. The prices of medicines set by the government included those on the EML of basic medical insurance schemes and were used for family planning and immunization. All prescription medicines in the basic health insurance medicine list—including chemical and Chinese traditional medicines—were priced by the NDRC; provincial pricing departments were responsible for setting the prices of nonprescription (over-the-counter, OTC) medicines in the basic health insurance medicine list. Prices of medicines excluded from government-set price lists were set by the market.

From October 2000 to April 2007, the central government adjusted drug prices nineteen times, with an average 21 percent reduction; as a result, pharmaceutical firms received 46.8 billion yuan less than they would have otherwise (see the appendix to chapter 12) (NDRC 2005). Based on such strong government action, we might assume continued intervention in the future.

How Pricing Policy Affects Drug Costs

Several recent studies have compared China's drug prices to those of other countries. One study, commissioned by the government, examined the prices of fifteen hundred drugs in sixteen countries. According to data provided by Intercontinental Marketing Services (IMS), China's drug prices are generally lower than those of the United States, United Kingdom, Japan, Canada, India, and South Korea. In contrast, a different study focusing on essential medicines found China's brand-name drug prices to be higher than international reference prices (defined as the median prices charged by nonprofit suppliers to low- and middle-income countries). Meanwhile, public-sector generic drug prices were generally similar to the benchmark. This latter study was based on a 2004 survey in Shandong Province, which employed methods developed by the World Health Organization (WHO) and Health Action International (HAI) (Sun 2005; Mendis et al. 2007).

It is uncertain whether these two report findings accurately reflect China's drug pricing status since they use different methods, comparator countries, drugs, and pricing samples. Moreover, because of the problem of combined prescribing and dispensing (*yi yao yang yi*), drug prices are inextricably linked to the prices of other health-care services in China.

Reducing administrative prices appears to have little effect on pharmaceutical spending growth. For example, controlling retail drug prices is not an effective way to contain hospital drug expenditures, according to a detailed study of two public hospitals (Meng et al. 2005).

Moreover, low prices have contributed to shortages of select medicines according to a recent NDRC report that surveyed 114 hospitals in 10 provinces as well as 3 large manufacturing firms (NDRC and Peking University Joint Research Group 2008).

Irrational Use of Medicine and the Behavior of Health-care Providers

The WHO has called attention to the irrational use of medicines worldwide (WHO 2002). In China the problem is closely linked with the incentive system for health-care providers.

The government has officially permitted hospitals to charge a 15 percent markup for drugs. But some evidence suggests that the actual markup of medicines in government hospitals in 2005 was much higher, at about 42 percent (Chinese Pharmacy Administration Association 2006). These markups stem, in part, from the regulation of other medical prices in China and the phenomenon of combined prescribing and dispensing. One detailed study using cost-accounting methods found that cost-recovery rates of official fees for health-care services in China were very low (16 percent for hospital registration, 25 percent for hospital bed and board, 30 percent for basic surgical operations, and 40 percent for general examinations and treatments). Fees were higher than costs for only 4 percent of assessed services (Liu et al. 2000; Meng et al. 2000; Eggleston et al. 2008). Moreover, government appropriations only provided an average of 8.2 percent of hospital revenue in 2003 (China National Health Economics Institute 2006). Hospitals therefore rely on pharmaceutical sales for a large share of their revenue.

Hospitals account for roughly four-fifths of all retail pharmaceutical sales. One study of seven public hospitals at the county level and higher found that only 29 percent of outpatients filled their prescriptions in retail drugstores rather than at the treatment hospital's pharmacy (Zhang 2003). Patients prefer hospital pharmacies over retail drugstores for several reasons: convenience, physician recommendation, nonstandardized prescriptions, and greater assurance of pharmaceutical quality. Therefore, hospitals have considerable market power in dispensing drugs and can encourage their physicians to overprescribe, since hospitals usually employ physicians at relatively low baseline salaries but with bonuses linked to profits (Liu and Mills 2003).

Such strong incentives have been blamed for exacerbating the inappropriate use of medicine in China. A project studying a sample of township health centers and village clinics in Chongqing and Gansu provinces determined that less than 2 percent of prescriptions were consistent with best practices, given the clinical indication (Zhang and Zhang 2000). In Henan, antibiotics constituted 70 percent of prescriptions in village clinics and town health centers. Another study found that 98 percent of outpatients with a common cold were prescribed antibiotics (Zhan et al. 1998). One study has estimated that approximately half of antibiotic prescriptions in China were medically unnecessary and implicated in more than one million children becoming deaf or suffering neurological disorders (Cheng 2005). Such prescribing patterns contribute to the global problem of antimicrobial resistance.

Policy Recommendations

China's health system reform has reached a critical stage; eight sets of new health reform proposals are being discussed hotly among the different stakeholders. Pharmaceutical reform is one of the key components of overall health-care reform, and China's pharmaceutical pricing strategy is to be changed once again. According to recent reports, the NDRC plans to regulate the prices of all prescribed medicines. The production cost of manufacturers will not be the only evidence used when setting medicine prices,[3] and the 15 percent markup for public hospitals will be abolished gradually. The impact of these possible policies is not clear but at least one point is: the government plans to strengthen its regulation of drug prices and to explore more scientific pricing methods.

Our analysis points to some specific recommendations for pharmaceutical policy reform. First, drug pricing changes should be implemented in conjunction with other health system reforms, especially those of public hospital financing, health insurance, and medicine distribution. Only changing profit incentives can fundamentally correct the problem of joined drug prescribing and dispensing practices. It is necessary to regulate the distribution system to truly reduce the markups along the distribution chain. Meanwhile, the capacity of health insurance payers to control physician prescription behavior should be further strengthened by changing the payment methods from fee-for-service to other alternatives such as capitation and case-based payment.

Second, the drug pricing method should be changed to abolish production cost pricing. Instead, reference pricing could be used to set the prices of generic medicines, using as reference, prices of other developing countries or international reference prices. For domestic and imported innovative medicines, prices can be set based on the results of pharmaceutical economic evaluation such as cost-effectiveness analysis.

Finally, the Chinese government should establish a regular and dynamic monitoring and evaluation mechanism for pharmaceuticals. Since most medicines in China are generics and the essential medicine system has not yet been set up, it is necessary to select some basic essential medicines from the WHO-recommended EML to monitor availability and price in both urban and rural areas.

Notes

[1] Numbers correct as of end of March 2006. See http://www.chinadataonline. org.

[2] This section and that on appropriateness draw from Sun et al. 2008. Also, see Chen and Wang 2002.

[3] http://www.chinapharm.com.cn/html/hyyw/1138176125218.html.

References

Chen, B., and H. Wang. 2002. China's pharmaceutical industry: Competitive features, marketing conditions and development strategy. *China Pharmacy* 13 (5): 260–62.

Cheng, W. 2005. The analysis of the characteristics and defects of China's pharmaceutical price system. *Shanghai Pharmaceuticals* 26 (12): 533–35.

China National Health Economics Institute. 2006. *China National Health Accounts report 2006.* Beijing: Ministry of Health.

Chinese Pharmacy Administration Association. 2006. *Changing the mechanism of hospitals supported by drug sales and guiding the healthy development of the medical and pharmaceutical industry with a scientific outlook of development.* Beijing: Chinese Pharmacy Administration Association.

Eggleston, Karen, Li Ling, Meng Qingyue, Magnus Lindelow, and Adam Wagstaff. 2008. Health service delivery in China: A literature review. *Health Economics* 17 (2): 149–65.

Jiang, D., and J. Zhang. 2006. The consideration of the development of GMP in China. *Chinese Pharmaceutical Management* 20 (4): 44–47.

Liang, Y. 2005. Drug representatives disclose the rebates related to the high drug prices. *Xi'an Medical Information* 4 (10): 4–6.

Liu, X., Y. Liu, and N. Chen. 2000. The Chinese experience of hospital price regulation. *Health Policy and Planning* 15 (2): 57–163.

Liu, X., and A. Mills. 2003. The influence of bonus payments to doctors on hospital revenue: Results of a quasi-experimental study. *Applied Health Economics and Health Policy* 2 (2): 91–98.

S. Mendis, K. Fukino, A. Cameron, R. Laing, A. Filipe, Jr., O. Khatib, J. Leowski, and M. Ewen. 2007. The availability and affordability of selected essential medicines for chronic diseases in six low- and middle-income countries. *Bulletin of the World Health Organization* 85 (4): 279–88.

Meng, Q., 2000. Rationalizing the health-care price system: Problems, causes, and adjustment. *Chinese Health Economics* 21 (5): 31–34.

Meng, Q., G. Cheng, L. Silver, X. Sun, C. Rehnberg. 2005. The impact of China's retail drug price control policy on hospital expenditures: A case study in two Shandong hospitals. *Health Policy and Planning* 20 (3): 185–96.

Ministry of Health (Statistic Information Centre). 2006. *Statistic bulletin of China's health development.*

National Development and Reform Commission. 2005. *Rule on drug comparative pricing.* http://www.pharmtec.org.cn/allpage/newsAll/content1.asp?id=1201000038.

National Development and Reform Commission and Peking University Joint Research Group. 2008. Research on the problem of shortages of inexpensive medicines. http://www.ndrc.gov.cn/zjgx/t20080408_203047.htm.

NDRC. *See* National Development and Reform Commission.

State Food and Drug Administration South Pharmaceutical Economic Institute. 2007. The competition of the top-100 pharmaceutical industries is challenging. *Medicine Economic News* (August 10), Guangzhou.

———. 2007. The competition of the top-100 pharmaceutical industries is challenging. The guideline comments for the Eleventh Development Plan of Pharmaceutical Industries, NDRC.

Sun, Q. October 2005. *A survey of medicine prices, availability, affordability and price components in Shandong Province, China.*

Sun, Q., M. Santoro, Q. Meng, C. Liu, and K. Eggleston. 2008. Pharmaceutical policy in China. *Health Affairs* (July) 27 (4): 1042–1050.

Wang, Q., and Qiu, J. 2006. Discussion and research on medicine price reform in China. *China Pharmacy* 17 (22): 1684–87.

Wang, Y. 2006. Price competition in the Chinese pharmaceutical market. *International Journal of Health Care Finance and Economics* 6 (2): 119–29.

WHO. *See* World Health Organization.

World Health Organization. 2002. Report: Promoting rational use of medicines: Core components. WHO/EDM/2002.3.

Zhao, Y., Y. Chen, and Q. Wan. 2006. Result on China National Health Accounts estimation for the year of 2004 and analysis of health-care financing. *Chinese Health Economics* 25 (3): 5–9.

Zhan S. K., S. L. Tang, Y. D. Guo, and G. Bloom. 1998. Drug prescribing in rural health facilities in China: Implications for service quality and cost. *Tropical Doctor* 28 (1): 42–48.

Zhang, L. 2003. Analysis of reasons for revenue loss and discussion of countermeasures for general hospital pharmacies. *Chinese Hospital Management* 23 (9): 45–47.

Zhang, N., and L. Zhang. 2000. The utilization of drugs in rural area and essential medicine policy in China. Chinese Rural Health Service Administration 20 (11): 43–45.

Zhang, Y. 2005. The current situation and future of the pharmaceutical distribution system in China. *Economic Theory and Management* 3 (1): 34–38.

PHARMACEUTICAL PRICING IN CHINA

Yanfen Huang and Yiyong Yang[1]

Along with market-oriented reforms of the health sector beginning in the early 1980s, China has experienced soaring pharmaceutical expenses and increasing difficulty providing access to medical services. In 2005 pharmaceuticals accounted for 44.19 percent of China's total expenditure on health, the highest percentage in the world (Hu 2007). Drug expenditure per capita increased from 36.59 yuan in 1990 to 316.78 yuan in 2005—an annual growth rate of 15.48 percent. These phenomena raise several questions: Why is China's pharmaceutical spending so high? How does the Chinese government regulate pharmaceutical prices? Has the government's pharmaceutical price regulation policy played a role in mitigating the increase of pharmaceutical expenditures? Are there problems with this policy, and if so, how can they be solved? Finding answers to such questions is the objective of this chapter.

While numerous studies in Chinese address China's pharmaceutical price regulation policy (most recently, Zhu 2007; Yu, Yu, and Tian 2007; Huang and Yang 2007), only a small number of English works deal with this topic. Meng et al. (2005) assess the impact of China's retail drug price control policy on hospital expenditures through a case study of two Shandong hospitals. Tian (2006) examines three aspects of the "drug price paradox": "pharmaceutical firms in collusion with hospitals" via pharmaceutical sales representatives; the "bundling of medical treatment and drugs," or even "super-bundling" in hospitals; and the evident government failure in pharmaceutical regulation. Wang (2005, 2006) focuses on the strategies of price competition in the Chinese pharmaceutical market. The weakness of these English works lies in their microanalytical focus on China's pharmaceutical price regulation policy and relative neglect of the larger factors that affect it.

This chapter fills the gap, presenting a detailed analysis of China's pharmaceutical price regulation, mainly from a macro-perspective. Having reviewed many policy documents of the National Development and Reform Commission (NDRC),[2] the government pricing agency, we provide an overview of China's pharmaceutical pricing over several decades. We then introduce the framework of China's pharmaceutical pricing regulation policy. After assessing the effects of the policy, we examine its problems and conclude with suggestions for further reform.

China's Pharmaceutical Pricing Policy: An Overview

As in other centralized economies, the prices of almost all Chinese commodities, including pharmaceuticals, were set by the government prior to the economic reforms of 1978. The government strictly controlled not only pharmaceutical approval, production, and distribution but also pharmaceutical pricing at every stage of the process including ex-factory, wholesale, and retail prices (Meng et al. 2005; Zhu 2007).

China's market-oriented reforms eventually included its pricing system, but not that of drugs until 1990. Before then, China's price reforms had achieved great success, deregulating by varying degrees the prices of 90 percent of commodities—including farm products, consumer goods, and the means of production. With such successes behind it, the Chinese government decided to reform pharmaceutical pricing in a market-oriented way. In 1990 the central government began to loosen its grip on pharmaceutical pricing, delegating this task to the price regulatory departments of the governments of provinces, autonomous regions, and municipalities directly under the central government. Subsequently, prices of pharmaceuticals skyrocketed, which led to high and abnormal prices and widespread concern (Zhu 2007).

Since 1996 the central government has again tightened its control of pharmaceutical prices through a series of laws and regulations. The former State Planning Commission (SPC)[3] formulated the Provisional Regulation for the Drug Price Administration (Policy Document no. 1590) in 1996, Supplementary Rules on Provisional Regulation for the Drug Price Administration (Policy Document no. 199) in 1997, and Notice on Improving Pharmaceutical Pricing Policy and Strengthening Pharmaceutical Price Administration (Policy Document no. 2196) in 1998. The so-called *three-systems reforms* were started in 1998 to coordinate the reforms of (1) the medical insurance system for staff members and workers in cities and towns, (2) the management system of medical institutions, and (3) the pharmaceutical production and distribution system. These reforms were expanded in 2000. The former SPC promulgated Guidelines for Reforming the Drug Price Administration (Policy Document no. 961) in July 2000 and Measures for the Government-Regulated Prices of Drugs (Policy Document no. 2142) in November 2000. These policy documents stipulated that the government should set the prices of some important pharmaceuticals, while drug manufacturers, wholesalers, and retailers were free to set the prices of other, less important drugs. These policy documents constitute the basic framework of pharmaceutical price regulation in China.

How China Regulates Pharmaceutical Prices

Based on the principle of combining macroeconomic control and market adjustment, pharmaceutical price regulation includes government-regulated[4] and market-determined prices. The government pricing agencies are the NDRC and its lower-level commissions or the price-managing departments in every province, autonomous region, and municipality.[5] These agencies regulate the prices of drugs listed in the *National Drug Catalog of Basic Medical Insurance and Worker Injury Insurance* and a few other special pharmaceutical products not listed in the catalog (including anesthetic drugs, psychoactive drugs, prevention and immunity drugs, contraceptives, and so on, which are produced and provided according to the government plan). The prices of other drugs are determined by the market. After being revised several times, the newest version of the catalog, released in 2004, includes more than 2,400 drugs, which account for 80 percent market share but only 20 percent of the total quantity of drugs sold in China (Zhu 2007).

For the drugs falling under government regulation, the NDRC stipulates maximum pharmaceutical retail prices (the final price charged to health-care users). In setting prices, the NDRC considers production costs as well as other factors such as supply and demand, therapeutic value, prices of similar drugs, and the desire to encourage research and development (R&D). Drug manufacturers can apply for "separate pricing" if any of their drugs satisfy the following conditions: (1) belong to the list of drugs for which the government sets prices; (2) are more effective or safer than similar drugs, or can shorten the period of treatment and reduce patients' expenditures significantly; and (3) have prices not suitable to be set according to the general price ratios indicated in the sixth item of the *Measures for the Government-Regulated Prices of Drugs.* The NDRC examines these applications for "separate pricing" on a case-by-case basis and, if the application is approved, sets the drug's maximum retail price accordingly.

To promote reasonable ex-factory and wholesale pharmaceutical prices through competition among drug manufacturers, wholesalers, and retailers, centralized medication bidding began in 1999 as a complementary reform. The appendix provides more detail about pharmaceutical pricing regulations, including the respective jurisdictions of national and provincial pricing agencies and the specific pricing formulas for ex-factory, wholesale, and retail prices of drugs produced domestically or imported.

The Limited Effectiveness of Price Regulations

Outcomes in three areas demonstrate the limited effectiveness of China's pharmaceutical price regulation policies: the failure of the government to reduce patients' pharmaceutical costs, the extremely high share of China's total health expenditure spent on pharmaceuticals, and overly high costs in the retail chain of regulated pharmaceutical prices

To reduce the burden on patients of high pharmaceutical expenditures, the NDRC has reduced the prices of pharmaceuticals up to twenty-four times by varying degrees since 1997 (see detailed description in appendix table 12.A), adjusting the prices of 87 percent of the drugs listed in the catalog of drugs priced by the central government. But these price-reducing measures have not solved the problem of high pharmaceutical expenses paid by patients. Soon after the NDRC issued the documents reducing prices, many drugs listed in the documents disappeared from hospital pharmacies and appeared in slightly modified forms as "new drugs" with similar therapeutic effects as the originals but at prices that were several times—sometimes more than ten times—higher (chapter 13, Zhang and Liu, in this volume; Zhu 2007; Yu, Yu, and Tian 2007); usually the only differences were dosage forms, specifications, and packaging. Some pharmaceutical manufacturers stopped producing the drugs listed in the price-reducing documents.

High Pharmaceutical Expenditures Have Not Been Effectively Controlled

Although the central government strengthened pharmaceutical price regulation in 1996, pharmaceutical expenditures have not been reduced. As shown in table 12.1, the average proportion of China's gross domestic product (GDP) spent on pharmaceuticals in the period 1996–2005 (2.16 percent) was higher than that spent in the period 1990–1995 (2.08 percent). Moreover, in the period 1990–2005, the percentage of total health expenditures spent on pharmaceuticals remained over 40 percent, which is much higher than the 17 percent average among the countries of the Organisation for Economic Co-operation and Development in 2005 (OECD 2007). Increased consumption and overpricing of pharmaceuticals are the major factors pushing up pharmaceutical expenditures and thus overall heath expenditures in recent years (Huang 2005). The growth in pharmaceutical expenditures raises concerns regarding the affordability of China's expanding health insurance coverage.

The High Proportion of Expenses in the Retail Chain of Regulated Drug Prices

A drug's retail price is the final price charged to patients. It includes costs from the production, wholesale, and retail links in the distribution chain. In China, retail markups make up an extremely high proportion of retail prices. According to Zhu (2007), the drug ex-factory price represents only 10 to 50 percent of the retail price, and markups for wholesalers account for another 3 to 20 percent. But profit margins for hospitals and brokerage fees paid to doctors and hospital administrators absorb 30 to 70 percent of drug retail prices. Table 12.2 shows, for example, that the markups in the retail chain account for 66 percent of the retail price of Omeprazole capsules, a much higher proportion of the price than for wholesalers (20 percent) and manufacturers (14 percent).

Why is China's pharmaceutical price regulation ineffective? Several problems follow.

1. *China's pharmaceutical price regulation is not integrated with the national essential medicine system.* The World Health Organization (WHO) defines essential medicines as those that satisfy the priority health-care

needs of the population. Essential medicines should be available within the context of functioning health systems at all times, in adequate amounts, in the appropriate dosage forms, with assured quality, and at a price the individual and the community can afford.[6] Essential medicines lists (EMLs) also guide the procurement and supply of medicines in the public sector and schemes that reimburse medicine costs, medicine donations, and local medicine production.

Table 12.1 Pharmaceutical Expenditures in China, 1990–2005

Year	1990	1991	1992	1993	1994	1995	1996	1997
Pharmaceutical spending as percentage of gross domestic product (GDP)	2.24	2.26	2.22	1.95	1.91	1.92	1.99	2.02
Pharmaceutical spending as a percentage of total expenditures on health	48.61	49.59	49.73	45.94	47.56	48.81	47.97	46.88
Year	1998	1999	2000	2001	2002	2003	2004	2005
Pharmaceutical spending as percentage of GDP	2.11	2.22	2.23	2.10	2.22	2.14	2.27	2.26
Pharmaceutical spending as a percentage of total expenditures on health	46.87	45.91	45.40	43.83	45.32	44.06	44.76	44.19

Source: China National Health Economics Institute 2006.

As mentioned above, China's list of government-regulated drugs is based on the *National Drug Catalog of Basic Medical Insurance and Worker Injury Insurance*, released in 2004. But while the national EML was released in 1996, there is still a lack of policies for essential medicines' production, distribution, usage, and related fiscal and tax policies. Moreover, the EML is not linked to clinical usage and compulsory enforcement. Therefore, when the government released documents listing reduced (select) pharmaceutical prices, manufacturers, wholesalers, and hospitals easily escaped from the regulations by changing dosage forms, specifications, and packaging types—and by charging higher prices for the resulting "new" drugs. Without the EML, the pharmaceutical price regulation cannot be effective.

2. *China's pharmaceutical price regulation is restricted by the fact that medical care services are supported by selling drugs and the monopoly position of hospitals in the drug retailing process.* Since the launch of the market-oriented reforms of 1978, government and social spending on health care and public health has declined. This situation can be demonstrated by total health spending, which is made up of three parts: government health appropriations, social health expenditure,[7] and out-of-pocket (OOP) health payments. From 1978 to 2005, government health appropriations—as a share of total spending—decreased from 32.16 percent to 17.93 percent; the share of social health expenditure fell from 47.41 to 29.87 percent; and the share of OOP payments increased from 20.43 percent to 52.21 percent (see figure 12.1).

Table 12.2 The Price Chain of Omeprazole Capsules (%)

Retail price composition	%
Markups in the retail chain (hospitals)	66
Profit margin for hospitals	30
Brokerage paid to doctors	30
Brokerage paid to hospital administrators	4
Expense for bidding	2
Markups in the wholesale chain	20
Cost of sales promotion (mainly paid to medicine deputies)	4
Profit margin for drug wholesalers	7
Profit margin for drug agents	5
Tax	4
Total expense of production chain (ex-factory price)	14
Production cost	6
Sales expense	1
Management cost	2
Cost of R&D	2
Profit of pharmaceutical manufacturers	2
Tax	1

Source: Yu, Yu, and Tian 2007.

Figure 12.1 Structure of China's Total Expenditure on Health According to Financing Sources, Using China's Definitions

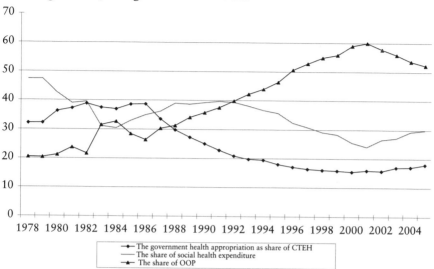

Source: China National Health Economics Institute 2006.
Note: CTEH = China's total expenditure on health; OOP = out-of-pocket payments.

Using the WHO definition,[8] the same pattern can be seen. As shown in table 12.3, in the period 1996–2005, the share of general government expenditure on health (GGEH) fell from 46.59 percent to 38.77 percent and the share of private expenditure on health increased from 53.41 percent to 61.23 percent. Compared with other countries, China's GGEH share is relatively low. Table 12.4 shows that in the year 2000, China's GGEH share (38.28 percent) was remarkably lower than the world average, the average of high-income countries, and the average of middle-income countries. It was almost exactly that of the average of lower-middle-income countries.

Because of a shortage of government funding in China's health sector, public hospitals are required to cover their own costs. Unfortunately, the prices for medical services are strictly controlled by the government, resulting in policy-induced deficits in all public hospitals.[9] To compensate for these losses, public hospitals are authorized to receive 15 percent commission for drug retailing. This mechanism is an incentive to health-care providers to administer more expensive drugs in larger quantities than might be necessary—in order to generate higher profits—a system that has come to be known as "medical care services supported by selling drugs" (*yi yao yang yi*). Table 12.5 shows that fiscal subsidies were less than 10 percent of the total revenue of China's general hospitals in the period 1999–2006, while drug revenue accounted for more than 40 percent of total revenue.

Table 12.3 Structure of Total Health Spending by Financing Source, Using WHO Definitions

	1996	1997	1998	1999	2000	2001	2002	2003	2004	2005
% of GGEH	46.59	44.24	41.81	40.89	38.28	35.57	35.83	36.23	37.97	38.77
% of PEH	53.41	55.76	58.19	59.11	61.72	64.43	64.17	63.77	62.03	61.23

Source: China National Health Economics Institute 2006.
Note: GGEH = general government expenditure on health; PEH = private expenditure on health.

Table 12.4 GGEH as a Percent of CTEH in Different Types of Countries, 2000

	World	High-income countries	Middle-income countries	Lower-middle-income countries	Low-income countries
Average percent of GGEH in CTEH	58.1	58.8	50.8	38.3	25.6

Source: World Bank 2003.

Table 12.5 Shares of Fiscal Subsidies and Drug-Dispensing Revenue in the Total Revenue of China's General Hospitals

	1999 (%)	2000 (%)	2001 (%)	2002 (%)	2003 (%)	2004 (%)	2005 (%)	2006 (%)
Fiscal subsidies	6.81	6.30	7.11	7.35	7.49	6.22	5.98	6.39
Drug-dispensing revenue	46.79	46.28	45.30	43.50	43.68	40.02	42.75	41.52

Source: Ministry of Health 2007.

Moreover, public hospitals have been able to extend their monopoly position over the provision of health-care services to the retail of prescription drugs. Since prescription drugs account for more than 80 percent of the total volume of pharmaceutical retail sales, public hospitals actually control the retail sales for most drugs, with market power bordering on monopoly vis-à-vis suppliers on the one hand and patients on the other. Public hospitals' market power is such that many pharmaceutical manufacturers and wholesalers have lost their bargaining power. Because it is hospital physicians—not patients—who choose which drugs to prescribe and in what quantities, they can substitute profitable for unprofitable drugs and can prescribe excessive quantities to earn more profits. Patients have little scope for "voting with their feet" or bargaining with public hospitals; as a result, supplier-induced overconsumption is considered to be an enormous problem.

3. *China lacks third-party purchasers that can effectively complement pharmaceutical price regulation.* In developed countries, medical insurance institutions play a very important role as third-party purchasers in pharmaceutical price regulation. Not only do they share drug expenses with patients, but they pay for the medical services of insured beneficiaries and supervise health-care providers. The mechanism of third-party purchasing can impel medical institutions to control expenses and improve their service quality. But China's medical insurance system is still in its infancy. Because so few people have medical insurance, the insurance funds are small; benefits are therefore limited, and patients still pay a large share of medical bills out of pocket. As a result, medical insurance institutions as third-party purchasers are limited in their ability to monitor medical providers. Moreover, China's medical insurance funds mostly reimburse providers on a fee-for-service basis according to submitted claims; this type of payment system is not effective for cost control.

4. *Problems in government drug-pricing methods.* Currently, China regulates pharmaceutical prices on a cost-plus basis, but this pricing method does not reflect patient demand or therapeutic effectiveness. Moreover, information asymmetry between government and pharmaceutical firms makes it difficult to ensure the authenticity and accuracy of cost accounting. It is possible for manufacturers and wholesalers to exaggerate costs and thereby raise pharmaceutical prices.

The current policy allowing new and special drugs to be priced separately is problematic. As mentioned above, although the pharmaceutical price regulation system was intended to encourage pharmaceutical manufacturers to invest in R&D, loopholes in the process have made it easy for pharmaceutical manufacturers and wholesalers to change unprofitable drugs into "new" drugs, driving pharmaceutical prices up and thereby circumventing pharmaceutical regulation.

Suggestions for Improvement

To improve China's pharmaceutical price regulation policy, the following reforms should be considered.

1. *Set up a national essential medicines system to provide a sound basis for pharmaceutical price regulation.* This is necessary for meeting the health-care needs of the population. To ensure supplies of effective and inexpensive drugs and provide a sound basis for pharmaceutical price regulation, the system should cover several related policies, including the choice of national essential medicines; the production, procurement, distribution, and pricing of the medicines; and the monitoring of their use and quality. A more detailed and comprehensive pharmaceutical price regulation system based on the essential medicines system should be set up to solve the problem of overpriced drugs.

2. *Increase government funding of China's health sector and separate pharmacies from hospitals.* The system of combined prescribing and dispensing is one of the chief causes of high pharmaceutical expenditures in China. Therefore, a series of measures should be implemented to eliminate this system. First, the governments of provinces, autonomous regions, and municipalities should increase budgetary appropriations for China's health sector and contribute a greater share of total health expenditures. Second, medical service prices should be raised to reflect the value of doctors' professional services. Third, to prevent hospitals from benefiting from drug sales, hospitals should be separated from dispensaries and drug prescribing split from dispensing. The separation of pharmacies from hospitals is also an important measure to weaken hospitals' monopoly position in drug retailing. All of these measures need to be done in conjunction with government fiscal reforms, medical provider reforms, and reforms of the pharmaceutical distribution system.

3. *Accelerate the development of China's medical insurance system, thereby strengthening the role of third-party purchasers.* China should encourage the development of the medical insurance system—including basic medical insurance for staff and workers in cities and towns, the new cooperative medical scheme in rural areas, and commercial insurance—and thereby promote the development of third-party purchasers as a check and balance on health-care providers. Compared to patients, medical insurance organizations as third-party purchasers have an advantage in gathering market information and applying professional knowledge, thus influencing the market more effectively. On the one hand, they share drug expenses with patients, and on the other, they check and supervise pharmaceutical

production, distribution, and use. In serving both functions, strong medical insurance organizations would promote a pharmaceutical market with a sound structure and ordered competition, weakening the monopoly position of health-care providers and enhancing the effectiveness of pharmaceutical price regulation.

4. *Improve governmental drug-pricing regulation.* The value of pharmaceuticals depends not only on their production costs but also on their value in treatment—including safety, convenience, affordability, and so on. The government should consider these factors when regulating prices. The methods of pharmacoeconomics, such as cost-effectiveness analysis, should be used in governmental drug pricing. For separately priced drugs, the government should set up a comprehensive index system that reflects each drug's quality and treatment effects, and strictly review all new drug applications to prevent firms from using the policy to raise drug prices by changing dosage forms, specifications, and packaging. As the role of third-party purchasers is strengthened, reference pricing could be used to encourage hospitals and patients to choose cheaper and unpatented drugs to help control pharmaceutical expenditures.[10]

To summarize, improving China's pharmaceutical price regulation policy is contingent on reforming health-care delivery, pharmaceutical distribution, and medical insurance. The government needs to coordinate all these reforms.

Appendix

Details of China's Pharmaceutical Price Regulations

Kinds of drugs regulated by the NDRC

(1) Western medicines that are in the prescription drugs list in the *National Drug Catalog of Basic Medical Insurance and Worker Injury Insurance*, 2004 edition (hereinafter referred to as the *Catalog*)

(2) Chinese traditional patent drugs that belong to the prescription drugs listed in the *Catalog*

(3) Anesthetic drugs not listed in the *Catalog* (including drugs managed as anesthetics), and first-class psychiatric drugs, contraceptives, and planned immunization drugs, which are produced and bought according to the government's mandatory plan and the drugs on patent

(4) All kinds of blood products not listed in the *Catalog* (referred to as plasma protein goods)

Kinds of drugs regulated by the governments at the province level (including autonomous regions and province-level municipalities)

(1) The over-the-counter (OTC)[11] drugs in the *Catalog* and the drugs listed by the localities' social medical insurance programs

(2) Anesthetic drugs and first-class psychiatric drugs

(3) Hospital-made medical preparations, ethnic drugs, and the Chinese herbal medicines listed in the *Catalog* according to the local situation

Forms of pricing

(1) The NDRC fixes the ex-factory prices, or port prices, for some drugs, including anesthetics listed in the *Catalog*, first-class psychiatric drugs, contraceptives, and planned immunization drugs

(2) The NDRC sets guiding prices for the other drugs listed in the *Catalog* in the form of maximum retail prices. The provincial governments set maximum retail prices for those drugs falling under their jurisdiction

(3) Policy allows separate pricing for some new and special drugs (see discussion in the main text)

Government pricing principles for drugs

When pricing pharmaceuticals, the government should take into account the state's macro, industrial, and public health policies. Specifically, the following principles should be adhered to:

(1) Ensure the drug producer can make up reasonable production costs and turn a reasonable profit. Government drug pricing needs general consideration of drug production costs, profit margins, and the prices of other drugs in the same class—or their substitutes. If necessary, the prices of the same drugs in international markets should also be taken into account. In principle, government drug pricing is based on the social average production cost, but the prices of oversupplied drugs are based on the social advanced production cost in which the total social drug demand could be satisfied.

(2) Take market factors into consideration. The reasonable drug price should be based on the actual relationship between demand and supply in the drug market.

(3) Reflect differences in the quality of drugs and their curative effects.

(4) Assign reasonably similar prices to the same kind of drugs produced in the same conditions, taking into account different kinds of dosage forms, specifications, and packaging types based on the effective component per unit.

(5) Encourage the R&D of new drugs. It is necessary in government drug pricing to differentiate between good manufacturing practice (GMP) drugs and non-GMP drugs, brand drugs and generic drugs, new high-quality brand drugs, and general drugs. Higher quality justifies a higher price.

Government pricing formulas

At present, Chinese governments generally use cost-plus pricing for drugs. In November 2000, the former State Development Planning Commission promulgated Measures for the Government-Regulated Prices of Drugs, which specifies the government pricing formula as follows:

(1) The retail price of domestic and imported drugs consists of the ex-factory price and the distribution margin. The manufacturer's ex-factory price (including tax) consists of production costs, period expenses,[12] profit, and tax. The retail price of imported drugs consists of the port price and the distribution margin. The port price (including tax) consists of cost, insurance, and freight (CIF); port charges (including customs clearance fee, inspection fee, drug testing fee, transportation fee, storage expense, and so on); and tax. The distribution margin consists of period expenses of wholesalers and retailers, profit, and tax.

The computational formulas for drug retail and ex-factory prices are as follows:

Drug retail price = ex-factory price including tax (port price including tax) × (1 + distribution margin rate)[13]

Ex-factory price including tax = (production cost + period expense) ÷ (1 − sales profit margin rate) × (1 + value-added tax [VAT])

The computational formula for port prices (including tax) of imported drugs is:

Port price including tax = CIF × (1 + tariff rate) × (1 + VAT) + port charges

Differentiated rates of drug sales cost (the ratio of drug sales cost to sales revenue) and the sales profit margin rate (the ratio of drug sales profit to sales revenue) should be introduced on the basis of the degree of innovation of the specific drug. Table 12.A shows the maximum rates of drug sales costs and the maximum sales profit margin rates for all kinds of drugs.

Appendix Table 12.A The Maximum Rates of Drug Sales Cost and the Maximum Sales Profit Margin Rates

Maximum rate of drug sales cost %		Maximum sales profit margin rate %	
The first class of new drug	30	The first class of new drug	45
The second class of new drug	20	The second class of new drug	25
The third class of new drug	18	The third class of new drug	18
The fourth class of new drug	15	The fourth class of new drug	15
The fifth class of new drug	12	The fifth class of new drug	12
General drug	10	General drug	10

Source: Measures for Government-Regulated Prices of Drugs.

(2) The retail prices of medicinal drugs prepared in hospitals shall be set in accordance with the principles of "cost compensation" and "marginal profit." The retail price consists of production cost and a maximum 5 percent markup. The computational formula is as follows:

Retail price = production cost × [1 + maximum 5 percent markup (profit-to-cost ratio)]

The ratio of Chinese medicine wastages in hospital pharmaceutical preparations is limited to no more than 20 percent and those of other medicines are limited to no more than 5 percent. When reselling pharmaceutical preparations, hospitals should set retail prices as the purchase price plus a maximum 5 percent markup.

(a) Ex-factory prices of "prepared slices of Chinese crude drugs" are equal to their wholesale prices. The computational formula is as follows:

(b) *Ex-factory price including tax (wholesale price including tax) = [original drug's purchasing price / (1 − attrition rate) + supplementary material expenses + other expenses] × (1 + rate of cost-profit) × (1 + VAT)*

In this formula, the attrition rate and other expense standards are determined by the NDRC based on the concrete situation of the manufacturers, and the rate of profit is 5 percent. The computational formula for retail prices of "prepared slices of Chinese crude drugs" is as follows:

Retail price = ex-factory price including tax × (1 + distribution margin rate)

Appendix Table 12.B Pharmaceutical Price Reduction by the NDRC since 1997

No.	Issuing time	Drug types subject to price reduction	Average percentage of price reduction (%)	Amount of money subject to price reduction (million yuan)
1	1997.1	47	15	200
2	1998.4	38	10	150
3	1999.4	21	20	200
4	1999.6	150	5	80
5	1999.8	2	15	12
6	2000.1	12	10	34
7	2000.6	9	15	120
8	2000.1	21	20	180
9	2001.4	69	20	200
10	2001.7	49	15	40
11	2001.12	383	20	300
12	2002.12	3	–	–
13	2003.3	199	15	200
14	2004.5	267	14	150
15	2004.6	107	–	–
16	2004.7	24	30	350
17	2005.1	22	40	400
18	2006.6	67	23	230
19	2006.8	99	30	430
20	2006.11	32	14.5	130
21	2007.1	354	20	700
22	2007.3	278	15	500
23	2007.4	188	–	160
24	2007.5	260	19	500

Source: Relevant policy documents.

Notes

[1] This research was supported by the National Natural Science Foundation of China (NSFC) under Grant 70673109.

[2] The NDRC is a macroeconomic management agency under the State Council of China, which studies and formulates policies for economic and social development, maintains a balance of economic aggregates, and guides overall economic system restructuring.

[3] The NDRC's predecessor was the State Planning Commission (SPC), which was founded in 1952. The SPC was renamed the State Development Planning Commission (SDPC) in 1998. After merging with the State Council Office for Restructuring the Economic System and part of the State Economic and Trade Commission in 2003, the SDPC was restructured into the NDRC.

[4] The forms of government price regulation include government-fixed prices (with the government setting commodities' prices directly) and government-directed prices (with the government setting a maximum price, a price floating range, and so on).

[5] Prior to 1990, the State Price Bureau was responsible for government pricing. After China's price reform achieved great success in the 1990s, the bureau was folded into the SPC, the predecessor of the NDRC. But some provinces, autonomous regions, and municipalities retained it as the price-managing department.

[6] See http://www.who.int/medicines/services/essmedicines_def/en/.

[7] The term *social health expenditure* includes social health insurance expenditures, extrabudgetary investment in the health sector, investments by private physician practices, and so on. According to the definition by the WHO, social health insurance expenditures belong to "general government expenditure on health;" extrabudgetary investment in the health sector and investment by private doctor practices can be included in "private expenditure on health."

[8] According to the definition of the WHO, general government expenditure on health is the sum of outlays by government entities to purchase health-care goods and services. It comprises the outlays on health by all levels of government and social-security agencies, as well as direct expenditure by parastatals and public firms. Private health expenditure is defined as the sum of expenditures on health by private insurance schemes and private social insurance schemes, private enterprises, nonprofit institutions, and households.

[9] To assure ordinary Chinese affordable access to medical services, the Chinese government set the prices for many general medical services lower than their costs. Although the government wants to raise prices for medical services, it is difficult in the current environment amid inflationary pressures (the consumer price index, CPI, increased 4.8 percent in 2007).

[10] Under reference pricing, social insurance institutions and insurance agents sort drugs into groups (by their primary active ingredients, pharmacological

functions, and therapeutic effectiveness) and then assign a price to each group. Pharmaceutical firms can set their own prices, but the insurers pay the reference price for the drug. If patients want the more expensive brands, they can pay the difference between the price and the lower reimbursement. If they use the cheaper ones, the saved money can be divided pro rata by patients, hospitals, and the paying institutions (insurers).

[11] The OTC drugs are judged according to the list of OTC, which is released by the State Food and Drug Administration.

[12] The term *period expense* refers to expense that cannot be inventoried; it is charged against sales revenue in the period in which the revenue is earned (also called period costs). Period expenses include sales, general, and administrative expenses.

[13] The drug circulation margin rate is checked and ratified by the NDRC based on the normal operating expenses and profits of drug wholesalers and retailers. The drug circulation margin rate is differenced: the higher rate is applied to drugs with a lower price, while the lower rate is applied to drugs with a higher price.

References

China National Health Economics Institute. 2006. *China national health accounts report*. Beijing, China.

Hu, Shanlian. 2007. Establishing national essential medicine policy [in Chinese]. *The Development Report on China's Health* 3. Social Sciences Academic Press, Beijing, China.

Huang, Yanfen. 2005. Study of China's health-care price [in Chinese]. *Price Theory and Practice* (May): 19–20.

Huang, Yanfen, and Xinbo Yang. 2007. Comparative study on the medicine price regulation between China's Mainland and Taiwan [in Chinese]. *Research on Economics and Management* (September): 18–21.

Meng, Qingyue, Gang Cheng, Lynn Silver, Xiaojie Sun, Clas Rehnberg, and Goeran Tomson. May 2005. The impact of China's retail drug price control policy on hospital expenditures: A case study in two Shandong hospitals. *Health Policy Planning* 20 (3): 185–96.

Ministry of Health. 2007. *China health statistical yearbook 2007*. Peking Union Medical College Press.

OECD. *See* Organisation of Economic Co-operation and Development.

Organisation of Economic Co-operation and Development. 2007. *Health at a glance 2007: OECD indicators*. http://www.oecd.org/document/11/0,334 3,en_2649_33929_16502667_1_1_1_37407,00.html.

Tian, Kun. 2006. Drug price paradox in China and its economics analysis. *Proceedings of the Third International Conference on Innovation and Management* 2:1867–73. Wuhan Univ. of Science and Technology Press.

Wang, Richard. Y. 2005. The Chinese pharmaceutical market at the crossroads: Pro-competition solutions to improve access, quality and affordability. *Applied Health Economy and Health Policy* 4 (3): 147–51.

———. 2006. Price competition in the Chinese pharmaceutical market. *International Journal of Health Care Finance and Economics* 6 (2): 119–29.

World Bank. 2003. *World Development Report 2004: Making services work for poor people.* Washington, D.C.: World Bank.

WHO. *See* World Health Organization.

World Health Organization. 2007. *The World Health Report 2006.* Geneva: WHO.

Yu, Li, Zou Yu, and Kun Tian. 2007. The paradox of high-priced China's medicine [in Chinese]. *Research on Economics and Management* (September): 10–17.

Zhu, Hengpeng. 2007. Abuses in the health-care system and distortions in pharmaceutical pricing [in Chinese]. *Social Science in China* (April): 89–103.

CHALLENGES TO CHINA'S PHARMACEUTICAL INDUSTRY AND THEIR POLICY IMPLICATIONS

Wei Wilson Zhang and Xue Liu

As China's pharmaceutical industry continues to expand, both regulatory agencies and the general public are paying increasing attention to its strategic development and impact on China's health-care system. In this chapter, we identify the challenges to ensuring pharmaceutical quality, cost control, and access in China. We also review industry behavior and incentives that may require future regulatory reform. Our premise is that international regulatory objectives (quality and safety, expenditure control, and access) are an appropriate lens through which to analyze China's pharmaceutical industry (Maynard 2003). China's experiences may also provide lessons for pharmaceutical industry development and regulation in other parts of the world.

Pharmaceutical Sector Development

During the past two decades, China's pharmaceutical sector has grown at an annual rate of 17.3 percent—almost twice as fast as its gross domestic product (GDP) (China International Capital Corporation 2008; see figure 13.1). The drug industry's share of GDP increased from 1.16 percent in 1999 to 2.26 percent in 2006 (figure 13.2). In 2007 its total production output reached 693 billion yuan, a 25.1 percent increase from 2006; its profit reached 63 billion yuan, a 55.6 percent increase from 2006 (Beijing TiangaoLaifu Consulting 2007).

China was home to the production branches and bases of 5,957 pharmaceutical companies at the end of 2006 (data from China Pharmaceutical Industry Association, CPIA 2007). About 25 percent of these were joint-venture and foreign companies; their market share was 27 percent nationally and about 60 percent in large cities (CPIA 2007). A close look at the hospital sector, which represents about 80 percent of pharmaceutical sales in China, shows that the market share of foreign and joint-venture pharmaceutical products made in China increased nearly 10 percent from 2002 to 2006; meanwhile, domestic products declined slightly and imported products decreased dramatically from 20 to 13 percent (figure 13.3). Foreign and joint-venture companies made rapid advances in the competitive market, increasing hospital sales by nearly 25 percent between 2002 and 2006.

Development of Pharmaceutical Regulation

The regulatory structure, once decentralized and fragmented, has become more centralized and integrated. One milestone was the 1998 establishment of China's State Food and Drug Administration (State FDA) as a vertically integrated and independent ministry-level regulatory agency. In 2008 the State FDA became part of the Ministry of Health in hopes of better coordinating regulatory activities.

Drug safety has been the top regulatory priority. About sixty laws and regulations have been implemented since 1985, covering drug approval, manufacture, distribution, promotion, and postmarket surveillance. But with over 5,000 manufacturers with different capacities, the pursuit of high quality often conflicts with local protectionism. Even unqualified manufacturers may receive good management practice (GMP) certification—a system-wide threat to drug safety.

Another potential threat is China's historically ambiguous definition of new drugs. From 1984 to 2005, a new drug was defined as "a drug not domestically manufactured" or an existing drug "with changed dosage, means of administration, and indications." As a consequence, many generic drugs varied only their dosage and administration to be approved as "new," then took advantage of the drug pricing policy to raise their cost. This loophole has seriously discouraged the research and development (R&D) of truly innovative drugs. Instead, competition has centered on the new drug approval process, resulting in corruption and public outrage. New drugs were redefined in 2005 as "drugs not sold in China," referring to new molecules or drugs only marketed in other countries. But, because drugs with new dosage amounts and means of administration are still regulated as "new drugs," the loophole remains.

In the next section, we share the results of a recent study we conducted in one of China's large metropolitan areas. Specifically, we focus on the challenges to quality, safety, cost control, and access found in the four segments of the pharmaceutical industry: R&D, manufacturing, distribution, and product utilization. We then analyze pharmaceutical industry incentives and behavior in light of current industrial and regulatory structures. Finally, we discuss the policy implications of our findings.

Challenges to Quality, Safety, Cost, and Access

Pharmaceutical safety and quality are of prime importance worldwide. Of the State FDA's three policy objectives (quality, expenditure control, and access), drug quality is the primary one—and the focus of the greatest public concern. Inadequacies in R&D, production, distribution, and utilization can often threaten the production of quality medications and the safety of their usage.

R&D

China's domestic pharmaceutical industry has focused on generic drugs, and lacks the R&D capacity for patentable drugs. Figure 13.4 illustrates the market share of different drug categories; the last two columns illustrate that patented drugs sold in China (currently and formerly on patent) come primarily from foreign-owned firms and imports.

Figure 13.1 Pharmaceutical Industry Output versus GDP Growth, 1995–2006

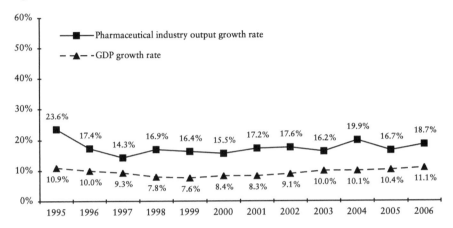

Source: Adapted from China International Capital Corporation 2008.

A poorly developed generic drug, if approved, can be a potential hazard. Most of the industry insiders we interviewed shared concerns about the bioequivalence of some generic drugs; reasons ranged from inadequate technical standards during drug development to inadequate capacity for reviewing the documentation during the drug-approval process—and rare cases of data manipulation during clinical trials. Industry-wide quality problems were said to arise from different standards for different drugs or drug groups and—perhaps most important—expired (or nonexistent) national standards for some drug ingredients.

Production

The number of pharmaceutical manufacturers in China decreased by 28 percent between 2000 and 2006, thanks to GMP implementation and recent mergers and acquisitions. The remaining 5,000 or so manufacturers face tremendous downward cost pressure, which can sometimes result in quality problems.

China has tried to implement strict GMP standards in its pharmaceutical industry, consistent with international best practices, but some operating manufacturers are still not in compliance. Our study identified cases of incomplete, untimely, or "selective" accreditation; failure to update accreditation following equipment changes; noncompliance with accreditation protocols; and data manipulation. In a few companies, GMP software incompatibility and staff incompetence were additional obstacles. Problems in production processes, often resulting from unsophisticated R&D, also contributed to inconsistent product quality.

In an effort to raise production standards, in 2006 China's regulatory agencies revoked the pharmaceutical production licenses of 5 manufacturers and the GMP certificates of 128 others, suspended the production of 168 manufacturers, and issued warnings to 2,025. This campaign identified production problems among about 50 percent of pharmaceutical manufacturers and pushed to enhance compliance with national standards.

Table 13.1 Pharmaceutical Industry Output, Sales and Profits, 2001–2004 and 2007 (billion yuan)

	2001	2002	2003	2004	2007
Production output	218.8	251.7	311.5	349.9	692.8
Sale	205.5	234.2	291.0	333.6	639.3
Profit	17.9	21.5	28.6	30.4	63.0

Source: 2001–2004 data from China Pharmaceutical Yearbooks; 2007 data from Beijing TiangaoLaifu Consulting, *China Pharmaceutical Report 2007*.

Figure 13.2 Share of Pharmaceutical Industry Output in China's GDP, 2001–2007

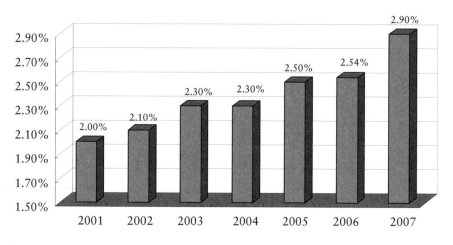

Source: National Statistics Bureau, China.

226

Distribution

We conducted a case study of drug distribution in one of China's largest metropolitan areas. The city under study has 3,864 pharmaceutical wholesale and retail companies, 165 of which exceed 20 million yuan in annual sales. Under such fierce competition and subsequent cost pressures, poor compliance with the generalized system of preferences (GSP) is the top threat to product quality in the pharmaceutical supply chain. One study found high rates of noncompliance in the areas of quality standards, staff training, drug storage, transfer tracking, and managerial capacity building in 2005 (Wu Zhengshan 2007). The supply chain in rural areas is an even bigger challenge, with chaotic and underregulated supply channels to many rural clinics and drugstores.

Figure 13.3 Shares of Domestic, Joint-venture, and Foreign-owned Pharmaceutical Firms and Imported Pharmaceutical Products in Hospital Drug Sales, 2002–2006

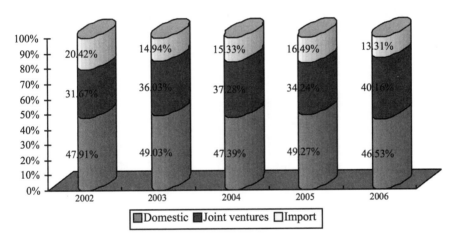

Source: Adapted from Huatai Securities 2008.

Transportation is often the weakest link in pharmaceutical distribution. The interviewed industry executives expressed concern about lack of oversight over transportation equipment requirements and record inspections, confirming recent findings that transportation problems are a threat to product safety (Wei 2006). These results are not surprising in the light of the low transportation fees from upstream companies, which leave downstream transportation entities few alternatives to cutting corners for profit. Finally (and even though we lack comparative data), the interviewed executives complained that the relatively long supply chain in China, which often involves more distribution enterprises than needed, makes it very difficult to trace and identify the source of the quality problems. These multiple links in the supply chain make it difficult to assure accountability and may even encourage opportunistic behavior in production and distribution (Xiao Guo 2007).

Appropriate Drug Utilization

Multiple factors confound efforts to assure the appropriate utilization of drugs in China (see Sun and Meng 2008). First, frequent changes to commercial name and dosage inevitably make it more difficult for physicians to prescribe accurately, which increases the likelihood of medication errors. In the city under study, out of 449 types of medications (chemical names) that were included in the centralized bidding process in 2004–2006, only 44 percent remained unchanged in name and dosage (figure 13.4). The high rate of change stems from a lack of industry standards and pressures to maintain market share in the face of centralized bidding.

Figure 13.4 Market Shares of Different Drug Categories in a Large Chinese City, 2004–2006

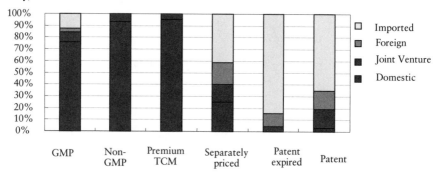

Source: A pharmaceutical bidding agency, 2004–2006.
Note: TCM = traditional Chinese medicine.

Second, direct-to-consumer advertising (DTCA) threatens drug safety when it conveys false or inaccurate information. While China only allows DTCA for over-the-counter (OTC) drugs, a 2006 study of 11,563 newspaper drug advertisements found that 56 percent illegally promoted prescription drugs. Other violations included the unauthorized DTCA of OTC drugs (26 percent) and manipulation of advertisement contents (7 percent). A study of DTCA on forty Chinese television channels showed similar patterns, with 31 percent of advertisements promoting prescription drugs, 34 percent featuring unauthorized DTCA, and 6 percent using manipulated contents (State FDA 2006). DTCA remains a source of inaccurate consumer information and thus a continuing threat to drug safety, as was illustrated by the findings of our 2007 research on newspaper drug advertisements (see table 13.2).

Third, the marketing personnel of pharmaceutical companies often provide inaccurate product information to physicians, mainly about prescription drugs. These representatives may come from production or distribution enterprises, and there is little regulatory requirement on their credentials. Based on our field study, we estimate that the average physician in a large hospital receives one visit from a drug marketing representative every two to three days, and over 50 percent of the promotional materials shown contain inaccurate or false information. The dissemination of inaccurate information is a serious threat to safe drug use, especially since clinical guidelines and utilization reviews are still rare in China.

A final threat to safe drug use could be solved by developing a comprehensive system for the mandatory reporting of adverse drug reactions in China, which can speed the identification of serious drug safety hazards.

Table 13.2 Results from a Study of Over-the-Counter (OTC) Drug Advertisements in May 2007

Major violations	Frequency (%)
No warning of side effects	100
Different from approved draft	94
No false or expired approval	72
No OTC sign	64
Advertisements for prescription drugs	56

Source: Authors' analysis of drug advertisements in 13 major Chinese newspapers during the first week of May 2007.

Expenditure Control

Rapidly escalating expenditure on pharmaceuticals is a leading concern for both the Chinese government and public. Hospitals (of which 95 percent are public) generate about 50 percent of their revenues from the sales of pharmaceuticals. In such an environment, some pharmaceutical companies use kickbacks, direct bribery, and corporate sponsorship to boost their hospital sales, exacerbating the social and individual burden of drug expenditure. According to statistics from the Ministry of Commerce, pharmaceutical kickbacks total about 773 million yuan per year, equivalent to about 16 percent of taxes generated from the pharmaceutical sector (*People's Daily* 2005).

Although drug prices have declined, the quantity index (by volume of drug usage) continues to grow. In the city we studied, the quantity of antibiotics used increased 4.19 times between 2002 and 2005, while that of circulatory system drugs increased 9.19 times (with a Paasche index of 14.23). These rates far exceed what one might predict by changes in total population and disease incidence (Jing Wu 2007). Increases in utilization and overall drug expenditure do not appear as obvious to consumers as price increases, and China's regulatory agencies have implemented few measures to contain the growth of overall drug utilization and expenditure. In general, the pharmaceutical industry has tried to offset the loss from price controls by boosting the overall quantity of drug usage. Drug expenditure control remains one of the greatest challenges to China's health-care system.

Access

Price cutting and the implementation of a bidding system have forced some inexpensive yet essential drugs out of the market. While one government report pointed out that less than 5 percent of drugs were affected, the interviewed hospital executives and pharmacy directors expressed concern that the recent unavailability of some inexpensive drugs (many with a long production history from well-established manufacturers) has, to some extent, affected clinical practice in large hospitals. Moreover, under the current environment, pharmaceutical companies have little incentive to develop "orphan" drugs, which are pharmaceutical agents developed specifically to treat a rare medical condition. The conditions for which orphan drugs are developed are known as orphan diseases. With some pediatric drugs, the related issue of access remains unresolved.

Corporate Behavior and Incentives

Competition in the pharmaceutical industry involves development of new drugs and the sales of existing drugs (Morse 2003). Without strong R&D capacity, Chinese pharmaceutical companies tend to compete on drug sales rather than innovation. Figure 13.5 provides a framework for understanding the motives and outcomes driving the Chinese pharmaceutical industry. Companies usually pursue profit by reducing production costs and increasing sales revenue. We therefore categorize corporate behaviors into those that promote lower costs, higher prices, or increased sales volume (see figure 13.6).

Controlling Production Costs

One of the primary reasons to be concerned about aggressive cost cutting in pharmaceutical firms is that inappropriate measures can lead to defective products, threatening patient safety.

On average, local companies spend only about 2 percent of sales on R&D (IMS Health 2004). As the quality of generic drugs is not obvious to physicians and patients, local companies may settle for the minimum quality standard (or fall below it) instead of bioequivalence. This, combined with lax regulation and occasional data manipulation, enables pharmaceutical companies to obtain State FDA approval at relatively low cost. Moreover, as "me-too" drugs, generic products have seen their clinical safety and effectiveness demonstrated in the

Figure 13.5 Framework for Analyzing Corporate Behavior in China's Pharmaceutical Industry

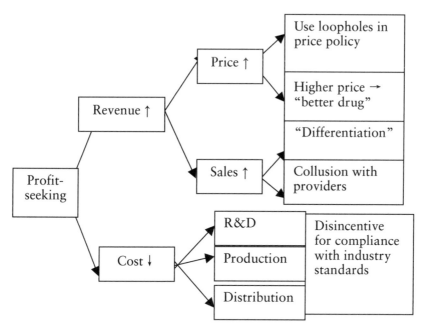

Source: Prepared by the authors.

clinical trials of their brand-name counterparts, which gives some generic manufacturers further incentive to cut corners on R&D.

Manufacturers have to strictly follow GMPs to produce reliable, high-quality drugs, and distribution entities have to do the same to guarantee effective storage and delivery. Inappropriate cost control over any of these links (such as inadequate production equipment or storage facilities) compromises drug quality and may help the entry of counterfeit drugs into the market.

Seeking Higher Prices

With the relative price inelasticity of many prescription drugs, a price increase can bring more profit to pharmaceutical companies. Moreover, consumers tend to link higher drug prices with better therapeutical effects, and may not view brand-name and generic versions of the same drug (or drugs) as interchangeable (Morse 2003). Thus, in addition to taking advantage of the existing loopholes in drug pricing policy, some Chinese pharmaceutical companies market their products as "superior" or "premium" drugs in the hope of securing a higher price. But instead of adopting technological innovation to improve the drugs,

231

some companies "innovate" by using a new commercial name for an existing product, or adding multiple dosage/name combinations, or aggressively marketing "new" drugs and withdrawing "old" products from the market.

Figure 13.6 Changes in Commercial Names and Drug Dosage Forms (from a sample of 449 drugs, 2004–2006)

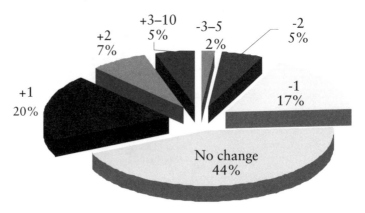

Source: A pharmaceutical bidding agency 2004–2006.
Notes: All 449 drugs (chemical names) were included in the bidding process of one pharmaceutical agency in 2004–2006.
+ refers to increase in commercial names, dosage, or both
– refers to decrease.

Increasing Sales Volume

One way to boost sales is to differentiate from existing drugs and mislead consumers into believing that a "new" drug has improved therapeutic effects. The past few years saw a growing number of new commercial names for the same drug, the same products with new dosage or package units, and aggressive marketing campaigns with inaccurate information.

Another technique, used more for prescription than OTC drug sales, is collusion with providers (hospitals and physicians). The standard 15 percent markup on pharmaceutical products dispensed by hospitals gives underfunded public hospitals strong incentive to sell more drugs. At the same time, pharmaceutical companies aggressively seek hospital sales by developing favorable relations with hospitals and physicians, resulting in widespread kickbacks. Such tactics have not only fueled escalating drug expenditures but, to some extent, encouraged the overuse and misuse of prescription drugs.

Because the development of new drugs is not the practical focus of market competition in China, competition has intensified over generic sales. The rising competitive pressure, coupled with an underdeveloped regulatory capacity and lack of clinical standards, has encouraged some pharmaceutical companies (mostly generic manufacturers) to focus on aggressive cost cutting and various underhanded tactics for raising prices and sales volumes.

Policy Implications

While industry structure often shapes firm behavior, we also need to consider how regulatory measures impact the industry. The evidence suggests that regulatory reform in China should focus on the direct and immediate supervision of corporate behaviors, along with a long-term policy focus on effective steps to change industry structure. The former should include tightening standards (especially for generic drugs); approving only bioequivalent drugs; adopting effective and proactive measures to enforce compliance with existing standards of production, distribution, and marketing; and closing policy loopholes that allow the superficial differentiation of drug products (Wang 2005). Quality and safety will and should remain the top priority. Instruments to consider include (1) reducing the number of manufacturers and intermediary companies along the supply chain and otherwise enhancing market consolidation and (2) encouraging the development of high-quality generic products and truly innovative brand-name drugs. As these changes unfold, the regulatory focus can gradually shift from catching the "bad guys" to promoting innovative products and R&D capacity. Given limited resources, however, it is more urgent to focus on assuring drug quality and safety; enforcing compliance with existing standards; and establishing an effective surveillance system to oversee the development, production, distribution, and marketing of pharmaceuticals in China.

References

Beijing TiangaoLaifu Consulting Firm. 2008. *China pharmaceutical report 2007.* http://www.reportbus.com/data/YYWS/YY/200803/data_80705.html.

China International Capital Corporation (CICC). 2008. *Pharmaceutical investment report.* Available for purchase from CICC.

China Pharmaceutical Industry Association. 2007. *Foreign and joint venture pharmaceutical companies in China.* http://www.bppa.org.cn.

CPIA. *See* China Pharmaceutical Industry Association.

Huatai Securities. 2008. *2008 pharmaceutical report.* Available for purchase from Huatai Securities.

Intercontinental Marketing Services (IMS) Health. May 2004. *IMS market prognosis, Asia 2004–2008.* London: IMS Health.

Xiao Guo, Li, and Xu Huawei. 2007. An analysis of Rx distribution abstract. *Journal of Changsha University of Science & Technology (Social Science)* 22 (1): 92–94.

Maynard, Alan, and Karen Bloor. 2003. Dilemmas in regulation of the market for pharmaceuticals. *Health Affairs* 22 (3): 31–41.

Morse, Howard. 2003. Product market definition in the pharmaceutical industry. *Antitrust Law Journal* 2:637.

People's Daily. 2005. October 14.

State Food and Drug Administration. 2006. State FDA briefing on advertisement surveillance.

Wang, Y. Richard. 2005. The Chinese pharmaceutical market at the crossroads, pro-competition solutions to improve access, quality and affordability. *Applied Health Economics Health Policy* 4 (3): 147–51.

Wei, Hua, and Huang Chuanhua. 2006. Paying attention to quality management of drug transportation and improving quality assurance system. *Chinese Pharmaceutical Affairs* 20 (7): 390–91.

Wu, Zhengshan. 2007. The analysis of drug distributor's GSP attestation following check. *Strait Pharmaceutical Journal* 19 (4): 105–07.

CHINA'S UNDERDEVELOPED DRUG REGULATION REGIME: A THREAT TO GLOBAL SAFETY?

Michael A. Santoro and Caitlin M. Liu

In May 2007 Zheng Xiaoyu, the former chief of China's State Food and Drug Administration (State FDA), was sentenced to death for taking $850,000 in bribes to facilitate the approval of myriad new drugs, including some that contained substandard or counterfeit ingredients. News of Zheng's July 2007 execution shocked the world, and the moment marked a potential watershed in China's regulation of its pharmaceutical industry.

In recent years, adulterated and misbranded drugs manufactured in China have resulted in hundreds of known deaths and an untold number of injuries, presenting a major threat to public health and safety worldwide. The year before public outcry in the United States over toxic pet food that sickened or killed thousands of dogs and cats, dozens of people in China had already died and more than a thousand fallen ill—some suffering permanent disabilities such as brain damage—from tainted pharmaceuticals (York 2007; Barboza 2007c). In Haiti a toxic ingredient sold by a Chinese chemical company killed over a hundred children (Bogdanich, Hooker, and Lehren 2007). In Panama tainted cough medicine ended up killing more than one hundred people. Instead of glycerin (a nonactive fluid used in many drug formulations), the cough medicine had been made with diethylene glycol, a cheap, toxic, industrial-grade fluid more commonly used in antifreeze (Bogdanich and Hooker 2007). The motive for substituting ingredients was simple greed. Diethylene glycol costs less than half what glycerin does. In South Asia investigators traced a flood of fake antimalarial drugs, containing starch, to an illegal factory in Guangdong Province in China. The counterfeit medication threatened to undermine global public health efforts to fight a disease that kills more than a million people each year (Bogdanich and Hooker 2008).

Tainted pharmaceuticals are slipping into the United States, too, through loopholes and gaps in the international drug safety regime. According to U.S. Congressional estimates, the United States currently imports as much as 80 percent of the active pharmaceutical ingredients used to manufacture prescription drugs—but has the capacity to inspect only 7 percent of the *known* manufacturing plants in China and other nations every year.[1] This leaves the policing of the drug pipeline to the pharmaceutical companies themselves—and to Chinese authorities. However, as we describe in this chapter, China's oversight of drug manufacturing and safety—notwithstanding the get-tough message its top officials wanted to send by executing Zheng—remains spotty and structurally deficient. As a result, there is a significant risk that major human tragedies such as those suffered in Panama and Haiti could occur in other parts of the world. Indeed, within a year of Zheng's execution, more than 140 people died when treated with the blood thinner heparin, whose active pharmaceutical ingredient was contaminated during its production in China.[2]

Shortly after Zheng's execution, the Chinese government released a new set of drug registration rules and announced a $1.1 billion plan to upgrade inspection offices and beef up enforcement actions to improve drug and food safety (*PharmAsia News* 2007). Aside from trying to reassure the Chinese public, the State FDA reforms of 2007 were also meant to assuage global concerns about the safety of Chinese imports in the aftermath of a series of highly publicized incidents involving defective consumer products, such as tainted toothpaste and lead-contaminated toys. Instead of inspiring greater confidence in the safety of Chinese manufacturing, however, Zheng's hasty execution raises questions about whether China is willing and able to institute thorough bureaucratic and institutional reforms. This chapter analyzes the 2007 reforms, evaluates their efficacy in stemming the tide of unsafe drugs, and concludes that China's regulatory system—and current bilateral efforts between China and the United States—are inadequate. Finally, we propose the first of what we hope will become a series of global policy reforms to make the pharmaceutical supply chain more transparent, hold responsible parties accountable, and improve safety for patients everywhere.

Regulatory Reforms of 2007

As chief of the State FDA from 1998 to 2005, Zheng oversaw the approval of an estimated 150,000 new drugs.[3] After Zheng's execution in May 2007, in an astonishingly swift and broad series of actions, the State FDA announced it had suspended 6,441 drug registration applications, cancelled 578 drug license numbers, and revoked the production permission certificates of 5 drug manufacturers and 1,202 medical appliance companies (Chuanjiao 2007). Officials also promised to review all 170,000 drug licenses in the country (*Pharma Marketletter* 2007a) and launch a five-year plan to restore public confidence and improve drug safety (*Pharma Marketletter* 2007b). As is typical of most regulation in China, the post-Zheng reforms announced by the State FDA came out in a piecemeal fashion, over the course of several months, through selective leaks to the state-run media as well as the foreign press. The following are the major components of the 2007 reforms:

- *More rigorous State FDA checks to be made during the drug application process.* Previously, the State FDA merely relied on the word of the drug manufacturer and only sometimes checked samples sent in by the company. The reforms provide that the State FDA will in the future verify the information supplied by pharmaceutical companies for drug applications, including having agents conduct on-site checks and authenticate records and statistics from preclinical and clinical trials. State FDA agents also must verify that factories are using the same production techniques as stated on their applications (*China Pharmaceutical & Health Technologies Newswire* 2007b). Firms that submit phony documents will face stiffer fines and penalties. Companies that obtained approval fraudulently will not be permitted to submit another drug application to the State FDA for another three to five years (Shankland 2007).

- *Regular rotation of key State FDA officials.* To discourage officials from developing cozy personal relationships with the pharmaceutical companies they are supposed to oversee, the State FDA will now regularly rotate key personnel. This has been touted as a key reform to thwart bribery and corruption (*International Pharmaceutical Regulatory Monitor* 2007).
- *More quality control by companies.* The new State FDA rules require drug manufacturers to conduct quality checks and monitor for adverse reactions. When confronted by a product with safety issues, the company must also conduct an investigation (*China Pharmaceuticals & Health Technologies Newswire* 2007a).
- *A clearer protocol for drug recalls and incentives for removing the most dangerous drugs from the market more quickly.* In the past, when a dangerous or defective consumer product surfaced in the Chinese marketplace, poorly defined government and private-sector roles in the recall process made a quick response impossible. Under the new regulatory regime, relevant duties and legal obligations are more clearly spelled out. Upon discovering that a drug is hazardous to health, manufacturers are asked to immediately stop selling the product, inform the public, and issue a recall. The most harmful and potentially deadly pharmaceuticals are to be recalled within twenty-four hours, while products that cause "temporary health problems" are to be recalled within two days. If a recall is issued for more benign reasons, such as improper product packaging, manufacturers have three days to issue a recall.
- *A stricter innovation standard for approving new drugs.* In the past, questionably "new," often substandard, drugs flooded into the Chinese consumer market with the State FDA's blessing. In fact, pharmaceutical companies had only made minor modifications to existing formulations, such as changing the recommended dosage or altering an ingredient (*China Pharmaceuticals & Health Technologies Newswire* 2007b). Companies did this because of financial incentives; drugs categorized as new were not subject to the government's price

caps (Barboza 2007b). Under the new regulations, minimal changes to an existing drug are no longer to be accorded new drug status. To ensure that a new drug application is based on actual innovation rather than mere repackaging, the State FDA will require companies to declare the drug's patent status and show that the new formula does not infringe on other pharmaceutical patents, which the agency promised would be posted on a government-run Web site (Shankland 2007).

The Chinese government's get-tough stance produced some results. In the immediate aftermath of Zheng's capital punishment and the prosecution of his deputies, new drug applications slowed to a trickle. By June 2007 the State FDA had approved only fourteen new drugs and five generic drugs, and analysts predicted that the number would fall even lower in 2008, as new regulations took effect (*China Pharmaceuticals & Health Technologies Newswire* 2007b). Chinese regulatory tactics are now focusing more on increasing penalties for wrongdoers. In October 2007, for example, the China Fine Chemicals Materials and Intermediate Association (CFCMIA) announced 774 arrests over a 2-month period as part of a nationwide crackdown on the manufacture and distribution of tainted food and drugs (Barboza 2007a). But it is one thing to discourage drugs from coming onto the market through occasional crackdowns, arrests, and executions. It is quite another to set up adequate bureaucratic systems and safeguards that will assure the public a steady supply of safe and effective drugs. For China to achieve this kind of regulatory effectiveness, it will have to address some of the more endemic problems underneath the current regulatory disarray.

Even before the reforms went into effect, State FDA officials were backing away from some of the more ambitious accountability measures. "Because the people who buy medication are scattered across the country and are hard to keep track of, companies probably will face difficulties recovering their drugs," State FDA spokeswoman Yan Jiangying told *China Daily* (Juan 2007). Rather than requiring recalls, as the State FDA had proposed earlier, the rules it ended up promulgating, in the agency's own words, were "voluntary." The State FDA now promises to impose lower fines or possibly exempt companies from punishment if they cooperate with the recall guidelines. Failure to comply could result in fines up to three times the value of the problematic drug or license revocation (*Xinhua News Agency*, December 12, 2007). Considering the enormous logistical troubles and expense of carrying out a recall—it cost the toy giant Mattel $29 million to recall its lead-contaminated toys in 2007 (Palmeri 2007)—some manufacturers, especially smaller ones, may well decide that is is cheaper to face the sanctions than to comply with the drug recall rules under China's new regulatory regime.

Endemic Problems and Challenges of Drug Regulation

Drug regulation in China must be understood within the broader context of the evolving status of law in the reform era. Western scholars often note the various obstacles to a true rule of law in China. In his seminal book on the subject, Stanley B. Lubman (1999) compared the place of law in China to a "bird in a cage." Another Western legal scholar compared the development of the rule of law in China to Mao's "long march" (Peerenboom 2002).

A fundamental problem with the rule of law in China is that the judiciary system lacks independence from the government and specifically the Communist Party. Under the Chinese Constitution, the courts have no power to interpret the meaning and constitutionality of laws made by the legislature at any level of government.[4] Accordingly, the courts are treated as agencies on par with other government agencies, and judges show great deference to the decisions of entities such as the State FDA. The influence and control of the Communist Party over virtually every aspect the government and society—including information disseminated by the domestic press—is difficult to overstate.[5]

The lack of an independent judiciary is the root cause of other problems endemic to the Chinese legal and regulatory system. There is no clear demarcation of power among various governmental agencies and national, provincial, and local governments. Moreover, there is almost a complete lack of transparency in legal reform and policymaking. In most cases, regulations become effective without prior public comment. Even after regulations become effective, they are often not even published and made available for review by affected parties.

The aforementioned shortcomings of the Chinese legal and regulatory system are evident in China's nascent drug regulation system. The national Ministry of Health (MOH) began provisional administration of new drugs in 1962. Regulations and quality-control measures evolved over much of the 1980s and 1990s. Power over approving new drug applications became vested in the State FDA, a national agency that also reviews clinical trials and oversees manufacturing inspections (Yin 2006). But the agency lacks jurisdiction over the production and distribution of chemicals that often wind up as ingredients in pharmaceuticals in Western countries—a huge legal loophole that essentially leaves many manufacturers of drug ingredients unregulated by even minimal standards (Bogdanich, Hooker, and Lehren 2007). Ostensibly, responsibility for product safety, including pharmaceuticals, is also vested in the General Administration of Quality Supervision, Inspection, and Quarantine (AQSIQ) and the CFCMIA. But as a result of undefined jurisdiction, there is often an oversight gap, and responsibility for drug safety falls by the wayside. For example, in October 2007, ABC News investigators contacted representatives of all three Chinese agencies to determine which one had jurisdiction over the case of the tainted cough medicine that resulted in more than one hundred deaths in Panama and the scandal involving counterfeit infant formula that caused thirteen babies in China's Anhui Province to die from malnutrition. None of the three agencies would acknowledge having regulatory power over either of the incidents.[6]

An additional challenge faced by Chinese regulators is the sheer number of companies they must oversee. China's pharmaceutical manufacturers and distributors are extremely dispersed. Thanks to the State FDA's efforts to close down plants that fail to meet good manufacturing practice (GMP) standards, China has about 3,500 pharmaceutical companies, down from more than 5,000 in 2004. But this is still an enormous number, making regulatory oversight and on-site inspections difficult.[7] Before there can be effective regulation, the Chinese pharmaceutical industry may have to undergo further consolidation.

Perhaps the most significant regulatory gap concerns chemical companies, which are neither certified nor inspected by Chinese drug regulators. Chemical companies from China supply active ingredients and, in some cases, finished products to drug manufacturers and distributors worldwide. There are approximately 80,000 chemical companies in China, and no one knows how many of these are involved in manufacturing drug ingredients. The State FDA has the power to inspect and certify any firm that identifies itself as a drug manufacturer. But if a chemical company does not apply for certification, the State FDA does not have the power to prevent that company from selling active pharmaceutical ingredients and finished drug products domestically or internationally. As a result, drug ingredients from unregulated Chinese chemical factories flow unchecked into international markets. Yan Jianling, who is also deputy director of policy and regulation at the State FDA, commented that such sales were "definitely against the law," but hastened to add that the agency has "never investigated a chemical company. We don't have jurisdiction." Chinese manufacturers understand this perfectly well. As Bian Jingya, an export manager for Changzhou Wejia Chemical Company, put it: "If you want to be regulated, they will regulate you. If you don't want to be regulated, they [won't]" (Bogdanich, Hooker, and Lehren 2007).

One has to wonder what is at the bottom of this regulatory abyss. As a formal legal matter, the State FDA's lack of jurisdiction over the manufacturing of active pharmaceutical ingredients by chemical companies can be easily fixed. Simply give the State FDA power to regulate the manufacturing and sale of all drugs and active pharmaceutical ingredients, right? Given the technical ease of fixing the jurisdiction problems, there are several ways to explain why a solution is not yet in place. First, it might just be the underdeveloped nature of China's legal and regulatory system. Pharmaceutical manufacturing is not the only area where there are overlapping jurisdictions and regulatory gaps. It will simply take time to coordinate efforts across national, provincial, and local levels. A second explanation is less benign. Does it benefit the Chinese government to allow these chemical companies unfettered access to global markets? Many of these chemical companies are partially owned by local and provincial governments or by individual Communist Party members. There seems to be little political enthusiasm—or will—to close obvious and significant regulatory loopholes even though reasonable solutions are within reach. Corruption continues to be a major problem in China, particularly at the provincial and local level, where companies can exert significant influence to block regulatory initiatives emanating from Beijing. As a traditional Chinese saying puts it: "The mountains are high and the emperor is far away." One Western pharmaceutical executive with long-standing experience in China cites this kind of corruption-based regional protectionism as a major impediment to the development of an effective drug-regulation system.[8]

Another impediment to the development of an adequate and responsive drug safety regime in China is the absence of an effective and independent court system where civil litigants, whether Chinese citizens or victims from overseas, can obtain monetary compensation for injuries they or their loved ones suffer from defectively manufactured products. A more robust civil law system that would allow the aggrieved to recover meaningful compensatory and punitive damages—whether for wrongful death, disabilities, or pain and suffering—from Chinese manufacturers and distributors would likely go a long way toward drug safety by creating stronger financial incentives for companies to think twice before unleashing something dangerous into the domestic or international marketplace. While laws and lawsuits to mitigate negligence and product defects are an integral part of safeguarding consumers, even in the United States and other developed nations, they are highly imperfect for compensating victims of dangerous pharmaceuticals, especially if the source of the problem comes from abroad.[9] In China the courts offer even less hope. Innocent consumers who have been victimized by unsafe and adulterated products have limited legal recourse to exact compensation from responsible companies. Only time will tell whether China's civil laws and court system will evolve to offer greater protections and remedies to injured consumers domestically and abroad (see Conk 2005).

The U.S.-China Drug Safety Pact

The world cannot wait for China to modernize its drug safety and efficacy regulation. That no other nations have been hit like Haiti and Panama is as much a matter of luck as of vigilance (Mathews and Burton 2008). But despite its legal and regulatory safety nets, the United States has its own loopholes when it comes to China. A U.S. Government Accounting Office study found that in 2007, the U.S. Food and Drug Administration (U.S. FDA) inspected just 13 of China's 714 known drug makers. By law each U.S. plant must be inspected every 2 years, but there is no such requirement for any foreign plants. Struggling with limited budgets and manpower, U.S. FDA Commissioner Andrew von Eschenbach admitted in Congressional testimony that the agency "must revamp our entire strategy, our entire game plan" (Mathews 2007).

With the Chinese and U.S. regulatory loopholes in mind, Henry Paulson, United States Treasury, and Wu Yi, China's top trade negotiator, met in Beijing in December 2007 and negotiated a broad product safety agreement that also covered pharmaceuticals. The agreement requires Chinese producers of certain drugs to register with the Chinese government and obtain an export license before exporting to the United States. But the agreement only applies to ten specifically designated products, including a growth hormone (oseltamivir), an antiviral drug, and the antibiotic gentamicin sulphate. Pharmaceutical ingredients not specifically listed are not covered by the agreement (Leow and Zhang 2007).

The 2007 bilateral pact is, to say the least, woefully inadequate to safeguard the safety and integrity of the pipeline of pharmaceuticals from China to the United States. It represents a tacit admission that China is, at this moment in its history, technically and politically incapable of assuring the safety and efficacy of active pharmaceutical ingredients and all those drugs not on the list of ten. The agreement calls for extensive technical consultation between the U.S. FDA and China's State FDA in acknowledgment of China's lack of expertise in setting up and administering an effective regulatory regime to prevent unlicensed facilities from manufacturing unsafe or ineffective pharmaceutical ingredients and finished drugs. The agreement stops short, however, of denying access to U.S. markets to unlicensed producers of drug categories not specifically referenced. The agreement is a political and economic compromise that leaves the U.S. public open to significant health and safety risks. One can only hope that China will be able to move quickly to shore up its regulatory capacity because, for now, the United States has proven unwilling to pressure its largest trading partner into speeding up the process.[10]

Conclusion: Toward Assuring Safe and Effective Drugs in China and the World

In the wake of a highly limited and flawed bilateral trade pact, China's drug industry remains a significant danger to its own citizens and the rest of the world. In the United States and Europe, one bulwark against regulatory loopholes is the vigilance of reputable pharmaceutical manufacturers and distributors seeking to ensure supply chain integrity. But other companies are so concerned with profits and suppressing costs that they end up pressuring their Chinese suppliers into taking perilous shortcuts in the manufacturing process and substituting cheaper ingredients.[11] Ultimately, regardless of where the ingredients or finished products are manufactured, drug companies bear both legal and moral responsibility for the safety and efficacy of products sold in the United States. The more reputable companies will endeavor to do their own site visits and batch testing to assure drug quality. These companies have, moreover, a strong interest in assuring that inferior and possibly dangerous counterfeit drugs do not make it into the global marketplace.

But will every company be vigilant? Will some companies, motivated by cost savings and outright greed, consign the possibility of lawsuits, fines, and loss of corporate reputation to the realm of acceptable business risk? As an increasing proportion of the world's drugs are manufactured in China[12] and sold over the Internet, how long will it be before international tragedy strikes again? Certainly no one could say it was not foreseeable. In January 2008, Shanghai police began investigating a Shanghai company that manufactured leukemia drugs contaminated with vincristine sulfate, which paralyzed 200 Chinese patients. Officials at Hualian, a division of the Chinese drug giant Shanghai Pharmaceutical, tried to cover up the cause of the contamination—an attempt to save money by storing the leukemia drug in the same refrigerator as another, highly toxic, drug. That same company, Shanghai Hualian, which exports to dozens of countries, is the sole manufacturer of the RU-486 abortion pill, which is sold in the United States and produced by a plant located an hour's drive from the facility where the contaminated leukemia drug was manufactured (Hooker and Bogdanich 2008). In the same month, January 2008, Baxter International, a U.S.-based pharmaceutical company, halted production of the blood thinner heparin after 350 allergic reactions and the deaths of 4 U.S. citizens were traced to ingredients manufactured in a Chinese facility never inspected by the U.S. FDA (Burton et al. 2008). The death toll from tainted heparin has since climbed to more than 140 people.

While luck and the threat of lawsuits offer some measure of imperfect protection in the United States and Europe, the rest the world—particularly Latin America, South Asia, and Africa—have already experienced tragedy stemming from China's lax standards.[13] Indeed, China's own people have suffered the most from the safety crisis. The execution of the former State FDA chief Zheng Xiaoyu in 2007 was a showy response to appease the Chinese people, but unless it is matched by a rapid advance in the honesty and technical abilities of the State FDA, tragedy will continue to strike wherever Chinese drugs and drug ingredients are sold.

Whereas the supply chain in the United States and Europe relies for the most part, but not exclusively, on reputable and well-established companies, the supply chain to poor countries is a shadowy morass of transshipments and shell companies. As *New York Times* reporters Walt Bogdanich and Jake Hooker painstakingly uncovered in their investigation, the counterfeit glycerin that killed 138 Panamanians passed through three trading companies on three continents—not one of them tested for safety or efficacy. The certificate accompanying the shipment was repeatedly altered, eliminating the name of the manufacturer and the previous owner. The Panamanian government, which bought the counterfeit product and mixed it into the cough syrup that killed their own citizens, did not even know where the product came from or who made it. They had no way of knowing that the factory that manufactured and misbranded the diethylene glycol was not certified to make pharmaceutical products (Bogdanich and Hooker 2007).

Assurance of a safe drug supply is not something that only the rich nations of the world deserve. Had the Panamanian government known where the adulterated drugs were coming from, it surely would have refused shipment of

243

the counterfeit products. While it may seem utopian at this stage, a reliable global system tracking the production, quality, and distribution of drugs is something that the poor and the rich can achieve together. As Dr. Henk Bekedam, the World Health Organization (WHO) representative in Beijing, stated: "This is really a global problem, and it needs to be handled in a global way" (Bogdanich and Hooker 2007). A big step toward such a solution would be to develop a tamper-proof drug-labeling system, ensuring that no matter where a drug or pharmaceutical ingredient is sold in the world, its source of manufacture will be known. While this would not necessarily guarantee product purity or authenticity, it would discourage manufacturers from shenanigans they could no longer hide from consumers. In the event of serious problems with the product, the information would also allow regulators to quickly identify companies in the supply chain and hold the responsible parties accountable. The technology to do this is quickly emerging. The U.S. FDA, concerned about counterfeiting, has asked pharmaceutical companies to develop a barcode scanning system for drugs sold in the United States, but nationwide efforts have been repeatedly stymied by complaints about the complexity and costs of such a system. The U.S. FDA now says it will develop a national standardized identification numbering system for tracking drugs by March 2010 (Pollack 2008). In the meantime, China has announced its own plan to introduce a barcode system: a fourteen-digit number on all packaging that would indicate, among other information, the product's country of origin, manufacturer, and specification (*China Pharmaceuticals & Health Technologies Newswire* 2008). Common sense tells us that these efforts need not only to be expedited but also extended to all drugs sold throughout the world. Justice demands that every citizen of the world, wealthy or poor, should be able to know and trust the medicine that goes inside his or her body. If there is to be free trade of potentially dangerous drugs and ingredients on a global scale, then there must be a global system and standard of safety to accompany such commerce. Until such a global system to assure safety, efficacy, and accountability is implemented, the flow of chemicals from China will remain a grave threat to global health and safety.

Notes

[1] U.S. Congress, House of Representatives, Committee on Energy and Commerce Subcommittee on Oversight and Investigations 2008. For a different estimate based on another analysis, see the conclusion of this volume (by F. M. Scherer).

[2] From January 1, 2007, to May 31, 2008, there have been at least 149 deaths related to allergic reactions to heparin that were reported to the U.S. government (U.S. FDA 2008). Whether or not shoddy or fraudulent Chinese manufacturing was responsible for the heparin deaths remains a source of dispute between China and the United States at the time of writing. While the U.S. FDA concluded that a key active ingredient of the deadly heparin had been contaminated during

its manufacturing process in China and that the contamination had caused the fatal allergic reactions among U.S. patients, Chinese regulators maintained that the Chinese-made ingredient, though tainted, did not cause the deaths, *Inside US-China Trade* 8 (17) (April 23, 2008).

[3] 150,000 is a phenomenal number, considering that the U.S. FDA approves fewer than 150 each year (Magnier 2007).

[4] Lubman (1999) discusses all of these factors and more in some detail.

[5] For an overview of the CCP and Chinese politics, see Lieberthal (2003).

[6] "Are Chinese Drugs and Chemicals Safe?" posted on *World Newser* on October 31, 2007, http://blogs.abcnews.com/theworldnewser/2007/10/are-chinese-dru.html.

[7] In another sign of market fragmentation, the top ten Chinese pharmaceutical producers control only about 20 percent of the domestic market, while the top ten international drug companies account for nearly half of global pharmaceutical sales (*Drug Week* 2008).

[8] Confidential interview with authors, November 14, 2007.

[9] In the United State, the legal doctrine of strict liability—the law in most states—allows victims to collect damages from distributors or retailers of a defective product even if the companies had no knowledge or reason to know that the product or ingredient they were passing on to consumers was injurious. But many state courts have adopted a "negligence safe harbor" exception for prescription drugs, which sometimes creates extraordinarily higher hurdles for injured plaintiffs to collect monetary damages from pharmaceutical companies (Madden 2000). Some states—notably New Jersey, Michigan, Missouri, Mississippi, and Texas—have also enacted "innocent seller" statutes protecting distributors from strict liability, which means a patient in those states may have little or no recourse against U.S. importers. According to interviews with seasoned U.S. litigators, it is virtually impossible for overseas litigants to obtain damages from Chinese manufacturers because of the lack of transparency and efficacy of China's current legal system (Liu 2007).

[10] An interesting legal question is whether the United States can restrict all pharmaceuticals from China under the World Trade Organization (WTO) accession protocols, unless China can demonstrate that its regulatory regime is sufficient for ensuring a safe system (Trebilcock and Howse 2005).

[11] According to one top executive at a leading U.S. importer of Chinese-made pharmaceutical ingredients, foreign buyers who experience problems in Chinese factories often have only themselves to blame, as they insist on paying such a low price that suppliers end up taking shortcuts in quality control and substituting cheaper ingredients (Tremblay 2008: 15–20).

[12] The chief scientific officer at U.S. Pharmacopeia, a standards-setting authority for prescription and over-the-counter (OTC) drugs, estimates that three-quarters of the pharmaceutical ingredients consumed in the United States are produced in China. Since the heparin deaths scandal, some U.S. and European pharmaceutical company executives initially expressed concerns

about sourcing from Chinese manufacturers. But once they found out that it could cost 40 percent more to buy from suppliers in other countries, they backed down and continued doing business in China (Tremblay 2008).

[13] Recent research shows that in Asia, 32 percent of malaria drugs on the market failed quality tests (*Los Angeles Times*, June 30, 2008, A12).

References

Barboza, David. 2007a. 774 arrests in China over safety. *New York Times*, October 30: A1.

———. 2007b. A Chinese reformer betrays his cause, and pays. *New York Times*, July 13: A1.

———. 2007c. Ex-Chief of China food and drug unit sentenced to death for graft. *New York Times*, May 30: A7.

Bogdanich, Walt, and Jake Hooker. 2007. From China to Panama, a trail of poisoned medicine. *New York Times*, May 6: A1.

———. 2008. Battle against counterfeit drugs has new weapon: Pollen. *New York Times*, February 12: A10.

Bogdanich, Walt, Jake Hooker, and Andrew W. Lehren. 2007. Chinese chemicals flow unchecked onto world drug market. *New York Times*, October 31: A1.

Burton, Thomas M., Anna Wilde Mathews, Nicholas Zamiska, and Gordon Fairclough. 2008. Heparin probe finds U.S. tie to Chinese plant. *Wall Street Journal*, February 15: B1.

China Pharmaceuticals & Health Technologies Newswire. 2008. Companies welcoming bar codes as weapons in the fight against fake drugs. May 12.

———. 2007a. China unveils new drug recall system. September 20.

———. 2007b. SFDA gets tough on new drug registration. September 25.

Chuanjiao, Xie. 2007. New quality measures praised. *China Daily*, September 12. http://www.chinadaily.com.cn/cndy/2007-09/12/content_6098831.htm.

Conk, George W. December 2005. People's Republic of China civil code: Tort liability law. Fordham Law Legal Studies Research Paper 892432. http://papers.ssrn.com/sol3/papers.cfm?abstract_id=892432.

Drug Week. 2008. Research and markets: Currently China has about 3,500 drug companies, falling from more than 5,000 in 2004. April 4.

Hooker, Jake, and Walt Bogdanich. 2008. Tainted drugs linked to maker of abortion pill. *New York Times*, January 31: A1.

Inside US-China Trade. 2008. U.S., Chinese delegations disagree over cause of Heparin reactions. 8 (17). April 23.

International Pharmaceutical Regulatory Monitor. 2007. China issues revised drug registration rules. 35 (8), August 15.

Juan, Shan. 2007. Rapid recall system for dangerous drugs. *China Daily*, September 21.

Leow, Jason, and Jane Zhang. 2007. Product-safety pacts put greater burden on Beijing. *Wall Street Journal*, December 12: A13.

Lieberthal, Kenneth. 2003. *Governing China: From revolution though reform*, 2nd ed. New York: W.W. Norton.

Liu, Caitlin. 2007. The next big import: Lawsuits. *Conde Nast Portfolio.com*, August 2.

Los Angeles Times. 2008. Deadly deception. June 30: A12.

Lubman, Stanley B. 1999. *Bird in a cage: Legal reform in China after Mao.* Stanford, CA: Stanford Univ. Press.

Madden, Stuart M. 2000. The enduring paradox of products liability law relating to prescription pharmaceuticals. *Pace Law Review* 21: 313.

Magnier, Mark. 2007. Chinese bribes: Better to give than receive. *Los Angeles Times*, August 10: A1.

Mathews, Anna Wilde. 2007. FDA's scrutiny of drug makers abroad faulted. *The Wall Street Journal*, November 2.

Mathews, Anna Wilde, and Thomas M. Burton. 2008. China plant played rule in drug tied to 4 deaths. *The Wall Street Journal*, February 14: A1.

Palmeri, Christopher. 2007. What went wrong at Mattel. *Business Week Online*, August 15.

Peerenboom, Randall. 2002. *China's long march toward the rule of law.* Cambridge: Cambridge Univ. Press.

Pharma Marketletter. **2007a.** 170,000 drug licenses face China SFDA review. February 9.

Pharma Marketletter. 2007b. SFDA: "unsatisfactory" drug regulations in China. July 18.

PharmAsia News. 2007. SFDA sticks to familiar theme during second press conference: Food and drug safety dominates discussion. August 20.

Pollack, Andrew. 2008. California delays start of drug-tracking program. *New York Times*, March 26: A4.

Shankland, Ben. 2007. New drug registration rules set to encourage innovation in China. *Global Insight Daily Analysis*, July 19.

Trebilcock, Michael J., and Robert Howse. 2005. *The regulation of international trade*, 3rd ed. London and New York: Routledge, 202–31.

Tremblay, Jean-Francois. 2008. Sourcing from China. *Chemical & Engineering News*, May 19: 15–20.

U.S. Congress, House of Representatives, Committee on Energy and Commerce Subcommittee on Oversight and Investigations. 2008. *Hearing on the food and drug administration's foreign drug inspection program.* 110th Congress, 1st session, April 22.

U.S. Food and Drug Administration. 2008. Information on adverse event reports and Heparin. http://www.fda.gov/cder/drug/infopage/heparin/adverse_events.htm.

World Newser, The. http://blogs.abcnews.com/theworldnewser/2007/10/are-chinese-dru.html.

Xinhua News Agency. 2007. China issues new recall method, encouraging voluntary drug recalls. December 12.

Yin, Hongzhang. 2006. Regulations and procedures for new drug evaluation and approval in China. *Human Gene Therapy*, October: 970.

York, Geoffrey. 2007. The face of Chinese cost-cutting. *The Globe and Mail*, July 3.

CROSS-CUTTING THEMES

PRESCRIBING CULTURES

AYURVEDIC PHARMACEUTICAL PRODUCTS: GOVERNMENT POLICY, MARKETING RHETORIC, AND RATIONAL USE

Maarten Bode[1]

This chapter is part of a broader study on the making of Ayurvedic-branded health products and their marketing in India. In a chapter published in a Routledge volume on orthodox and heterodox medical forms, I analyzed the marketing rhetoric of large Ayurvedic manufacturers. A structural analysis of interviews and promotional materials uncovered three themes in the marketing of Ayurvedic products: tradition, modernity, and nature (Bode 2002). In an article published a few years later, I described and analyzed the making and selling of Ayurvedic brands and their popularity among the Indian urban educated middle class as devices for taking away the "toxics of westernisation" (Bode 2006). In this chapter, I discuss the Indian government's attempts to regulate the definition, production, and sale of Ayurvedic medicines. In the 1970s the Indian government and its Ministry of Health came to the conclusion that regulation was necessary because a growing Ayurvedic industry had substantially replaced the making of medicine by Ayurvedic physicians (*vaidyas*) themselves. Since then, government committees have overseen modern laboratory tests to validate the quality, purity, and potency of standardized Ayurvedic formulas.

The next section provides a brief introduction to Ayurvedic medicines and how they are important carriers of tradition. I then move on to government legislation and the diminishing role of the Ayurvedic physician due to the proliferation of over-the-counter (OTC) Ayurvedic medicines. Finally, I turn to the issue of the rational use of Ayurvedic medicines, including such important aspects as quality, nontoxicity, use, and effectiveness. I discuss the images and notions used by large Ayurvedic manufacturers to establish the worth of their medicines. The case of *chyawanprash*—India's most successful Ayurvedic medical product—serves as an example. Next, I ask how and to what extent the insights and methods of modern pharmacology can improve the rational use of Ayurvedic medicines. The chapter ends with some policy suggestions.

Ayurvedic Products and Their Legacy

Ayurveda is a rational tradition in which natural and moral symbols are used to define, negotiate, and treat illnesses. Images from nature play an important role in nosology, aetiology, and therapy. The therapeutic objectives of Ayurveda are, for example, ripening and expelling accumulated humors, fortifying the body's innate healing capacity, cleaning its channels, feeding and lubricating its tissues, and lifting blockages in the flow of humors and waste products, to mention just a few. Ayurveda's qualitative concepts link the physical body to other spheres of life, including psychology, social interaction, ecology, and myth. Somatic, psychological, existential, and soteriological categories such as hot, cold, dry, wet, *dehaprakriti* (natural constitution), *sattva* (pureness, mental peace), and *svasthya* (health, literally "being established in yourself"), to mention a few examples, are arranged according to Ayurvedic humoral logic. A sophisticated system of correspondence is used to code empirical knowledge of the physical world. Observations on somatic and mental ailments, the biological effects of herbs, and the results of therapeutic measures are interrelated and explained in Ayurvedic parlance. The results have been laid down in a large body of medical and pharmacological texts linking empirical observations with humoral notions. A vast corpus of texts compiled over a period of two thousand years deals with aetiology, nosology, and therapy. Ayurvedic canons mention roughly ten thousand medical formulas and two thousand ingredients and claim that the system offers a truly authentic and humane way of treating illness. Its practitioners and supporters say that Ayurveda is beyond the whims of modern science and commerce because it has retained the essence of illness aetiology:

> In the medical context, Ayurveda classifies diseases as being those caused by *vata*, *pitta* and *kapha*. Any disease can be understood in terms of how it affects the *doshas* singly or in combination. Such an approach is useful not only in disease of yore, but also new diseases of today and tomorrow. (Balasubramanian 2000)

Here it is stated that Ayurvedic knowledge holds for all time. Though pathogens (such as viruses, bacteria, hypercholesteria, high blood pressure, and so on) are not denied as etiological explanations, the imbalance of the humors is seen as the root cause of all somatic illnesses and as the ultimate consequence of unwholesome thinking and acting.[2] Ayurveda sees itself as a natural medical practice because it seeks grounding in the essence of human nature and uses medicines made of natural substances such as plant materials, minerals, and metals.

Currently, 90 percent of industrially manufactured Ayurvedic products on the Indian market are branded commodities. Only 10 percent are classical medicines for which compositions, preparation methods, and indications of use come from the Ayurvedic canons known as *samhitas* and *nighantus*. Ayurvedic brands are officially classified as Patent and Proprietary Ayurvedic Medicines. Branded products sold as OTC consumer goods dominate the market; they represent 75 percent of the sales of Ayurvedic health products, which grew from $7 million in 1980 to approximately $700 million in 2000. In the same year, sales of biomedical drugs in India totaled approximately $7 billion. Ayurvedic soaps, hair oils, toothpastes, shampoos, creams, and other cosmetics all fall under the category of Patent and Proprietary Ayurvedic Medicines and totaled, approximately, an additional $200 million in sales. It is therefore realistic to say that Ayurvedic therapeutic substances, in the form of branded health products and classical medicines, sell at roughly one-tenth the rate of their biomedical counterparts. To put these data into perspective, we must realize that these do not include Ayurvedic medicines that are made by practitioners—some highly educated and others illiterate—for the benefit of their own patients. Such herbal and mineral remedies do not fall under the government regulations for indigenous medicines; the regulations only apply to Ayurvedic industries selling their products on the market either directly to consumers or to Ayurvedic and biomedical practitioners.[3]

Though there are almost eight thousand Ayurvedic manufacturers, the large majority of these firms are cottage industries (that is, with a yearly turnover of $250,000 or less). At the same time, a small number of firms account for a large part of the business, leading to a rather concentrated industry—ten Ayurvedic firms produce 60 percent of all Ayurvedic pharmaceutical products. One manufacturer, Dabur India Limited, accounts for 20 percent of the total sales of Ayurvedic commodities in India.

Large manufacturers thrive on selling branded medical products—classified as fast-moving consumer goods (FMCG)—to middle- and upper-middle-class consumers in urban areas. Apart from offering "natural" and "authentic" solutions for managing chronic diseases and other ailments (including diabetes, arthritis, asthma, stomach and skin complaints, high blood pressure and high cholesterol levels, dysmenorrhoea and leucorrhoea, menopausal symptoms, and the loss of vitality and virility), these products are sold as solutions to the iatrogenic effects of environmental pollution and hectic lifestyles marked by fast food, alcohol consumption, and "synthetic" (Western) medicines.

Manufacturers often design branded products by taking a classical formula, adding a few herbs, and applying an industrial production process (see Bode 2006 and Bode 2008 for examples). According to government regulations, a product qualifies as a classical Ayurvedic medicine only if the composition, manufacturing, and indications for its use come from one of fifty-seven Ayurvedic texts that have been selected by the Ayurvedic Pharmacopoeia Committee. For a Patent and Proprietary Ayurvedic Medicine, however, it is sufficient if the ingredients can be found in this selection of texts. The formula, its manufacturing process, and the conditions for which the product is marketed do not have to be derived from the classic texts. This definition leaves ample room for manipulation because controversy surrounds which substances constitute authentic Ayurvedic ingredients. To mention just two examples: uncertainties about the identity of ingredients as well as regulatory loopholes have led—hilariously enough—a health product like Vick's VapoRub (a nose de-blocker made by a foreign firm) and a line of expensive cosmetics under the name of Shahnaz Husain to carry

"Ayurvedic Proprietary Medicine" on their labels. Favorable tax treatment for indigenous medicines and the commercial appeal of the name *Ayurveda* underlie manufacturers' desire to sell diverse products under the category.

Government Legislation and the Bypassing of the Ayurvedic Physician

Before the twentieth century, Ayurveda was largely a local tradition, and the fame of healers depended upon (secret) family recipes tailored to specific patients and diseases. Physicians usually did not ask for consultation fees; instead, they made their earnings on the sale of therapeutic substances that they prepared themselves. This practice changed as an Ayurvedic industry began in the second half of the nineteenth century and gained momentum in the first decades of the twentieth century. Therapeutic indexes and price lists from the first half of the twentieth century suggest that *vaidyas* were important buyers of industrially produced Ayurvedic medicines. Ayurvedic physicians treated these products as half-fabricates to which they added their own ingredients.[4] In this way they created "authentic" therapeutic substances tailored to the needs of their patients. Even when they did not change the composition of a factory product, physicians hid the names of the manufacturers of the substances they were distributing. Out of fear of harming their reputation as inventors and composers of therapeutic substances, traditional physicians often kept silent about the industrial origin of their medicines. This obfuscation was possible because Ayurvedic remedies were not often prepacked. Patients were served *churnas* (powders), *batis* (hand-rolled pills), *kashayams* (decoctions), *avehlas* (jams), *arks* (distillates), as well as other traditional forms from large containers that did not bear the name of the manufacturer. Formulas were packed by the dose, and, for their distribution, practitioners depended upon recycled materials such as used bottles for liquid preparations and newspapers for powders and hand-rolled pills. This practice continues till today, albeit in dwindling numbers, even as prepacked products gain the upper hand.

Since the 1970s and intensifying in the 1990s, branded Ayurvedic products (mostly marketed as FMCG) have proliferated. The Indian government has taken note of this commodification of traditional formulas:

> The practice of the individual physician identifying drugs and preparing medicines himself for the use of his patients has been largely supplanted by the Pharmaceutical Industry. . . . He (the physician) prefers to buy it straight from the market. Even the patient . . . prefers purchasing a readymade drug from a manufacturer instead of obtaining it from his own physician. [Therefore] some sort of uniformity in the manufacture of Ayurvedic medicines should be brought about. . . . In view of the present trend of commercialisation in the preparation and marketing of Ayurvedic medicines . . . the Government of India considered it expedient to utilise the existing law which controls the standards of allopathic drugs, namely

the Drugs and Cosmetic Act, 1940, to also control, in a limited measure, the Ayurvedic, Siddha and Unani drugs by amending the Act. (Ayurvedic Pharmacopoeia Committee 1978)

The commodification of indigenous medicines has given Indian authorities a rationale for regulating the production and marketing of these remedies. In 1976 indigenous pharmaceuticals were, in part, brought under the Indian Drugs and Cosmetics Act originally passed to cover Western therapeutic drugs and cosmetics. The government wanted to regulate the identity, quality, manufacturing, and marketing of Ayurvedic herbal and mineral products in the Indian market. As I have said before, Ayurvedic physicians who made their medicines for the sole benefit of their patients were exempted from these regulations, as were hospitals and Ayurvedic colleges. In the introduction of the second edition of the Ayurvedic Formulary of India, published in 1978, the government emphasized that the rise of the Ayurvedic industry necessitated standards and quality control. But at that time the application of the Drugs and Cosmetics Act to Ayurveda was mainly a symbolic measure because manufacturers of Ayurvedic commodities (and their medical products) did not fall under the jurisdiction of the Central Drug Controller, and therefore the Ayurvedic industry did not have to prove the safety and efficacy of its products. The industry only had to deal with local food authorities, who were known for being too lenient. To my knowledge, when it comes to Indian indigenous medical products, even today there is no effective government infrastructure for law enforcement; the government, both at the central and state levels, has very limited facilities for testing drugs and registering adverse reactions. There is also no tradition of visiting production units and sales points or imposing sanctions on Ayurvedic and other indigenous medicines in case of bad-quality products or unethical marketing.

In 1995 the Department of the Indian Systems of Medicine was created to advance India's medical traditions. One important objective was the establishment of standards to guarantee the quality of ingredients, production processes, and end products. The 2001 publication of the Draft National Policy for Indian Systems of Medicine, which formulates new guidelines for good manufacturing practice (GMP) standards, represents a modest step. The document was rectified in 2003 and includes rules for hygienic storage and production methods, a list of machines needed for good manufacturing, and procedures for quality control (such as batch registration) with the aim of holding manufacturers accountable in cases of calamities.[5] But only time can tell if this policy will improve the quality of Ayurvedic medical products.

India generally lacks institutes that can link Ayurveda and its medicines to the practices and insights of modern pharmacology. Research performed by the Department of Clinical Pharmacology of the Seth GS (Gordhandas Sunderdas) Medical College and KEM (King Edward Memorial) Hospital Mumbai (formerly Bombay) since the 1990s is among few exceptions. This pioneering work has now resulted in three centers for registering and analyzing adverse drug effects for Ayurvedic medicines. Even more exceptional is the researchers' respect for the tenets of classical humoral pharmacology while at the same time utilizing the techniques and concepts of modern pharmacology (Gogtay et al. 2002; for adverse drug reactions, see especially Thatte et al. 1993).

In contrast, government research on Indian medical traditions—which started in 1962 with the foundation of the Central Council for Research of Indian Medicine (CCRIM)—has been insensitive to the ontological and epistemological differences between humoral medicine and pharmacology and its modern counterparts, which work within the paradigm of logical positivism. Despite some brave attempts, so far no academic bridge has been built between humoral and modern medicine and pharmacology. Virtually no community of scientists is working to bridge the gap between modern pharmacology and humoral medical forms such as Ayurveda and traditional Chinese medicine.[6]

Patented and Proprietary Ayurvedic Medicines and Their Marketing

Advertisements for branded Ayurvedic products appear prominently on billboards, in local newspapers and glossy magazines, and on television. The manufacturers of Ayurvedic products also distribute brochures, booklets, and CDs to spell out the worth of their goods. To attract consumers, advertisements tap into Indian notions of health and disease, including popular humoral ideas such as the need for good digestion and the health benefits of fruits, herbs, and roots. The industry's marketing activities evoke a wide spectrum of ideas and images. But a structural analysis of promotional materials and my interviews with marketers reveal two key themes.

The first theme—symbolized by a *rishi* (seer) sitting in a test tube—is the simultaneous invocation of tradition and modernity. The importance of both concepts is not difficult to detect in printed material as well as in conversations with people from the industry. Images of modern research and production technology are as important for the marketing of Indian indigenous pharmaceuticals as are references to tradition. Pestles and mortars are placed next to computers. Deities accompany pictures of the latest equipment used for chemical laboratory analyses. Company brochures contain images of modern factory buildings and halls equipped with production machinery such as huge metallic containers, electric ovens, and packing machines.

The second theme is the natural, wholesome quality that Ayurvedic manufacturers claim for their products. Ayurvedic pharmaceuticals are represented as "completely natural." Natural ingredients such as fruits, flowers, vegetables, leaves, and roots decorate labels, advertisements, and other promotional material. Ayurvedic manufacturers promise that their medicines make you feel good as an Indian because Ayurvedic substances, notions, and practices are "your history, your culture, your body, and your health." They associate their brands with the natural, wholesome, and authentic. Marketing rhetoric claims that Ayurvedic formulas lead people back to their "true" natures and "establish people in themselves", that is, activate the body's innate healing mechanism and revitalize body, mind, and spirit. Manufacturers state that their products and Ayurveda in general sustain and improve somatic, mental, and social integration. In contrast, modern medicines and Western influences (such as alcohol, fast food, and the environmental degradation caused by industrialization) undermine Indian bodies and mentalities. Ayurvedic manufacturers claim that their products are integrative and give people "what they really are and what they really need" and therefore make them effectively modern.

In their marketing discourse, Ayurvedic manufacturers link their brands to the "truth and wholesomeness" of tradition. Himalaya, India's second-largest manufacturer of Ayurvedic products, chose an actress in the garb of an Indian grandmother as the figurehead when, in 2001, the company launched Ayurvedic Concepts, its new line of OTC Ayurvedic products. India's largest Ayurvedic manufacturer, Dabur, stresses the health benefits traditionally ascribed to common substances, such as spices, fruits, and vegetables, which are also important ingredients of Ayurvedic medicines.[7] Manufacturers also link their products to Hindu myths and epics (representing Ayurveda as nectar received from and used by the gods) as well as to India's glorious Buddhist and Hindu civilizations.

At the same time, large manufacturers boast their use of modern science and technology in production and quality monitoring. They tout modern production and research facilities to differentiate their products from those produced by small manufacturers and cottage industries. The following excerpt from Dabur product leaflets aimed at the urban English-educated middle class, is an example of this marketing strategy:

Dabur India Limited is an ISO 9002 certified organisation. Stringent computer controlled quality assurance methods are followed in the company. This ensures that only the best raw material enters the system and only the standardised end final product reaches the consumer.

Applications of modern science such as process engineering and analytic chemistry are part of the activities of at least the larger Ayurvedic firms. In this way large manufacturers like Dabur and Himalaya seek to distinguish themselves from the backwardness that also clings to Ayurveda and its medicines. Though urban English-educated Indians see Ayurveda and its medicines as part of their cultural heritage, they also doubt their current relevance for treating serious diseases and the conditions under which Ayurvedic medicines are currently manufactured. By invoking the prestige of modern science and technology in their marketing rhetoric, large manufacturers like Dabur and Himalaya want to remove these doubts and consequently increase the attractiveness of their indigenous pharmaceuticals for the English-educated middle class.

In the next sections, I go beyond marketing rhetoric to discuss what modern pharmacology should and can contribute to the quality of Ayurvedic medicines and their use in India today.

A Case Study: Ayurveda's Most Popular Medicine

Chyawanprash is India's best-selling Ayurvedic health product with a market that in 2002 amounted to $70 million; Dabur is its largest producer, with 60 percent market share. Because of heavy advertising on television and in the print media, this product has had a great impact upon the popular image of traditional medicine in India. The tonic is named after a sage who was its first user. The sage obtained the tonic from the *ashvins*, the physicians of the gods, after losing his eyesight and vigor due to an overcurious and sexually demanding princess. *Chyawanprash* is a medicine used in one of the eight Ayurvedic subdisciplines called *rasayana*, an Ayurvedic branch that deals in promotive therapies with the objective of increasing the self-healing potential of the human body.

From its name, one would guess that we are talking about a classical formula that has been sanctioned by use over centuries. But Dabur Chyawanprash is actually a Patent and Proprietary Ayurvedic Medicine. Dabur changed its formula and patented its production process. The firm has popularized the formula's indications of use and converted the tonic into a daily necessity "to fight the stress and strain of modern city life." A large advertisement campaign on India's national television and in other prominent media such as the weekly *India Today* (which sells almost twenty million copies) made the public familiar with Dabur Chyawanprash. Dabur decided to keep the formula's classical name for marketing because *chyawanprash* is such a well-known name, although Dabur always precedes the name with that of the company. Himalaya, the second-largest Ayurvedic manufacturer after Dabur, holds 7 percent of the market; they decided to give their *chyawanprash* the name Geriforte.

Modern medical notions and references to Hindu culture frame Dabur Chyawanprash. Two quotations taken from advertisements for the product illustrate this:

Modern Science has ample evidence today to prove that the unique immuno-modulatory action of Dabur Chyawanprash restores the balance of antibodies. . . . It has powerful anti-oxidants which neutralise the harmful effects of modern living. Protecting you from illness. Making you stronger. From within . . . Based on the 3000-year old Ayurvedic recipe in Caraka Samhita, fortified with 48 herbs, roots, fresh fruits and minerals. Completely natural, free from side effects. (*India Today*, May 10, 1999)

Based on the original recipe laid down in the *Caraka Samhita*, Dabur Chyawanprash is an Ayurvedic tonic with 48 fruits, roots, herbs and minerals.

Every ingredient collected at their freshest best. Enriched with *Amla*, Nature's richest source of Vitamin C. (*Woman's Era,* January 1998)

The ads call attention to *amalaki* or *amla* (Phyllanthus emblica Linn) known traditionally as "the mother" (*dhatri*) because of the health-protecting properties ascribed to the berry. There is no apparent contradiction between modern and traditional ideas. Ayurveda is represented as the mother of all forms of medicine and therefore is said to encompass all biomedical notions. According to its manufacturer, Dabur Chyawanprash works from "deep within." It is common practice in India to assert that Ayurvedic products take away the cause of an ailment by activating the body's innate capacity to heal itself. In contrast, Western drugs are said to merely suppress symptoms—to sweep the dust under the carpet, so to speak. Their usage is compared to printing money in times of inflation, only making the problem worse.

Chyawanprash is traditionally used as one of the elements of an elaborate rejuvenation treatment in which regimen and therapeutic procedures are as important as medical substances. Patients go through elaborate purification procedures (depletion), after which their bodily tissues (*dhatus*) and disease immunity is rebuilt (repletion) and their humors (*doshas*) are rebalanced so that the patient becomes "established in himself" (*svasthya*). Within a humoral discourse, *chyawanprash* is used in cases of asthma (*svas*), involuntary semen loss, diabetes (*madhuprameha*), wind-blood (*vata-rakta*), and so on. The medicine is also said to develop the intellect, to enhance speech, and to improve the complexion of its users. According to tradition, *chyawanprash* fights emaciation and fixes "semen fault" and "urine fault," especially in cases of consumption caused by too much sexual activity and indulgence in "unwholesome" thoughts, actions, and the intake of "improper" food and drink (see, for example, Lata 1990).

If we look at the scientific evidence regarding the efficacy of *chyawanprash* in, for example, PubMed and the Annotated Bibliography of Indian Medicine, we find only four research articles that deal with the formula.[8] The journals publishing these research studies do not seem to be peer reviewed. The research designs and their validity are also not convincing. One of the clinical studies using ten human volunteers gives some evidence that *chyawanprash* lowers blood sugar and cholesterol; another study suggests that *chyawanprash* has immuno-modulating properties; and a third claims that the formula cures "smoker lungs." In its promotional material for Dabur Chyawanprash, the firm quotes some of these research findings. In short, we can say that modern scientific evidence for the efficacy of *chyawanprash* is meager indeed.

Compared to pharmacognostic and pharmacological research on Asian medical formulas, research articles that deal with their ingredients are more convincing. This is true for *amalaki*, the primary ingredient among the forty-eight used in *chyawanprash*. According to the scholarly humoral discourse on *amalaki,* the gooseberry has the following biological effects: it is astringent,

259

bitter, digestive, aphrodisiac, laxative, diuretic, and a tonic; cures diseases caused by morbid *kapha*, *vata*, and *pitta* (*tri-doshic*); takes away thirst, burning sensation, vomiting, fever, and blood impurities; and is useful in cases of cough, diabetes, jaundice, leucorrhoea, nausea, hyperacidity, and anorexia (Sivarajan and Balachandran 1994).

A PubMed search for *amalaki* yielded 122 research articles. In addition I have looked at pharmacognostic and pharmacological research on *amalaki* as it appeared in a review article (Balick 2001). Here we find five research articles that deal with the berry and address several topics: *amalaki*'s physical-chemical fractions; pharmacological animal models that experimentally induce inflammations in joints and stomachs of rats and rabbits; models that expose rats to mental stress through cold exposure and frustrating learning tasks; and clinical studies with human subjects that show *amalaki*'s antibacterial, antihypercholesterol, immuno-modulating, and antihepatitis effects. These findings offer some evidence regarding the efficacy of *amalaki* in the treatment of hyperlipidemia, hypercholesterol, forgetfulness, stress reduction, hyperacidity, viral hepatitis, and other bacterial and viral inflammations. However, a recent publication of the World Health Organisation (WHO) concludes that positivistic research on Asian medicinal substances suffers from "inadequate standardization, unacceptable preclinical toxicology studies, and inappropriate, uncontrolled, and badly designed clinical trials" (Chaudhury and Chaudhury 2002; Bode 2008).[9]

In conclusion, modern pharmacology does provide some evidence, though meager, that supports the efficacy of *chyawanprash*'s main ingredient. We also know that both *chyawanprash* and *amalaki* have been in use in India for medical purposes for many centuries, suggesting that the biological and physiological effects explained in scholarly and popular humoral logic has been put to empirical test by many patients. But the efficacy of these products only holds when other tenets of Ayurveda are followed, such as the simultaneous use of *anupans* (a drink taken with or after a medicine) and other medicines as well as food and behavioral restrictions and guidelines. Such tenets are not necessarily followed by patients using products in the category Patent and Proprietary Ayurvedic Medicines. These medicines are mainly sold as OTC remedies for "modern" ailments such as stress, arthritis, and hypercholesteria. Though Dabur Chyawanprash might profit from the formula's cultural potency (symbolic effectiveness) in the sense that its name instills trust in its effects, it is reasonable to state that the formula's empirical effectiveness is highly contingent upon humoral diagnostic expertise and its use within a wider Ayurvedic therapeutic regime.

Rational Use of Ayurvedic Drugs: Some Policy Implications

The patent medicine Dabur Chyawanprash is classified in India under the category FMCG. In my earlier work I raised doubts about the appropriateness of the label Ayurveda for products for which the Indian government has created the category Patent and Proprietary Ayurvedic Medicines. Using the term "Indian herbal-mineral medicine" would be more appropriate.[10] As we have seen, the category Patent and Proprietary Ayurvedic Medicines has been corrupted through products that have nothing to do with Ayurveda as a knowledge tradition posing an alternative to biomedicine. Those who want to keep Ayurveda as an alternative and complementary device for treating illnesses should support improving its rational use in terms of identity, quality, and use. Therefore it would be wise if the Indian government rethinks its categorization. Why not align with international conventions and rename these products "Indian herbal-mineral health products" or "Indian herbal-mineral food additives?" This would be in line with recent statements from Indian pharmacological authorities that Ayurvedic brands are in fact new products in terms of composition, manufacturing, and indications of use, and therefore should undergo pharmacological testing before entering the market (Gogtay et al. 2002:1015).

Modern pharmacology should be employed to ensure the quality of the Ayurvedic medications available in the market. Stricter regulations for quality will protect patients and consumers from medicines and health products that contain too high a proportion of heavy metals and pesticides. Such toxicities have been reported in the West; surely these mishaps also occur in India.[11] In addition, the inroads modern science has made into Indian society make it almost mandatory to turn to modern pharmacology for validating Ayurvedic pharmacological ideas and practices like the link between the taste (*rasa*) of a medical substance and its biological effects—one of the basic tenets of Ayurvedic pharmacology (*dravyagunasastra*).[12] These kinds of correlation studies are also necessary for validating traditional processing techniques such as Ayurveda's elaborate detoxifying procedures. The ethical marketing of Ayurvedic medicines also deserves government attention. Undue and unethical claims, such as selling Ayurvedic medicines as a cure for diseases like cancer and AIDS or promising customers that the ingestion of a Ayurvedic product greatly increases the chance of having male offspring, must be contested. Other measures that are necessary for Ayurveda to be taken seriously as an alternative and complementary medicine are the standardization of its formulas and the obligation of manufacturers to mention the true list of ingredients on their labels (which is currently rare). Ayurvedic medical products must also have inserts stating their shelf life, recommended doses, and safety warnings.

The profitability of the OTC Ayurvedic brands is associated with a shortage of classical Ayurvedic medicines on the Indian market. Ayurvedic physicians who work within the paradigm of humoral pharmacology have complained that their patients increasingly have difficulty buying the classical medicines they prescribe.[13] Production figures also suggest a relative shortage. I estimate that in 2000 the sales of classical Ayurvedic medicines amounted to $70 million, less than one-tenth of the total sales of products that go under the name *Ayurveda*. A more realistic way of defining Ayurvedic medicines might partially remedy this problem. Large manufacturers are also worried about their products losing their image as a medicine and being "reduced" to "health supplements" or "bioceuticals." It seems wise to reserve the label *Ayurvedic medicine* only for products whose composition, manufacturing, and indications of use are sanctioned by the fifty-seven Ayurvedic canons selected by the Department of Indian Systems of Medicine.

Ayurveda would also benefit from the implementation of GMPs. The Department of Indian Systems of Medicine came forth with new GMP regulations and quality controls in 2001 and 2003. But the Indian government's monitoring and surveillance systems fall far short of enforcing this new policy. Therefore, civil society—in the form of consumers, nongovernmental organizations (NGOs) such as the Voluntary Health Association of India (VHAI), Ayurvedic practitioner organizations, as well as individual Ayurvedic manufacturers—should work alongside the government to address this problem.[14] Raising awareness about the rational use of Ayurvedic medicines among consumers, manufacturers, medical practitioners, pharmacists, and druggists should be a priority. Too often these parties think "never mind if they [Ayurvedic medicines] are ineffective, they will be safe"; in contrast, all parties should be warned that pharmacology teaches "if a drug is effective, it is most likely to produce a side effect" (see Gogtay et al. 2002).

Discussion

In this chapter, I have argued for using the insights and methods of modern pharmacology to make Ayurveda acceptable as an alternative and complementary form of medicine. But this strategy will work only when we take classical Ayurvedic ideas and practices seriously, without hastily "translating" these ideas into biomedical logic. It is common to consider positivistic proof as the sole legitimate evidence regarding the effectiveness of medicines that are part of humoral paradigms. However, modern pharmacology and biomedicine should not be the sole arbiters of this debate. We must take classical Ayurvedic pharmacological practices and theories seriously and opt for Ayurvedic-based evidence as a supplement to evidence-based medicine.

I suggest that we pose the following questions. First, does modern pharmacology and biomedicine have proof for everything that works in medical treatment? Second, is such proof the only indication of worth? Third, does that which can be explained within the paradigm of modern pharmacology exhaust the mechanisms of action that account for medical success? If we seek a real alternative to biomedicine should we not acknowledge that the therapeutic objectives of Ayurvedic medicines differ from their biomedical counterparts? Should we not honor Ayurvedic mechanisms of action, such as unblocking the flow of humors and the expulsion of waste products; improving the body's innate healing capacity by balancing the somatic functions expressed by Ayurveda's three humors; removing toxins; and advancing the formation of good-quality tissues? Why not take these treatment objectives seriously instead of discrediting them because they fall outside the paradigm of positivistic pharmacology and are beyond its research procedures?

If we want to keep Ayurveda as an alternative and complementary means of looking at the body, its ailments, and their cures, we should take notice of traditional practices that still exist in India today. Ethnographic research such as that conducted by the joint Japanese-Indian Program for Archiving and Documenting Ayurvedic Medicine (PADAM), in which scholarly Ayurvedic physicians are extensively interviewed and videotaped, is a good example of the kind of research needed. The project documents Ayurvedic medical practices and their therapeutic goals (see Bode 2009). Another initiative that is worth mentioning is the rapid assessment methodology of the Foundation for the Revitalisation of Local Health Traditions (FRLHT), which has the objective of validating local Indian health practices and notions. When we want to understand for whom, how, and when Ayurvedic treatment works, it also makes sense to review the many ethnographic studies that describe and analyze these practices. In an article in which I build on ethnographic research done in India over the past four decades, I discuss the physiological, metaphysical, and regimental aspects of the effectiveness of Ayurvedic medicines (Bode 2009). Apart from health claims backed up by long-term use and modern pharmacological research on ingredients of Ayurvedic formulas, Ayurvedic medicines embody cultural power. When we try to understand the treatment effects of Ayurvedic medicinals, why not take this "meaning response" into account (Moerman 2002)? Especially in cases of chronic illness for which Asian medical traditions are increasingly called upon, a revaluation of symbolic mechanisms of action that are too often disqualified as placebo effects—treatment effects that cannot be explained within the paradigm of modern pharmacology—seems appropriate. After all, a medicine must prove itself in the bodies and minds of individual patients.

Notes

[1] I especially thank Dr. Anita Wagner for her comments on this chapter as part of the workshop at Stanford University where the chapters of this volume were discussed.

[2] The Sanskrit word *dosha* means both somatic humor and fault (of the body).

[3] *Vaidyas* who make medicines for the sole benefit of their patients and consequently do not fall under the jurisdiction of the central government form a hybrid category of part-time and full-time practitioners, generalists,

and specialists. Among them are consultants for ailments (such as jaundice, shortness of breath, digestive problems, and so on) as well as snakebite healers and traditional birth attendants. Their numbers are not known; depending upon what is considered to fall under the disputed category of "Ayurveda," estimates suggest between five hundred thousand and one million practitioners belong either to the codified or oral Ayurvedic tradition. See Shankar (2004).

[4] Interview with marketing manager, Zandu Pharmaceuticals Ltd., Mumbai, April 1996.

[5] See http://indianmedicine.nic.in/ for more specific information on these rules and regulations.

[6] See Bode (2008:142–59) for a more detailed analysis of this state of affairs.

[7] Dabur India Limited is the largest manufacturer of Ayurvedic medicinals. In 2000 the firm sold Ayurvedic products worth $200 million, mainly in India.

[8] http://www.indianmedicine.ub.rug.nl.

[9] Modern pharmacological research usually ascribes *amalaki*'s biological efficacy to its cytoprotective and immuno-modulating activity. See, for example, Dahanukar and Thatte 1997, pp. 363–64.

[10] Bode (2008:57–59). The term "Indian herbal-mineral medicine" was suggested in an interview I conducted in 2000.

[11] See Saper et al. 2004; Gogtay et al. 2002. A third example is the fact that in 2007 the Dutch food authorities drew the attention of the public to the toxicity of some Ayurvedic medical products available through distributors, Ayurvedic physicians, and Internet sites.

[12] Though rare, this kind of work is in progress, for example, in the laboratory of the Foundation for the Revitalisation of Local Health Traditions, Bangalore. See http://www.frlht.org.

[13] This scarcity was confirmed by statements of two very senior Ayurvedic physicians at the first conference of the Ayurvedic Drug Manufacturers Association in 1999.

[14] For an analysis of the (in)capacity of the Indian government to regulate India's health services and a plea for involving India's civil society, media, and provider organizations in this endeavor, see Peters and Muraleedharan 2008.

References

Ayurvedic Pharmacopoeia Committee. 1978. *The Ayurvedic formulary of India*, First edition, Part I. Delhi: Department of Health, Government of India, 1978, xxvii–xxvii.

Balasubramanian, A. V. 2000. Scientific basis of Indian systems of medicine. *The Hindu Folio*, October 8, 46–47.

Balick, Michael J. 2001. Therapeutic plants of Ayurveda: A review of selected clinical and other studies for 166 species. *Journal of Alternative and Complementary Medicine* 7 (5): 405–516.

Bode, Maarten. 2002. Indian indigenous pharmaceuticals: Tradition, modernity and nature. In *Plural medicine, tradition and modernity, 1800-2000*, ed. Waltraud Ernst, 184–203. London: Routledge.

———. 2006. Taking traditional knowledge to the market: The commoditization of Indian medicine. *Anthropology & Medicine* 13 (3): 25–36.

———. 2008. *Taking traditional knowledge to the market: The modern image of the Ayurvedic and Unani industry, c. 1980–2000.* Hyderabad: Orient Longman.

———. 2009. The effectiviness of Ayurvedic medical treatment: Humoral pathology, modern science and soteriology. *Electronic Journal of Indian Medicine* (eJIM) 2 (1). http://www.indianmedicine.ub.rug.nl.

Chaudhury, Ranjit Roy, and Mandakini Roy Chaudhury. 2002. Standardization, pre-clinical toxicology and clinical evaluation of medical plants, including ethical considerations. In *Traditional Medicine in Asia*, ed. Ranjit Roy Chaudhury and Uton Muchtar Rafei, 209–26. New Delhi: SEARO Regional Publications 39, World Health Organization, Regional Office for South-East Asia.

Dahanukar, S. A., and Thatte, U. M. 1997. Current status of Ayurveda in phytomedicine. Review article. *Phytomedicine* 4 (4): 359–68.

Gogtay, N. J., H. A. Bhatt, S. S. Dalvi, and N. A. Kshirsagar. 2002. The use and safety of non-allopathic Indian medicines. Review article, *Drug Safety* 25 (14): 1005–19.

Lata, W. S. 1990. *Svasth jivan* (Healthy life). Bombay: Leopard Investments.

Moerman, Daniel E. 2002. *Meaning, medicine and the "placebo effect."* Cambridge, MA: Cambridge Univ. Press.

Peters, David H., and V. R. Muraleedharan. 2008. Regulating India's health services: To what end? What future? *Social Science & Medicine* 66 (10): 2133–44.

Saper R. B., S. N. Kales, J. Paquin, M. J. Burns, D. M. Eisenberg, R. B. Davis, and R. S. Phillips 2004. Heavy metal content of Ayurvedic herbal medicine products. *Journal of the American Medical Association* 292 (23): 2868–73.

Shankar, Darshan. 2004. Community-based oral health traditions in rural India. In *Challenging the Indian Medical Heritage*, ed. Darshan Shankar and P. M. Unnikrishnan. Ahmedabad: Centre for Environmental Education, 24.

Sivarajan, V. V., and I. Balachandran. 1994. *Ayurvedic drugs and their plant sources*. Delhi: Oxford and IBH Publishing Co., 28–9.

Thatte, U. M., N. N. Rege, S. D. Phatak, and S. A. Dahanukar. 1993. The flipside of Ayurveda. *Journal of Postgraduate Medicine* 39 (4): 179–82.

PHYSICIANS AND PHARMACISTS IN COMPARATIVE HISTORICAL PERSPECTIVE: THE CASE OF SOUTH KOREA

Karen Eggleston and Bong-Min Yang[1]

Since the edict of Palermo in 1231, if not earlier, Europeans have been separating the diagnosis and treatment of disease from the preparation of medicine. In other parts of the world, by contrast, professional boundaries between physicians and pharmacists remain fluid. In South Korea (hereafter Korea) and other countries in East Asia in particular, physicians have traditionally prescribed *and* dispensed medicine. Even today, revenues from dispensing drugs represent a large share of physician income in China and some other nations with longstanding herbal medicine traditions.

What accounts for such historical differences? This chapter seeks to understand the social, cultural, and economic forces behind physician dispensing as an institution. We argue that the roles of physicians and pharmacists coevolve with other social institutions, including patient and provider beliefs, indigenous approaches to illness and healing, contracting and enforcement mechanisms, and intellectual property rights. Thus, a constellation of factors shapes the legal and practical extent of physician services and medicine dispensing—and their overlap—in any given community and point in time.

Our primary goal is to explain why the roles of physicians and pharmacists are integrated in some societies and separate in others. In the process, we discuss the relative efficiency and social desirability of these two alternatives. We conclude that, while there need not be a linear movement from integration to separation, the increasing capabilities of medical technology, rising health-care costs, and the expanding role of third-party payers (such as national health insurance programs) might make such a change desirable.

The next section lays out the conceptual background for the study, including the definition of institutions and the primary components of a model that explains the integration of prescribing and dispensing. We describe the historical role of physicians in Korea and their relationship to pharmacists, and compare the Korean experience with that of Europe and the United Kingdom. We then situate these historical narratives within the conceptual framework of social institutions and their evolution. Drawing on insights from a game theoretic model (Eggleston 2008), we attempt to show that culture and history shape the development and dissolution of integrated prescribing and dispensing.

Physician Dispensing as an Institution

As noted in the introduction to this book, economic theory does not predict that medicine prescribing and dispensing are more efficient if separate. From a societal perspective, it might even be preferable that a single health-care provider both diagnose and treat a patient. After all, integrating the two tasks saves the cost of visiting an additional provider. But integrating diagnosis and treatment also implies a conflict of interest that may tempt providers to recommend medicines (at least in part) because of their profit margins rather than their clinical appropriateness.

In this chapter we seek to understand how and why societies have "chosen" separation or integration as a social institution governing the provider-patient relationship. First, what do we mean by "institution"? D. C. North defines institutions as "the humanly devised constraints that structure political, economic and social interaction" and therefore "provide the incentive structure of an economy" (1991:97). We draw on this definition in describing the "humanly devised constraints" that structure clinical reality across societies.

For some research questions, putting *beliefs* at the center of the analysis can prove fruitful. Even in many standard microeconomic models of expert services, customer beliefs or expectations play an important role in defining equilibria. Aoki (2001) convincingly argues that, for many questions, "understanding the process of institutional change may be tantamount to understanding the ways in which the agents revise their beliefs in a coordinated manner" (2001:4). We draw on this concept to analyze how beliefs about the role of physicians in traditional herbal medicine led to the current model of modern physician dispensers—and how this, in turn, has been affected by recent reforms to separate diagnosis and dispensing.

Aoki develops the following definition of an institution:

> An institution is a self-sustaining system of shared beliefs about how the game is played. Its substance is a compressed representation of the salient, invariant features of an equilibrium path, perceived by almost all the agents in the domain as relevant to their own strategic choices. As such it governs the strategic interactions of the agents in a self-enforcing manner and in turn is reproduced by their actual choices in a continually changing environment (2001:26).

Greif (2006:30) defines an institution as a system of rules, beliefs, organizations, and norms that regulate social behavior—a definition that also brings beliefs and norms to the fore. In applying Grief's definition to physician dispensing, we examine actual individual and group behavior, rather than assuming that formal rules embody and guide behavior. This distinction can be important. For example, Kleinman (1980:13) describes how Taiwan's legal restrictions on joint prescribing and dispensing were routinely ignored in the 1970s, with pharmacists freely doing both.

To illustrate his argument, Greif (2006) asks us to consider the rules regulating the use of credit cards and the prosecution of defaulters. These work in conjunction with organizations (credit card companies and legal authorities) and beliefs and norms ("belief in the credit card company's ability to screen cardholders, impose legal punishment, and damage one's credit history") to give rise to regular social behavior ("impersonal exchange without cash among sellers and holders of credit cards") (Greif 2006:38).

The institutions of physician-dispensing integration and separation can be understood analogously. Rules define who can legally prescribe and dispense drugs. Organizational players include professional associations and legal authorities. Beliefs held by both patients and providers (traditional and modern physicians, apothecaries, herbalists, and so on) shape doctor-patient interactions. Drugs may be seen to embody the medical skill of the expert or, alternatively, to represent only one aspect of treatment, separable from diagnosis. Associated with these beliefs are internalized norms of how and when to seek medical care (and from whom), and beliefs about whether health professionals legitimately make a living from diagnosing and/or dispensing medicine. These alternative bundles of rules, organizations, beliefs, and internalized norms give rise to regularities of social behavior that either integrate or separate the diagnosis/ prescribing and treatment/dispensing functions.

With this as background, we ask the following questions: How did physician dispensing become an institution in Korea and other parts of East Asia? How and why did the separate roles of physicians and pharmacists evolve in the West? And, finally, how and why have East Asian countries initiated policy reforms to separate prescribing and dispensing, and how has this process (in terms of proximate causes and recent effects) differed from the earlier European experience?

Prescribing and Dispensing in Korea: A Historical Perspective

During the Yi Dynasty (1392–1910), formal treatment patterns came with the advent of herbal medicine physicians, the opening of herbal medicine markets (*Yak-young-si*) throughout the Korean Peninsula, and the publication of diagnosis and treatment books for both physicians and households.[2] By the second half of the Yi Dynasty, the average civilian had access to treatment, whether through herbal medicine dealers or acupuncture practitioners. Many such local health-care providers were self-educated or self-proclaimed, and nearly all dispensed medicine.

Meanwhile, the herbal physicians of the royal family and the palace residents were selected through a national examination system and, in fact, did separate prescription from dispensation (the royal physicians prescribed medicine and their assistants dispensed it). That the two practices were separated in the treatment of the elite may indicate that this was considered an important and desirable aspect of medical treatment even at that time. Role differentiation

269

and specialization appeared, but only for the most privileged, and all under the supervision of the herbal medicine physicians.

The Introduction of Western Medicine

After years of conflict, both within the Yi Kingdom and with outside colonial powers (including Russia, Japan, the United States, and China), Korea finally opened its doors to foreign trade and social influence in 1886. Western religion and medicine were two of the most salient and influential imports to Korea at that time. In 1890 the governing body of the Daehan Jae-guk[3] (then called Tong-gam-bu), under the influence of foreign powers, opened the first Western medicine clinic. Named Daehan Clinic, it introduced not only Western-style treatment but, in 1899, the first Western medicine physician training program, though its few graduates had limited influence (Shin 2001).

Between 1910 and 1945, Japan occupied the Korean Peninsula, administering colonial rule through the Cho-sun Governing Bureau. This bureau created a completely new health-care environment as part of Japan's goal of modernizing the peninsula. In 1912 a new law, the Order on Medicine and Medicine Marketing, attempted to introduce three fundamental changes: (1) the establishment of pharmacology as a separate medical profession, (2) the abolition of the herbal medicine tradition,[4] and (3) the expansion of physician training in Western medicine (Shin 2002). As the traditional system was phased out, Western medicine practitioners were allowed to provide both Western and herbal medicine services; traditional physicians who were trained prior to 1912 were allowed to practice as "traditional medicine medical practitioners" until they ceased to work.

These changes significantly altered Korea's health-care system and the boundaries of the medical profession in several respects. First, a traditional practice that for centuries had served the Yi Kingdom's palace residents and upper classes was destined to disappear from Korean society. Second, even though they could practice until their retirement, herbal medicine doctors were forced to accept the lower status of "practitioners." Third, many Koreans who once sought treatment from traditional physicians now turned in greater numbers to the herbal medicine dealers who were more readily available and comparatively inexpensive. With these changes, four types of providers were available to dispense drugs: Western medicine physicians, pharmacists, traditional medicine practitioners, and herbal medicine dealers. As the number of traditional practitioners declined over time, their role as provider-dispensers gradually faded. The concept of a pharmacist as a dispenser of Western biomedicine was established in Korea during the early part of this period. But the first Korean pharmacist of Western medicine was not trained until 1920 (Shin 2002), and by 1945, when Korea gained independence from Japan, there were still only about three hundred pharmacists in the country (Pharmacist Association for Healthy Society, PAHS, 1993). This small number, relative to

Korea's population, reveals that the role of pharmacists in dispensing drugs must have been very limited at the time.

Meanwhile, although the number of Western medicine physicians was increasing, they remained scarce and costly, primarily treating Japanese residents and elite Koreans. The average Korean simply could not afford their services (Shin 2002).

Among the four types of providers, inexpensive and readily available herbal medicine dealers were the most widely used. By law, dealers were allowed to sell only herbal drugs, but in practice they also made medicines and provided dosing information for treatment. Although the Cho-sun Governing Bureau recognized this discrepancy—evident in several official documents—the colonial government knew that herbal medicine dealers were deeply rooted in Korean tradition (Shin 2002) and so did not attempt to enforce restrictions on their dispensing practices. In fact, given the shortages of both traditional medicine practitioners and Western medicine physicians and pharmacists, the governing bureau was forced to allow the herbal medicine dealers to offer diagnoses to patients.

From historical accounts we can deduce that the Korean public patronized herbal medicine dealers for two interlinked reasons: lower cost and wider availability. As a result, the number of dealers increased rapidly during the early twentieth century. Their proliferation was largely unregulated, even as some started to trade and dispense Western medicines (Yang 2006).

Role delineations did exist to some extent among physicians, pharmacists, traditional medicine practitioners, and herbal medicine dealers. Some physicians only prescribed and some herbal medicine dealers and pharmacists only dispensed according to prescriptions. But, in most cases, drug prescribing and dispensing were integrated. It was common for physicians to treat patients and dispense drugs at their own offices, while medicine dealers offered diagnosis and then sold the "appropriate" drugs (Higa 1932).

1945–1989: The Practice of Western Medicine Expands

After Japan withdrew from the Korean Peninsula in 1945, the United States played an influential role in restructuring Korean society. In the arena of health care, this meant that Western biomedicine was front and center. After the Korean War of 1950–1953, the Korean government established eleven new schools of pharmacy in just two years (1954–1955), greatly increasing the number of pharmacists in the country (PAHS 1993). New medical schools were opened as well. Following the U.S. pattern, physicians were mostly trained as specialists; relatively few became general practitioners. Yet, as the country developed economically, demand for health care—primary care in particular—grew rapidly. With Western-trained physicians unable to meet demand, the relatively abundant pharmacists stepped in to fill the void at dispensaries across the country (PAHS 1993).

Pharmacists in Korea essentially played the role of primary caregivers for nearly four and a half decades. They responded to medical inquiries by making a diagnosis, then dispensing drugs. Most Koreans accepted this tradition as the health-care norm. Many, in fact, liked it because, when ill, they could obtain medical advice and medicine very easily, quickly, and inexpensively. Because most treatments were reasonably effective, few Koreans questioned pharmacists' authority or judgment.

Pharmacists too had little hesitation. They were happy with the revenues they earned and enjoyed their role as primary care provider. They could legally dispense any kind of drug to a patient without a prescription. The pharmacist's right to dispense was enshrined in the Pharmaceutical Affairs Law of 1953.[5]

The Korean government also reestablished the tradition of herbal medicine; a four-year college of Korean medicine opened its doors in 1953. As of 2008 there were eleven schools of traditional medicine, all of which were fully accredited six-year medical education programs in universities. As the number of traditional practitioners increased, the professional boundaries between pharmacists, Western-style doctors, and traditional doctors coevolved with new social structures that further transformed the roles of health-care providers.

1989–2000: From the Birth of National Health Insurance to Separation Reform

Expanding from the employee insurance programs of various sectors, Korea achieved universal coverage with the 1989 introduction of a national health insurance (NHI) scheme. After this, the entire Korean population was covered by either social insurance or the tax-financed Medicaid program. But alongside the expansion of coverage came a rapid increase in health service utilization and other pressures that threatened the NHI's financial sustainability. NHI authorities became more acutely aware of problematic practices such as high pharmaceutical spending, especially after the NHI funds were merged into a single fund in 1999. Researchers and health authorities singled out the misuse and overuse of drugs as key threats to both public health and health system efficiency.

Since the story of Korea's reforms separating prescription from dispensation is the topic of another chapter in this book (chapter 1, Kwon), we will only briefly sketch the pre-reform evolution of those practices.

As the number of traditional medicine schools—and their graduates— increased, post-1953, traditional physicians became increasingly vocal critics of pharmacists dispensing herbal medicine. This conflict escalated into a prominent social issue in the early 1990s. Traditional medicine physicians argued that pharmacists should not touch the herbal medicine domain because they were not schooled or trained in it, while the pharmacists said they could.

Civil society played a prominent role in resolving the issue. After a series of struggles, including strong resistance from both Western and herbal medicine physicians, prescribing and dispensing became legally separated. The ultimate implications of this change remain important topics of social policy research. What is already apparent, however, is that resistance to the separation policy is deeply rooted in the Korean tradition of integrated physician dispensing. In this, Korea has much in common with its East Asian neighbors.

Physicians and Pharmacies in Europe

The functions of medicine prescribing and dispensing coevolved somewhat differently in Europe. Some historians, referring to ancient Egypt and Hammurabi's Code in early Mesopotamia, suggest that their separation dates back 4,000 years (Court 2005:21). Apothecary shops appeared in the Middle East around 850 AD. As Arab scholars emigrated to Europe, they introduced many important concepts, including the separation of pharmacology and medical diagnosis. Then Frederick II of Hohenstaufen (emperor of Germany and king of Sicily) issued the Edict of Palermo in 1231. This not only states that medicine and pharmacology are separate professions requiring particular skills and responsibilities but also stipulates government control over many aspects of market entry, contracting, and payment. For example, physicians and apothecaries are not to enter into business relationships, and the number of apothecaries, their locations, and prices are all subject to government oversight. "The idea that the diagnosis and treatment of disease should be separated from the preparation of medicines soon spread across continental Europe" (Anderson 2005:40).

Central and local European government authorities as well as professional guilds regulated pharmacies and their separation from physician practices (Sonnedecker 1976:68). In France, for example, some guilds included pharmacists alongside surgeons and barbers. Other guilds were only for pharmacists, who were not distinguished from "spicers" (dealers in Eastern herbs and spices). The overlapping functions of pharmacists and spicers continued into the eighteenth century (Sonnedecker 1976:70). Meanwhile, disputes over the professional boundaries of pharmacists and physicians were common. The 1777 Royal Declaration in France established professional pharmacies and prohibited competing organizations (such as religious hospitals and societies) from selling drugs. Thus, a clear delineation between prescribing and dispensing, with the latter function reserved for pharmacists, took hundreds of years to consolidate.

Yet the experiences of Italy, France, and Germany should not lead one to assume that the separation of prescribing from dispensing predated social insurance in all countries with Western medical traditions. Britain provides a good counter example.

In 1617 King James I signed a charter establishing London apothecaries. Interestingly, and not unlike traditional medicine physicians in East Asia, the English apothecary "understood that he was not permitted to charge for his consultation, and was quite prepared to rely on the sale of drugs and medicines for his profit" (Worling 2005:60). Physicians "bitterly resented the encroachment of the apothecaries. The position was complicated, because the apothecaries' charter did not specifically prevent them from examining and treating patients, although it was accepted that they could not charge for their services, only for the medicines supplied" (Worling 2005:64). Note that even in areas where the law was ambiguous, there was a shared belief in proper actions: "it was accepted" that apothecaries could only charge for drugs. This social institution itself shaped the legal rules defining professional boundaries. The apothecaries won a case brought against one of them for providing medical advice to a patient because "their Lordships accepted the argument that it was contrary to custom and against the public interest to prevent the apothecaries from giving advice and treatment" to the poor and middle classes (Worling 2005:66). The House of Lords' decision was based both on adherence to the status quo institution (the physicians' case was "contrary to custom") as well as a judgment about social efficiency ("against the public interest"). Thus, the apothecaries of England and Wales integrated prescribing and dispensing and developed into the general practitioners of today.

It was only with the rise of the welfare state and third-party payments that pharmacists obtained legal authority over dispensing in England. The National Insurance Bill of 1911 and the insurance scheme implemented two years later separated prescribing and dispensing for insured patients (Hunt 2005). Physicians could still dispense for uninsured dependents and in rural areas with no pharmacy. Although the rural exception continues today, the separation of prescribing and dispensing spread with universal coverage under the National Health Service after World War II.

Integration or Separation? A Theory

One promising framework for understanding these contrasting historical accounts is to embed an economic theory of firm boundaries (Hart and Moore 1990; Hart 1995) in a game theoretic model of physician dispensing as an equilibrium institution (Eggleston 2008). The theory of firm boundaries is useful because the question of integration or separation is a familiar one in theories of vertical integration. When do physicians vertically integrate with pharmacists instead of "contracting out" dispensing services? Game theory helps us to understand a given structure as a self-enforcing institution (Greif 2006). Combined, these theories can be useful for explaining how different organizational forms evolve and develop their own supporting professional norms. In particular, an economic approach requires that the analyst specify the objectives and constraints of all parties; the model thus explicitly incorporates a multilevel approach to derive, rather than stipulate, what is socially "optimal."

Using this framework and the notion of institutions defined earlier, we can construct a theory of the integration of prescribing and dispensing in

East Asia. Shared beliefs are central. Patients believe that physicians provide diagnosis altruistically, to serve the sick and demonstrate their skill. Meanwhile, physicians make a living by selling the cure (the drug) for the diagnosed illness. The physician's diagnostic skill is embedded in the process of prescription. Payment is for the tangible output of the encounter—the medicine itself. These beliefs uphold integration as an institution that offers patients the convenience of "one-stop shopping" while protecting and rewarding the physician's most valued skill—the dispensing of (secret) herbal medicine compounds. Provider abuse of asymmetric information to increase profits is held in check partly by demand-side constraints (as patients that pay out of pocket for treatment do not have unlimited ability and willingness to pay) and partly by professional norms and reputational considerations. As Iizuka (2007) demonstrates empirically, the financial incentive to dispense profitable medications does not obviate physician altruism toward patients and effective demand-side constraints on prescribing, as manifest by taking account of patient's copayments. In other words, Iizuka's evidence from Japan shows that doctors, when deciding what drugs to prescribe and dispense, consider both their own profit *and* what patients have to pay.

When pressures toward specialization push toward separation—but patients still pay for diagnostic services out of pocket and expect medication as the primary output—physicians can hire or supervise pharmacists (as in the Korean royal court). Dispensing is then partially separated from prescribing, but the principle of bundling remains deeply embedded. Many physicians in China, for example, function like owners, with equity tied to the profits of hospitals or clinic pharmacies. This model is consistent with the belief that physician value derives largely from dispensing a customized medicinal cure.

The institution of physician dispensing also appears to be linked historically to the relatively weak or ineffective legal regulation of contracting and property rights. The most famous herbal medicines remain secret recipes (*mifang*), at least in part because physicians and drugmakers fear expropriation. Since patients largely believe that the cure comes from the correct mixture and preparation of herbal medicines—and not the physician's diagnostic or other treatment expertise—both patients and physicians would expect patients to self-medicate if they knew the recipe or had direct access to a prepared medication with some knowledge of the symptoms or illness it treats. In the language of game theory, the provider expects the patients to "defect" in all the subsequent periods once the inducement to "cooperate" in the market exchange of "money for *mifang*" is broken by revealing secret knowledge. This expectation is made all the more real by the lack of effective contract enforcement. Physician dispensing originated in societies with few effective sanctions against people who stole the compounding secrets of potent mixtures to market them under new names (as well as weak or nonexistent legal restrictions on obtaining medicines only by prescription). Indeed, appropriating secret recipes from the imperial court pharmacy appears to be the basis of probably the most famous traditional herbal brand in China, Tong Ren Tang (Cochran 2006:18). Once in hand, owners jealously guard such knowledge. The proprietors of Tong Ren Tang employed only relatives in an effort to keep recipes secret over generations (Cochran 2006:23).

It is a misconception to think that physician dispensing and secret formulations give providers all the power in clinical encounters. In fact, almost all societies with physician dispensers also host active markets for self-medication through herbalists and drugstores. Together with ineffectual protection of herbal medicine innovations, faith in the efficacy of self-medication and the associated supply of over-the-counter drugs generally creates significant competition for physician dispensers. The institution of physician dispensing has thus developed in part to protect the physicians' investments in creating effective new herbal medicines by paying the provider directly to dispense the secret formula.

Recent debates about the separation of prescribing and dispensing in Korea, Taiwan, and elsewhere appear to corroborate these conjectures. For example, a central concern voiced by the Korean physicians opposing separation was the worry that pharmacists would misuse prescriptions to engage in "quasi-prescribing" (see Kwon and Reich 2005; Kwon 2008). To some extent, even contemporary physicians in Korea do not believe that their position is secure, instead fearing that once information is more symmetrical, pharmacists and patients will expropriate their knowledge and thus undercut their professional autonomy and ability to make a living.

Since patients expect to pay for medicine, not a physician's evaluation and management services, it is difficult to break from the institution of physician dispensing while individual patients bear the majority of medical costs. As the organizational arrangements surrounding the clinical encounter transform—with the introduction of social insurance and large third-party payers that pay for the majority of services—these shared beliefs will gradually change. Spurring a new, shared belief to regulate behavior is the challenge. As policymakers strive to cut rising health-care costs and wasteful overuse—while making the fruits of medical and pharmaceutical innovation available to all—the logic of specialization and separating economic interests comes to the fore.

Via strategic purchasing, patient education, and so on, policymakers seek to change the shared belief that patients pay for medication, not the diagnosis and evaluation skills of medical professionals. Gradually, patients and providers will reconstruct their shared beliefs about their functions and associated income streams. But reform will take time and entail conflict, as professional identities and powerful economic interests are threatened by the separation of prescribing and dispensing. Furthermore, the modernizing of herbal medicine—through standardized manufacturing processes, packaging, and marketing—fosters patients' ability to self-medicate and threatens to put dispensing physicians out of business.

Why did Europe separate prescribing from dispensing earlier than East Asia? Clearly, one contributing factor was the absence of a strong identification of medical skill with compounding medications. The protection of property rights and the ability to regulate dispensing (including, in some cases, medicine prices and pharmacy locations) also contributed to this separation. As in the case of many other institutional innovations that took root in Europe, these ideas were "borrowed from medieval Italian city states or Islam or Byzantium and then elaborated upon" (North 1991:105). Early on, apothecaries and pharmacists developed a relatively high social rank that allowed their profession to stake an exclusive claim on the role of dispensing.[6] This socioeconomic status derived in part from pharmacists' association with the commercially vital spice trade. Thus, ironically, both the independence and integration of the pharmacy profession in the East and the West appears inextricably linked to Eastern herbs and medications.

Conclusion

In sum, shared beliefs regarding the medical profession, the potency of drugs, and the property rights of "secret formulas" (mifang) have sustained the institution of physician dispensing and continue to shape clinical reality in East Asia. Our specific hypotheses, derivable from formal modeling (Eggleston 2008), are as follows:

- The institution of physician dispensing in East Asia is consistent with the longstanding belief that specialized medical knowledge is embodied in medication, which is thus the expected outcome (or "product") of a patient-doctor interaction.
- As a consequence of this belief, both patients and providers place low value on the diagnostic, evaluative, and managerial services of physicians (relative to the tangible output of medication) and systematically pay less (or not at all) for these services. Thus, seeking medical expertise to obtain proper medication—but self-medicating if the medication and information on its proper use is available directly—become patient norms.
- Professional norms coevolve to place primary importance, during clinical encounters, on describing how the patient should prepare and eat the medicine, while preserving the secrets of the medication mixture. These norms are linked to ineffective contracting and enforcement mechanisms for property rights over "secret formulas." Social norms accept higher prices for effective herbal remedies (analogous to patent rights to spur innovation) while delegitimizing payment for diagnostic services.
- Separating physician diagnosis from dispensing (and readjusting prices to reflect the physician's diagnostic, evaluation, and management efforts) only becomes feasible when patients no longer are paying out of pocket (and expecting the main service to be a drug) or change their beliefs. But

beliefs are likely to change more slowly than the pace of technological change in medicine (as seen in the past several decades)—and slower than policymakers' efforts to control costs.

- The development of a large third-party payer, such as NHI in Korea, changes the rules of the game and encourages legislating the separation of prescribing and dispensing. Professionals and patients thus have to change their shared beliefs to fit this new organizational model. The design of the legal reform itself and the reality of clinical practice are the legacy of the physician-dispensing institution.

We conclude with a brief return to the normative question of relative optimality. Separation of prescribing and dispensing is neither innately pernicious nor inherently modern and efficient. It is not a panacea for the appropriate use of medications.

To suggest that the integration of prescribing and dispensing leads to inherently more ethically questionable exploitation of asymmetric information would be to stretch the truth. Certainly, difficult questions about regulating the practice of provider ownership in ancillary medical organizations and self-referral are not unheard of in societies with a long history of separating prescribing and dispensing. A prime example might be the proliferation of diagnostic imaging technologies (such as the CAT scan and MRI) and the regulation of self-referral practices. U.S. physicians evading self-referral restrictions by using imaging technology in their own practices bear a striking resemblance to Taiwanese physicians evading the separation of prescribing and dispensing laws by hiring pharmacists to dispense in their own clinics (Chou et al., 2003, report the latter phenomenon). The beliefs about medical skill sets and appropriate integrated skills may differ, but the potential for a conflict of interest is no less—to the detriment of patients and the socially desired allocation of resources.

The financial incentives associated with prescribing a certain medication may change as a consequence of separation but not necessarily shift toward the socially optimal goal. Physicians may no longer have strong incentives to prescribe according to relative profitability. They may instead have incentive to ignore costs altogether and prescribe whatever patients and colleagues view as the highest-quality drug, regardless of cost-effectiveness or affordability. For some patients this may be desirable. Indulging patient moral hazard and adhering to perceived quality as the sole criterion may strengthen the agency relationship and physician-patient trust. For society as a whole, however, resources may still be allocated inappropriately.

Finally, population aging and the increasing burden of chronic disease have spurred innovative thinking about health-care delivery, such as utilizing pharmacists as convenient and inexpensive coordinators of chronic disease management. A limited reintegration of the prescribing and dispensing functions, enabling and legitimizing the pharmacists' role of giving advice about treatment options and patient self-management, might be appropriate. In the end, policies most likely to be effective should both respect historical and cultural legacies while pushing the envelope to shape system incentives so that they reward prescribing, dispensing, and other activities according to their contribution to social value.

Notes

[1] The authors would like to thank participants of the March 2008 coauthors' meeting at Stanford University for comments on this chapter, especially Maarten Bode and Soonman Kwon.

[2] The *Gu-min-bang* (emergency treatment booklet) and the *Dong-eui-bo-gam* (treatment text for physicians and the upper class) were published to deepen the understanding of the importance of medicine and acupuncture, and the general public was encouraged to rely on them (Shin 2001).

[3] The Yi Dynasty, under Western countries' influence, established a new government called Daehan Jae-gook. King Go-jong continued his role as a dictator of this new governing body until 1910.

[4] The Korean government reinstated the system of traditional physicians in 1953.

[5] This law was valid until June 2000. The law was then amended, making drug dispensing without a prescription illegal. The Separation Law was implemented in July 2000 as part of the health reform agenda; see Kwon (2008).

[6] "The Italian pharmacist was always considered a patrician" (Sonnedecker 1976:59). Similarly, "the social status of the French *apothicaire* from the 14th to the 18th century was doubtless that of a patrician" (Sonnedecker 1976:70).

References

Anderson, Stuart. 2005a. Pharmacy in the medieval world, 1100 to 1617 AD. In Anderson 2005b, chapter 3, 37–56.

———. 2005b. *Making medicines: A brief history of pharmacy and pharmaceuticals*. London: Pharmaceutical Press.

Aoki, Masahiko. 2001. *Toward a comparative institutional analysis*. Comparative Institutional Analysis Series. Cambridge and London: MIT Press.

Chou, Y. J., W. C. Yip, C. H. Lee, N. Huang, Y. P. Sun, and H. J. Chang. 2003. Impact of separating drug prescribing and dispensing on provider behaviour: Taiwan's experience. *Health Policy and Planning* 18 (3) (Sep): 316–29.

Cochran, Sherman. 2006. *Chinese medicine men: Consumer culture in China and Southeast Asia*. Cambridge and London: Harvard Univ. Press.

Court, William. 2005. Pharmacy from the ancient world to 1100 AD. In Anderson 2005b, 21–36.

Eggleston, K. 2008. Comparative institutional analysis of the integration of diagnosis and treatment in health care markets: Evidence from physician dispensing in East Asia. Working paper, Asia Health Policy Program, Walter

H. Shorenstein Asia-Pacific Research Center, Stanford Univ.

Greif, Avner. 2006. *Institutions and the path to the modern economy: Lessons from medieval trade.* Political Economy of Institutions and Decisions series. Cambridge and New York: Cambridge Univ. Press.

Hart, O. 1995. *Firms, contracts, and financial structure.* New York: Oxford Univ. Press.

Hart, O., and J. Moore. 1990. Property rights and the nature of the firm. *The Journal of Political Economy* 98 (6): 1119–58.

Higa, Kiyoshi. 1932. Essay on physicians of Cho-sun (Korea). Joong-Oe Eu-sa Shin-bo, July 28th.

Hunt, John A. 2005. Pharmacy in the modern world, 1841 to 1986. In Anderson 2005b, 77–94.

Iizuka, T. 2007. Experts' agency problems: Evidence from the prescription drug market in Japan. *RAND Journal of Economics* 38 (3): 844–62.

Kleinman, A. 1980. *Patients and healers in the context of culture: An exploration of the borderland between anthropology, medicine and psychiatry.* Univ. of California Press.

Kwon, Soonman, and Michael R. Reich. 2005. The changing process and politics of health policy in Korea. *Journal of Health Politics, Policy and Law* 30 (6) (12): 1003–25.

North, D. C. 1991. Institutions. *The Journal of Economic Perspectives* 5 (1): 97–112.

PAHS. *See* Pharmacist Association for Healthy Society

Pharmacist Association for Healthy Society. July 1993. Future direction of traditional Korean medicine, where to go? [in Korean]. Pharmacist Association for Healthy Society. Seoul.

Shin, D. W. 2001. Medicine for civilians in the history of Korean medicine [in Korean]. *Critique on Society (Sa-hoe Bi-pyung)* 29, Na-nam Publishing Company, 93–106.

———. 2002. Health policy during Japanese colony [in Korean]. *Korean Culture* 30: 333–70.

Sonnedecker, G. 1976. *Kremers and Urdang's history of pharmacy.* Philadelphia, PA: American Institute History of Pharmacy.

Worling, Peter. 2005. Pharmacy in the early modern world, 1617 to 1841 AD. In Anderson 2005b, chapter 5, 57–76.

Yang, J. P. 2006. Changing environment of medicine and the role of herbal medicine dealers during 1880–1910 period [in Korean]. *Korean Journal of Medical History* 15 (December 2006): 189–209.

Prescribing Patterns in Australia: Determinants and Implications for the Asia-Pacific

Siaw-Teng Liaw

This chapter analyzes prescribing patterns in Australia and how they are influenced by a complex interplay of intrinsic and extrinsic factors under the National Medicines Policy (NMP). The quality use of medicine (QUM) requires a multidisciplinary approach, including contributions from the government, the pharmaceutical industry, health professionals, consumers, and researchers. Strategies to contain costs often conflict with those to promote quality health care and medicine use, creating significant tension at the clinical level. Well-implemented electronic prescribing and decision-support systems are possible and will effectively promote safety and quality. This chapter discusses the relevance and applicability of such systems to Australia and other Asia-Pacific nations.

The Prescribing Environment in Australia

The Pharmaceutical Benefits Scheme (PBS) and Medicare Australia subsidize medicines and health services, respectively. Both put a cap on individual annual spending on medicine and health care, after which citizens receive free services. The Repatriation PBS (RPBS) provides veterans with free medicine. Prescription medicines included in the PBS may (1) be unrestricted, (2) be restricted to specific conditions, or (3) require permission to prescribe to specific eligible patients. Doctors telephone a central agency for permission, a time-consuming clerical process seen by doctors as a cost-containment strategy (Liaw et al. 2003).More recently, a streamlined authority codes scheme was introduced to allow doctors to prescribe authority-required drugs from a list of (cheaper) drugs, using a drug group number available online and bypassing the phone-approval process.

The majority of Australian general practitioners/family physicians (GPs/FPs) use computers to prescribe and print scripts (McInnes et al. 2006). The Australian government promotes this through practice incentives payments (PIPs) for the use of information and communication technology (ICT), such as the Internet-based Medicare Online[1] and Medicare Easyclaim,[2] and subsidies to use ICT infrastructure such as Broadband for Health. The National E-Health Transition Authority (NEHTA)[3] was established to develop interoperability standards for the sharing of health information as well as a national electronic health record (EHR) system, HealthConnect (Health Insurance Commission,

HIC, 2008), which has a medicine component (MediConnect). As more evidence supports the cost-effectiveness of computerized decision support (see, for example, Kawamoto et al. 2005) and proposed strategies to promote a national e-health and decision-support program (National Electronic Decision Support Taskforce, NEDST, 2002), the future is likely to involve e-commerce, e-prescribing, and decision-support systems.

Prescribing Patterns

Case Study: Medicine Use in the PBS

Dr. Karen Lee, a GP/FP, was working through her busy Monday patient list when she was interrupted by a call from the local pharmacist. She had prescribed acyclovir, an authority-required medication, without using the appropriate prescription form during a Sunday morning home visit. The visit was to a 23-year-old patient who had been suffering painful shingles for 24 hours. Dr. Lee hadn't used an authority-required prescription form because she could not access the "authority hotline" after hours.

Dr. Lee assured the pharmacist that an authorized script would be mailed to him as soon as possible, put down the phone, and cursed inwardly since filling one out would take time—and she was already running late!

Dr. Lee hurried through her consultation with the elderly diabetic. As she used her clinical information system to generate repeat scripts for this patient's prescriptions, she found herself appreciating the computer-generated information on the myriad regular and restricted prescribing requirements. If only she could send the prescription directly to the pharmacist instead of waiting for the printed copy! She ignored the computer's usual warning about the possible interaction between the diclofenac (nonsteriodal anti-inflammatory drug, NSAID) and the antidiabetics that this elderly patient was taking. She did not have the time to discuss the issues of adherence and appropriate use of medicine, but she printed the medicine information for the patient to study at home.

She found the software's pop-up advertisements a nuisance, but she'd heard the software company's claim that these kept the system's price down at a reasonable level.

Now for the authority-required medicine form she'd promised over the phone. Dr. Lee first checked the Medicare Web site for the streamlined authority codes scheme to see if acyclovir was on the list of (cheaper) drugs that did not need the time-consuming phone approval. To her disappointment, it was not. She then rang the toll-free number. The usual recording said that the lines were busy and that someone would be with her shortly. She spent the next fifteen minutes listening to piped music and a recorded message every three minutes, before putting down the phone. This process was repeated twice before she got through. She went through the motions, paraphrased the words as required by the PBS to the administrative person at the end of the phone, received the authority number for the acyclovir prescription, printed the script, signed it, and arranged for it to be sent to the pharmacist.

By this time, Dr. Lee was even further behind in her Monday schedule . . . and she needed to finish on time, so that she would not be late picking up her children from school before going off to a drug-company-sponsored educational event organized through her local Division of General Practice (supported financially by the Australian government).

As prescribers and gatekeepers to the Australian health system, GPs/FPs such as Dr. Lee shape Australia's prescribing patterns. The domains of general/ family practice—first-contact care, continuity of care, coordinated and integrated care, comprehensive care—and the patient-doctor relationship (Buetow 1995) form a framework for the examination of prescribing patterns and the QUM (Anastasio, Dutro, and Parent 1986).

Australian GPs/FPs conducted more than 100 million consultations in 2006–2007, managing about 1.5 problems per encounter (Britt et al. 2008). The exponential increase from 5.4 million consultations in 1999–2000 reflects an aging population with chronic diseases such as diabetes, cancer, cardiovascular disease, and mental health problems. While respiratory diseases remain the most prevalent problem in general practice, there has been a decrease in the management of upper respiratory tract infections, probably related to ongoing public education on how to self-limit viral illnesses with symptomatic treatments. In some other Asia-Pacific countries, where antibiotics are freely available without prescription, self-management of acute respiratory infections often involves antibiotics, which can lead to widespread antibiotic resistance (Hui et al. 1997) or self-harm; in fact, some over-the-counter (OTC) drugs available without prescription in these countries have been withdrawn in Europe and North America (Greenhalgh 1987).

Overall, GPs/FPs prescribed 83.3 prescriptions per 100 encounters in 2006–2007, down from 94 in 1999–2000. At least 1 medicine was prescribed, supplied, or advised in over half the cases (Britt et al. 2008). Extrapolating to the 103 million GP/FP encounters claimed from Medicare in 2006–2007, it is estimated that the Australian GPs/FPs prescribed more than 85 million medicines (82 percent), supplied 9.1 million medicines directly to the patient (8.8 percent), and recommended medicines for OTC purchase on 9.6 million occasions (9.2 percent). This represents half of the PBS-subsidized pharmaceuticals and one-fifth of the OTC purchases (table 17.1).

In Australia, cardiovascular medicines (55.6 million to 59.8 million prescriptions) were the most prescribed PBS-subsidized medicines in 2003–2005, followed by medicines for the nervous system, alimentary tract, infections, musculoskeletal

Table 17.1 All PBS and Nonsubsidized Pharmaceuticals Prescribed, by ATC Group

ATC group	2003 (Number of scripts)		2004 (Number of scripts)		2005 (Number of scripts)	
	PBS/RPBS	Non-PBS	PBS/RPBS	Non-PBS	PBS/RPBS	Non-PBS
A. Alimentary tract	22,740,691	2,850,999	24,440,087	3,016,850	25,049,634	3,063,200
B. Blood and blood forming	6,055,450	571,578	6,832,327	649,604	6,982,053	771,841
C. Cardiovascular	55,636,433	3,550,849	59,739,321	4,245,356	59,775,680	6,622,648
D. Dermatologicals	3,197,628	2,174,243	3,252,060	2,475,662	3,097,776	2,556,379
G. Genitourinary	4,757,566	6,230,972	4,459,829	6,561,123	4,125,163	6,359,089
H. Hormonal	2,598,636	918,520	2,717,339	1,055,169	2,707,859	1,166,942
J. Antiinfectives	12,630,131	9,184,888	12,989,871	10,683,031	12824919	11,406,277
L. Antineoplastic	1,200,722	816,18	1335278	84,236	1,431,572	94,423
M. Musculoskeletal	13,069,783	2,038,056	13,111,616	2,172,133	10,639,123	2,442,114
N. Nervous system	35,150,198	7,214,871	36,804,032	7,852,334	36,314,641	8,630,443
P. Antiparasitic	1,129,459	372,692	1,158,838	439,173	790,462	468,753
R. Respiratory system	10,847,076	3,315,126	10,763,850	3,301,679	10,521,188	3,153,888
S. Sensory organs	8,034,353	1,700,054	8,430,985	1,962,634	8,506,734	1,971,560
V. Various	692,364	18,639	678,975	17,814	663,368	15,317
Other	317,151	1,778,849	334,720	1,816,467	339,623	1,527,959
Total scripts	178,057,641	42,001,954	187,049,128	46,333,265	183,769,795	50,250,833
Total (PBS + non-PBS)	*220,059,595 scripts*		*233,382,393 scripts*		*234,020,628 scripts*	

Source: Australian Statistics on Medicines 2004–2005.

Notes: ATC is the drug classification based on anatomy, therapy, chemistry (ATC); PBS = Pharmaceutical Benefits Scheme; RPBS = Repatriation Pharmaceutical Benefits Scheme; non-PBS = the drug is not in the PBS schedule, and therefore not subsidized.

system, respiratory system, sensory organs, blood and blood-forming system, genitourinary system, skin, endocrine system, cancers, and parasitic infections (Commonwealth Department of Health and Aged Care 2005).

An increasing number of medicines are not subsidized by the PBS/RPBS because either (1) the total costs of listed medicines are equal to or less than the statutory copayment; (2) they are dispensed through private prescriptions for items not listed in the PBS/RPBS or do not meet the PBS/RPBS dispensing criteria; or (3) they are OTC medicines such as aspirin, cough and cold medicines, vitamins and minerals, some herbal and other complementary medicines, and medical nondurable goods. Increasing copayments could increase financial stress, leading to reduced access to medicines or substitution with cheaper and less effective alternatives—potentially compromising safety and quality (Sweeny 2007).

Of the nonsubsidized medicines, the anti-infectives are the most prescribed, followed by medicines for the nervous system, cardiovascular system, genitourinary system, respiratory system, alimentary tract, skin, musculoskeletal system, sensory organs, endocrine system, blood and blood-forming system, parasitic infections, and cancers. Nonsubsidized cardiovascular medicines increased at a greater rate than genitourinary medicines, consistent with the overall rate of increase in cardiovascular diseases.

From 2003 to 2005, prescriptions of nonsubsidized nervous system medicines increased from 17 to 19 percent. The pattern is similar for paracetamol and codeine with paracetamol (Commonwealth Department of Health and Aged Care 2005). This complements the finding that the prescribing of celecoxib decreased (with a concomitant increase in meloxicam), reflecting an effort to manage patients with chronic musculoskeletal problems in the midst of concerns about the safety of Vioxx (Britt et al. 2008).

Prescriptions of nonsubsidized anti-infectives increased from 42 percent in 2003 to 47 percent in 2005. While the overall rate of antibiotic prescribing has not changed significantly since 2001–2002, the reported prescribing rate of amoxicillin and cephalexin continued to increase (Britt et al. 2007). Amoxicillin and cephalexin were among the top ten prescribed drugs in Australia in 2004–2005 by daily defined dose (table 17.2) and prescription count (table 17.3) but not in terms of cost (table 17.4). The most expensive medicines were statins and proton pump inhibitors.

The decreased GP/FP prescribing of ranitidine and omeprazole, counteracted by an increase in esomeprazole, reflects a common pharmaceutical industry practice of producing variations of the same old drug. The decrease in diuretics prescriptions (with a concomitant increase in combination angiotensin-converting enzymes [ACEs], inhibitors, and diuretics) reflects an increasing trend in combination medications (Britt et al. 2007), an issue present in some developing countries, especially in the private sector (Greenhalgh 1987).

In general, the fall in GP/FP prescriptions between 1999 and 2000 is related to the wider availability of some medications for OTC purchase, the increasing availability of combination medications, changes in GP/FP prescribing behavior, and the broadening of government initiatives such as the free supply of selected vaccines (Britt et al. 2008).

Table 17.2 Top Ten Medicines (defined daily dose (DDD)/1,000 population/day)

Top 10 medicines 2004	2004 DDD/1,000/day	2005 DDD/1,000/day	Top 10 medicines 2005
1. Atorvastatin	90.917	106.830	Atorvastatin
2. Simvastatin	54.716	57.490	Simvastatin
3. Ramipril	35.333	38.034	Ramipril
4. Diltiazem HCL	34.787	30.996	Diltiazem HCL
5. Salbutamol	27.400	26.176	Salbutamol
6. Omeprazole	21.284	20.140	Omeprazole
7. Irbesartan	30.006	21.893	Irbesartan
8. Frusemide	20.494	19.647	Frusemide
9. Aspirin	18.514	19.269	Aspirin
10. Sertraline	17.649	17.790	Sertraline

Source: Australian Statistics on Medicines 2004–2005.
Note: Total DDD/1,000/day is calculated based on combined data from the PBS/RPBS database and the pharmacy guild survey.

Table 17.3 Top Ten Medicines by Prescription Count

Top 10 medicines 2004	Total scripts 2004	Total scripts 2005	Top 10 medicines 2005
1. Atorvastatin	7,718,626	8,533,868	Atorvastatin
2. Simvastatin	6,236,140	6,329,242	Simvastatin
3. Paracetamol	4,908,374	4,729,588	Paracetamol
4. Amoxycillin	4,809,835	4,981,940	Amoxycillin
5. Omeprazole	4,517,212	4,323,201	Omeprazole
6. Salbutamol	4,317,044	4,166,844	Salbutamol
7. Atenolol	4,087,266	4,151,893	Atenolol
8. Codeine+ Paracetamol	3,964,510	4,038,763	Codeine+ Paracetamol
9. Irbesartan	3,635,606	3,780,906	Irbesartan
10. Cefalexin	3,498,816	3,730,428	Cefalexin

Source: Australian Statistics on Medicines 2004–2005.
Note: Total scripts = total scripts prescribed from PBS/RPBS data + total scripts prescribed from pharmacy guild survey data.

Table 17.4 Top Ten Medicines by Cost to the Australian Government

Top 10 medicines 2004	Total cost 2004 (A$)	Total cost 2005 (A$)	Top 10 medicines 2005
1. Atorvastatin	507,316,672	574,426,634	Atorvastatin
2. Simvastatin	417,906,953	400,703,647	Simvastatin
3. Omeprazole	220,866,475	202,379,149	Omeprazole
4. Salmeterol+ Fluticazone	193,330,502	198,963,992	Salmeterol+ Fluticazone
5. Olanzepine	154,713,064	192,732,358	Esomeprazole
6. Esomeprazole	153,336,176	173,060,819	Clopidogrel
7. Clopidogrel	150,990,376	156,019,723	Olanzepine
8. Pravastatin	139,827,498	126,981,644	Pravastatin
9. Pantoprazole	119,871,009	126,406,633	Pantoprazole
10. Alendronic acid	115,377,255	126,177,262	Alendronic acid

Source: Australian Statistics on Medicines 2004–2005.
Note: Total cost = daily defined dose (DDD)/1,000/day from PBS/RPBS data + total scripts prescribed from PBS/RPBS data.

Australian Medicine Policy

Explaining prescribing patterns in Australia, as elsewhere, requires an understanding of the national economy and governance, the NMP, and the complex interplay of intrinsic and extrinsic factors that determine doctors' prescribing behaviors (Greenhalgh and Gill 1997) and consumers' needs.

Formalized in 1996, the Australian NMP is described further by Hans Löfgren in chapter 6 of this volume. The four tenets of the NMP are:

(1) The availability of medicines that meet appropriate standards of quality, safety, and efficacy, while allowing the introduction of new products to the Australian market in a timely manner
(2) The provision of timely access to the medicines that Australians need, at a cost that individuals and the community can afford
(3) The achievement of high QUM
(4) The maintenance of a responsible and viable pharmaceutical industry

The NMP addresses the main determinants of pharmaceutical expenditure: (1) the subsidy amount, medicines subsidized, people subsidized, and size of copayment; (2) the cost of drug development and dispensing; and (3) the appropriateness of use. The NMP encompasses a mix of educational, managerial, and regulatory strategies within a cost-effectiveness model, emphasizing the links among government, industry, prescribers, and dispensers.

The Australian Pharmaceutical Advisory Council (APAC), which includes representation from all the major professional and consumer groups involved in pharmaceutical issues in Australia, has a broad charter to develop, promote, influence, and assist in the implementation of the NMP in Australia.

Quality Use of Medicine (QUM)

The National Strategy for QUM (Commonwealth Department of Health, Housing, and Community Services 1992) is multidisciplinary, emphasizing that doctors, pharmacists, nurses, and consumers all play a role in promoting the QUM. The National Prescribing Service (NPS) was formed to provide independent advice to the government and independent information to health professionals and consumers. In January 2008, the online QUM Map Project[4] listed 1,429 QUM projects in Australia. These range across disciplines; hospitals and general practices; regulatory, managerial, and educational strategies; and QUM attributes, which include efficacy, equity, safety, appropriateness, and cost (Holden and Wilson 1996).

The safety dimension is important. An estimated 16 percent of hospitalized patients suffer an adverse drug event (ADE); 50 percent of such events are preventable (Wilson and Van Der Weyden 2005). About 10.4 percent of the 17.5 million people who make 95 million visits to their GP/FP annually will experience an ADE. About 1 million of these events are moderate or severe; 138,000 require hospitalization (Miller, Britt, and Valenti 2006). Over half (56 percent) of preventable ADEs occur during drug ordering (prescribing) and 4 percent when drug orders are filled (dispensing) (Leape et al. 1995).

QUM research includes data collection and monitoring systems (linking drug utilization, health services, and clinical information) to examine cost-effectiveness, safety, quality, and appropriate prescribing of medicines, including those used off-label and outside PBS-approved indications (called *leakage*). Such research guides the development and administration of pharmaceutical policy (Tang 1996; World Health Organization, WHO, 1985). The main sources of information about Australian prescribing activities are the Australian Statistics on Medicines (ASM, Commonwealth Department of Health and Aged Care 2005) and the Bettering the Evaluation And Care of Health (BEACH), report on "General Practice Activity in Australia" (Britt et al. 2007). The ASM data set is derived from PBS utilization data and does not include a large proportion of public hospital drug use, OTC purchases, or the supply of highly specialized drugs to outpatients through public hospitals. These national data sets are insufficient to understand the QUM beyond prescribing rates; information is incomplete on some classes of drugs, patient characteristics, and indications for use. In contrast, the information from the electronic prescribing packages of participating GPs/FPs, which includes diagnosis data, enables an assessment of the appropriateness of therapy (Robertson et al. 1999).

Variations in health and medicine policies and prescribing and dispensing environments in the Asia-Pacific make it difficult to extrapolate findings across the region. Poorer countries are often characterized by limited access to and nonavailability of medicines, relatively underdeveloped health-care systems, inadequate financial resources, lack of national drug legislation, ineffective implementation, and self-medication involving many potent drugs available without prescription (Bapna, Tripathi, and Tekur 1996). Nevertheless, there must be universal benchmarks in defining and measuring the QUM in relation to health outcomes.

Appropriate Prescribing and the QUM

Appropriateness refers to decision-making that maximizes the net individual health gain within a society's available resources (Buetow et al. 1997). It incorporates a biopsychosocial approach to the QUM and health care (Liaw et al. 2003). Indicators of inappropriate prescribing include:

- Adverse medication events (Barraclough 2001; Fletcher 2000; Wilson and Van Der Weyden 2005)
- Underuse of appropriate medicines, for example, prophylactic aspirin, hormone replacement therapy (HRT), nicotine substitutes, beta-blockers after myocardial infarction, steroids in asthma (Kerr 1994)
- Leakage of restricted medicines, for example, proton pump inhibitors used outside recommended guidelines (McManus et al. 1998; Pillans et al. 2000)
- Nondispensing of prescribed medicines (Gardner et al. 1996)
- Continued prescription of superseded medicines (Britten et al. 1995; Britten et al. 2000)
- Inappropriate use of OTC medicines (Erwin, Britten, and Jones 1997)
- Overprescribing, polypharmacy, and adverse events (National Health Strategy 1992; Pillans and Roberts 1999)
- Doctor shopping—that is, seeking advice and, often, drugs of dependence from multiple doctors (HIC 2000)
- Use of more expensive medications with no clear advantages (Barrie 1996)

Prescribing and the QUM

A dimension of appropriate prescribing is off-label and unlicensed prescribing (Stafford 2008; Liaw et al. 2004). Off-label prescribing describes the use of regulatory authority-approved medicines that are used outside the terms of their manufacturer's product information (PI), with respect to dose, indication, age, route of administration, contraindication, and duration of therapy. "Unlicensed" drug use occurs when the medicine is used without a manufacturer's PI. Off-label prescribing is significant because it permits clinicians to explore the innovative use of existing medicines, access potentially valuable medications, and adopt new practices based on emerging evidence. It is often the only mechanism available to treat "orphan" conditions with no ongoing R&D, but it implicitly condones the use of medicines without fully evaluating safety and efficacy. When it involves newer, expensive drugs, health-care costs increase. While off-label prescribing is legal in Australia, its promotion is not.

It is estimated that one-fifth (21 percent) of office-based prescribing in the United States is off-label, particularly in the case of anticonvulsants and some cardiac medications. Most (73 percent) off-label prescribing has little or no scientific support (Radley, Finkelstein, and Stafford 2006). In Australia more than half (63 percent) of a random sample of active prescribers reported that they sometimes prescribed off-label in both community and hospital settings, with no resulting harm (Liaw et al. 2004). Their responses to ten off-label prescribing scenarios—ranging from coloxyl for softening ear wax to aldara for warts—suggested that the decision to prescribe off-label products was influenced by the risks and benefits to the specific patient group, familiarity with the medicine and its appropriateness, awareness of the prescribing practice, and belief that the patients were informed. This measured approach to off-label and unlicensed prescribing is reassuring. But a rational policy on off-label and unlicensed prescribing must be developed and adopted by the regulatory bodies, profession, and industry. Proposed strategies include postmarketing surveillance of the off-label uses of medicines with analyses and dissemination, appropriate marketing of medicines stipulating stage-4 comparator clinical trials, requiring information about the anticipated off-label uses as part of a drug's review for initial approval (Stafford 2008), and education programs supported by a compendium of off-label use in common practice (Liaw et al. 2004).

Patient-prescriber Relations and Their Impact on the QUM

Prescribing behaviors result from individual physicians addressing the needs of individual patients with particular illnesses. The doctor-patient relationship and the expectations and perceptions of patients are important determinants of prescribing behavior (Liaw et al. 2003; Webb and Lloyd 1994) and are often valued over the cost of medicines (Stevenson et al. 1999). Patients' perceptions are related to their hopes and education as well as the education and characteristics of the doctor (Britten and Ukoumunne 1997). Doctors often (25 percent) misperceive patients' expectations (Cockburn and Pitt 1997). Misunderstandings occur when the doctor is unaware of the patient's information, patients withhold information, the doctor's information is not understood by the patient, conflicting information is given or there is disagreement over the attribution of side effects, or there is no communication about the doctor's treatment recommendations (Britten et al. 2000). Addictive drugs (for example, opioids and benzodiazepines) pose significant dilemmas, especially if the patients' medications were commenced elsewhere and the patient does not have an established relationship with the prescribing doctor (Bendtsen et al. 1999a, 1999b).

Higher prescribing rates are generally found among busier practitioners who see more difficult patients; high-volume medical practices often use prescription to terminate purposefully short visits (Soumerai, McLaughlin, and Avorn 1989). Prescribing medications as placebos for self-limiting conditions (Bradley 1991; Webb and Lloyd 1994) can lead to inappropriate expectations or demands. Compared to low prescribers, Canadian high prescribers were more likely to be male, trained in Canada, qualified by the College of Family Physicians of Canada (CFPC), practice on more days, and see and bill more patients per day (Davidson, Molloy, and Bedard 1995). In one study, high prescribers had 50 percent more patients with heart disease, asthma, diabetes, and thyroid disease than low prescribers did (McGavock 1988). High prescribers and high-cost generators were also less likely to shift to generic prescribing (Avery et al. 2000a; Avery et al. 2000b), suggesting that strategies to reduce spending on antibiotics must focus on high prescribers (Steffensen, Schonheyder, and Sorensen 1997).

Patient attributes (such as age, social class, ethnic group, medical or paramedical background, and how well known the patient is to the doctor) can influence prescribing behavior (Bradley 1991). In Hong Kong the use of prescription drugs among the elderly is associated with the presence of chronic disease, poor self-perceived health, and being female and a resident in institutions. The use of nonprescription drugs is associated with joint pain, dissatisfaction with living arrangements, and age (Woo et al. 1995). The patient's medical condition and health status were the most important factors determining care decisions (Scott and Shiell 1997); the diagnosis was the major influence in prescribing in New Zealand (Davis, Yee, and Millar 1994). But when the doctor was unclear about the need for anti-infectives (Miller et al. 1999) or proton pump inhibitors (Boath and Blenkinsopp 1997), patient demands were seen to influence prescribing, regardless of indications. Demands from other health professionals, such as a standing order for sedatives and psychoactive drugs in nursing homes, also play a role.

Self-treatment, defined as "diagnosing a health problem, choosing medication or treatment and administering this without professional assistance," is prevalent in developing countries, even when a variety of established health services are available (Brieger, Ramakrishna, and Adeniyi 1986). The implications are significant when potent medicines are available without prescription (Bapna, Tripathi, and Tekur 1996). According to a study by Hui et al. (1997), before Chinese parents sought medical care for acute respiratory infections, many of the children in the counties (47 percent), townships (25 percent), and villages (18 percent) had already used antibiotics obtained without prescription. This practice had cost, safety, and quality impacts in the poorer, rural (Zhan et al. 1998), and more affluent urban areas of many Asia-Pacific countries (Quah 1985). Prescription-only drugs were used widely to self-medicate in culturally specific ways, suggesting that local drug-use patterns must be studied before introducing interventions (Greenhalgh 1987).

Strategies to Promote the QUM

The growing evidence supporting complex and multifaceted interventions (Gill et al. 1999; Horowitz 1999; Roter et al. 1998) suggests that promoting the QUM is most likely to succeed when it employs a blend of educational, managerial, and regulatory strategies (Hogerzeil 1995)—including the use of enabling ICT (Liaw and Schattner 2008)—relevant to the particular needs of health professionals and patients.

Regulatory strategies

NMPs balance public health, public expenditure, and industry interests (see Löfgren, chapter 6 of this volume). Australia and most other Asia-Pacific nations have such policies, usually based on the WHO Action Programme on Essential Drugs and Vaccines (Ess, Schneeweiss, and Szucs 2003; WHO 1988a, 1991), which includes national drug policies, essential drug lists, the WHO Certification Scheme, ethical medicines promotion, and operational research and training (WHO 1984). The Australian PBS/RPBS, along with Medicare Australia, has kept prices relatively low through monopsony purchasing (Harvey and Murray 1995; Johnston and Zeckhauser, chapter 7 of this volume). The availability of cheap generics in the international market has put pressure on PBS pricing arrangements (Löfgren 2007a). The balance of public and private health-care funding is another issue that influences the PBS and QUM (Richardson and Segal 2004).

Evidence of a new medicine's efficacy and safety is universally required for licensing. For listing in the Australian PBS, a pharmaceutical firm must submit a comprehensive evaluation, including its cost-effectiveness (Bloor, Maynard, and Freemantle 1996; Drummond, Jonsson, and Rutten 1997). Ontario, Canada, has similar policies (Angus and Karpetz 1998). Evaluation must consider contextual and methodological issues such as variability and proper choice of comparators (Salkeld, Davey, and Arnolda 1995). Pharmaceutical manufacturers criticize the use of comprehensive, comparative, and cost-effectiveness evaluations, saying they represent cost containment (Bell 1995; Towse and Wells 1995) and may delay access to new medicines, restrict prescribing choice, and reduce funding for pharmaceutical research (Clear and Grobler 1998; Drummond, Jonsson, and Rutten 1997).

Pricing policies include product price control, reference pricing, and profit control. Some countries place a limit on drug costs or otherwise control the profits of drug manufacturers, wholesalers, and retailers (Bloor, Maynard, and Freemantle 1996). Reference-based pricing can limit the use of therapeutically equivalent medicines from the same class (Bourgault et al. 1999; Grootendorst and Holbrook 1999). For example, New Zealand subsidizes only the cheapest representative of a class of drug. Budgetary restrictions also affect physicians' prescribing behavior (Ess, Schneeweiss, and Szucs 2003).

Patients' demand for drugs can be managed by limiting subsidies, setting copayments, and otherwise designing incentives for the patient's appropriate use of medicine (Ess, Schneeweiss, and Szucs 2003). Some countries reimburse according to the seriousness of the medical condition (Freemantle and Bloor 1996). China uses some economic incentives for both health-care providers and consumers (Dong et al. 1999; Sun and Meng, chapter 11 of this volume). The 30 Baht Health Insurance Scheme in Thailand covers medicine dispensed during hospital visits (Ratanawijitrasin, chapter 4 of this volume).

To promote QUM in developing countries, policymakers must consider inherent politicoeconomic and infrastructural disadvantages, such as poor access to health services and poor control of drug quality (Alubo 1985). Entrepreneurial activities often complicate the regulation of modern drug producers, sellers, prescribers, dispensers, and users (Fabricant and Hirschhorn 1987). The absence of effective regulatory controls can increase the average consumption of medicines, including sales of drugs without a prescription (Bazin 1982). Developing countries need comprehensive quality control and surveillance systems to detect poor-quality and mislabelled medicines (Binka and Wieniawski 1985). Supporting developing countries to produce low-cost, high-quality essential drugs can reduce dependence on the multinational drug industry (Chetley 1985, 1986) and prevent global disasters stemming from unsafe medicines (Santoro and Liu, chapter 14 of this volume).

In many Asia-Pacific countries, the doctor traditionally both prescribes and dispenses medicine, which is seen as the necessary outcome of any doctor-patient interaction (Bode, chapter 15 of this volume). This has persisted even with the advent of Western medicine (Eggleston and Yang, chapter 16 of this volume). Nevertheless, attempts are being made to limit prescribing to doctors and to develop clinical pharmacy services to dispense medicines as a strategy to remove financial conflicts of interest (Wang, Chen, and Lau 1993; Kwon, chapter 1 of this volume; Iizuka, chapter 2; Tomita, chapter 3; Hsieh, chapter 5). To promote the QUM, it is also important to develop pharmacy training programs to ensure the safety and quality of dispensing.

An integrated, interprofessional, and intersectoral approach to the QUM is broadly applicable. For example, national treatment guidelines for sexually transmitted diseases (STDs) in Myanmar need to be complemented by infrastructure and systems to monitor the quality of available anti-infectives (Prazuck et al. 2002). Successful implementation of the WHO case-management program for paediatric pneumonia requires an integrated approach to improving the recognition of childhood pneumonia by parents, promoting earlier presentation to health services, and assuring the availability and rational use of anti-infectives in primary care (Shimouchi et al. 1995). Regulations should be complemented by managerial and educational strategies.

Managerial strategies

There is conflict between the responsibilities of the GP/FP as a personal doctor versus those as a manager of primary health care within a cost-containment framework (McCormick 1996). This can negatively impact the doctor-patient relationship (Newdick 1998) or compromise patient privacy (Liaw et al. 2003). Managerial strategies include prior-authorization requirements to reduce the inappropriate use of nonsteroidal anti-inflammatory drugs in the United States (Smalley et al. 1995); formulary restrictions to reduce indiscriminate antibiotic prescribing (Anassi et al. 1995; Lesar and Briceland 1996; Rifenburg et al. 1996; Vlahovic-Palcevski, Morovic, and Palcevski 2000); therapeutics committees (Weekes and Brooks 1996); and forcing doctors to nominate two generic medications before being able to prescribe a brand-name drug (Ahluwalia et al. 1996; Jones et al. 1996).

Generic or off-patent medicines are believed to be more cost-effective and thus to promote more equitable care (Shrank et al. 2007). But a significant delay between patent expiry and the availability of a generic (Kesselheim, Fischer, and Avorn 2006) and "pseudo-generics" can present problems (Probyn 2004). Strategies to promote generics include differential subsidies (Mager and Cox 2007) and allow pharmacists to substitute generic drugs for proprietary brands (Mott and Cline 2002). While Australian pharmacists receive government incentives to dispense generics (Kalisch, Roughead, and Gilbert 2007), there are no similar incentives for consumers or prescribers (Löfgren 2007b).

Local formularies have reduced costs for new and repeat prescriptions in general practice in the United Kingdom (Dowell, Snadden, and Dunbar 1995; Tomson, Wessling, and Tomson 1994), in managed care organizations in the United States (Lyles and Palumbo 1999), and in the health care system of many developing countries (WHO 1991). Continued peer-review and educational interventions enhance the benefits of formularies (Wyatt et al. 1992).

Weiss et al. (1996) find that GPs/FPs in the United Kingdom are more concerned with overt pressures to prescribe generics and have their prescribing patterns compared with their peers, than with funding arrangements. Whether remuneration is time or content based makes little difference to prescribing, counselling, or treatment in general practice in developed countries (Scott and Shiell 1997). In developing countries, where regulation is not as stringent, financial incentives may have stronger effects on prescribers and dispensers of medicine (Fabricant and Hirschhorn 1987).

The roles of pharmacists are expanding (Benrimoj and Frommer 2004) to include medication reviews in residential aged-care facilities (Roberts, Bateman, and Smith 1997; Roughead 2000), development of formularies, and review of repeat prescriptions (Hamley et al. 1997). These roles are related to the Australian models of interprofessional care in the hospitals and community (Roughead 2000). Some evidence suggests that pharmacist involvement in therapeutic monitoring improves adherence to medicines and reduces costs for asthma (Blackbourn and Sunderland 1987) and for lipid-lowering drug therapy (Peterson et al. 2004). Pharmacists accompanying physicians to visit patients with complex medical conditions reduce costs and simplify medicine regimes without reducing the quality of care (Jameson, Vannoord, and Vanderwoud 1995). Pharmacists employed in primary care practices control prescribing costs sufficiently to offset their employment costs (Rodgers et al. 1999). But while doctors are happy to see pharmacists provide information on medicines or perform simple health checks, they are less happy to see them involved in prescribing decisions (Chandler 2000; Nathan and Sutters 1993).

Drug company promotions can influence prescribing behavior directly as well as via patients and consumers (Orlowski and Wateska 1992). Promotional strategies by the manufacturers of ACE inhibitors and calcium channel blockers helped weaken the impact of the Canadian hypertension guidelines (Huston and Campbell 1998). The pharmaceutical industry in developing countries is charged with indiscriminate promotion, excessive prices, and provision of nonessential drugs (Breckenridge 1986). Drug company warnings of side effects and contraindications in patient package inserts are seldom passed on to the patient in developing countries and are often written in a language the patient does not speak—making grassroots education of patients and doctors essential to promoting appropriate drug use (Greenhalgh 1986).

Educational strategies

Most doctors are conservative prescribers (Taylor and Bond 1991), tending to work from a personal formulary of medicines that they have come to know and understand. Understanding this behavior and the importance of individualized and multifaceted interventions (Gill et al. 1999; Horowitz 1999; Roter et al. 1998) is important in designing and implementing medical education and vocational training strategies to promote behavior change. Three models of prescribing behavior change have been described: accumulation, challenge, and continuity. The *accumulation* model describes incremental shifts in perception. The *challenge* model describes change arising from a dramatic or conflictual clinical situation. In the *continuity* model, change is driven by education, cost pressures, and an accumulated understanding of the actions of the medication (Armstrong, Reyburn, and Jones 1996).

In Australia objective information and an independent formulary is provided by the *Australian Medicines Handbook* and bimonthly editions of *The Australian Prescriber*, and guidelines for clinical decision-making provided by the *Therapeutics Guidelines*, published and updated regularly by expert groups convened by Therapeutic Guideline Limited. Many countries have also developed or purchased online medicine-information services. Information-sharing strategies must recognize that colleagues are an important influence and may serve to effectively prompt the prescribing of a new drug (Christensen and Wertheimer 1979).

Providing feedback on prescribing is more effective when combined with other strategies. Government-sponsored feedback, based on aggregated prescribing data, to Australian GPs/FPs made no impact on prescribing levels of indicator medications (O'Connell, Henry, and Tomlins 1999). Neither did practice profiling and feedback to alter antibiotic prescribing for viral upper respiratory infections in the United States (Mainous et al. 2000). Providing cost information to GPs/FPs may change their behavior in all service areas (Beilby and Silagy 1997) but helping them choose less expensive medications does not necessarily reduce pharmaceutical costs (Vedsted, Nielsen, and Olesen 1997). A drug-cost manual for interns in a U.S. hospital reduced drug expenses (Frazier et al. 1991) but placing price stickers on the vials of medications used by anaesthetists did not (Horrow and Rosenberg 1994). The measurable impact during the feedback phase often disappears once the feedback stops (McGavock 1998). Feedback is effective when combined with reflection (Lassen and Kristensen 1992), peer review (Lagerlov et al. 2000) and prescription analysis, a visit by a pharmacist, a local bulletin, or a locally compiled preferred medication list (Ferguson, Salmond, and Maling 1995).

Academic detailing is effective in the case of GPs/FPs (Braybrook and Walker 1996; Newton-Syms et al. 1992), especially for the prescribing of benzodiazepines by GP/FP registrars (Zwar et al. 1999) and antibiotics (Ilett et al. 2000). Academic detailing by the Australian HIC borrows heavily from the techniques of pharmaceutical representatives and includes the principles of reciprocity, commitment, consistency, social validation, authority, friendship, and exclusivity (Roughead, Harvey, and Gilbert 1998).

Clinical audits have been used to influence physicians' prescribing behaviors with some success (de Vries et al. 1999; de Vries et al. 1996; Jaski et al. 2000; McElnay et al. 1995). But these require access to best practice guidelines and adequate and relevant clinical information, which is only cost-efficient when online information resources and structured EHRs are available. The Australian NPS online clinical audit program[5] provides prompt and useful feedback, but audit data has to be entered manually, a tedious and error-prone process. Much sociotechnical research and development (R&D) is required before clinical information systems can be used for clinical audits and clinical decision support automatically and accurately (NEDST 2002).

Electronic prescribing and decision-support systems

A clinical decision-support system (CDSS) can potentially provide relevant information to the right person at the right time and right place, highlight abnormal values, check for allergies or drug-drug/drug-disease interactions, and make patient-specific recommendations. Physician order entry (POE) and e-prescribing systems are a type of CDSS used to automate the process of drug ordering/prescribing, assist in generating and communicating computerized scripts, and review the prescriptions produced. They can reduce medication errors—a significant cause of iatrogenic injury, death, and costs in hospitals (Kohn, Corrigan, and Donaldson 2000; Leape and Berwick 2005). Computer-assisted prescriptions contain fewer errors than handwritten prescriptions, requiring less pharmacist clarifications (Bizovi et al. 2002). Bates et al. (1998 and 1999) find that pharmaceutical decision support in allergy alerts and suggested drug doses significantly reduce medication errors and potential ADEs in the short and long term. Clinicians are often unaware of clinically significant ADEs that are identified by an alert system (Raschke et al. 1998). In addition, "alert fatigue" is a very real problem—clinicians dismiss or override between 49 percent to 96 percent of drug safety alerts (van der Sijs et al. 2006).

A CDSS can enhance clinical performance in drug dosing, preventive care, and other aspects of medical care (Hunt et al. 1998; Johnston et al. 1994; Sullivan and Mitchell 1995). According to Kawamoto et al. (2005), most (66 percent) CDSSs significantly improve clinical practice, especially if they automatically provide recommendations (rather than just assessments) at the time and location of decision-making within the clinical workflow. Also important are providing periodic performance feedback, sharing recommendations with patients, and requesting that reasons for not following recommendations be documented (Kawamoto et al. 2005). Clinician and other stakeholder involvement were critical to good system design and successful implementation (Liaw et al. 2006).

In the past decade the Australian government has encouraged the majority of Australian GPs/FPs to adopt electronic script printing (Liaw and Tomlins 2005). But computerized tools and protocols are often not user-friendly (Young and Beswick 1995). While promising, computer-based intervention requires careful development and implementation within a comprehensive conceptual framework of intrinsic and extrinsic determinants of technology diffusion and adoption. The Australian approach has been to build national infrastructure, provide a supportive environment, and develop interoperability standards to encourage the computer industry to build a national shared EHR and standards-based e-health system. A national e-health implementation agency is being mooted to complement the National E-Health Transition Authority, whose role is to develop the required standards. A key question is whether the government should build a standards-based reference implementation of the EHR to proactively engage the software industry or continue to only define the specification requirements and leave implementation to the industry. Whatever the approach, medication-management and decision-support programs must incorporate the QUM and health outcomes. Prescriber-patient-dispenser relationships need to be enhanced to promote best practices. And promoting change is important.

Despite demonstrated benefits from well-designed electronic and nonelectronic information management and decision-support systems across a wide range of health-care environments (Kohn, Corrigan, and Donaldson 2000), the safety and quality of medicines used remains highly imperfect in Australia (Barraclough 2001), the United States (Leape and Berwick 2005), and the rest of the world (WHO 2004).

Conclusion

Prescribing patterns in Australia are influenced by a complex interplay of factors that shape the four tenets of the NMP. The integration of the four tenets of Australia's NMP and an intersectoral approach to the QUM are essential to minimize the financial stress of copayments, to improve equity of access to medicines, and to maximize safety and the QUM. The QUM requires a multidisciplinary approach, including contributions from the government, the pharmaceutical industry, the health profession, consumers, and researchers. Well-implemented e-prescribing and decision-support systems can promote safety and the QUM.

The Australian experience is relevant to other Asia-Pacific nations, even while we recognize that applicability will vary according to the economy, financial resources, culture, health traditions, health and medicines policies, epidemiology, and sociodemographics of the given society. Fundamental issues include self-medication and the separation of prescribing from dispensing among traditional and Western-medicine practitioners. It is important to enhance self-care skills, encourage use of safer alternatives, discourage indiscriminate use of potent medicines such as antibiotics, and encourage the seeking of professional help in case of serious diseases.

International harmonization of the benchmarks specified by the WHO Essential Drugs Program (WHO 1988a, 1988b) is important to promote national QUM programs. This is probably best done within the context of health-funding reform, health insurance system improvement, authoritative best-practice guidelines, quality improvement protocols, and international collaboration (Zhang and Harvey 2006). In developing countries, a list of essential drugs appropriate to local health needs must be complemented by an efficient supply of quality medicines; health professionals trained in the QUM; strategies to improve adherence; and systems to monitor the use of medicines and provide feedback to patients and providers, guide policy, control inventory, and support QUM research. Reducing the number of unlabelled drugs, restricting access to nonprescription drugs, improving access to doctors, and patient education are all important measures that will improve the QUM (Woo et al. 1995).

The role of the pharmaceutical industry in promoting the QUM is compromised by the inappropriate promotion of profitable current, outdated, or even unsafe drugs in developing countries. Investment in the quality control of imported drugs and production of low-cost, high-quality essential drugs can reduce reliance on the multinational drug industry. Regulatory strategies are essential but must be complemented by managerial and educational strategies within an international framework to enable effective policing of compliance to regulations.

Historical, social, economic, regulatory, managerial, and educational factors determine prescribing patterns in Australia and other Asia-Pacific nations. Therefore, to understand and promote the QUM requires a holistic explanatory framework that incorporates intrinsic and extrinsic factors, including public institutions, the pharmaceutical industry, the health profession, and consumers. There are many useful international and Australian lessons and strategies relevant to the promotion of medicine safety and the QUM in the Asia-Pacific region.

Notes

[1] http://www.medicareaustralia.gov.au/provider/business/online/medicare-online.shtml.

[2] http://www.medicareaustralia.gov.au/provider/medicare/claiming/easyclaim/index.shtml.

[3] http://www.nehta.gov.au.

[4] http:///qummap.net.au.

[5] http://audit.nps.org.au.

References

Ahluwalia, J. S., M. L. Weisenberger, A. M. Bernard, and S. E. McNagny. 1996. Changing physician prescribing behaviour: A low-cost administrative policy that reduced the use of brand name nonsteroidal anti-inflammatory drugs. *Preventive Medicine* 25: 668–72.

Alubo, S. O. 1985. Drugging the people: Pills, profits and underdevelopment in Nigeria. *Studies in Third World Societies* 24: 89–113.

Anassi, E. O., C. Ericsson, L. Lal, E. McCants, K. Stewart, and C. Moseley. 1995. Using a pharmaceutical restriction program to control antibiotic use. *Formulary* 30 (November 1995): 711–14.

Anastasio, G. D., M. P. Dutro, and L. S. Parent. 1986. Applying family medicine concepts to prescribing. *Family Medicine* 18 (5): 259.

Angus, D. E., and H. M. Karpetz. 1998. Pharmaceutical policies in Canada—Issues and challenges. *Pharmacoeconomics* 14 (Suppl 1): 81–96.

Armstrong, D., H. Reyburn, and R. Jones. 1996. A study of general practitioners reasons for changing their prescribing behaviour. *British Medical Journal* 312 (7036): 949–52.

Avery, A. J., S. Rodgers, T. Heron, R. Crombie, D. Whynes, M. Pringle, D. Baines, and R. Petchey. 2000a. A prescription for improvement? An observational study to identify how general practices vary in their growth in prescribing costs. *British Medical Journal* 321 (7256): 276–81.

Avery, A. J., R. V. Wetzels, S. Rodgers, and C. O'Neill. 2000b. Do GPs working in practice with high or low prescribing costs have different views on prescribing cost issues? *British Journal of General Practice* 50 (451): 100–04.

Bapna, J. S., C. D. Tripathi, and U. Tekur. 1996. Drug utilisation patterns in the third world. *Pharmacoeconomics* 9 (44): 286–94.

Barraclough, B. H. 2001. Safety and quality in Australian healthcare: Making progress. The newly formed Australian council for safety and quality in health care has ambitious plans. *Medical Journal of Australia (MJA)* 174: 616–17.

Barrie, W. 1996. Cost-effective therapy for hypertension. *Western Journal of Medicine* 164 (4): 303–09.

Bates, D. W., J. M. Teich, J. Lee, D. Seger, G. J. Kuperman, N. Ma'Luf, D. Boyle, and L. Leape. 1999. The impact of computerized physician order entry on medication error prevention. *Journal of American Medical Informatics Association* 6 (4): 313–21.

Bates, D. W., L. L. Leape, D. J. Cullen, N. Laird, L. A. Petersen, J. M. Teich, E. Burdick, M. Hickey, S. Kleefield, B. Shea, V. M. Vander, and D. L. Seger. 1998. Effect of computerized physician order entry and a team intervention on prevention of serious medication errors. *Journal of the American Medical Association* 280 (15): 1311–16.

Bazin, M. 1982. Drug regulation in Brazil: Troubles building. *Nature* 295 (5845): 90.

Beilby, J. J., and C. A. Silagy. 1997. Trials of providing costing information to general practitioners—a systematic review. *Medical Journal of Australia* 167 (2): 89–92.

Bell, K. D. 1995. Support for trials of promising medications through the Pharmaceutical Benefits Scheme. *Medical Journal of Australia* 162 (8): 447.

Bendtsen, P., G. Hensing, C. Ebeling, and A. Schedin. 1999a. What are the qualities of dilemmas experienced when prescribing opioids in general practice? *Pain* 82 (1): 89–96.

Bendtsen, P., G. Hensing, L. McKenzie, and A. K. Stridsman. 1999b. Prescribing benzodiazepines—A critical incident study of a physician dilemma. *Social Science and Medicine* 49 (4): 459–67.

Benrimoj, S. I., and M. S. Frommer. 2004. Community pharmacy in Australia. *Australian Health Review* 28 (2): 238–46.

Binka, J. Y., and W. Wieniawski. 1985. Quality control: Think small. *World Health* [monograph]: 10–13.

Bizovi, K. E., B. E. Beckley, M. C. McDade, A. L. Adams, R. A. Lowe, A. D. Zechnich, and J. R. Hedges. 2002. The effect of computer-assisted prescription writing on emergency department prescription errors. *Academic Emergency Medicine* 9 (11): 1168–75.

Blackbourn, J. L., and V. B. Sunderland. 1987. Impact of pharmacist intervention on oral theophylline therapy in adult inpatients. *Drug Intelligence and Clinical Pharmacy* 21: 811–16.

Bloor, K., A. Maynard, and N. Freemantle. 1996. Lessons from international experience in controlling pharmaceutical expenditure III: Regulating industry. *British Medical Journal (BMJ)* 313: 33–35.

Boath, E. H., and A. Blenkinsopp. 1997. The rise and rise of proton pump inhibitor drugs—Patients perspectives. *Social Science and Medicine* 45 (10): 1571–79.

Bourgault, C., E. Elstein, J. Le Lorier, and S. Suissa. 1999. Reference-based pricing of prescription drugs: Exploring the equivalence of angiotensin converting-enzyme inhibitors. *Canadian Medical Association Journal (CMAJ)* 161 (3): 255–60.

Bradley, C. P. 1991. Decision making and prescribing patterns—A literature review. *Family Practice* 8 (3): 276–87.

Braybrook, S., and R. Walker. 1996. Influencing prescribing in primary care—A comparison of two different prescribing feedback methods. *Journal of Clinical Pharmacy and Therapeutics* 21 (4): 247–54.

Breckenridge, A. M. 1986. The pharmaceutical industry and developing countries. *British Journal of Clinical Pharmacology* 22: 27S–29S.

Brieger, W. R., J. Ramakrishna, and J. D. Adeniyi. 1986. Self-treatment in rural Nigeria: Community health education diagnosis. *HYGIE* 5: 41–46.

Britt, H., G. C. Miller, J. Charles, C. Bayram, Y. Pan, J. Henderson, L. Valenti, J. O'Halloran, C. Harrison, and S. Fahridin. 2008. General practice activity in Australia 2006–07. In *General Practice Series* no. 21; AIHW cat. no. GEP 21. Canberra: Australian Institute of Health and Welfare.

Britt, H., G. C. Miller, J. Charles, Y. Pan, L. Valenti, J. Henderson, C. Bayram, J. O'Halloran, and S. Knox. 2007. General practice activity in Australia 2005–06. In *General Practice Series* no. 19; AIHW cat. no. GEP 19. Canberra: Australian Institute of Health and Welfare.

Britten, N., and O. Ukoumunne. 1997. The influence of patients' hopes of receiving a prescription on doctors' perceptions and the decision to prescribe: A questionnaire survey. *British Medical Journal* 315 (7121): 1506–10.

Britten, N., F. A. Stevenson, C. A. Barry, N. Barber, and C. P. Bradley. 2000. Misunderstandings in prescribing decisions in general practice: Qualitative study. *British Medical Journal* 320 (7233): 484–88.

Britten, N., S. Brant, A. Cairns, W. W. Hall, I. Jones, C. Salisbury, A. Virji, and A. Herxheimer. 1995. Continued prescribing of inappropriate drugs in general practice. *Journal of Clinical Pharmacy and Therapeutics* 20 (4): 199–205.

Buetow, S. A. 1995. What do general practitioners and their patients want from general practice and are they receiving it—A framework. *Social Science & Medicine* 40 (2): 213–21.

Buetow, S. A., B. Sibbald, J. A. Cantrill, and S. Halliwell. 1997. Appropriateness in health care—Application to prescribing. *Social Science and Medicine* 45 (2): 261–71.

Chandler, J. 2000. GPs and pharmacists: An uncertain partnership. *Victorian General Practice Divisions Quarterly* 3 (Winter): 9–12.

Chetley, A. 1985. Drug production with a social conscience: The experience of GPL. *Development Dialogue* 2: 94–107.

———. 1986. Health action international. *New Internationalist* 165:24–25.

Christensen, D. B., and A. I. Wertheimer. 1979. Sources of information and influence on new drug prescribing among physicians in an HMO. *Social Science and Medicine* 13: 313–22.

Clear, P. R., and M. Grobler. 1998. Regulating the pharmaceutical industry—Australian scheme has disadvantages. *British Medical Journal* 316 (7126): 227.

Cockburn, J., and S. Pitt. 1997. Prescribing behaviour in clinical practice—Patients expectations and doctors perceptions of patients expectations—A questionnaire study. *British Medical Journal* 315 (7107): 520–23.

Commonwealth Department of Health and Aged Care (in conjunction with the Pharmaceutical Benefits Advisory Committee, Drug Utilisation Sub-Committee, PBAC DUSC). 2005. *Australian statistics on medicines 2004–5.* Canberra: Australian Government Publishing Service (AGPS).

Commonwealth Department of Health, Housing, and Community Services (in conjunction with PHARM). 1992. *A policy on the quality use of medicines.* Canberra: AGPS.

Davidson, W., D. W. Molloy, and M. Bedard. 1995. Physician characteristics and prescribing for elderly people in New Brunswick—Relation to patient outcomes. *Canadian Medical Association Journal* 152 (8): 1227–34.

Davis, P. B., R. L. Yee, and J. Millar. 1994. Accounting for medical variation—The case of prescribing activity in a New Zealand general practice sample. *Social Science and Medicine* 39 (3): 367–74.

de Vries, C. S., N. M. Vandiepen, T. F. J. Tromp, and L. T. W. de Jong-van den Berg. 1996. Auditing GPs prescribing habits—Cardiovascular prescribing frequently continues medication initiated by specialists. *European Journal of Clinical Pharmacology* 50 (5): 349–52.

de Vries, C. S., T. F. J. Tromp, W. Blijleven, and L. T. W. de Jong-van den Berg. 1999. Prescription data as a tool in pharmacotherapy audit (I) general considerations. *Pharmacy World and Science* 21 (2): 80–84.

Dong, H., L. Bogg, C. Rehnberg, and V. Diwan. 1999. Health financing policies. Providers' opinions and prescribing behavior in rural China. *International Journal of Technology Assessment in Health Care* 15 (4): 686–98.

Dowell, J. S., D. Snadden, and J. A. Dunbar. 1995. Changing to generic formulary—How one fundholding practice reduced prescribing costs. *British Medical Journal* 310 (6978): 505–08.

Drummond, M., B. Jonsson, and F. Rutten. 1997. The role of economic evaluation in the pricing and reimbursement of medicines. *Health Policy* 40: 199–215.

Erwin, J., N. Britten, and R. Jones. 1997. General practitioners views on the over-the-counter availability of H-2-antagonists. *British Journal of General Practice* 47 (415): 99–102.

Ess, S. M., S. Schneeweiss, and T. D. Szucs. 2003. European healthcare policies for controlling drug expenditure. *Pharmacoeconomics* 21 (2): 89–103.

Fabricant, S. J., and N. Hirschhorn. 1987. Deranged distribution, perverse prescription, unprotected use: The irrationality of pharmaceuticals in the developing world. *Health Policy and Planning* 2: 204–13.

Ferguson, R. I., C. E. Salmond, and J. B. Maling. 1995. The Nelson prescribing project—A programmed intervention in general practice in New Zealand. *Pharmacoeconomics* 7 (6): 555–61.

Fletcher, M. 2000. The quality of Australian health care: Current issues and future directions. *Health Financing Series* vol 6. Commonwealth Department of Health and Aged Care.

Frazier, L. M., J. T. Brown, G. W. Divine, G. R. Fleming, N. M. Philips, W. C. Siegal, and M. A. Khayrallah. 1991. Can physician education lower the cost of prescription drugs? A prospective controlled trial. *Annals of Internal Medicine* 115 (2): 116–21.

Freemantle, N., and K. Bloor. 1996. Lessons from international experience in controlling pharmaceutical expenditure: 1. Influencing patients. *British Medical Journal* 312 (7044): 1469–71.

Gardner, T. L., S. M. Dovey, M. W. Tilyard, and E. Gurr. 1996. Differences between prescribed and dispensed medications. *New Zealand Medical Journal* 109 (1017): 69–72.

Gill, P. S., M. Makela, K. M. Vermeulen, N. Freemantle, G. Ryan, C. Bond, T. Thorsen, and F. M. Haaijer-Ruskamp. 1999. Changing doctor prescribing behaviour. *Pharmacy World and Science* 21 (4): 158–67.

Greenhalgh, T. 1986. Drug marketing in the third world: Beneath the cosmetic reforms. *Lancet* 1: 1318–20.

———. 1987. Drug prescription and self-medication in India: An exploratory survey. *Social Science and Medicine* 25: 307–18.

Greenhalgh, T., and P. Gill. 1997. Pressure to prescribe—Involves a complex interplay of factors. *British Medical Journal* 315 (7121): 1482–83.

Grootendorst, P., and A. Holbrook. 1999. Evaluating the impact of reference-based pricing. *Canadian Medical Association Journal* 161 (3): 273–74.

Hamley, J. H., S. H. Macgregor, J. A. Dunbar, and J. A. Cromarty. 1997. Integrating clinical pharmacists into the primary health-care team—A framework for rational and cost-effective prescribing. *Scottish Medical Journal* 42 (1): 4–7.

Harvey, K., and M. Murray. 1995. Medicinal drug policy. In *The politics of health: The Australian experience*, ed. H. Gardner. Melbourne: Churchill Livingstone, 238–83.

Health Insurance Commission. 2000. *Doctor shopping.* Canberra: HIC.

———. 2008. *MediConnect.* Medicare Australia 2008. http://www.medicareaustralia.gov.au/provider/patients/mediconnect.shtml.

HIC. *See* Health Insurance Commission.

Hogerzeil, H. V. 1995. Promoting rational prescribing—An international perspective. *British Journal of Clinical Pharmacology* 39 (1): 1–6.

Holden, J., and R. Wilson. 1996. The quality of prescribing in general practice. *International Journal of Health Care Quality Assurance* 9 (5): 17–23.

Horowitz, A. M. 1999. Challenges of and strategies for changing prescribing practices of health-care providers. *Journal of Public Health Dentistry* 59 (4): 275–81.

Horrow, J. C., and H. Rosenberg. 1994. Price stickers do not alter drug usage. *Canadian Journal of Anaesthesia* 41 (11): 1047–52.

Hui, L., X. S. Li, X. J. Zeng, Y. H. Dai, and H. M. Foy. 1997. Patterns and determinants of use of antibiotics for acute respiratory tract infection in children in China. *Pediatric Infectious Disease Journal* 16: 560–64.

Hunt, D., R. Haynes, S. Hanna, and K. Smith. 1998. Effects of computer-based clinical decision support systems on physician performance and patient outcomes. A systematic review. *Journal of the American Medical Association* 280 (15): 1339–46.

Huston, P., and N. R. Campbell. 1998. Influencing prescribing patterns. *Canadian Family Physician* 44: 221–23.

Ilett, K. F., S. Johnson, G. Greenhill, L. Mullen, J. Brockis, C. L. Golledge, and D. B. Reid. 2000. Modification of general practitioner prescribing of antibiotics by use of a therapeutics adviser (academic detailer). *British Journal of Clinical Pharmacology* 49 (2): 168–73.

Jameson, J., G. Vannoord, and K. Vanderwoud. 1995. The impact of a pharmacotherapy consultation on the cost and outcome of medical therapy. *Journal of Family Practice* 41 (5): 469–72.

Jaski, M. E., J. G. Schwartzberg, R. A. Guttman, and M. Noorani. 2000. Medication review and documentation in physician office practice. *Effective Clinical Practice* 3 (1): 31–34.

Johnston, M. E., K. B. Langton, R. B. Haynes, and A. Mathieu. 1994. Effects of computer-based clinical decision support systems on clinician performance and patient outcome—A critical appraisal of research. *Annals of Internal Medicine* 120 (2): 135–42.

Jones, D. L., K. Kroenke, F. J. Landry, D. J. Tomich, and R. J. Ferrel. 1996. Cost savings using a stepped-care prescribing protocol for nonsteroidal anti-inflammatory drugs. *Journal of the American Medical Association* 275 (12): 926–30.

Kalisch, L. M., E. E. Roughead, and A. L. Gilbert. 2007. Pharmaceutical brand substitution in Australia–Are there multiple switches per prescription? *Australian and New Zealand Journal of Public Health* 31 (4): 348–52.

Kawamoto, K., C. A. Houlihan, E. A. Balas, and D. F. Lobach. 2005. Improving clinical practice using clinical decision support systems: A systematic review of trials to identify features critical to success. *British Medical Journal* 330 (7494): 765–72.

Kerr, C. P. 1994. Eight underused prescriptions. *American Family Physician* 50 (7): 1497–04.

Kesselheim, A. S., M. A. Fischer, and J. Avorn. 2006. Extensions of intellectual property rights and delayed adoption of generic drugs: Effects on Medicaid spending. *Health Aff (Millwood)* 25 (6): 1637–47.

Kohn, L. T., J. M. Corrigan, and M. S. Donaldson. 2000. *To err is human: Building a safer health system.* Washington, D.C.: National Academy Press.

Lagerlov, P., M. Loeb, M. Andrew, and P. Hjortdahl. 2000. Improving doctors' prescribing behaviour through reflection on guidelines and prescription feedback: A randomised controlled study. *Quality in Health Care* 9:159.

Lassen, L. C., and F. B. Kristensen. 1992. Peer comparison feedback to achieve rational and economical drug therapy in general practice: A controlled intervention study. *Scandinavian Journal of Primary Health Care* 10 (1): 76–80.

Leape, L. L., and D. M. Berwick. 2005. Five years after to err is human, what have we learned? *Journal of the American Medical Association* 293: 2384–90.

Lesar, T. S., and L. L. Briceland. 1996. Survey of antibiotic control policies in university-affiliated teaching institutions. *Annals of Pharmacotherapy* 30 (1): 31–34.

Leape, L. L., D. W. Bates, D. J. Cullen, J. Cooper, H. J. Demonaco, T. Gallivan, R. Hallisey, J. Ives, N. Laird, G. Laffel, et al.. 1995. Systems analysis of adverse drug events. ADE prevention study group. *Journal of the American Medical Association* 274 (1): 35–43.

Liaw, S. T., and P. Schattner. 2003. Electronic decision support in general practice. What's the hold up? *Australian Family Physician* 32 (11): 941–44.

———. 2008. eConsulting. In *Methods in Molecular Medicine. Clinical bioinformatics*, ed. R. Trent, Totowa, NJ: Humana Press, 353–73.

Liaw, S. T., and R. Tomlins, eds. 2005. Chapter 12. Developments in information systems. In *General Practice in Australia 2004*, ed. CDOHF Services, May 2005. Canberra: AGPS.

Liaw, S. T., E. Deveny, I. Morrison, and B. Lewis. 2006. Clinical, information and business process modeling to promote development of safe and flexible software. *Health Informatics Journal* 12 (3): 199–211.

Liaw, S. T., E. Tan, C. Pearce, and K. Stewart. 2004. *Off-label and unlicensed prescribing—Prevalence and perceptions of doctors.* Final report, March 19, 2004. Canberra: Commonwealth Department of Health and Aged Care.

Liaw, S. T., C. Pearce, P. Chondros, B. McGrath, L. Piggford, and K. Jones. 2003. Doctors' perceptions and attitudes to prescribing within the authority prescribing system. *Medical Journal of Australia* 178: 203–06.

Löfgren, H. 2007a. The global biopharma industry and the rise of Indian drug multinationals: Implications for Australian generics policy. *Australia and New Zealand Health Policy* 4: 10.

———. 2007b. Reshaping Australian drug policy: The dilemmas of generic medicines policy. *Australia and New Zealand Health Policy* 4: 11.

Lyles, A, and F. B. Palumbo. 1999. The effect of managed care on prescription drug costs and benefits. *Pharmacoeconomics* 15 (2): 129–40.

Mager, D. E., and E. R. Cox. 2007. Relationship between generic and preferred-brand prescription copayment differentials and generic fill rate. *American Journal of Managed Care* 13 (6, Part 2): 347–52.

Mainous, A. G., W. J. Hueston, M. M. Love, M. E. Evans, and R. Finger. 2000. An evaluation of statewide strategies to reduce antibiotic overuse. *Family Medicine* 32 (1): 22–29.

McCormick, J. 1996. Death of the personal doctor. *Lancet* 348 (9028): 667–68.

McElnay, J. C., M. G. Scott, J. Y. Sidara, and P. Kearney. 1995. Audit of antibiotic usage in a medium-sized general hospital over an eleven-year period—The impact of antibiotic policies. *Pharmacy World and Science* 17 (6): 207–13.

McGavock, H. 1988. Some patterns of prescribing by urban general practitioners. *British Medical Journal Clinical Research Edition* 296 (6626): 900–02.

———. 1998. Prescribing feedback and its use in self-regulation. *Australian Prescriber* 21 (1): 4–5.

McInnes, D. K., M. R. Kidd, and MR. D. C. Saltman DC. 2006. Use of computers to improve patient safety and quality of care in Australian general practice: A national survey. *Medical Journal of Australia.* 185(2): 88–91, 2006.

McManus, P., J. Marley, D. J. Birkett, and J. Lindner. 1998. Compliance with restrictions on the subsidized use of proton pump inhibitors in Australia. *British Journal of Clinical Pharmacology* 46 (4): 409–11.

Medicare Australia. *Streamlined authority process, 2007.* http://www.medicareaustralia.gov.au/provider/pbs/doctor/streamlined-authority-process.shtml.

Miller, E., L. D. MacKeigan, W. Rosser, and J. Marshman. 1999. Effects of perceived patient demand on prescribing anti-infective drugs. *Canadian Medical Association Journal* 161 (2): 139–42.

Miller, G. C., H. C. Britt, and L. Valenti. 2006. Adverse drug events in general practice patients in Australia. *Medical Journal of Australia* 184 (7): 321–24.

Mott, D. A., and R. R. Cline. 2002. Exploring generic drug use behavior: The role of prescribers and pharmacists in the opportunity for generic drug use and generic substitution. *Medical Care* 40 (8): 662–74.

Nathan, A., and C. A. Sutters. 1993. A comparison of community pharmacists and general practitioners opinions on rational prescribing, formularies and other prescribing related issues. *Journal of the Royal Society of Health* 113 (6): 302–07.

National Electronic Decision Support Taskforce. 2002. *Report to health ministers: Electronic decision support in Australia.* Canberra: National Health Information Management Advisory Council.

National Health Strategy, Australia. 1992. *Issues paper no. 3: The future of general practice.* Canberra: Commonwealth Department of Health, Housing, and Community Services.

NEDST. *See* National Electronic Decision Support Taskforce.

Newdick, C. 1998. Primary care groups and the right to prescribe. *British Medical Journal* 317 (7169): 1361–64.

Newton-Syms, F. A., P. H. Dawson, J. Cooke, M. Feely, T. G. Booth, D. Jerwood, and R. T. Calvert. 1992. The influence of an academic representative on prescribing by general practitioners. *British Journal of Clinical Pharmacology* 33 (1): 69–73.

O'Connell, D. L., D. Henry, and R. Tomlins. 1999. Randomised controlled trial of effect of feedback on general practitioners' prescribing in Australia. *British Medical Journal* 318 (7182): 507–11.

Orlowski, J. P., and L. Wateska. 1992. The effects of pharmaceutical firm enticements on physician prescribing patterns. There's no such thing as a free lunch. *Chest* 102 (1): 270–73.

Peterson, G. M., K. D. Fitzmaurice, M. Naunton, J. H. Vial, K. Stewart, and H. Krum. 2004. Impact of pharmacist-conducted home visits on the outcomes of lipid-lowering drug therapy. *Journal of Clinical Pharmacy and Therapeutics* 2004; 29: 23–30.

Pillans, P. I., and M. S. Roberts. 1999. Overprescribing: Have we made any progress? *Australian and New Zealand Journal of Medicine* 29 (4): 485–86.

Pillans, P. I., P. A. Kubler, J. M. Radford, and V. Overland. 2000. Concordance between use of proton pump inhibitors and prescribing guidelines. *Medical Journal of Australia* 172 (1): 16–18.

Prazuck, T., I. Falconi, G. Morineau, V. Bricard-Pacaud, A. Lecomte, and F. Ballereau. 2002. Quality control of antibiotics before the implementation of an STD program in Northern Myanmar. *Sexually Transmitted Diseases* 29 (11): 624–27.

Probyn, A. J. 2004. Some drugs more equal than others: Pseudo-generics and commercial practice. *Australian Health Review* 28 (2): 207–17.

Quah, S. R. 1985. Self-medication in Singapore. *Singapore Medical Journal* 26: 123–29.

Radley, D. C., S. N. Finkelstein, and R. S. Stafford. 2006. Off-label prescribing among office-based physicians. *Archives of Internal Medicine* 166 (9): 1021–26.

Raschke, R. A., B. Gollihare, T. A. Wunderlich, J. R. Guidry, A. I. Leibowitz, J. C. Peirce, L. Lemelson, M. A. Heisler, and C. Susong. 1998. A computer alert system to prevent injury from adverse drug events: Development and evaluation in a community teaching hospital. *Journal of the American Medical Association* 280 (15): 1317–20.

Richardson, J. R. J., and L. Segal. 2004. Private health insurance and the pharmaceutical benefits scheme: How effective has recent government policy been? *Australian Health Review* 28 (1): 34–47.

Rifenburg, R. P., J. A. Paladino, S. C. Hanson, J. A. Tuttle, and J. J Schentag. 1996. Benchmark analysis of strategies hospitals use to control antimicrobial expenditures. *American Journal of Health-System Pharmacy* 53 (17): 2054–62.

Roberts, S. J., D. N. Bateman, and J. M. Smith. 1997. Prescribing behaviour in general practice—The impact of promoting therapeutically equivalent cheaper medicines. *British Journal of General Practice* 47 (414): 13–18.

Robertson, J., D. Henry, T. Dobbins, A. Sprogis, R. Terry, and M. Ireland. 1999. Prescribing patterns in general practice. A comparison of two data sources. *Australian Family Physician* 28 (11): 1186–90.

Rodgers, S., A. J. Avery, D. Meechan, S. Briant, M. Geraghty, K. Doran, and D. K. Whynes. 1999. Controlled trial of pharmacist intervention in general practice: The effect on prescribing costs. *British Journal of General Practice* 49 (446): 717–20.

Roter, D. L., J. A. Hall, R. Merisca, B. Nordstrom, D. Cretin, and B. Svarstad. 1998. Effectiveness of interventions to improve patient compliance—A meta-analysis. *Medical Care* 36 (8): 1138–61.

Roughead, E. E., K. J. Harvey, and A. L. Gilbert. 1998. Commercial detailing techniques used by pharmaceutical representatives to influence prescribing. *Australian and New Zealand Journal of Medicine* 28 (3): 306–10.

Roughead, L. 2000. *PHARM and APAC: A decade of developing sustainable activities that improve health outcomes for consumers.* Canberra: Department of Health and Aged Care.

Salkeld, G., P. Davey, and G. Arnolda. 1995. A critical review of health-related economic evaluations in Australia: Implications for health policy. *Health Policy* 31 (2): 111–25.

Scott, A., and A. Shiell. 1997. Do fee descriptors influence treatment choices in general practice—A multilevel discrete choice model. *Journal of Health Economics* 16 (3): 323–42.

Shimouchi, A., D. Yaohua, Z. Zhonghan, and V. B. Rabukawaqa. 1995. Effectiveness of control programs for pneumonia among children in China and Fiji. *Clinical Infectious Diseases* 21 (Suppl 3): S213–S217.

Shrank, W. H., M. Stedman, S. L. Ettner, D. Delapp, J. Dirstine, M. A. Brookhart, M. A. Fischer, J. Avorn, and S. M. Asch. 2007. Patient, physician, pharmacy, and pharmacy benefit design factors related to generic medication use. *Journal of General Internal Medicine* 22 (9): 1298–304.

Smalley, W. E., M. R. Griffin, R. L. Fought, L Sullivan, and W. A. Ray. 1995. Effect of a prior-authorization requirement on the use of nonsteroidal antiinflammatory drugs by Medicaid patients. *New England Journal of Medicine* 332 (24): 1612–17.

Soumerai, S., T. McLaughlin, and J. Avorn. 1989. Improving drug prescribing in primary care: A critical analysis of the experimental literature. *The Millbank Quarterly* 67 (2): 268–69.

Stafford, R. S. 2008. Regulating off-label drug use—Rethinking the role of the FDA. *New England Journal of Medicine* 358 (14): 1427–29.

Steffensen, F. H., H. C. Schonheyder, and H. T. Sorensen. 1997. High prescribers of antibiotics among general practitioners—Relation to prescribing habits of other drugs and use of microbiological diagnostics. *Scandinavian Journal of Infectious Diseases* 29 (4): 409–13.

Stevenson, F. A., S. M. Greenfield, M. Jones, A. Nayak, and C. P. Bradley. 1999. GPs' perceptions of patient influence on prescribing. *Family Practice* 16 (3): 255–61.

Sullivan, Frank, and Elizabeth Mitchell. 1995. Has general practitioner computing made a difference to patient care? A systematic review of published reports. *British Medical Journal,* September 311 (7009): 848–52.

Sweeny, K. 2007. Trends and outcomes in the Australian pharmaceutical scheme. Working Paper No. 36, Pharmaceutical Industry Project, Centre for Strategic Economic Studies, Victoria University of Technology, Melbourne.

Tang, Jingbo. 1996. Clinical drug evaluating: Meaning and methods. *China Pharmacy* 7 (6).

Taylor, R. J., and C. M. Bond. 1991. Change in the established prescribing habits of general practitioners: An analysis of initial prescriptions in general practice. *British Journal of General Practice* 41 (347): 244–48.

Tomson, Y., A. Wessling, and G. Tomson. 1994. General practitioners for rational use of drugs. Examples from Sweden. *European Journal of Clinical Pharmacology* 47 (3): 213–19.

Towse, A., and N. Wells. 1995. Promoting cost effective prescribing—Cost effectiveness studies may not be cost effective. *British Medical Journal* 311 (6997): 126.

van der Sijs, H. et al. 2006., *Overriding of drug safety alerts in computerized physician order entry. Journal of the American Medical Informatics Associaiton,* 2006. 13 (2): 138–-47.

Vedsted, P., J. N. Nielsen, and F. Olesen. 1997. Does a computerized price comparison module reduce prescribing costs in general practice. *Family Practice* 14 (3): 199–203.

Vlahovic-Palcevski, V., M. Morovic, and G. Palcevski. 2000. Antibiotic utilization at the university hospital after introducing an antibiotic policy. *European Journal of Clinical Pharmacology* 56 (1): 97–101.

Wang, H. C., L. Y. Chen, and A. H. Lau. 1993. Pharmacy practice and education in the People's Republic of China. *Annals of Pharmacotherapy* 27 (10): 1278–82.

Webb, S., and M. Lloyd. 1994. Prescribing and referral in general practice—A study of patients expectations and doctors actions. *British Journal of General Practice* 44 (381): 165–69.

Weekes, L. M., and C. Brooks. 1996. Drug and therapeutics committees in Australia: Expected and actual performance. *British Journal of Clinical Pharmacology* 42 (5): 551–57.

Weiss, M. C., R. Fitzpatrick, D. K. Scott, and M. J. Goldacre. 1996. Pressures on the general practitioner and decisions to prescribe. *Family Practice* 13 (5): 432–38.

WHO. *See* World Health Organization.

World Health Organization. 1984. Essential drugs for the world. *World Health* (July): 1–31.

———. 1985. *Guidelines for evaluating an essential drugs programme.* Geneva: WHO.

———. 1988a. *Guidelines for developing national drug policies.* Geneva: WHO.

———. 1988b. *Rational use of drugs—(review of implementation of WHO's revised drug strategy).* Geneva: WHO.

———. 1988c. *The world drug situation.* Geneva: WHO.

———. 1991. *The use of essential drugs—model list of essential drugs (fifth list).* Geneva: WHO.

———. 2008 (accessed). The launch of the World Alliance for Patient Safety. "Please Do Me No Harm." 2004. http://www.who.int/patientsafety/launch/en.

Wilson, R. M., and M. B. Van der Weyden. 2005. The safety of Australian healthcare: Ten years after QAHCS. *Medical Journal of Australia* 182 (6): 260–61.

Woo, J., S. C. Ho, Y. K. Yuen, and J. Lau. 1995. Drug use in an elderly Chinese population: Prevalence and associated factors. *Gerontology* 41: 98–108.

Wyatt, T. D., P. M. Reilly, N. C. Morrow, and C. M. Passmore. 1992. Short-lived effects of a formulary on anti-infective prescribing—The need for continuing peer review? *Family Practice* 9 (4): 461–65.

Young, A., and K. Beswick. 1995. Protocols used by U.K. general practitioners, what is expected of them and what solutions are provided. *Computer Methods and Programs in Biomedicine* 48 (1–2): 85–90.

Zhan, S. K., S. L. Tang, Y. D. Guo, and G. Bloom. 1998. Drug prescribing in rural health facilities in China: Implications for service quality and cost. *Tropical Doctor* 28: 42–48.

Zhang, Y., and K. J. Harvey. 2006. Rational antibiotic use in China: Lessons learnt through introducing surgeons to Australian guidelines. *Australia and New Zealand Health Policy* 3 (1): 5.

Zwar, N. A., J. Wolk, J. J. Gordon, R. W. Sanson-Fisher, and L. Kehoe. 1999. Influencing antibiotic prescribing in general practice: A trial of prescriber feedback and management guidelines. *Family Practice* 16 (5): 495–500.

CROSS-CUTTING THEMES

ACCESS AND INNOVATION

INSURANCE SYSTEMS IN THE ASIA-PACIFIC REGION: IMPROVING APPROPRIATE USE OF AND ACCESS TO MEDICINES

Anita Wagner and Dennis Ross-Degnan[1]

L ack of affordable access to life-saving medicines contributes to the tremendous inequity in health between industrialized and developing countries. Improving access to medicines would help to prevent mortality and morbidity, catastrophic illness effects, low quality of life, and large-scale economic and health system losses (World Health Organization, WHO, 2004). Economic factors are often the biggest barriers to medicines access. Health insurance programs[2] that cover both care *and* medicines can improve access to and encourage better use of medicines, thus significantly reducing the burden of disease and poverty. Health insurance programs exist in most Asia-Pacific countries, though with important differences in their stage of development, organization, financing, scale, and covered services.

Health insurance programs enroll a defined member population for which they usually have data on health-care needs and use of services. Programs can use these data to design policies that promote cost-effective care. They can also use their power as large-scale purchasers to offer medicines at affordable prices and structure contracts and benefit policies to encourage better prescription and use patterns. Evidence-based policies intend to promote medicines access that is both scaleable and sustainable. The Medicines and Insurance Coverage (MedIC) initiative of the WHO Collaborating Center in Pharmaceutical Policy (WHOCCPP) aims to improve the health of the poor by supporting the design, implementation, evaluation, and routine monitoring of medicines policies for vulnerable populations across the world.

In this chapter, we first look at MedIC initiative activities in the Philippines. We then describe the need for medicines in the Asia-Pacific region, focusing on chronic conditions. Medicines coverage is important for acute conditions as well; however, assuring affordable access to medicines for lifelong treatment is particularly challenging, both for patients and health insurance programs. We then discuss the mix of public and private health-care financing in the region. Next, we describe the potential role of health insurance programs and list insurance policy options that can promote a balance between equitable

313

access to medicines, appropriate use, and affordable cost. We conclude with a description of the global MedIC initiative.

A case study in the Philippines illustrates a key point to be elaborated in this chapter: health insurance programs exist in developing and transitional countries, but many do not cover available, important medicines. Those programs with available data generate evidence for medicines policy decision-making.

Case Study: An Outpatient Medicine Benefit for Chronic Conditions in the Philippines

The Philippines, like several other Asia-Pacific countries, has committed to providing health insurance to the country's entire population.[3] The National Health Insurance Act (NHIA) established the Philippine Health Insurance Corporation (PhilHealth) in 1995, with the goal of achieving universal coverage. One of PhilHealth's mandates is to further an efficient, high-quality national health-care system. In 2006 an estimated 79 percent of the population (68 million) were insured by PhilHealth.[4] Members belong to one of four categories, each with different contribution parameters: formally employed workers, indigents (government-sponsored members), nonpaying members (retirees), and individually paying members. PhilHealth partially reimburses its members (and their dependents) for the cost of inpatient care, while providing very limited outpatient benefits (for maternal care and tuberculosis treatment) that do not include medication coverage for chronic conditions. Hypertension has become a major contributor to morbidity, mortality, and increased health-care expenditures in the Philippines. Two out of ten Filipinos over twenty years old (an estimated 7.76 million in 2003) have been diagnosed with hypertension (Gatbonton 2006). Sixty-one per hundred thousand deaths were attributed to hypertension in 1996 (WHO Collaborating Center for Surveillance of Cardiovascular Diseases 2009). Given the low socioeconomic status of most Filipinos—48 percent of the population lives on less than $2 per day (Population Reference Bureau 2006)—and the high cost of medications in the country (Batangan et al. 2006), the regular use of antihypertensive medicines is not affordable for many patients.

PhilHealth and MedIC initiative collaborators have estimated the cost to PhilHealth of inpatient care for hypertension and its complications. Using PhilHealth inpatient claims for discharges between July 1, 2002, and December 31, 2005, we found that PhilHealth reimbursed $56 million for 446,628 hospitalizations for hypertension-related diagnoses incurred by 360,016 patients during 3.5 years; 42 percent of admissions were for essential or secondary hypertension, 19 percent for hypertensive heart or renal disease, and 39 percent for other potential consequences of untreated hypertension. Among 60,659 patients who were admitted during the first 18 months of the study with a diagnosis of essential or secondary hypertension, 9 percent were hospitalized again for treatment of subsequent problems; older individuals (over forty years), men, dependents (versus primary members), and the employed (versus those in the private membership category) were more likely to be hospitalized again, as were those whose first admission during the study period was for consequences of hypertension (versus essential or secondary hypertension) (Wagner et al. 2008). In a follow-up survey of members recently discharged with a diagnosis of hypertension, we found that many were recommended antihypertensive medication treatment after their hospitalization but could not afford to buy it (unpublished data).

Inpatient care for hypertension and its consequences is expensive; hospitalizations could be avoided by using regular antihypertensive pharmacologic therapy. Given that PhilHealth is responsible for building an efficient health-care system, PhilHealth and its partners are now implementing pilot interventions to test the feasibility and efficacy of an outpatient hypertension-treatment program, with medicines benefits targeting different member groups as a first step toward the development of a broad-scale chronic-disease medicines benefits scheme in the Philippines.

The Need for Medicines to Treat Chronic Diseases in the Asia-Pacific Region

Chronic diseases—diabetes, hypertension, and cardiovascular disease—are the major causes of illness and death worldwide, including the Asia-Pacific region, and their rates are growing (Mathers and Loncar 2006; see also Birt 2006). For example, about 24 million Chinese over the age of 20 had diabetes in 2007, and about 47 million are forecasted to have it by 2025 (International Diabetes Federation 2009). In India diabetes prevalence will increase from 5.9 percent (36 million people) to 8.1 percent (73 million) in the same time period. In 23 of 45 Asia-Pacific countries, diabetes will affect more than 10 percent of the adult population by 2025 (figure 18.1).

Suboptimal blood pressure is the number-one risk factor for death throughout the world (WHO 2002), leading to stroke, heart attack, and heart failure. More than a quarter of the world's adult population—nearly 1 billion people—had hypertension in the year 2000 (Kearney and others 2005); with an estimated increase to 29 percent (or 1.56 billion) by 2025. In China and India alone, the number of individuals with hypertension is estimated to increase to more than 500 million by 2025. Worldwide, about 7.8 million premature deaths were attributed to high blood pressure in 2001 (Lawes 2008). The Asia-Pacific Cohort Studies Collaboration (APCSC) (Woodward et al. 2006) has found that, after adjusting for other risk factors, the risk of stroke and coronary heart disease due to high blood pressure is considerably greater in Asia than in Australia and New Zealand (Asia Pacific Cohort Studies Collaboration 2005). Similarly, more than 60 percent (35 million) of all deaths in 2005 were caused by cardiovascular disease, cancer, chronic respiratory diseases, and diabetes; 16.6 million of global deaths are caused by cardiovascular disease alone; with 80 percent of these deaths occurring in low- and middle-income countries

Figure 18.1 Prevalence of Diabetes Mellitus in 2003 and Predicted Prevalence in 2025 in Asia-Pacific Countries

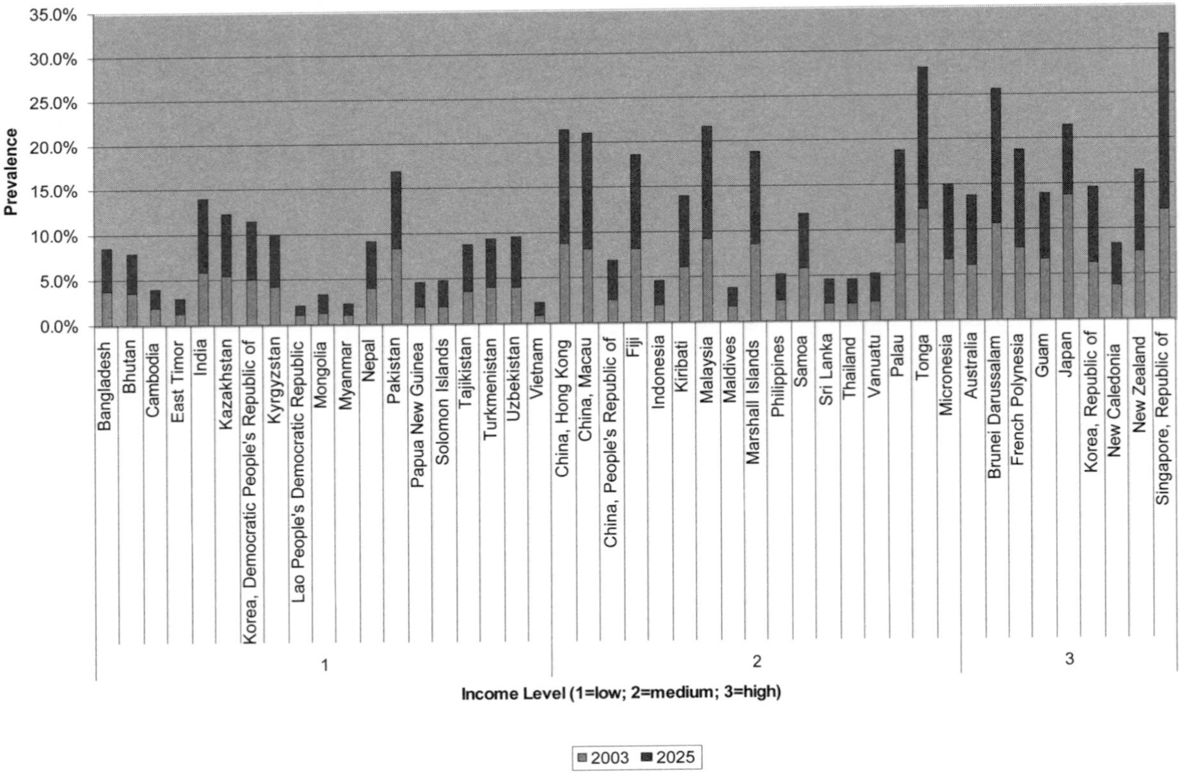

Source: International Diabetes Federation 2009.

(Puska, Mendis, and Porter 2003). Among the twenty-three developing countries which suffer 80 percent of the chronic disease burden, nine are located in the Asia-Pacific region (Bangladesh, Burma, China, India, Indonesia, Pakistan, Philippines, Thailand, and Vietnam) (Abegunde et al. 2007). In sum, the Asia-Pacific region carries about half the world's burden of cardiovascular disease (Martiniuk et al. 2007), where related deaths range from less than 20 percent in countries such as Indonesia, Philippines, and Thailand to roughly 20 to 30 percent in Hong Kong, urban China, Japan, Korea, and Malaysia (Khor 2001).

The macroeconomic consequences of chronic disease are profound (Suhrcke et al. 2006; Abegunde et al. 2007). In 2006 economic losses (foregone gross domestic product [GDP]) because of diabetes, coronary heart disease, and stroke in Asia-Pacific countries ranged from $20 million in Vietnam to over $1 billion in India. In the period 2006–2015, the cumulative loss of GDP due to chronic diseases is projected to be $14 billion in China and $17 billion in India (Abegunde et al. 2007).

While appropriate diet, exercise, and other measures are crucial to preventing chronic disease, millions of patients already suffer from these conditions. Effective medicines exist to treat chronic conditions and, when used appropriately, substantially decrease morbidity and save lives. Pharmaceutical treatment for hyperglycemia, hypertension, and hyperlipidemia for patients with diabetes reduces both macrovascular (heart disease, stroke) and microvascular complications (blindness, kidney disease, and nerve damage, which can lead to amputations). Pharmacotherapy for hypertension reduces the incidence of stroke by 35 to 40 percent, heart attack by 20 to 25 percent, and heart failure by more than 50 percent (Neal, MacMahon, and Chapman 2000). It thus prevents costly inpatient care as these diseases progress. But for treatment to be effective, patients need to take necessary medicines regularly. Consequently, they need continued, affordable access to appropriate medicines.

Like other effective health-care interventions, pharmacotherapy is underutilized in many countries, and the poor, who need them most, make the least use of the interventions that are available (O'Donnell 2007). Many factors on the supply and demand side of health care are responsible for underuse (Neal, MacMahon, and Chapman 2000), including the high cost of services and medicines in health-care financing systems that rely on out-of-pocket (OOP) spending. Ensuring access to essential medicines is of crucial importance to individuals, health-care organizations, governments, and society as a whole. Allocating a portion of health system resources to medicines is an efficient way to increase the value in health achieved for the money spent.

Financing Health Care and Medicines in the Asia-Pacific Region

Table 18.1 displays health-care financing data from 39 Asia-Pacific countries. Per capita health expenditures vary widely; in 2004 they were below $30 in most low-income countries—lower than what is needed to provide the essential

Table 18.1 Health-care Financing in Asia-Pacific Countries, 2004

Member state	Country income level (1=low, 2=middle, 3=high)	Per capita total expenditure on health at average exchange rate (US$)	General government expenditure on health as % of total expenditure on health	Private expenditure on health as % of total expenditure on health	Social security expenditure on health as % of general government expenditure on health	Out-of-pocket expenditure as % of private expenditure on health	Private prepaid plans as % of private expenditure on health
Bangladesh	1	14	28.1	71.9	0.0	88.3	0.1
Bhutan	1	15	64.2	35.8	0.0	100.0	0.0
Cambodia	1	24	25.8	74.2	0.0	85.4	0.0
India	1	31	17.3	82.7	5.6	93.8	0.8
Kyrgyzstan	1	24	40.9	59.1	14.6	94.3	n/a
Lao PDR	1	17	20.5	79.5	12.1	90.3	0.5
Mongolia	1	37	66.6	33.4	38.6	92.3	0.0
Myanmar	1	5	12.9	87.1	3.2	99.4	0.0
Nepal	1	14	26.3	73.7	0.0	88.1	0.0
Pakistan	1	14	19.6	80.4	0.0	98.0	n/a
Papua New Guinea	1	30	84.3	15.7	0.0	46.4	6.2
Solomon Islands	1	35	94.5	5.5	0.0	55.9	0.0
Tajikistan	1	14	21.6	78.4	0.0	97.3	0.0
Timor-Leste	1	44	78.9	21.1	0.0	25.6	0.0
Uzbekistan	1	23	46.6	53.4	n/a	96.2	0.0
Vietnam	1	30	27.1	72.9	16.9	88.0	2.9
China	2	71	38.0	62	55.2	86.5	5.5
Fiji	2	148	62.3	37.7	0.0	100.0	n/a

Indonesia	2	33	34.2	65.8	10.8	74.7	5.9
Kazakhstan	2	109	59.8	40.2	0.0	100.0	n/a
Kiribati	2	112	93.0	7.0	0.0	100.0	0.0
Malaysia	2	180	58.8	41.2	0.7	74.1	13.2
Maldives	2	180	81.4	18.6	29.2	100.0	0.0
Marshall Islands	2	272	97.0	3.0	15.7	100.0	0.0
Micronesia	2	156	85.7	14.3	n/a	40.0	n/a
Palau	2	656	91.2	8.8	0.0	100.0	0.0
Philippines	2	36	39.8	60.2	23.8	77.9	12.1
Samoa	2	109	76.8	23.2	1.2	78.0	0.0
Sri Lanka	2	43	45.6	54.4	0.2	84.0	8.8
Thailand	2	88	64.7	35.3	10.2	74.7	16.5
Tonga	2	117	79.5	20.5	n/a	84.9	0.4
Turkmenistan	2	124	68.9	31.1	6.1	100.0	0.0
Vanuatu	2	58	76.8	23.2	0.0	57.5	n/a
Australia	3	3,123	67.5	32.5	0.0	61.6	20.4
Brunei Darussalam	3	473	79.7	20.3	n/a	100.0	n/a
Japan	3	2,831	81.0	19.0	78.6	93.4	1.7
New Zealand	3	2,040	77.4	22.6	0.0	76.1	22.6
Republic of Korea	3	787	51.4	48.6	79.6	76.0	8.0
Singapore	3	943	34.0	66.0	25.9	96.9	n/a

Source: WHO 2008.

Notes: Turkmenistan: estimates derived from limited sources. OECD countries: From OECD Health Data (October 2006) and corresponding national sources. Japan: 2004 ratios estimated by WHO. Republic of Korea: Expenditures were reclassified between out-of-pocket and private prepaid plans. Thailand: Published data reclassified to distinguish between social security and other health insurance schemes. China: Estimates do not include Hong Kong and Macao Special Administrative Regions. In some cases the sum of government and private expenditures on health may not add up to 100 because of rounding.

health-care interventions according to the Commission on Macroeconomics and Health (WHO 2003). By contrast, per capita health expenditures were between $100 and $200 in most middle-income countries and much higher in high-income countries.

In all countries, patients pay for a substantial proportion of health care out of pocket. In general, households in poorer countries pay a higher percentage out of pocket than those in wealthier countries. In twelve of the low- and middle-income Asia-Pacific countries listed, at least 60 percent of health-care expenditures were funded privately, that is, out of pocket, because private health insurance (the alternative private funding source) plays a negligible role in these countries. Percentages paid out of pocket are lower in the high-income countries with social health insurance systems (Australia, Japan, and New Zealand); in South Korea, relatively high OOP spending likely stems from high copayments for care (O'Donnell et al. 2008).

Medicines consume the largest proportion of OOP health-care expenditures, ranging from 21 percent in China[5] to 69 percent in Nepal (table 18.2). This share is higher among poor households, among those who do not incur catastrophic health-care expenditures (expenditures greater than 40 percent of available income after paying for food), and among the uninsured (figure 18.2).

Large OOP spending on health care has a negative impact on households (Van Doorslaer et al. 2007). In at least 10 percent of households in Bangladesh, China, India, Nepal, and Vietnam, such spending consumes more than one-quarter of household resources after paying for food (Van Doorslaeret al. 2007). High OOP payments require households to make difficult choices: forego needed medical care, pay for care from limited resources needed for food, sell assets, or borrow money—pushing them further into poverty. A 2003 survey in China found that 30 percent of poor households attributed their poverty to health-care costs and the inability to afford insurance or pay for medical treatment (World Bank 2005).

Social health insurance is at varying stages of development in the Asia-Pacific region. Some high- and middle-income countries (Australia, Japan, South Korea, New Zealand, Singapore, Thailand, and Taiwan) have universal social health insurance systems (O'Donnell et al. 2008). In other countries (China, Indonesia, Kyrgyz Republic, Philippines, Vietnam, Mongolia), existing insurance programs cover parts of the population, and several have a declared goal of reaching universal coverage in the near future (Philippines, Vietnam, Mongolia) (O'Donnell et al. 2008). Some countries, such as the Lao People's Democratic Republic (PDR) and Cambodia, have just begun to implement health insurance programs targeting different population groups in an attempt to reach universal coverage in the longer term (Howell 2006).

Increasing health insurance coverage in the Asia-Pacific region is crucial to decrease OOP health-care payments and mitigate their detrimental health and economic consequences. But to achieve this goal efficiently, health insurance programs will need to provide well-designed medicines coverage. At the moment, individuals pay for medicines, especially those used for outpatient treatment, in most Asia-Pacific countries—even those with social health insurance systems (O'Donnell et al. 2008; see also Van Doorslaer et al. 2007). Designing and implementing medicines coverage in insurance systems requires understanding the role that medicines can play in achieving health-care objectives.

Table 18.2 Percentage Distribution of Out-of-pocket Health-care Payments in Asia-Pacific Countries, by Type of Medical Service

	Medicines	Inpatient care	Outpatient care	Care by traditional or alternative healers	Other
Bangladesh	67.1	6.3	8.1	5.0	13.6
China	21.3	43.1	25.9	1.0	8.7
India	44.4	25.4	16.9	3.3	9.9
Kazakhstan	67.5	6.1	1.8	1.4	23.2
Lao PDR	47.8	25.2	10.1	10.7	6.2
Myanmar	47.8	11.9	26.6	5.2	8.4
Nepal	68.8	13.9	4.3	1.5	11.5
Pakistan	45.5	21.2	14.5	7.0	11.8
Philippines	50.2	24.4	9.8	1.0	14.5
Sri Lanka	36.1	28.7	14.7	1.7	18.8
Malaysia	28.8	22.7	14.3	5.2	28.9
Vietnam	37.0	27.2	21.9	5.0	8.9
Median	46.7	23.6	14.4	4.2	11.7
25th percentile	36.8	13.4	9.4	1.5	8.9
75th percentile	48.4	25.9	18.2	5.2	15.6

Source: World Health Survey 2002, http://www.who.int/healthinfo/survey/en.

Stakeholders in the Pharmaceutical Sector

A network of pharmaceutical sector stakeholders with different and sometimes conflicting agendas interact in complex ways to determine access to and utilization of medicines (Bennett et al. 1994, figure 18.3).

The central actors in the pharmaceutical system are consumers, prescribers, and the government. In simple terms, consumers seek care from a variety of health-care providers (if and when they decide to do so) and utilize available health-care services, including medicines, if they feel they need and are able to afford them. Providers give care, offer advice, and prescribe medicines; their decisions about which medicines to prescribe depend on their prior knowledge, experience, institutional constraints, and economic incentives for prescribing one medicine versus another. The government is responsible for broad legislative and regulatory policy, and decides, among other things, which medicines enter the country, how much they cost, through what public and private outlets they are dispersed, and by which types of health-care professionals.

Ideally, consumer organizations and professional societies link their constitutents to governments by providing information, support, and oversight. But in many low- and middle-income countries, consumer organizations and professional societies are nonexistent, weak, or ineffective in fulfilling these functions.

Figure 18.2 Percentage of Medicine Expenditures Paid Out of Pocket by Household Income Group, Presence of Catastrophic Health Expenditure, Insurance Status, and Urban/Rural Location in Twelve Asia-Pacific Countries

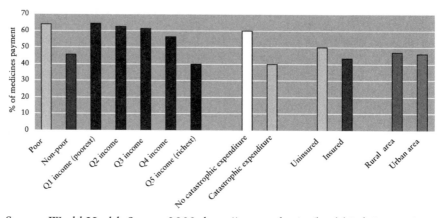

Source: World Health Survey 2002, http://www.who.int/healthinfo/survey/en.
Note: Countries included are Bangladesh, China, India, Kazakhstan, Lao PDR, Myanmar, Nepal, Pakistan, Philippines, Sri Lanka, Malaysia, and Vietnam.

Perhaps the dominant role in determining access to and use of medicines belongs to the pharmaceutical industry, which broadly includes manufacturers, importers, wholesalers, and distributors of pharmaceutical products. Medicines enter the pharmaceutical marketplace via a drug registration process by which the government approves companies to market products, under a trade name or as generics. After registration, companies and their representatives are free—within the constraints of government regulations—to distribute and promote medicines to health-care providers. Industry decisions dominate the pharmaceutical market: which products to register; whether to import or manufacture them locally; how much to charge different customers; how to distribute products; how to promote specific products to prescribers, dispensers, and to consumers; and what economic incentives to offer so these parties use more of their products. The pharmaceutical industry thereby exerts a powerful influence on treatment recommendations of health-care providers, on individuals' choice of medicines, and thus on overall patterns of consumption.

Figure 18.3 The Role of Health Insurance in the Pharmaceutical Sector

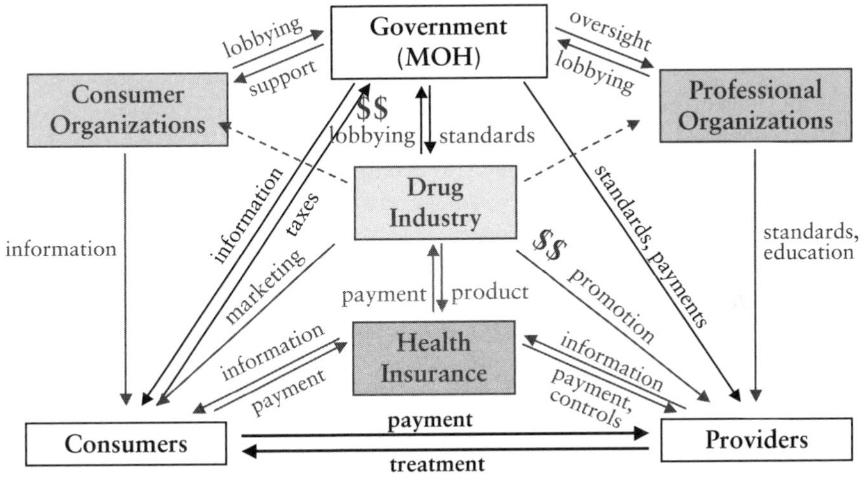

Source: Modified from Bennett et al. 1994.
Note: MOH = Ministry of Health.

From a societal perspective, the main goal of each stakeholder should be to achieve the best positive health outcomes for the money spent on health care and to do so equitably. However, achieving this goal is difficult: The pharmaceutical sector is characterized by information asymmetry between industry and government, between sellers and purchasers, and between patients and health providers. Interactions between national and institutional policy structures and industry influences determine the degree to which medicines are used in a clinically optimal and cost-effective manner. In countries where government regulation is insufficient or lacks enforcement and where consumer and professional organizations are weak, the pharmaceutical industry is the source of most information on medicines (Vancelik et al. 2007).

Health insurance organizations can strategically advance the societal goals of equitable access to medicines at affordable costs, with a greater likelihood of positive health outcomes for the money spent on medicines. They can do this by providing unbiased information about effective care and appropriate use of medicines to health-care providers and consumers, assembling data on illness and health-care utilization patterns to target key problems and population groups, and monitoring health-care practice and data dissemination to improve the quality of care.

Determinants of Medicines Use and Cost

Within the context of the multistakeholder pharmaceutical system, supply- and demand-side factors combine to determine the selection, price, and volume of medicines used, and whether their purchase—by individuals, insurance programs, or governments—has positive health and economic effects.

Key supply-side factors that contribute to high medicines costs include: (1) the market entry of innovative but costly treatments that do not meet clinical needs; (2) marketing pressure to increase sales of costly products for which less costly, equally beneficial, alternatives exist; (3) lack of government and private purchaser leverage in negotiating medicines prices; (4) lack of generic competition; (5) lack of transparency and accountability in pricing and supply; (6) economic incentives for individual providers or health institutions to prescribe and dispense greater numbers of medicines or more profitable high-cost medicines; and (7) regulators' inability to ensure quality, especially of locally manufactured generic products.

Some of the key demand-side factors that escalate medicines costs include: (1) aging populations with chronic illnesses (such as cardiovascular diseases, diabetes); (2) spreading epidemics (such as HIV/AIDS and malaria); (3) increasing purchasing power and demand for health care in growing economies; (4) lack of trust in locally produced generic products and demand for costly, imported products; (5) patient demand for specific products as a result of previous recommendations by health-care providers, exposure to advertisements, or other types of drug promotion; (6) lack of health provider awareness of and adherence to evidence-based standard treatment guidelines; (7) lack of organizational capacity to assess the quality or cost-effectiveness of treatment; and (8) lack of coordination between inpatient and outpatient care.

To enhance value for money, medicines need to reach patients at the right time, at an affordable cost, and for the necessary duration. Supply- and demand-side policy interventions are needed to accomplish this objective (O'Donnell 2007). Health insurance programs have the unique potential to affect the factors driving high costs and substandard use of medicines, especially in the private sector. Insurance programs can provide unbiased information about medicines to patients and providers; decide which medicines to cover; use their power as large-scale purchasers to expand access to medicines at more affordable prices; leverage better prescribing by clinicians and more cost-effective use by consumers; promote use of generic medicines; build performance standards into provider accreditation or contracting; monitor both the cost and quality of pharmaceutical care; implement programs to assist patients in using medicines in a clinically effective way; and, in pursuing these options, design insurance-based financing for medicines that is both scaleable and sustainable.

Medicines Coverage Policies in Health Insurance Programs

Insurance programs can use an array of tools to influence the way medicines are used by prescribers, dispensers, and patients (figure 18.4). These policy interventions typically include education for health-care providers and members, strengthening of management systems, positive and negative financial incentives, and restrictions on practice.

Figure 18.4 Framework for Insurance Intervention Options to Improve Access to and Use of Medicines

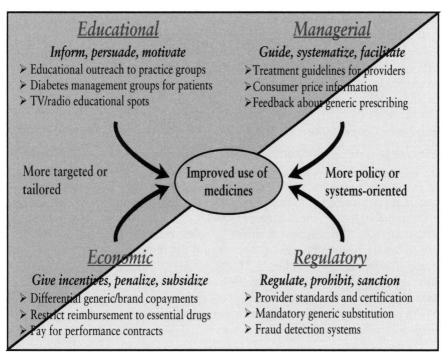

Source: Ross-Degnan et al. 1992.
Note: Derived from an intervention framework to improve use of medicines developed by the International Network for Rational Use of Drugs, http://www.inrud.org/.

Educational Interventions

Health insurance programs can educate health-care providers and patients about known problems. Tailored interventions often combine educational outreach with managerial support such as standard treatment guidelines and formularies. For example, a tailored educational program could target members who have multiple chronic illnesses, such as hypertension and diabetes, and the providers who care for them. Patients with multiple illnesses cause high system costs and have high morbidity and mortality rates; well-managed medication regimens can lead to demonstrable short- and long-term improvements. The Australian government conducts large-scale educational outreach (academic detailing) through pharmacists who instruct office-based primary-care prescribers on the relative value of different medicines to promote evidence-based prescribing for target populations (Weekes et al. 2005).

Interventions by insurance programs to improve medicines use can also be more systems oriented. For example, an educational program could be developed to inform providers and members about the demonstrated quality and superior value of generic medicines, which might be combined with a formulary that lists generic medicines, economic incentives in the form of lower cost sharing to encourage patients to demand them, and performance-based incentives for providers who prescribe target rates of generic products.

Managerial Interventions

Managerial interventions are intended to guide prescribers and patients in their choice of medicines and their appropriate use. Commonly used examples of managerial interventions are formularies, standard treatment guidelines, and disease-management programs. Standard treatment guidelines suggest preferred therapeutic classes to prescribers; formularies list preferred drugs within classes (Management Sciences for Health 1997). Disease-management programs coordinate pharmacotherapy and other treatment approaches and target those program members with the greatest need for and highest cost of care. All three interventions need to be based on evidence of safety, efficacy, and cost-effectiveness of recommended treatments. Insurance programs can monitor health provider and patient utilization patterns, provide feedback on prescribing patterns, and facilitate systems that encourage desired practices.

Economic Interventions

In general, interventions have greater long-term impact on behavior when the economic incentives of institutions, providers, and patients can be aligned. Such incentives can, over time, shift practice toward desired outcomes. For example, tiered copayment structures under which patients pay less for preferred generic medicines and more for nonpreferred brand products can encourage patients to demand generic prescribing and dispensing. Pay-for-performance programs

(O'Kane 2007) can provide economic rewards for health providers who achieve desired prescribing patterns, such as higher rates of generic prescribing or of prescribing first-line medicines recommended by standard treatment guidelines for common chronic diseases.

As large-scale purchasers, health insurance programs can negotiate prices for high-quality products from pharmaceutical manufacturers, thereby decreasing medicines prices. With their purchasing leverage, programs can also demand more complete disclosure of information from manufacturers, including formal cost-effectiveness data.[6]

Regulatory Interventions

Health insurance programs contract with health-care institutions, health-care providers, product suppliers, and patients. Via contracts, programs can regulate provider access and member reimbursements for care delivered. Many insurance systems accredit health-care providers based on documented standards of their educational background and practice experience; they can implement requirements beyond licensing criteria implemented by government regulatory authorities, for example, demanding continuing education or documented quality assurance processes (Philippine Health Insurance Corporation 2004). Similarly, contracts can determine the pharmacy retail outlets in which insurance program members are able to fill prescriptions, allowing programs to exert influence over standards of practice in pharmacies as well. For example, if generic substitution is legally allowed, insurance programs can make generic use a requirement for medicines dispensed to members and design contracts so that accredited pharmacies do not suffer a consequent economic disadvantage.

The Medicines and Insurance Coverage (MedIC) Initiative

Routine enrollment and claims data enable health insurance programs to monitor the utilization and cost of medicines, increase transparency, maintain efficiency, and design policies to increase the quality of care and promote equity. But established and emerging programs often lack the capacity, tools, and networks to use existing data in evidence-based medicines policymaking. Recognizing the increasing prevalence and the potential of insurance programs, experts from seventy countries at the Second International Conference on Improving Use of Medicines (ICIUM)[7] recommended medicines coverage through health insurance as a key global strategy to improve access to essential medicines, especially for the poor (ICIUM 2004). To facilitate this strategy, the WHOCCPP[8] began the global MedIC initiative. MedIC's goal is to improve the health and economic well-being of people in developing and transitional economies by improving the availability and affordability of essential medicines through health insurance programs. MedIC initiative staff work with policymakers and analysts in health insurance programs across the world to generate evidence for effective medicines policy.

327

The MedIC initiative has four core objectives: (1) to build capacity through training programs in the design, implementation, management, and evaluation of medicines policies; (2) to collaborate with health-care organizations and insurance programs in designing, implementing, evaluating, and monitoring policy interventions to improve medicines use among vulnerable populations; (3) to develop, test, and disseminate locally relevant standard performance indicators of cost, affordability, equitable access, and quality use of medicines (QUM); and (4) to establish global and regional networks for health insurance programs to share expertise, tools, and model medicines coverage policy portfolios.

Capacity Building

The WHOCCPP launched the MedIC initiative in the fall of 2007, with its inaugural course on Medicines Policy Analysis in Health and Insurance Systems in Manila. Thirty-eight officials from ministries of health, insurance programs, and nongovernmental organizations in twelve countries participated (Wagner and Ross-Degnan 2007). In the short term, the MedIC initiative offers courses in various regions to expand insurance programs' capacity to design, implement, and evaluate evidence-based medicines policies. In the longer term, the training program will incorporate both in-person learning collaboratives and on-the-job mentoring, as well as Web-based tutorials and online interactive learning.

Target audiences for MedIC training programs include managers and policymakers who develop, implement, and monitor medicines policy in insurance systems, including governmental and private insurance programs, self-insured employers, donors, and regulatory officials. Participants develop the skills needed to extract and analyze data generated from pharmacy and medical claims, formulate and implement interventions based on evidence, monitor and evaluate intervention effects, and present and disseminate results to policymakers.

Technical Collaboration

The MedIC initiative's core activity is the provision of technical support to health insurance organizations in developing and transitional countries that are interested in implementing policies to increase access to and appropriate use of medicines by their enrollees. Insurance organizations are at different levels of evolution in terms of their medicines benefits, policy structures, and data systems. Some countries have full-fledged national social insurance coverage, while others are moving toward that goal by incrementally adding coverage for target groups. For example, although Vietnam established a social health insurance system in 1992, coverage is only at 9 percent and is slowly including the poor, informal workers, minorities, students, and children through health-care funds and voluntary health insurance schemes (Ekman et al. 2008). To maximize the impact of expanded coverage, insurance programs need to systematically examine their effects on the utilization of public health facilities and private health-care providers, on health and medicines expenditures, and on QUM. Establishing and expanding community-based health insurance (CBHI) schemes are another way of reaching universal coverage, as evident in the Lao People's Democratic Republic (Howell 2006). Whether CBHI can improve access to and use of medicines among vulnerable groups is unknown (Vialle-Valentin et al. 2008). Their success may depend on establishing linkages with drug sellers of high-quality, low-cost essential medicines. Policy analysis in this context should focus on changes in vulnerable groups' utilization after insurance coverage and the impact of purchasing agreements with systems supplying affordable medicines.

Potential interventions in different settings will depend upon existing benefit structures, reimbursement policies, quality-improvement programs, health-care and pharmaceutical systems characteristics, and enrollee populations. Examples of policy interventions include: extending a defined outpatient medicines benefit scheme to children or another vulnerable group (for example, poor members with high-risk conditions such as tuberculosis, HIV infection, diabetes, or hypertension); creating formularies with tiered copayments or reference prices to increase use of generic medications or preferred brands; or establishing performance-based compensation for providers linked to defined quality standards with periodic feedback on performance indicators.

Standard Performance Measures

To successfully manage medicines benefits, insurance organizations must undertake a range of complex functions. These include regular, real-time analyses of: (1) members, providers, and vendors; (2) types and quantities of care, including medicines, reimbursed; and (3) economic and health impacts of policy changes on different member groups. In this process, insurance programs must continually make decisions about which medicines to reimburse, for which patients and providers, and with which restrictions. They must also evaluate the impact of coverage decisions on members' health, utilization, and spending.

Using well-constructed performance measures (derived from routine data), insurance program managers and policymakers can monitor their efforts toward specific policy objectives and ensure financial accountability and sustainability. Industrialized countries have developed several model sets of health-care and insurance systems performance measures, including those of the Organisation for Economic Co-operation and Development (OECD) (Mattke, Epstein, and Leatherman 2006), the National Committee for Quality Assurance (NCQA), and the Healthcare Effectiveness Data and Information Set (HEDIS).[9] Existing performance measures are often inappropriate for resource-poor, developing and transitional countries and do not acknowledge the fact that medicines represent a much larger component of OOP health expenditures in these countries. Finally, except for performance measures developed by the Australian National

Prescribing Service (NPS) (Quality Use of Medicines and Pharmacy Research Centre 2003), few measures currently used in industrialized countries focus on medicines access and use.

MedIC initiative staff will work with partner insurance programs to develop and field-test candidate measures of cost, affordability, equity in access, quality use, and health outcomes, based on routine data in their systems. Measures that prove relevant and feasible in local settings can be included in models for other regions to adapt.

Information Sharing and Networking

To stimulate the sharing of expertise, experience, and tools, the MedIC initiative will facilitate the creation of regional MedIC networks. These networks will allow members to interact in person and electronically. The approach will be modeled on the International Network for Rational Use of Drugs (INRUD), a highly successful network facilitated by the WHO and international partners (Ross-Degnan et al. 1992). MedIC network members will share information (about use, cost, and clinical guidelines), tools (such as standardized drug coding, disease classification, monitoring systems, and analysis programs), and evidence of intervention effects over the Internet, in technical project meetings, and through regional and global conferences.

Summary

All countries in the Asia-Pacific region have a critical and growing need for affordable and reliable access to appropriate medicines—from the perspectives of individual health, household economic security, health-care system efficiency, and economic productivity. Established and emerging health insurance systems in the Asia-Pacific region can design medicines coverage policies to address many of the supply- and demand-side factors in the pharmaceutical system that impede affordable access to quality medicines. We believe that the development of evidence-based medicines policies in existing and emerging insurance systems is key to achieving societal health goals for the large populations in Asia-Pacific countries. The MedIC initiative seeks to support the development, implementation, and evaluation of evidence-based medicines coverage policies in the Asia-Pacific region.

Notes

[1] We gratefully acknowledge the support of Sarah Lewis, who compiled and analyzed data reported in this chapter and of Joyce Cheatham, who reviewed the edited version. The Department of Population Medicine (DPM) at Harvard Medical School supports Wagner, Ross-Degnan, Lewis, and Cheatham through its Accelerating MedIC Grant. We thank Karen Eggleston, Gordon Moore,

Michael A. Santoro, and Stephen Soumerai for their critical review of an earlier version of this chapter.

[2] The term *insurance* in this document refers to all types of health insurance programs, including private, public, for-profit, and not-for-profit programs and organizations, in particular those which include the poor. Health insurance programs pool risks across populations and pay part of or all health-care expenses for their defined populations of members (and possibly dependents) from premiums contributed by individuals, employers, nongovernmental organizations, and/or government. The services and goods covered by health insurance programs and the restrictions that apply to coverage vary widely. In this chapter, we assume that a medicines benefit would be provided, in addition, to coverage of basic health-care services; we are not considering schemes that only cover medicines.

[3] Implementing rules and regulations of the National Health Insurance Act (NHIA) of 1995 (Republic Act No. 7875), http://www.philhealth.gov.ph/download/IRR2004.pdf. See also Oberman et al. 2006.

[4] Philippine Health Insurance Corporation Statistics.

[5] We believe the relatively low reported percentage of household spending on medicines in National Health Accounts data from China can be explained by the inclusion of the relatively high percentage of spending on medicines in hospitals in the inpatient category (43.2 percent of inpatient costs are for medicines).

[6] Australian Pharmaceutical Medical Benefits Scheme. http://www.health.gov.au/internet/main/publishing.nsf/Content/Pharmaceutical%20Benefits%20Scheme%20(PBS)-1.

[7] See International Conference on Improving Use of Medicines, Chiang Mai, Thailand (March 30–April 2), http://www.icium.org/icium2004.

[8] See World Health Organization Collaborating Center on Pharmaceutical Policy, http://www.whoccpp.org.

[9] HEDIS and quality measurement, http://www.ncqa.org/tabid/59/Default.aspx.

References

Management Sciences for Health. 1997. Treatment guidelines and formulary manuals. In *Managing drug supply. The selection, procurement, distribution, and use of pharmaceuticals*, ed. J. D. Quick, J. R. Rankin, R. O. Laing, R. W. O'Connor, H. V. Hogerzeil, M. N. G. Dukes, A. Garnet second edition, 137–49. West Hartford, CT: Kumarian Press.

Abegunde, D. O., C. D. Mathers, T. Adam, M. Ortegon, and K. Strong. 2007. The burden and costs of chronic diseases in low-income and middle-income countries. *Lancet* 370: 1929–38.

Asia Pacific Cohort Studies Collaboration. 2005. A comparison of the associations between risk factors and cardiovascular disease in Asia and Australasia. *European Journal of Cardiovascular Prevention and Rehabilitation* 12: 484–91.

Batangan, D. B., C. Echavez, A. A. Santiago, A. C. de la Cruz, and E. Santos. 2006. *The prices people have to pay for medicines in the Philippines.* Report from the WHO/HAI Medicines Prices Project. World Health Organization/Health Action International, Geneva, Switzerland. http://www.haiweb.org/medicineprices/surveys/200502PH/sdocs/survey_report.pdf.

Bennett, S., G. Dakpallah, P. Garner, L. Gilson, S. Nittayaramphong, B. Zurita, and A. Zwi. 1994. Carrot and stick: State mechanisms to influence private provider behavior. *Health Policy and Planning* 9: 1–13.

Birt, M. P. 2006. Chronic neglect. *Foreign Policy* (September/October). http://www.foreignpolicy.com/story/cms.php?story_id=3551&print=1.

Ekman, B., N. T. Liem, H. A. Duc, and H. Axelson. 2008. Health insurance reform in Vietnam: A review of recent developments and future challenges. *Health Policy and Planning* 23: 252–63.

Gatbonton, P. 2006. The unfit Filipino. *Pinoy Health.* http://www.globalpinoy.com/pinoyhealth/ph_feature/FE092605.php.

Howell, Fiona. 2006. Development of social health insurance in Lao PDR. Presentation at the Conference on Extending Social Health Insurance to Informal Workers, Manila, Philippines, October 18–20.

ICIUM. *See* International Conference on Improving Use of Medicines.

International Conference on Improving Use of Medicines. 2004. Chiang Mai, Thailand (March 30–April 2). http://www.icium.org/icium2004.

———. International Conference on Improving Use of Medicines. 2004. Chiang Mai, Thailand (March 30–April 2). Recommendations on insurance coverage. http://www.icium.org/icium2004/recommendations.asp.

International Diabetes Federation. 2009. *Diabetes atlas.* http://www.eatlas.idf.org.

International Network for Rational Use of Drugs. http://www.inrud.org/.

Kearney, P., M. Whelton, K. Reynolds, P. Muntner, P. K. Whelton, and J. He. 2005. Global burden of hypertension: Analysis of worldwide data. *Lancet* 365: 217–23.

Khor, G. L. 2001. Cardiovascular epidemiology in the Asia-Pacific region. *Asia-Pacific Journal of Clinical Nutrition* 10: 76–80.

Lawes, C. M. M., S. Vander Hoorn, A. Rodgers. 2008. Global burden of blood-pressure-related disease, 2001. *Lancet* 371: 1513–18.

Martiniuk, A., C. Lee, C. M. Lawes, H. Ueshima, I. Suh, T. H. Lam, D. Gu, V. Feigin, K. Jamrozik, T. Ohkubo, M. Woodward; Asia-Pacific Cohort Studies Collaboration. 2007. Hypertension: Its prevalence and population-attributable fraction for mortality from cardiovascular disease in the Asia-Pacific region. *Journal of Hypertension* 25: 73–79.

Mathers, C. D., and D. Loncar. 2006. Projections of global mortality and burden of disease from 2002 to 2030. *PLoS Med* 3(11): e442. doi:10.1371/journal. pmed.0030442. http://www.pubmedcentral.nih.gov/articlerender.fcgi?tool =pubmed&pubmedid=17132052.

Mattke, S., A. M. Epstein, and S. Leatherman. 2006. The OECD health care quality indicators project: History and background. *International Journal of Quality Health Care* 18 (Suppl. 1): 1–4.

National Committee for Quality Assurance. various years. Healthcare data and information set (HEDIS). http://www.ncqa.org/tabid/59/Default.aspx.

Neal, B., S. MacMahon, and N. Chapman. 2000. Effects of ACE inhibitors, calcium antagonists, and other blood-pressure-lowering drugs: Results of prospectively designed overviews of randomized trials. Blood Pressure Lowering Treatment Trialists' Collaboration. *Lancet* 356: 1955–64.

O'Donnell, O. 2007. Access to health care in developing countries: Breaking down demand side barriers. *Cad Saúde Pública* 23: 2820–34.

O'Donnell, O., E. van Doorslaer, R. P. Rannan-Eliya, A. Somanathan, S. R. Adhikari, B. Akkazieva, D. Harbianto, C. C. Garg, P. Hanvoravongchai, A. N. Herrin, M. N. Huq, S. Ibragimova, A. Karan, S. M. Kwon, G. M. Leung, J. F. Lu, Y. Ohkusa, B. R. Pande, R. Racelis, K. Tin, K. Tisayaticom, L. Trisnantoro, Q. Wan, B. M. Yang, Y. Zhao. 2008. Who pays for health care in Asia. *Journal of Health Economics* 27: 460–75.

O'Kane, M. E. 2007. Performance-based measures: The early results are in. *Journal of Managed Care Pharmacy* 13 (2 Suppl. B): S3–S6.

Oberman, K., M. R. Jowett, Maria O. O. Alcantara, E. P. Banzon, and C. Bodart. 2006. Social health insurance in a developing country: The case of the Philippines. *Social Science and Medicine* 62: 3177–85.

Philippine Health Insurance Corporation. 2004. Quality assurance research and policy development group: Benchbook on performance improvement of health services. ed. Wystan de la Peña. Philippines.

Population Reference Bureau. August 2006. *World population data sheet.* Washington, DC. http://prb.org/pdf06/06WorldDataSheet.pdf.

Puska, P., S. Mendis, and D. Porter. 2003. *Cardiovascular disease facts.* Geneva, Switzerland. World Health Organization. http://www.who.int/hpr/NPH/ docs/gs_cvd.pdf.

Quality Use of Medicines and Pharmacy Research Centre. September 2003. *Measurement of the quality use of medicines component of Australia's national medicines policy. Second report of the national indicators.* Report for the Australian Government Department of Health and Aging, University of South Australia. http://www.health.gov.au/internet/main/publishing.nsf/ Content/AC9F1C85C978FB0CCA256F1800468E76/$File/qumnmp.pdf.

Ross-Degnan, D., R. Laing, J. Quick, H. M. Ali, D. Ofori-Adjei, L. Salako, and B. Santoso. 1992. A strategy for promoting pharmaceutical use: The international network for rational use of drugs. *Social Science and Medicine* 35: 1329–41.

Suhrcke, M., R. A. Nugent, D. Stuckler, and L. Rocco. 2006. *Chronic disease: An economic perspective*. London: Oxford Health Alliance. http://www.oxha.org.

Van Doorslaer, E., O. O'Donnell, R. P. Rannan-Eliya, A. Somanathan, S. R. Adhikari, C. C. Garg, D. Harbianto, A. N. Herrin, M. N. Huq, S. Ibragimova, A. Karan, T. J. Lee, G. M. Leung, J. F. Lu, C. W. Ng, B. R. Pande, R. Racelis, S. Tao, K. Tin, K. Tisayaticom, L. Trisnantoro, C. Vasavid, Y. Zhao. 2007. Catastrophic payments for health care in Asia. *Health Economics* 16: 1159–84.

Vancelik, S., N. E. Beyhun, H. Acemoglu, and O. Calikoglu. 2007. Impact of pharmaceutical promotion on prescribing decisions of general practitioners in Eastern Turkey. *BMC Public Health* 7: 122. http://www.biomedcentral.com/1471-2458/7/122.

Vialle-Valentin, C. E., D. Ross-Degnan, J. Ntaganira, and A. K. Wagner. 2008. Medicine coverage and community-based health insurance in low-income countries. *Health Research Policy and Systems* 30 (6): 11.

Wagner, A. K., and D. Ross-Degnan. 2007. *Medicines and insurance coverage (MedIC) initiative course on medicines policy analysis in health and insurance systems*. Final report, November 17. http://www.whoccpp.org/training/medic2007/MedIC_in_Manila_Course_Report_Nov_19_2007.pdf.

Wagner, A. K., M. Valera, A. J. Graves, S. Laviña, and D. Ross-Degnan. Costs of hospital care for hypertension in an insured population without an outpatient medicines benefit: An observational study in the Philippines. *BMC Health Services Research*. 29(8): 161.

Weekes, L. M., J. M. Mackson, M. Fitzgerald, and S. R. Phillips. 2005. National prescribing service: Creating an implementation arm for national medicines policy. *British Journal of Clinical Pharmacology*. 59: 112–16.

Woodward, M., Barzi, A. Matiniuk, X. Fang, D. F. Gu, Y. Imai, T. H. Lam, W. H. Pan, A. Rodgers, I. Suh, S. H. Jee, H. Ueshima, R. Huxley. 2006. Cohort profile: The Asia-Pacific Cohort Studies Collaboration. *International Journal of Epidemiology*. 35: 1412–16.

World Bank. 2005. *Rural health in China. Briefing note #3. China's health sector—Why reform is needed*. Beijing: World Bank Office.

WHO. *See* World Health Organization.

World Health Organization. 2002. *World health report 2002: Reducing risks, promoting healthy life*. Geneva, Switzerland: WHO. http://www.who.int/whr/2002/en/index.html.

———. 2003. *Investing in health. A summary of the findings of the Commission on Macroeconomics and Health*. Commission on Macroeconomics and Health (CMH) Support Unit. http://www.who.int/macrohealth/infocentre/advocacy/en/investinginhealth02052003.pdf.

———. 2004. *Regional macroeconomics and health framework*. New Delhi: WHO Regional Office for South East Asia. http://www.who.int/macrohealth/documents/en/RegionalMacroeconomicsandHealthFramework.pdf.

World Health Organization Collaborating Center for Surveillance of Cardiovascular Diseases. 2009. *Global cardiovascular infoBase*. Division of Cardiology, University of Ottawa. http://cvdinfobase.ca.

World Health Survey. 2002. http://www.who.int/healthinfo/survey/en/.

DEBATING DRUG ACCESS AND R&D INCENTIVES

John H. Barton

The global pharmaceutical market fails to meet global medical needs. True, the current development and supply system provides many drugs suited to the requirements of the most wealthy nations. But it develops very few to meet the needs of the poorest, many of whom cannot even afford those products that have been developed.

This gap might be bridged by:

- Providing financial incentives—whether via international donors or the pricing systems of developed nations—for research that targets the needs of low-income developing nations
- Protecting research-based pharmaceuticals against excessive price regulation in developed markets
- Creating an efficient generic market in the poorest regions of the world, even for drugs that are still on-patent in developed countries
- Eliminating tax and customs barriers, strengthening controls on corruption and drug counterfeiting, and otherwise streamlining the supply of drugs to developing nations.

Each effort responds to an underlying trend that will continue to sway the world market until it is mitigated. The aim is a "win-win" situation in which all parties benefit: patients in both developed and developing nations and stakeholders of both research-based and generic pharmaceutical industries. This goal will be most readily met through reciprocal commitments acceptable to taxpayers in developed nations.

Background

The 1984 Hatch-Waxman Act resolved several problems in the U.S. pharmaceutical market[1] and is thus a good model to look at. It benefited the research-based industry by extending patent terms to mitigate time lost during the drug registration process. It also helped create the vibrant U.S. generic drug industry that has since helped reduce overall drug prices. The act boosted generics by allowing the U.S. Food and Drug Agency (U.S. FDA) to approve generic drugs biologically equivalent to clinically tested drugs going off patent. Several provisions designed to facilitate generic entry have since given rise to bizarre licensing agreements and serious antitrust concerns (see, for example,

U. S. Federal Trade Commission 2002). But these provisions are not central to the basic concept of the legislation, nor to its benefits, which include the growth of the generic industry from 19 percent (by unit) of the U.S. market in 1984 to 42–43 percent after 1995 (Berndt 2002).

What is the possibility of a parallel global compromise today?

Table 19.1 World Pharmaceutical Market Share by Sector

Nation type: Sector	2000 share (%)	Estimated 2016 share (%)
High-income: public	33.2	37
High-income: private	45.5	37
Middle-income: public	5.5	7
Middle-income: private	13.3	15
Low-income: public	0.7	2
Low-income: private	1.7	2

Note: The year 2000 column is calculated directly from tables 5.1 and 5.3 in World Health Organization (WHO) figures. The year 2016 column has been estimated, by the author, based on assumptions that are described in the paper. Clearly, the numbers are uncertain, the assumptions in the 2016 estimates are heroic, and the actual numbers will differ from drug to drug. But the *trend* is, almost certainly, correctly estimated.

Developed nations are the primary movers of the world's pharmaceutical market and thus decide the focus of pharmaceutical research. This places a unique responsibility on the governments of these nations, many of which are the biggest purchasers in their respective markets. It is almost certain that, as estimated in table 19.1, the percentage of the market controlled by governments and subject to public-sector price control will increase radically.

The U.S. market is particularly significant in this regard. The United States made up, as a purchaser, 52.9 percent of the world pharmaceutical market (by value) in 2000, up from 18.4 percent in 1976 (WHO 2004). Within the United States, the government's share in purchasing pharmaceuticals has already grown from 18 percent in 1990 to a projected 39 percent in 2007 (Kaiser Family Foundation 2006). It is likely that this role will increase as the U.S. health-care sector is reformed. A recent study (K. Davis et al. 2007) suggests that the health sector's share of the U.S. gross national product (GNP) will rise from 16 percent in 2005 to 20 percent in 2015. The same study also shows that health insurance premiums have grown 81 percent since 2000, while median family income has increased only 11 percent. Such trends will—sooner than later—prompt politicians and other policymakers to change the system. In this context, drug prices are a leading candidate for reform.[2] In the long term, the government will almost certainly be given a larger role in the market and will use this to press for reduced pharmaceutical prices. What the government does is likely to be imitated by private health insurers. In sum, the U.S. government is the dominant factor shaping *global* demand for pharmaceuticals and pharmaceutical research.

Encouraging the Research-based Pharmaceutical Industry

To encourage innovation, the governments of developed nations must promise that they will pay an adequate price for pharmaceuticals and not force prices down so far as to discourage innovation. Such harm may already have been done to the U.S. childhood vaccine industry (Institute of Medicine 2004), and the spread of reference pricing in other nations suggests a broad risk. An ideal government commitment would give the industry enough confidence to invest in research while, at the same time, satisfying the needs of taxpayers, patients, and doctors.

An excellent starting point is laid out in a recent market study on British pharmaceutical purchases (U.K. Office of Fair Trading 2007). It calls for a "value-based approach to pricing, which would ensure that the price of drugs reflect their clinical and therapeutic value to patients and the broader National Health Service." Such an arrangement is fair to both the pharmaceutical industry and the taxpayers supporting national health care. The United Kingdom is not the only nation doing this: the approach was pioneered by Australia, and several European public health agencies are already taking into account the therapeutic value of drugs and requiring cost-effectiveness studies as part of their procurement processes (Ess, Schneeweiss, and Szucs 2003).

Analyzing cost-effectiveness simply compares the costs and benefits of one drug against an alternative treatment or drug. Given that several treatments may apply to a particular indication, it may be wise to measure cost-effectiveness not against current competitors but instead against whatever treatment was prevalent several years (perhaps as many as seven) prior. This would reward alternative directions of innovation that reached the market at the same time. It is also important to do the cost-effectiveness calculations with a minimum value of a "quality adjusted life year" (QALY). Any formal arrangements would probably apply only to the public sector, but a parallel private-sector market also serves to drive innovation (and one will certainly survive in the United States).

New Drug Research

To promote global equity, it is crucial for public-sector purchasers in developed nations to take into account diseases found only in developing nations. An "international orphan drug" approach to these drugs would require that public health authorities in developed nations pay extra—beyond cost-effective pricing—for such drugs when procuring them for travelers and military personnel. This is because the benefits to this small market are only a portion of the social value of such drugs. To effectively promote the dissemination of important drugs, various buyers must share the research costs equitably.

Important recent changes in this market are driven by the rise of donor funding, especially for treating the human immunodeficiency virus (HIV), tuberculosis, and malaria. Since 2000 an international public sector has grown—funded, for example, by the Global Fund to Fight AIDS, Tuberculosis, and Malaria (GFATM); by the U.S. President's Emergency Program for AIDS Relief (PEPFAR); and by the Bill and Melinda Gates Foundation (B&MGF). Economic development will certainly increase the role of the private sector in these areas, but the major trend (see table 19.1) will be an increasing role for donor funds—assuming they continue to grow. They will be the world's most important buyers of drugs for certain diseases and vaccines. However, their total expenditures on drugs will be no more than 1 to 2 percent of total developed nation spending—but perhaps double that of the poorest nations.

These funds should reasonably pay the majority of the research cost of the "international orphan drug" products whose application is primarily in developing nations. A cost-benefit-based price for a term of ten to twelve years comparable to an effective patent term is rational. This may be a very high return—but this area is where research is probably the most beneficial to society. There should, of course, be adjustments for the extent to which the research costs of these products are covered by front-end foundation or public-sector funding in developed nations. This amounts to a less formal version of the "advance purchase commitment" put forward during the 2006 G-8 summit in St. Petersburg, Russia. Under that concept an advance commitment would be made to pay for a predefined large amount of purchases from the successful developer of a new drug or vaccine for a specific predefined need; the payment requirement proposed here would achieve the same goal through the regular behavior of purchasing agencies rather than through a special promise.[3] Similarly, it would seek to achieve the same goal as the priority review voucher system described by Grabowski, Ridley, and Moe in chapter 20 of this volume.

Generic Drugs for the Poorest

For drugs whose research costs can be recovered in developed nations, there should be generic alternatives available for purchase by international donor funds and by the public and private sectors of the poorest nations. In low-income nations with deficient health infrastructure, patients must often obtain pharmaceutical products on their own—and generally lack resources to do so. Moreover, overall drug quality is terrible; as much as 15 percent—in some cases even 50 percent—of available pharmaceuticals are bogus.[4] And the prices faced by patients in developing nations are often far higher than world market prices (Richards 2006).[5] To counter this trend, more generic drugs—or brand-name drugs at low prices—should be made available to developing nations. The registration process might be similar to that in developed nations' postpatent generic markets. To achieve this goal, pharmaceutical producers would need to offer differential pricing or encourage generic firms to compete. The low prices would be available to consumers in low-income nations, and for products for which research costs can be recovered in the developed world. The low-priced drugs would also be available to global donors. The net cost to global donors (who will, in large part, be taxpayers in developed nations) is thus kept as low as possible by keeping procurements at generic price levels, except when higher prices are needed to encourage research on diseases only prevalent in developing nations. The arrangement, of course, requires strong barriers to stop the flow of low-cost generic products back to developed nations until their branded alternatives go off-patent in those nations.

Such a low-cost generic market may require some encouragement to develop. The TRIPS-Doha arrangements that allow generics in low-income nations have been only somewhat successful. Thus, the number of HIV patients receiving antiretrovirals in Africa was reported to be about 1.3 million in 2007— only 28 percent of those requiring treatment (WHO 2007). Generics are apparently covering some 65 percent of this African market (Chien 2007). This helps, but is nowhere close to meeting the actual need. The primary sources of such drugs are still Indian and South African suppliers. Save for a 2007 Canadian license to Apotex, the TRIPS-Doha mechanisms have not brought in new suppliers. The current success of Indian exporters may well depend, in part, on the availability of an Indian market to cover start-up and fixed costs, which are certainly not as high as research costs but are nevertheless significant. Hopefully, global donor funds (and their ability to offer prices that cover start-up costs) will help build a strong generic market. In the vaccine sector, for example, the United Nations International Children's Emergency Fund (UNICEF) has used its buying policies to supply about 40 percent of the world's childhood vaccines, with a new generation of Indian vaccine manufacturers making that nation the world's second-largest supplier (UNICEF 2005).

A Free Market for All

The poorest nations can help build a strong generic market while at the same time encouraging innovation. All nations receiving the benefit of the generic market must help make it open and transparent. This will help grow the generic market large enough to attract the substantial investments that are needed to provide economies of scale and to satisfy good manufacturing practice (GMP) requirements. The free market would require eliminating all tariffs, taxes, and, as far as possible, regulatory barriers. The most difficult task in this context is ensuring product safety and quality review (Hill and Johnson 2004). There is no reason for every nation to organize its own product safety review. The review process is expensive, it may become a basis for corruption, and it slows product entry. To harmonize regulatory review worldwide would be ideal but, in spite of the efforts of the International Conference on Harmonization, this goal is a long way off.

One sensible model is that all nations benefiting from the new generic drug market would accept a WHO-defined review process. This would depend on existing leading regulatory agencies but would be flexible enough to make exceptions in specific cases. Along with the rest of the world, member nations would commit to fixing the problems of substandard drugs and corruption in distribution chains. International collaboration in this regard is crucial, since countering corruption can be more a matter of obtaining technical assistance than of adopting new laws.

Middle-income Nations

It is in middle-income nations that current patent battles are being fought most fiercely. This is primarily because their markets are likely to grow the most over the next few decades—as real incomes and purchasing power rise. The pharmaceutical industry correctly sees these as its future markets. This is why the United States is pressuring nations such as Colombia and Thailand to strengthen intellectual property right (IPR) protection (see Oxfam 2006). At the same time, nations such as Brazil and Thailand (see Ratanawijitrasin, chapter 4 of this volume) have programs for national production of drugs through compulsory licenses of products still on patent.

When they reach a certain income level, these nations must be treated as developed nations and must pay their full share of research costs. Moreover, they will, at some point of development, face pressure from their own industries for stronger patent protection. Yet, they are home to many poor people. For example, there are more people living in absolute poverty in South Asia than in Africa (Chan and Ravallion 2004). And some middle-income markets may assist in making a generic market economically feasible for the poorest.

Particularly since these nations will be crucial in developing a new pharmaceutical regime, there needs to be a special set of rules for the middle-income tier. For example, the public sector (or, if the market could be so divided, the poorest) in these nations could be allowed access to developing nations' low-cost generic market, while the private sector would be subject to the same patent standards as developed nations. Yet, the actual nature of these markets—as described in the rest of this volume—make such a distinction problematic. Often, the public-sector market is used to subsidize other aspects of medical care; frequently the only market available to the poorest is a high-priced private market. And so another option might be to create a postpatent generic market that would become available sooner than in the high-income nations. Or there may be other ways of dividing the market, as exemplified by GlaxoSmithKline's recent efforts in Africa, where the firm provides a lower price to specific institutions, such as nongovernmental organizations (NGOs) that directly serve the poor (GSK 2007). Or it may be possible to provide some of these nations, especially India and China, greater opportunities to participate in research and production for the rest of the world.

Implementation

The efforts outlined at the beginning of this chapter seek to promote health equity around the world in a way that is negotiable and benefits all parties. There are many ways to implement such initiatives. The following are put forward as suggestions:

(1) Public-sector drug-buying authorities, such as those in the United States and Europe, would commit themselves to developing detailed mechanisms to ensure that they pay a price that reflects the clinical value of drugs, as measured by national health needs, and also to covering an appropriate share of research costs for their purchases of new products of primary value to the developing nations.

(2) Low-income developing nations, as well as global funds such as GFATM and PEPFAR, would be permitted to purchase generic or low-price versions of all drugs including those on patent. The global funds would pay prices that cover an appropriate share of research costs for new products of primary value to developing nations.

(3) Middle-income nations would, generally, be subject to the rules for high-income nations, but would be entitled to low prices for their poor or to reduce patent terms for pharmaceuticals by some years from those currently required by TRIPS.

(4) All nations would prohibit the trade of substandard drugs, would cooperate with generic and research pharmaceutical firms to help suppress it, and would help prevent the reverse flow of generic drugs from low-income to high-income nations.

(5) Beneficiaries of new generic pricing would remove all legal tax, duty, and similar barriers to the import and marketing of pharmaceuticals. They would further agree to accept new drugs upon approval by a new process that would be based on the standards defined by U.S. and European regulatory authorities.

(6) Donor nations would commit themselves to supporting the global funds at a defined level.

(7) These national commitments would be set down in both international agreements and national legislation. The agreement might take the form of a code within the World Trade Organization (WTO). (This would assure the industry that a nation's failure to live up to its commitment could be brought before a WTO panel, and thus provide some check against future legislation seeking to drive down pharmaceutical prices.)

This overall proposal is quite different from many of those suggested before. Each of the components is economically defensible. And the likely perceived political costs and benefits are reasonably balanced among the different communities.

Unavoidable Issues

Whether or not these proposals are packaged as suggested, many aspects of them are likely to be implemented in one way or another in national health policies and in the actions of international donors. The underlying issues must be faced:

- Demand for drug access versus that for research incentives, whether patent based or otherwise.
- The industry effects of cost-effectiveness pricing and price controls in major developed-nation markets.
- The growing role of foundations, such as the GFATM and PEPFAR, in shaping research incentives for diseases specific to the poorest.
- The likelihood that patents will lose economic relevance in contrast to governmental and other institutional purchase policies.
- The changing role of middle-income nations as they become host to major research innovation as well as production and purchase.
- Pressures to unify markets to support research of and investment in both generic and patent-protected products.

Notes

[1] Drug Price Competition and Patent Term Restoration Act of 1984, Pub. L. No. 98–417.

[2] Administrative costs are also an important reform area. They make up 25 to 30 percent of medical costs. See, for example, Woolhandler, Campbell, and Himmelstein 2003 (31 percent); Kahn et al. 2005 (25 percent).

[3] For an analysis of such commitments, see Grace 2006.

[4] Calculated from WHO 2004.

[5] Richards 2006. The underlying study was undertaken for the WHO and Health Action International 2006.

References

Berndt, E. 2002. Pharmaceuticals in U.S. health care: Determinants of quantity and price. *Journal of Economic Perspectives* 16 (4): 45–66.

Chan, S., and M. Ravallion. 2004. *How have the world's poorest fared since the early 1980s?* Washington, DC: World Bank.

Chien, C. 2007. HIV/AIDS drugs for Sub-Sahara Africa: How do brand and generic supply compare? PloS ONE 2 (3) (March 14): e278.

Davis, K; C. Schoen, S. Guterman, T. Shih, S. Schoenbaum, and I. Weinbaum. 2007. *Slowing the growth of U.S. health-care expenditures: What are the options?* January. New York:The Commonwealth Fund, Commission on a High Performance Health System.

Ess, S., S. Schneeweiss, and T. Szucs. 2003. European healthcare policies for controlling drug expenditure. *Pharmacoeconomics* 21 (2): 89–103.

GlaxoSmithKline. 2007. *GSK corporate responsibility report 2007*. Brentford, Middlesex, UK.

Grace, C. July 2006. *Developing new technologies to address neglected diseases: The role of product development partnerships and advanced market commitments*. London: Department for International Development (DFID) Health Resource Center.

Hill, S., and K. Johnson. May 2004. *Emerging challenges and opportunities in drug registration and regulation in developing countries*. London: DFID Health Systems Resource Center.

Institute of Medicine. 2004. *Financing vaccines in the 21st century: Assuring access and availability*. Washington, D.C.

Kahn, J., R. Kronick, M. Kreger, and D. Gans. 2005. The cost of health insurance administration in California: Estimates for insurers, physicians, and hospitals. *Health Affairs* 24: 1629–39.

Kaiser Family Foundation. June 2006. *Prescription drug trends*. Menlo Park, CA, and Washington, D.C.

Oxfam. November 2006. Patents v. patients; Five years after the Doha Declaration. Briefing paper 95. http://www.oxfam.org/sites/www.oxfam.org/files/Patents%20vs.%20Patients.pdf.

Richards, T. 2006. The great medicines scandal. *British Medical Journal* 332 (June 10): 1345–46.

U.S. Federal Trade Commission. July 2002. *Generic drug entry prior to patent expiration; An FTC study*. Washington D.C. http://www.ftc.gov/os/2002/07/genericdrugstudy.pdf.

U.K. Office of Fair Trading (OFT). February 2007. *The pharmaceutical price regulation scheme*. http://www.oft.gov.uk/shared_oft/reports/comp_policy/oft885.pdf.

UNICEF. *See* United Nations International Children's Emergency Fund.

United Nations International Children's Emergency Fund. 2005. *Supply division annual report* 2005. http://www.unicef.org/supply/files/SD_AnnualReport_2005.pdf.

WHO. *See* World Health Organization.

Woolhandler, S., T. Campbell, and D. Himmelstein. 2003. Costs of health-care administration in the United States and Canada. *New England Journal of Medicine* 349 (August 31): 768–75.

World Health Organization. 2004. *The world medicines situation*. http://www.searo.who.int/LinkFiles/Reports_World_Medicines_Situation.pdf.

———. 2007. *Towards universal access: Progress report April 2007*. Geneva.

World Health Organization and Health Action International. 2006. *Price, availability and affordability; An international comparison of chronic disease medicines*. WHO-EM/ED8/068/E. Cairo.

Encouraging Innovative Treatment of Neglected Diseases through Priority Review Vouchers

Henry G. Grabowski, David B. Ridley, and Jeffrey L. Moe[1]

Tropical diseases cause substantial suffering and loss of life around the world. Africa rightly receives considerable attention in its efforts to fight them, but other regions too have limited resources to mitigate their impact. Fortunately, the developing nations of the Western Pacific (excluding Australia, Japan, New Zealand, and the Republic of Korea) have a disease rate (18 percent of the global average) below their share of the world's population (24 percent). But they have only 2 percent of the world's health resources (World Health Organization 2007:19).

A recent shift in U.S. policy could help fight tropical diseases in developing Western Pacific countries and elsewhere. In September 2007 the U.S. Congress enacted the Food and Drug Administration Amendments Act of 2007, which increased funding for the research and development (R&D) of treatments for neglected tropical diseases including malaria, leishmaniasis, Chagas disease, and tuberculosis (TB). Introduced into Congress by Senators Sam Brownback and Sherrod Brown (Brownback 2007), the law is based on the policy proposal and economic analysis of this chapter's authors (Ridley, Grabowski, and Moe 2006). One of its provisions involves awarding a transferable priority review voucher (PRV) to any company that gains U.S. Food and Drug Administration (U.S. FDA) approval for a new pharmaceutical or biological treatment targeting a neglected tropical disease. The bearer of this voucher is entitled to a priority review (instead of a standard one) for another drug product submitted for U.S. FDA approval.[2]

A PRV thus speeds the process of getting a new drug to market. The U.S. FDA's target review times for priority and standard drugs are six and ten months, respectively, but the *actual* median review time (since 2000) is about seven months for priority drugs and fifteen months for standard drugs (table 20.1). In an earlier analysis we found that a difference of several months can be worth hundreds of millions of dollars for pharmaceutical products with large expected sales (Ridley, Grabowski, and Moe 2006).

PRVs raise a number of interesting questions for both policymakers and analysts. How will the PRV market evolve? How will vouchers be administered by the U.S. FDA? And how effective will they be in promoting the R&D of tropical disease treatments? Other important issues to consider are how the vouchers will complement other public and private incentives, and whether they will have any important unintended consequences. Under the new law, companies that use the voucher will be required to pay a supplemental review fee so that the FDA can recoup the resource costs associated with additional priority reviews. The additional user fee is intended to prevent a PRV from slowing the review process for other drugs in the U.S. FDA queue.

In this chapter we consider several important aspects of the new PRV law. We first provide background information on tropical diseases in developing countries and how the vouchers complement other push-and-pull incentive programs directed at mitigating these diseases. We then consider the PRV law in more detail and examine regulatory issues in administering it. After analyzing the economic value of a PRV under different scenarios, we summarize our findings and discuss some key issues for further analysis.

The PRV and Other Incentives for Treating Neglected Diseases

Under the Food and Drug Administration Amendments Act of 2007, companies that make treatments for any of sixteen tropical diseases are eligible to receive PRVs.[3] The law also states that vouchers can be obtained for treatment of "any other infectious disease for which there is no significant market in developed nations and [which] disproportionately affects poor and marginalized populations, designated by regulation of the Secretary."

The major obstacle to stimulating the R&D of new medicines for neglected diseases is low-income nations' inability to pay for such medicines. Average spending on health services in low-income countries was about $29 per capita in 2003.[4] This barrier is compounded by others, including ineffective policies and inadequate medical infrastructure, both of which impede the efficient delivery of drugs and other medical supplies. Insufficient revenue and infrastructure on the demand side are coupled with the high fixed cost of R&D on the supply side. As a consequence, relatively few drugs have been developed to address the high global disease burden posed by tropical diseases (WHO 2004).

Figure 20.1 shows diseases that are highly concentrated in developing countries. Some of these, such as malaria and TB, have large annual global burdens and are the subject of targeted public-private development partnerships (PDPs) and other initiatives. The PRV law could complement existing programs. At the same time, a large number of tropical diseases have substantial disease burdens in the aggregate but are targeted by few drug development efforts. These diseases could garner more interest and attention as a result of the new PRV law.

Push and Pull Incentive Programs

Public and private strategies for stimulating R&D of treatments for neglected diseases are usually designated as "push" or "pull" programs. Strategies in the "push" category involve R&D cost sharing and subsidies such as tax credits,

Figure 20.1 Annual Global Burden of Disease versus Share of Burden in Developing Countries, 2005

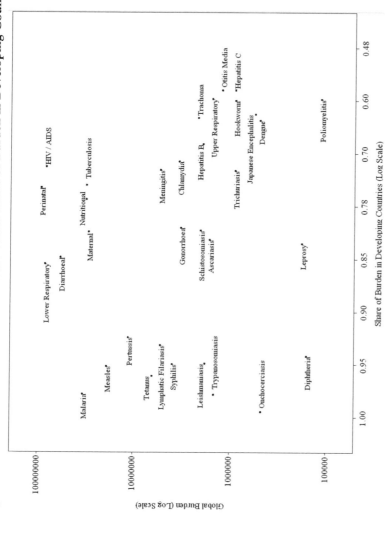

Source: Authors' calculations based on World Health Organization data (2006) on disability-adjusted life years lost from disease.

research grants, and PDPs. "Pull" programs involve a specified prize or reward for research outputs—for example, guaranteed purchase arrangements for developing and gaining approval for new drugs for neglected diseases. The PRV is a market-oriented pull mechanism that can be combined with push mechanisms such as orphan drug tax credits.

Push and pull mechanisms have well-known benefits and limitations. Push mechanisms allow direct donor control over product development and might be especially beneficial at the earliest stages of the research process, when scientific and commercial risks are substantial and the feasibility of the product is uncertain. On the other hand, push mechanisms that are controlled by a central agency can suffer from asymmetric information and a misalignment of incentives across donors and developers, leading to resource inefficiencies.

Pull strategies reward output and do not require donor funding except at specific milestones, such as regulatory approval or market distribution. Pull strategies are designed to create market incentives through commitments to particular outcomes. Two potential limitations, however, are the credibility of the commitment and the substantial time involved in pharmaceutical R&D programs, which can span a decade or more.

A prominent example of a market-oriented pull strategy is the advanced market commitment (AMC) for stimulating R&D for neglected diseases, developed by Michael Kremer and his colleagues (Kremer 2002; Berndt and Hurwitz 2005). The concept was adopted in 2007, when five countries (Canada, Italy, Norway, Russia, and the United Kingdom) along with the Gates Foundation committed $1.5 billion to launch the first AMC for a pneumococcal vaccine for disease strains prevalent in developing countries. This pilot program provides for seven to ten years of funding with the goal of creating sustainable supply conditions in developing countries. It is estimated that a vaccine meeting the AMC criteria could save the lives of 5.4 million children by 2030 (GAVI Alliance 2007).

One successful program that uses both push and pull incentives is the U.S. Orphan Drug Act (ODA), passed in 1983. This provides tax credits, subsidies, and other benefits such as market exclusivity to stimulate R&D of treatment for diseases not prevalent in the United States (Grabowski 2005). It has been very successful in encouraging new drug treatments for rare illnesses such as Gaucher's disease and Wilson's disease. Neglected diseases also qualify for orphan drug status because of their rare occurence in the United States, but there have been relatively few drugs developed under the ODA for tropical diseases—even widespread killers like malaria.[5] The combination of orphan drug subsidies, together with the prize of a transferable PRV, could provide a more powerful set of incentives to increase R&D in this area.

The PRV as a Complement to Other Incentive Programs for Neglected Diseases

One advantage of the PRV is that it can complement other push and pull strategies. Many PDPs support a portfolio of development projects dedicated to particular neglected diseases. A PRV could be a valuable addition by providing resource support and incentives to private partners. For example, nonprofit foundations engage a variety of public and private institutions with novel contractual relationships to support their clinical development programs. In effect, the PRV could be a *quid pro quo* for performing the expensive late-stage trials. Alternatively, if the PDPs retained ownership of the PRV on a successful approval, they could auction it to the highest bidder and use the funds for further research.

The PRV also complements the charitable and good-will activities of for-profit corporations. Some important drugs that target neglected diseases have been developed under the philanthropic programs of major pharmaceutical firms. The most prominent example is Merck's development and donation of the drug ivermectin for river blindness. Other important corporate initiatives in progress target filariasis, trachoma, and leprosy (Grabowski 2005). The PRV could help broaden the scope of R&D on neglected diseases and complement the philanthropic motivation of these programs.

The PRV could reinforce other pull mechanisms as well, such as AMC programs that provide purchase guarantees for malaria or TB vaccines that meet particular specifications (Berndt and Hurwitz 2005). However, the PRV's most important function might be to encourage R&D of treatments for lower-profile neglected diseases without large, dedicated funding. In particular, the voucher could encourage drug developers to apply what they have learned about one set of neglected diseases to another set. It could also allow smaller biotech firms to demonstrate the importance of innovative new therapies.

The U.S. FDA's Role in Administering the PRV

To earn a PRV, researchers must develop a molecule (pharmaceutical or biological) that contains an active ingredient not previously approved by the U.S. FDA. This precludes new formulations, new indications, and fixed combinations of previously approved drugs. The PRV, once awarded, can be sold or transferred to another party. To use the PRV, however, the bearer must notify the U.S. FDA 365 days before filing the new drug application (NDA) on which it is to be applied. This then binds the party to the supplemental priority user fee. The U.S. FDA will calculate and publish this fee each year, based on its assessment of the average cost to review priority drugs. The user fee for new drug applications requiring clinical data was $1,178,000 for the 2008 fiscal year (Federal Register, Prescription Drug User Fee Rates for Fiscal Year 2008).

Under priority review, the target for U.S. FDA action is six months from the date of NDA submission. This does not mean that the application must be accepted or rejected in this period. Rather, the U.S. FDA can approve, reject, or deem the drug "approvable," in which case the drug application is returned to the sponsor to correct deficiencies and perhaps perform additional tests (Berndt et al. 2005). The U.S. FDA, therefore, retains considerable discretion in the review of all drug applications.

351

U.S. FDA actions in administering the priority review of voucher drugs will affect the value of the voucher. If, for example, U.S. FDA reviewers tend to label these drugs approvable rather than approved—whether because of minor deficiencies or excess risk aversion—this would significantly diminish the value of the PRV and its efficacy as an incentive for R&D. Such a risk appears to be the biggest concern of companies that are considering participating. Given that R&D is high-cost, high-risk, and can stretch over long time periods, there must be a credible expectation that the PRV will in fact speed drug approval. Many companies might wait to see if this is the case before initiating new R&D programs targeting neglected diseases—and the markets for vouchers could be slow to develop.

Potential Unintended Consequences

There are concerns that the PRV program could slow the review of other drugs or, alternatively, that the faster reviews will not be thorough, with the consequence that voucher drugs pose greater safety risks. Charging the special user fee and requiring 365-day advance notification for PRV drugs should provide the U.S. FDA with sufficient resources to handle the extra workload and not delay the review of other drugs. In addition, since priority review does not lower the approval criteria for safety or efficacy, it should not increase safety risks, provided that adequate resources are available to undertake the faster reviews.

Several recent studies investigate whether the fast review track, established under the Prescription Drug User Fees Act (PDUFA), has led to greater safety risks. The legislation introduced review time targets and also gave the U.S. FDA significantly more resources to undertake new product reviews. Berndt et al. (2005) find that the proportion of new drug withdrawals remained unchanged after the implementation of drug user fees in 1994. Similar findings are reported by the U.S. FDA (2005) and the Tufts Center for the Study of Drug Development (2005). On the other hand, Mary Olson (2004, 2008), in a multiple regression analysis, finds that drugs with faster review times are subject to more adverse events. But her results are subject to some data limitations and potentially confounding factors.

Grabowski and Wang (2008) analyze the effect of review times on adverse events, controlling for global launch lags, drug novelty, and utilization. Their results indicate that drugs first approved abroad are subject to fewer adverse events than those first approved in the United States. This suggests that U.S. FDA reviewers benefit from spillover knowledge of the drug's effects in actual clinical practice with large patient populations—in addition to the data obtained from controlled patient trials. From a policy perspective, however, PRVs are unlikely to affect the country of initial launch, since the vast majority of commercially important new drugs since the mid-1990s have been either launched in the United States or worldwide (Grabowski and Wang 2008). After controlling for global launch lags and other factors such as drug novelty and utilization,

Grabowski and Wang find no significant relation between review times and adverse events.

In the deliberations leading to the passage of the Food and Drug Administration Amendments Act of 2007, Congress considered several policy options to enhance drug safety, including elimination of the U.S. FDA review time targets. However, these targets were designed to reduce the lengthy delays of the pre-user fee period, and there is evidence of significant health benefits from the timely access to new medicines under user fees (Philipson, Berndt, Gottshalk, and Sun 2008). So instead of rolling back these targets, Congress chose to institute new post-marketing safety measures. This is consistent with the recommendations of an array of experts including the Institute of Medicine (2007) and former FDA commissioner Mark McClellan (2007).[6] The 2007 law dedicates a significant percentage of drug user fees to enhancing post-market surveillance and information disclosure. It also gives the FDA expanded risk-management tools.

The Value of PRVs

The PRV is valuable from three perspectives. First, the company awarded the voucher can either choose to enjoy its benefits or, upon sale, their monetary equivalent.[7] Second, the company that uses the voucher receives a speedier drug review. Third, people around the world benefit from the new drugs and vaccines encouraged by the PRV program.

The Value of a Priority Review

In an earlier analysis (Ridley, Grabowski, and Moe 2006), we considered the corporate advantages of obtaining a PRV. We showed that roughly half the blockbuster drugs introduced in the 1990s—that is, drugs that had $1 billion in annual sales by the fifth year after launch—received a standard rather than a priority review. But between 1992 and 2002, priority reviews were, on average, twelve months faster than standard reviews. To estimate the value lost in those twelve months, we used as our baseline the after-tax stream of income for the representative top-decile product from a comprehensive sample of new drugs introduced in the period 1990–1994 (Grabowski, Vernon, and DiMasi 2003). We found that getting such a product to market a year earlier was worth more than $300 million (Ridley, Grabowski, and Moe 2006).

The value of the voucher decreases as the difference between the priority and standard review times decreases. In 2006 the difference in median review times was seven months, not twelve (table 20.1). The PRV's value would be positively affected, however, if the voucher (1) increased a drug's time on the market (rather than just shifting it forward) and (2) created early mover advantages vis-à-vis a competitor. Given the workings of the Hatch-Waxman Act on patent restorations, we assume that effective patent life will remain unchanged. Specifically, we assumed that a faster U.S. FDA review time will be exactly offset by less patent term restoration under the rules of the Hatch-Waxman Act for many products. In Ridley, Grabowski, and Moe (2006), therefore, we estimated only the time value of money, assuming the voucher product's income stream was unchanged and shifted forward in time by exactly one year.

There are many situations in which effective patent life will be increased by a product's earlier entry into the market. In several scenarios, the PRV will effectively put the product on the market sooner and increase its patent life by the time difference between the priority and standard review—that is, the drug will have an earlier market entry but the same patent expiration date. A longer patent life could be worth a substantial amount in the case of a top-decile product.

Early-mover advantages are another source of value that we abstracted from our 2006 analysis. These advantages, which accrue to companies that beat competitors to introduce a new class of therapeutics, can be substantial in the pharmaceutical field. The fact that the PRV is transferable and can be sold to the highest bidder could greatly enhance its value if a bidding war were to occur between rival firms developing competing drugs in the same class. We will now consider the increase in PRV value from extra patent life and early-mover advantages in more detail.

Effective Patent Life

Under the Hatch-Waxman Act, new molecular entities are eligible for patent restoration associated with losses in effective patent life during clinical development and U.S. FDA review. Half the time lost in clinical development and all the time lost during U.S. FDA review is added to the effective patent life—subject to two constraints: (1) the maximum patent extension time is five years, and (2) the extension is capped by an effective patent life of fourteen years from the date of first approval. Only one patent is eligible for patent restoration (usually the core product or composition-of-matter patent). Process patents are not eligible for restoration.

As noted in our 2006 analysis, we assumed that the earlier market entry afforded by a PRV will be exactly offset by reduced patent restoration time (Ridley, Grabowski, and Moe 2006). For example, drugs subject to the fourteen-year cap on effective patent life will have a fixed fourteen-year effective patent life with or without the PRV. This fixed effective patent life would also hold true when the extension is relatively short and neither of the Hatch-Waxman constraints hold (for example, restored patent time is less than five years and effective patent life less than fourteen years). On the other hand, products with lengthy development and review times typically reach the five-year Hatch-Waxman limit on patent time extensions prior to a fourteen-year effective patent life. Such products would gain an extended patent life from a PRV.[8]

There are several other scenarios in which a product could gain a longer patent life from a speedier U.S. FDA review. Especially relevant examples are products whose market exclusivity periods are not determined by their effective patent life expiration date. For example, a product's life could be ended prior to the expiration of its extended patent period if it were successfully challenged by a generic competitor. Alternatively, a product's sales could be significantly curtailed if a superior product were introduced. In other cases, a product's effective patent life might extend beyond that determined by the patent extension formula due to other patents or regulatory factors.

Empirical analysis of effective patent life

To determine the relevance of these patent-life scenarios, we examined the experiences of blockbuster products encountering initial generic competition in the five-year period 2002–2007. In particular, we focused on the subsample of all new molecular entities that received a standard U.S. FDA review. We then selected products that had $1 billion in sales or more in the year immediately proceeding generic entry. There were eleven products that met these criteria in 2002–2007 (see table 20.2)[9]

Of these eleven products, four had an extended patent life of fourteen years under Hatch-Waxman, plus an additional six months for undertaking pediatric clinical trials.[10] As discussed, the patent life for these projects would have been the same with or without the PRV. On the other hand, two products (Coreg and Ambien) reached the five-year constraint prior to a fourteen-year effective life. These products would have obtained increased patent life from an earlier launch with a PRV.[11] In the case of another five products listed in table 20.2 (Paxil, Celexa, Allegra, Norvasc, and Protonix), the outcome is less clear. This is because their generic entry points were determined by patent litigation rather than the Hatch-Waxman patent life formula.

An earlier launch date also shifts forward the first point in time that a generic firm can file an abbreviated new drug application (ANDA) with a patent challenge (a so-called Paragraph Four certification, indicating that the generic firm believes the patent is invalid or noninfringed). Under Hatch-Waxman, the first generic firm that files an ANDA and successfully challenges the innovator's patent receives 180 days of exclusivity (Berndt et al. 2007). The earliest permitted filing date for an ANDA with a patent challenge is four years after the U.S. FDA approves the innovator's product.[12] But the actual timing of ANDA challenges depends on a variety of factors, including the size of the commercial opportunity, the perceived vulnerability of the innovator's patents, regulatory considerations, and the parties' resources and constraints. The timing of generic entry from a successful patent challenge spans a wide spectrum from 6.3 to 14.7 years after the introduction of the innovator's product. This range reflects the myriad factors at work in these situations.

In their analysis of market exclusivity periods for new molecular entities challenged by generic entry in the period 1995–2006, Grabowski and Kyle (2007) suggest that many would have obtained increases in effective patent life from a PRV. In particular, the mean annual market exclusivity for drugs with sales above $100 million varies between ten and twelve years (Grabowski and

Kyle 2007). Most products had shorter lifetimes than the fourteen-year effective patent life extension limit (or the limit of fourteen years and six months with pediatric exclusivity), due to a variety of factors including licensing delays, lengthy preclinical or clinical development times after the core patents were filed, regulatory delays, and successful patent challenges.

Based on our historical analysis, many products can expect to increase their effective patent life through the PRV. Because the PRV can be traded, the evidence of longer exclusivity increases the voucher's market value.

A stylized example

To obtain further insights into the expected values associated with increased patent life from a PRV, we developed a stylized example, illustrated in figure 20.2. In this example, we assume that a product without a PRV will have a lifetime of eleven years, at which point the product loses the entire market to generic competitors.[13] The PRV is assumed to permit the innovator company to gain entry into the market seven months earlier (this is the average difference between the priority and standard review, given in table 20.1).

Figure 20.2 The Priority Review Voucher Shifts Sales Forward and Increases Effective Patent Life

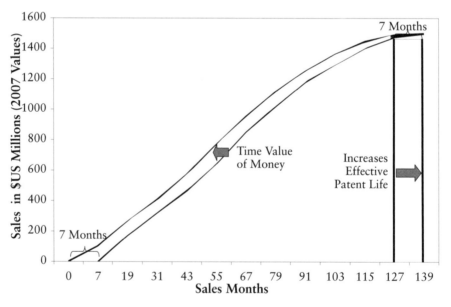

Source: Authors' stylized example based on sales patterns of blockbuster drugs.

Table 20.1 Approval Time (Months) for Priority and Standard NMEs and New BLAs, 2000–2006

Year	Total standard review median	Total priority review median	Differences in total median time	Standard U.S. FDA review median	Priority U.S. FDA review median	Differences in median U.S. FDA review
2000	19.9	6.0	13.9	15.4	6.0	9.4
2001	19.0	6.0	13.0	15.7	6.0	9.8
2002	15.9	16.3	-0.4	12.5	13.8	-1.3
2003	23.3	6.7	16.4	13.8	6.7	7.1
2004	24.7	6.0	18.8	16.0	6.0	10.0
2005	23.0	6.0	17.0	15.8	6.0	9.8
2006	13.7	6.0	7.7	12.5	6.0	6.5
Mean	20	8	12	15	7	7

Source: http://www.fda.gov/cder/rdmt/NMEapps93-06.htm.
Notes: NME = new molecular entity; BLA = biologic license application. Beginning in 2004, these figures include new BLAs for therapeutic biologic products. Total review time is the full time from an NDA's filing date to U.S. FDA approval. U.S. FDA review time refers to the subperiod when the NDA is under active review (i.e., not counting the period when an NDA is returned to the sponsor to clarify issues or correct omissions prior to a decision.)

Early-mover Advantages

The advantages of first entry have long been recognized. Theoretical work by Schmalensee (1982) shows that once consumers use a new product and become familiar with it, they might be reluctant to use a newly introduced competitor. In the case of pharmaceuticals, being first to market means that physicians will have time to become familiar with the therapeutic qualities of a drug before competitors enter the scene and, even after, they will often think of the first entrant as the best.

Research on the pharmaceutical industry also provides empirical evidence that first-movers have an advantage over later entrants, all else equal. In an early, oft-cited analysis, Bond and Lean (1977) studied two prescription drug markets (diuretics and antianginals) and concluded that the "the first firm to offer and promote a new type of product received a substantial and enduring sales advantage." More recently, in analyses of sales of serotonin-specific reuptake inhibitors (SSRIs) and H2-receptor antagonists, Berndt and colleagues found that order of entry had significant effects on market share (Berndt et al. 1997, 2002). Their analysis of the H2 blockbuster market, for example, finds that all else being equal, the $(n+1)$th entrant can expect sales about 40 percent lower than those of the nth entrant (Berndt et al. 1997).

Table 20.2 Standard Review Drugs with More than $1 Billion in Sales in the Year Before Generic Entry

	Chemical name	Generic entry	FDA approval	Market exclusivity[a]	Generic trigger event
1	Zestril/Prinivil (lisinopril)	06/2002	12/1987	14 years, 6 months	14-year Hatch-Waxman EPL
2	Paxil (paroxetine)	09/2003	12/1992	10 years, 8 months	Litigation
3	Celexa (citalopram)	10/2004	07/1998	6 years, 3 months	Litigation
4	Allegra (fexofenadine)	09/2005	07/1996	9 years, 2 months	Litigation
5	Pravachol (pravastatin)	04/2006	10/1991	14 years, 6 months	14-year Hatch-Waxman EPL
6	Zocor (simvastatin)	06/2006	12/1991	14 years, 6 months	14-year Hatch-Waxman EPL
7	Zoloft (sertaline)	08/2006	12/1991	14 years, 6 months	14-year Hatch-Waxman EPL
8	Norvasc (amlodipine)	03/2007	07/1992	14 years, 8 months	Litigation
9	Ambien (zolpidem)	04/2007	12/1992	14 years, 4 months	5-year Hatch-Waxman extension
10	Coreg (carvedilol)	09/2007	09/1995	12 years	5-year Hatch-Waxman extension
11	Protonix (pantoprazole)	12/2007	02/2000	7 years, 11 months	Litigation

Source: FDA Web site, Drugs@FDA; Company Annual Reports and Press Releases.
Note: [a] All the products in the table except Protonix were granted a six-month pediatric exclusivity extension to their patent expiration date; this is reflected in the values for market exclusivities.

To the extent that companies are involved in a competitive race to introduce a new class of therapies, the value of a PRV—especially for a bidder firm projected to be second in the race—could increase significantly with the expected long-term gains in market share from an earlier introduction. In certain scenarios, the value of the early-mover status could be substantially higher than either the time value of money or increased effective patent life. Since the PRV can be banked and sold to the highest bidder, its market exchange value will depend on the demand for and supply of vouchers at any point in time As discussed, expectations and attitudes toward risk as well as the negotiating and bargaining strength of the participants in this market are likely to play an important role in the market value of the PRV.[16]

The PRV's Value to the Developer of a New Tropical Medicine

To motivate the development of a new drug for a neglected disease, the price of the PRV must exceed the R&D costs that the organization expects to incur for developing and gaining drug approval. For a profit-making entity, the clinical development costs would be eligible for the 50 percent tax credit that comes with an orphan drug designation. Sale of the voucher to a third party would, in turn, be subject to the corporate income tax. These revenues total several hundred million dollars and would obviously support many neglected disease programs.

In the case of nonprofit PDPs, the PRV could be a valuable item to trade in exchange for support services. For example, a private firm might be willing to fund the phase 3 trials of a drug in its portfolio in exchange for obtaining the PRV in the event of a successful product approval. Alternatively, as stated earlier, a PDP that has significant funding for its phase 3 trials from foundations and philanthropic sources could bank the PRV and eventually auction it to the highest bidder. It could then plow back the revenues into further work on other components of its R&D program. In either event, the PRV could become a major source of R&D funding for PDPs with programs targeting neglected diseases.

As discussed in our 2006 analysis, we believe the cost of neglected disease R&D could be significantly less than the $800 million mean estimated cost of researching and developing new chemical entities.[17] This is true even without the R&D tax credits from the Orphan Drug Act. First, infectious disease indications frequently have higher probabilities of success, shorter timelines, and lower R&D costs than the mean case. Second, drugs for neglected diseases need not undergo comparative trials for formulary and reimbursement purposes. Third, there are substantial spillover possibilities from other R&D programs associated with bioterrorism and from public efforts by the U.S. military to support vaccine and drug development for pathogens in foreign countries. These products could be investigated following clinical trials in these public programs. All of these factors suggest that a PRV, valued at several hundred million dollars, could be a valuable stimulus to increase R&D activity on neglected diseases, just as the ODA stimulated a dramatic increase in research targeting rare genetic diseases in developed countries.

Global Social Welfare

New pharmaceuticals and biologicals that address diseases for which adequate treatments are not currently available offer immense societal benefits. A common threshold for health interventions in the poorest countries is $100 per disability-adjusted life year (DALY), a fraction of the value used in more developed countries. Even utilizing this low DALY value per day, the benefits could be enormous for products that significantly reduce the disease burden for the sixteen neglected diseases targeted by the Food and Drug Administration Amendments Act of 2007. In addition, other diseases that disproportionately affect developing countries—as shown in figure 20.1—are likely to be added to the list of targets for the PRV in future regulatory actions.

Another potential benefit is that drugs sped to market by the PRV will be sooner available in the United States. Several of the blockbuster drugs that received standard reviews in the 1990s went on to be leaders in their therapeutic class (including Zocor, Norvasc, and Ambien). If people in the United States are given access to a voucher-applied product seven months earlier than expected, this could lead to significant increases in consumer and producer surplus. Quantifying these potential gains is an empirical task for future researchers.

Conclusion

In 2007 Congress created a novel voucher award program to stimulate the R&D of treatment for neglected diseases. The PRV program became effective in September 2009. The first voucher was awarded to Novartis in conjunction with the U.S. FDA approval of the anti-malarial drug Coartem in April 2009.[18] We estimate that in a well-functioning market, a PRV could be worth hundreds of millions of dollars based on the value of faster reviews, increases in effective patent life, and early-mover advantages vis-à-vis competitors. The vouchers therefore could be a powerful stimulant for developing and filing new U.S. FDA drug applications relevant to neglected diseases.

The voucher program complements other push and pull mechanisms such as PDPs and AMC incentive programs. Given that drugs targeting tropical diseases such as malaria and dengue fever are eligible for orphan drug status in the United States, a 50 percent tax credit would also be applicable to the clinical trial costs for these diseases. The PRV, in combination with these credits, provides substantial incentives for companies to investigate a wider set of neglected diseases beyond those already targeted by dedicated programs.

The costs of the program appear to be small compared to potential benefits. The biggest concerns are the possibility of the PRV program slowing other U.S. FDA approvals, or subjecting patients to increased safety risks due to the faster reviews of voucher drugs. But users of the priority review program will pay an additional user fee and must give the U.S. FDA 365 days' advance notice to allow the agency time to allocate its resources for the expedited reviews. Furthermore, priority review does not involve a lower standard for approval and does not entitle the bearer to an actual approval in six months, only a decision in that time period. At the same time, however, for priority reviews to be an effective market-oriented pull mechanism, there must be a credible expectation that the program will be administered in the spirit of the law's objective, and that voucher drugs will not be subject to inordinate delays unrelated to a product's efficacy or safety.

To achieve the ultimate public health objective of reducing the large disease burden associated with tropical diseases, new medicines and vaccines emerging from the PRV program must be distributed to the relevant developing countries. This, of course, requires more than U.S. FDA approval. Nevertheless, development and approval of new medicines are essential first steps in the process.

As the U.S. FDA approves more medicines for tropical diseases, these drugs will likely be eligible for support by both governmental and nongovernmental initiatives (such as that of the Gates Foundation) to improve the welfare of people in developing countries. The U.S. government has also announced a $350 million program over five years for Neglected Tropical Disease Control to provide integrated treatment for seven neglected tropical diseases, including lymphatic filariasis (elephantiasis); schistosomiasis (snail fever); trachoma (eye infection); onchocerciasis (river blindness); and three soil-transmitted helminthes, or STHs (hookworm, roundworm, and whipworm). This program is being coordinated by USAID in collaboration with the CDC and World Health Organization (USAID Health 2009). As was true for the U.S. Orphan Drug Act, Europe and Japan could pass their own variants of the PRV.[19] These initiatives could also be integrated with other evolving programs for the distribution of established therapies to countries with low ability to pay.

Notes

[1] We appreciate helpful comments from Toshiaki Iizuka, Karen Eggleston, Hector Rincon, and participants at the Pharmaceuticals in the Asia-Pacific Stanford University Conference.

[2] Section 1102 of the Act titled Priority Review to Encourage Treatments for Tropical Diseases.

[3] The sixteen diseases are tuberculosis, malaria, blinding trachoma, buruli ulcer, cholera, dengue/dengue haemorragic fever, dracunculiasis (guinea-worm disease), fascioliasis, human African trypanosomiasis, leishmaniasis, leprosy, lymphatic filariasis, onchoceciasis, schistosomiasis, soil-transmuted helmithiasis, and yaws.

[4] Per capita spending is estimated using WHO data on health-care spending in 2003, WHO data on population and population growth rates from 2005, and World Bank data on country income classification for 2004.

[5] As of July 2003, there were only twelve orphan drugs approved in the United States targeted specifically to tropical diseases (Grabowski 2005; Kettler 2000).

[6] As various analysts have pointed out, serious adverse events that occur with relatively low incidence are only observable after regulatory approval in large patient populations rather than in the controlled premarket clinical trials that typically involve a few thousand individuals (Institute of Medicine 2007; Grabowski and Wang 2008). Post-marketing safety activities have been relatively underfunded in both the public and private sector (Ridley, Kramer, Tilson, et al. 2006).

[7] The company awarded the voucher and its user are not necessarily the same company, since the firm that generates the PRV might choose to auction or trade it to another company rather than utilize the PRV itself.

[8] Assume, for example, that the formula on clinical development time and review time yielded a restoration time of six years. In this case, the five-year cap would be effective and added onto the original patent expiration date under either priority or standard review. Hence, an earlier approval of seven months would also expand effective patent life by the same seven months.

[9] Information on Hatch-Waxman times for specific drugs are available on the U.S. Patent Office's Web site (http://www.uspto.gov/web/offices/pac/dapp/opla/term/156.html). Information on the dates of initial generic launch were obtained from IMS data collected through 2005 (Grabowski and Kyle 2007) and also from sources on the Internet, such as Silver (2007). These latter sources also contained information on entry based on the successful challenges of branded firm patents.

[10] A product can be granted an additional six months exclusivity for undertaking clinical trials and gaining an approved label for pediatric utilization. For an analysis of the value of six months' pediatric exclusivity for a selective group of products, see Li, Eisenstein, and Grabowski, et al. (2007).

[11] In the case of Ambien, the five-year extension time under Hatch-Waxman plus pediatric exclusivity yields an effective patent life of fourteen years and four months. Hence the extra time offered by a PRV would only be two months before it reaches the fourteen-year, six-month constraint under Hatch-Waxman.

[12] There is a period of between 5–7.5 years before an ANDA filed with a patent challenge can be effective. Under the Hatch-Waxman Act there is a five-year period (the innovator's "data exclusivity" period) in which a generic can not enter with an ANDA filing. In addition, for ANDAs filed with a patent challenge, there is a stay of up to thirty months while the matter is being resolved in the courts. If the matter is still active after this stay, the generic firm may enter at risk or wait until a District Court rules on the validity and/or infringement of the innovator's patents (Gryta 2008).

[13] Products with sales in excess of $1 billion typically lose more than 90 percent of their sales to generic competitors within a matter of months (Grabowski 2004; Silver 2007). But where only a generic product enters with a six-month Hatch-Waxman exclusivity because of a successful product challenge, the innovator firm will typically license an authorized generic (Berndt et al .2007). This strategy enables the innovator to capture some of the lost sales

from generic entry (albeit at reduced margins) for a short period of time before commodity pricing sets in with multiple generic entrants. We abstract from authorized generics in this stylized example, and assume that the originator firm loses all of the product's sales at the time of generic entry.

[14] For discounting purposes, this analysis treats the year 0 as the first seven months of product life and then each year after that is discounted based on an 11 percent cost of capital, compounded from the start of each calendar year. If one adopts an end-of-year calendar timing convention, total value would be $550 million in this stylized example instead of $599 million. The value of the additional sales in this stylized example before discounting is $874 million.

[15] To obtain present values of income, one would need to subtract the variable costs of production, marketing, taxes, and other fees (see Grabowski, Vernon, and DiMasi 2002). A company-specific prelaunch analysis for a new product correspondingly would need to include the product's forecasted sales revenues over its expected lifetime as well as the relevant contribution margins, cost of capital, marginal tax rates, and so on.

[16] It is not clear at this point whether there would be any requirement for transactions between firms to be publicly transparent in terms of the exchange of the PRV.

[17] This estimate includes discovery research and clinical development expenses as well as the costs of failed candidates, all capitalized to the date of marketing.

[18] Since the program was only implemented in September 2008, the initial approvals are expected to be products already approved elsewhere, or in the late stages of development, prior to their introduction here or abroad. Coartem had been approved outside the United States prior to 2009, and Novartis has made it available on a nonprofit basis in several low-income countries. For Coartem, one potential benefit of this initial voucher award is to provide information to market participants on the U.S. FDA's behavior toward priority review under the PRV program. Novartis has not indicated yet how it plans plan to utilize the voucher.

[19] In Japan, for example, priority review is granted for drugs treating orphan and other serious diseases (Japan Pharmaceutical Manufacturers Association 2007: 32–33).

References

Berndt, Ernst R., and John A. Hurvitz. 2005. Vaccine advance-purchase for low-income countries. *Health Affairs* 24(3): 653–65.

Ernst R. Berndt, Ashoke Bhattacharjya, David N. Mishol, Almudena Arcelus, and Thomas Lasky, 2002. An analysis of the diffusion of few antidepressants: variety, quality, and marketing efforts. *The Journal of Mental Health Policy and Economics* 5: 3–19.

Berndt, Ernst R., Linda T. Bui, David H. Lucking-Reiley, and Glen L. Urban. 1997. The roles of marketing, product quality, and price competition in the growth and composition of the United States antiulcer drug industry. *The Economics of New Goods,* ed. Timothy F. Bresnahan and Robert J. Gordon. Chicago: University of Chicago Press, 277–328.

Berndt, Ernst R., Adrian H. Gottschalk, Thomas J. Philipson, and Matthew W. Strobeck. 2005. Industry funding of the FDA: Effects of PDUFA on approval times and withdrawal rates. *Nature Reviews: Drug Discovery* 4(7): 545–54.

Berndt, Ernst R., Richard Mortimer, Ashoke Bhattacharjya, Andrew Parace, and Edward Tuttle. 2007. Authorized generic drugs, price competition, and consumers' welfare. *Health Affairs* 26(3): 790–99.

Bond, Ronald S., and David F. Lean. 1977. Sales promotion and product differentiation in two prescription markets. *Staff report to the Federal Trade Commission,* February.

Brownback, Sam. 2007. Eliminating neglected diseases: Impact of published paper. *Health Affairs* 26 (5): 1509.

DiMasi, Joseph A., Ronald W. Hansen, and Henry G. Grabowski. 2003. The price of innovation: New estimates of drug development costs. *Journal of Health Economics,* 22 (2): 151–85.

Federal Register October 12, 2007. Prescription drug user fee rates for fiscal year 2008. 72 (197): 58103–6. http://www.fda.gov/oc/pdufa.

GAVI Alliance. 2007. *Advanced market commitments for vaccines.* http://www.vaccineamc.org/news_launch_event_01.html.

Grabowski, Henry G. 2005. Increasing R&D incentives for neglected diseases: Lessons from the orphan drug act. In *International public goods, and transfer of technology under a globalized intellectual property regime,* ed. K. E. Maskus and J. H. Reichman. Cambridge: Cambridge University Press: 457–80.

Grabowski, Henry G., and Margaret Kyle. 2007. Generic competition and market exclusivity periods in pharmaceuticals. *Managerial and Decision Economics* 28:491–502.

Grabowski, Henry G., John Vernon, and Joseph A. DiMasi. 2002. Returns on research and development for 1990s new drug introductions. *PharmacoEconomics* 210 (Suppl. 3): 11–29.

Grabowski, Henry G., and Wang Y. Richard. 2008. Do faster FDA drug reviews adversely affect patient safety? An analysis of the 1992 Prescription Drug User Fee Act. *Journal of Law and Economics:* 377–406.

Gryta, Thomas. 2008. Generic-drug industry grows bolder about launches. *Wall Street Journal.* February 6: B12.

Institute of Medicine. 2007. *The future of drug safety.* National Academies Press, Washington, DC.

Japan Pharmaceutical Manufacturers Association. March 2007. Pharmaceutical Administration and Regulations in Japan. http://www.nihs.go.jp/mhlw/jouhou/yakuji/yakuji-e0703.pdf.

Kettler, Hannah E. 2000. Narrowing the gap between provision and need for medicines in developing countries. *London office of Health Economics.*

Kremer, Michael. 2002. Pharmaceuticals and the developing world. *Journal of Economic Perspectives* 16: 67–90.

Li, Jennifer S., Eric L. Eisenstein, Henry G. Grabowski, Elizabeth D. Reid, Barry Mangum, Kevin A. Schulman, John V. Goldsmith, M. Dianne Murphy, Robert M. Califf, and Daniel K. Benjamin Jr. 2007. Economic return of clinical trials performed under the pediatric exclusivity program. *Journal of the American Medical Association* 297(5): 480–88.

McClellan, Mark. 2007. *Fundamental improvements in drug safety for the 21st century: Time for systemic, electronic infrastructure. AEI-Brookings Joint Center for Regulatory Studies.* Statement of testimony to the U.S. Senate HELP Committee on March 14, 2007. http://aei-brookings.org/admin/authorpdfs/ redirect-safely.php?fname=../pdffiles/Testimony_07-9_topost.pdf.

Olson, Mary K. 2004. Are novel drugs more risky for patients than less novel drugs? *Journal of Health Economics* 23: 1135–58.

———. 2008. The risk we bear: The effects of review speed and industry user fees on new drug safety. *Journal of Health Economics* 27: 175–200.

Philipson, Thomas J., Ernst R. Berndt, Adrian Gottshalk, and Eric Sun. 2008. Cost-benefit analysis of the FDA: The case of the prescription Drug User Fee Acts. *Journal of Public Economies* 92: 1306–25.

Ridley, David B., Henry G. Grabowski, and Jeffrey L. Moe. 2004. Developing drugs for developing countries. *Health Affairs* 25 (2): 313–24.

Ridley, David B., Judith M. Kramer, Hugh H. Tilson, Henry G. Grabowski and Kevin A. Schulman. 2006. Spending on post-approval drug safety. *Health Affairs* 25(2): 429–36.

Schmalensee, Richard. 1982. Product differentiation advantages of pioneering brands. *American Economic Review* 72(3): 349–65.

Silver, Richard. 2007. A Wall Street perspective on generics. Lehman Brothers presentation at the 2007 GPhA Annual Meeting. March 1–3, 2007. http:// www.gphaonline.org/AM/CM/ContentDisplay.cfm?ContentFileID=593

Tufts Center for Study Development. 2005. Drug safety withdrawals in the U.S. not linked to speed of FDA approval. *Impact Report* 7(5).

U.S. Food and Drug Administration, Center for Drug Evaluation and Research. 2005. CDER *Report to the Nation: 2004*. http://www.fda.gov/cder/reports/ rtn/2004/rtn2004.htm.

USAID Health. *Infectious Diseases, Neglected Tropical Diseases*. 2009. http:// www.usaid.gov/our_work/global_health/id/ntd_main.html.

World Health Organization. 2004. *World Health Report*.

———. 2006. Projected DALYs for 2005, 2015 and 2030 by country income group under the baseline scenario. http://www.who.int/healthinfo/statistics/ bodprojections2030/en/.

———. 2007. *World health statistics*. http://www.who.int/whosis.

CONCLUSION:
A CRITICAL REVIEW
OF THE DYNAMICS AND REGULATION
OF ASIAN PHARMACEUTICAL INDUSTRIES

F. M. Scherer

The work assembled in this book provides broad and deep insights into the pharmaceutical industries of Asia. By my calculations, the nations on which the book focuses were home to some 2.6 billion individual human beings in the year 2000, or 42.8 percent of the world's population. Among the nations analyzed are several highly developed entities and some (comprising the bulk of the population covered) still marked by low average incomes per capita. In several of the less wealthy nations, recent economic growth has been rapid, so the provision of health care, including modern pharmaceuticals, to their citizens poses especially immediate challenges.

Desiring a broad overview of the condition of Asia's pharmaceutical industries, I sought statistics on pharmaceutical sales and domestic pharmaceutical production volumes in the individual nations. My search yielded only partial success. In a 2004 report, the World Health Organization (WHO) estimated the dollar value (at prevailing exchange rates) of pharmaceutical production *in* a substantial sample of nations.[1] I italicize *in* since, presumably, the difficult task of disentangling the production of multinationals outside their home bases and assigning it to the host country was attempted—how successfully, one does not know. Table 21.1 lists the values for 1997, the last year covered, for the top twenty nations and for other Asian nations on which data were available. For many nations there are data gaps—for Russia, Ireland, Israel, Poland, the Czech Republic, and Hungary among possibly substantial producers, and for Taiwan and Vietnam among Asian nations. And there is reason to believe that some nations' industries have expanded significantly during the past ten years, rendering the figures somewhat outdated.

Recognizing that many Asian nations have experienced rapid economic development through export-oriented strategies, I also obtained evidence on the relative success of Asian countries in exporting to the world's most lucrative market for pharmaceuticals: the United States. My curiosity on this point was heightened by recent reports in diverse newspapers, one of them quoted in chapter 14 (Santoro and C. Liu), that the United States imports some 80 percent of the pharmaceuticals or "active pharmaceutical ingredients" (whatever that means) consumed domestically.[2]

Table 21.1 Estimated National Pharmaceutical Production Value, 1997

Country	Millions of dollars
United States	97,505
Japan	56,768
United Kingdom	23,326
Germany	23,088
France	22,518
Switzerland	20,000[a]
Spain	16,038
India	6,012
Canada	5,561
Italy	4,938
South Korea	4,815
Denmark	4,596
Sweden	4,391
Netherlands	3,536
Singapore	3,012
Mexico	2,973
Belgium	2,656
Portugal	2,460
Austria	2,352
Australia	2,261
Other Asia-Pacific countries	
Indonesia	1,314
Philippines	1,147
Thailand	741[b]
Pakistan	711
Bangladesh	320
China	214
Malaysia	178
Myanmar	129
New Zealand	95[c]
Sri Lanka	9[b]

Source: World Health Organization 2004, Appendix table 20.1.
Note:
[a] Estimated from report text.
[b] Value for 1991.
[c] Value for 1985.

Figure 21.1 Leading Pharmaceutical Importers into the United States, 2006

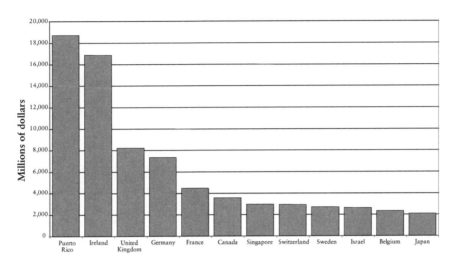

Source: U.S. Census Bureau, "U.S. Imports from All Countries from 2002 to 2006 by 5-Digit End-Use Code;"and "Shipments from Puerto Rico to the United States by Schedule B Commodity and Method of Transportation: Census Year 2006."

The results of my investigation are summarized in figure 21.1.[3] Total U.S. pharmaceutical imports were on the order of $82 billion in 2006. By any measure, this falls far short of the 80 percent reported in the press. According to the Annual Survey of Manufactures (ASM) for 2006, the value of pharmaceutical, medicinal, and biological product shipments from U.S. establishments in the same year was $158 billion. Exports from U.S. producers were roughly $31 billion. Thus, the total U.S. market for pharmaceuticals must have approximated the value of imports ($82 billion) plus domestic plant shipments ($158 billion) minus the value of exports ($31 billion), or $209 billion. Admitting that a considerable but unknown amount of double counting may reside in that total,[4] imports are found to be roughly 39 percent of the total, not 80 percent.

More importantly for our immediate concern, only two Asia-Pacific nations—Singapore and Japan—are among the top twelve pharmaceutical importers to the United States. Singapore, ranked seventh in figure 21.1, like Puerto Rico and Ireland, draws pharmaceutical manufacturing in part because of its unusually low corporate income tax rates.[5] It has also made a major effort to attract science-based biotechnology enterprises. Among Asia-Pacific nations not included in figure 21.1, India placed 16th, shipping to the U.S. imports of $799 million; China 17th with $676 million; Australia 21st with $305 million; South Korea 23rd with $63 million; and Taiwan 24th with $36 million. Imports from other Asian nations—notably, Thailand, the Philippines, Hong Kong, Indonesia, Malaysia, and New Zealand—totaled $41 million.

India

Most surprising to me was the relatively weak performance of India suggested by the figure 21.1 data. After Italy ended its policy of denying patent protection for pharmaceutical products in 1978, India moved forward to become the world's leading exporter of generic drugs, seizing a first-mover advantage by supplying drugs in patent-free markets (including its home market) long before product patents expired in the principal industrialized nations. Indian pharmaceutical firms, with estimated global sales of $32 billion in 2007, have been particularly aggressive in supplying antiretrovirals at steeply discounted prices to AIDS care-providers in low- and middle-income nations, accounting for 69 percent of the total antiretroviral supply (by quantity) to such nations between 2005 and 2006.[6] Cipla, the leading manufacturer of low-priced antiretrovirals, originated 51 percent of the total Indian supply. Altogether, India is said to have seventy-five plants approved by the U.S. Food and Drug Administration (U.S. FDA) for supply to the American market—the most of any nation other than the United States itself.[7] The forte of Indian companies during the 1990s and early 2000s was low-price generic drugs (see chapter 8, Chatterjee). For example, in February 2008 U.S. pharmacies began selling cetirizine hydrochloride (brand-name, Zyrtec), whose patent expired in the United States on December 25, 2007. Prior to the appearance of that formulation on the shelf of my local pharmacy, my copayment alone for the drug was $35 for thirty tablets per month. The price to my health insurer was presumably a multiple of that figure. My price for the over-the-counter (OTC) formulation was $19.99 for 120 tablets—that is, a price reduction for me as copayer of 86 percent. Because so many Indian drug exports are made at prices much lower than those at which patented and branded drugs are supplied in the United States, it would not be unreasonable to suggest that the quantity impact of Indian products is several times the $799 million dollar value implied by the data underlying figure 21.1. Indeed, the WHO reports (2004:4) that "India . . . accounts for about 1 percent of the world's production by value, but 8 percent by weight."

Forced under the Uruguay Round Treaty to begin issuing already backlogged pharmaceutical product patents in March of 2005, Indian suppliers lost their first-mover advantage in new generic drug markets and now have to compete with others who wait until U.S. or European patents expire. Some Indian firms have undertaken efforts to discover and develop their own new drugs for the world market.[8] A leader among them is Ranbaxy, which in 2007 expended 6.4 percent of its sales dollars on research and development (R&D).[9] By then Ranbaxy had several of its own new drugs in various stages of testing and had entered into several joint R&D arrangements with multinational drug companies. Similarly, Dr. Reddy's Laboratories reported in its 2007 annual report an R&D/sales ratio of 6.0 percent after netting out contributions from joint venture partners and four new drug molecules, all developed in cooperation with other companies, in clinical or preclinical testing.[10]

My own experience suggests that Ranbaxy has powerful research and manufacturing capabilities. During the 1990s the Eli Lilly Company sought a second source for its antibiotic Ceclor (cefaclor), whose manufacture entails a particularly intricate ten-stage process. Ranbaxy was one of the half dozen finalists chosen from companies all around the world. Thus, India's pharmaceutical producers are already a significant influence in world markets (ignoring the Ayurvedic products analyzed by Bode in chapter 15) and bid fair, despite the loss of generic sales advantages, to continue making inroads in the future.

Japan

Japan, ranked only 12th in figure 21.1, with 2006 imports to the United States of $2.05 billion, was also surprising, although less so. The data listed in table 21.1 agree with Tomita's statement (chapter 3) that Japan, with a high level of industrial development and a population of 128 million, is the world's second-largest pharmaceutical market. My surprise was less than what it might have been because I had followed the pioneering research by L. G. Thomas (1996), mentioned in none of the chapters.[11] Thomas found that among nine major pharmaceutical-producing nations in 1985, Japan had the second-largest share of sales summed across the companies at home in those nine nations (see figure 21.2). To be sure, Japan had a considerably larger population than any of the other nations in the sample other than the United States. Domestic demand alone might be sufficient to account for the indicated differences. But Thomas then went on to compute the percentage of national firms' 1985 sales achieved in nations among the nine—but *outside* their home markets. The results are arrayed in figure 21.3. Switzerland, Sweden, and the Netherlands, with small home markets but proficient pharmaceutical firms, do well. So do England and Germany, with similarly strong home-based firms and home markets of middling size. The United States also fares well, especially when one takes into account the enormous size of its home market. But France and Italy are underachievers, and Japan shows up particularly poorly as an export generator.

Thomas adduces several explanations for the differences in national industries' export performance. The most important new insight in his study, from the perspective of an American who had heard repeated complaints about the testing burdens and costs imposed upon pharmaceutical companies by the 1962 Kefauver-Harris Act reforms, was that the changes forced U.S. companies to focus their efforts on highly promising molecules and to minimize work on "me-too" drugs of low incremental therapeutic potential. During the 1950s, forty to seventy "new" drugs were being introduced into the U.S. market every year; after Kefauver-Harris strengthened standards of proof for efficacy and safety and increased clinical testing costs, the average introduction rate dropped

Figure 21.2 National Companies' Shares of Nine-nation Market

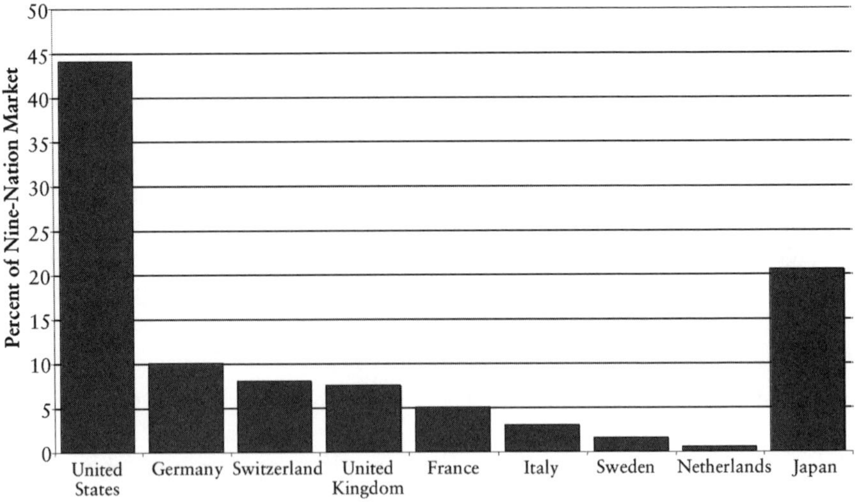

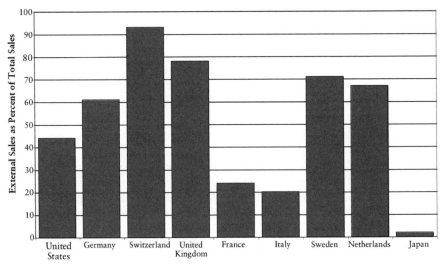

Source: Thomas 1996.

Figure 21.3. Percent of Multinational Drug Company Sales Outside the Home Market

Source: Thomas 1996.

below twenty per year.[12] But the post-1962 drugs approved were those that showed exceptional promise during testing and, having overcome such high hurdles, they went on to succeed in world markets. Italy and France, on the other hand, had very low product-approval thresholds at the time (since superseded by those nations' inclusion under the European Agency for the Evaluation of Medicinal Products, now called the European Medicines Agency, EMA). Thomas characterized French policies as "the French impressionist school" of drug safety regulation. The changes since 1985 undoubtedly underlie France's stronger performance, evident in figure 21.1.

Thomas explains Japan's particularly weak performance in 1985 as the result of several conditions. For one, he includes Japan among the nations with low standards for new drug product approval—a judgment I have not seen evidence to overturn on the basis this book. Second, he observes (p. 111) that Japan's producers fragmented their innovative effort to focus on "minor local products," while only 10 percent of their innovations were characterized as "global products."[13] This explanation is consistent with analyses showing that Japanese pharmaceutical producers were induced to stress minor "me-too" innovations by the tendency of price regulators to allow higher retail prices for drugs that could claim any innovative component at all and by the parallel tendency of prescribing physicians to favor products with the highest retail profit margins. To this I would add a third, more speculative, hypothesis. Japan is home to some of the world's most capable biotechnical companies, who among other things collaborated in the creation of synthetic erythropoietin and the enzymes needed to produce high-fructose corn syrup. I have reason to believe that mainline Japanese pharmaceutical firms also have strong technological skills. I believe it could be shown that many pharmaceutical products invented by Japanese companies have been licensed for sale in the United States and Europe by multinationals at home outside Japan. My speculative hypothesis is that Japanese firms find the challenges of surmounting U.S. FDA approval hurdles and establishing extensive sales networks in the United States sufficiently formidable that they have emphasized licensing rather than direct sale. It is far from clear why this should be so; European firms have not been intimidated by the entry barriers. Unfortunately, no chapter here illuminates this aspect of Japanese industrial performance.[14]

Physician Dispensing in General

If there is an overriding theme in this book, it is the dominant role physicians play in dispensing the medicines they prescribe, rather than allowing specialization of functions, with physicians making prescription decisions and pharmacists dispensing the desired products. This theme is addressed in chapters 1 (Kwon), 2 (Iizuka), 3 (Tomita), 5 (Hsieh), 10 (Li and Reimers), 11 (Sun and Meng), 12 (Huang and Y. Yang), and 16 (Eggleston and B-M. Yang). This practice has predominated in nations with ancient medicine traditions (including China, South Korea, Japan, Taiwan, and India) in which practitioners made and dispensed medicines—and appears to have been carried on as modern science-based pharmaceuticals entered the health-care picture.

Dispensing of pharmaceuticals by physicians has thrived in part through tradition, but also, and probably more importantly, because it is profitable. Influenced perhaps by traditional norms, public health-care reimbursement authorities have tended to allow only low fees for diagnostic activity by physicians, assuming tacitly or explicitly that physicians will earn their bread with the profit margins on drugs they dispense.

Eggleston and B-M. Yang suggest some possible advantages to this approach. Miscommunication may be avoided—a benefit that must be appreciated by any American who has received an illegible prescription from his or her physician. But this is less likely to occur as computers generate readable prescriptions and transmit them electronically to pharmacies (see also chapter 17 by Liaw). There may be economies of scope in combining prescription and dispensing at one locale, although countervailing economies of specialization seem equally plausible. And the placebo effect known to exist even with the most high-powered science-based pharmaceuticals may be stronger when the prescribing physician pops the pill or squeezes the syringe. On the other hand, there are compelling disadvantages. Assuming that physicians will glean a significant part of their income from prescriptions, government price controllers and price-setting drug manufacturers allow generous margins between wholesale and retail prices, which in turn encourage physicians to overprescribe medications generally and in particular to substitute high-priced, high-margin innovative drugs for older but equally effective entities. For antibiotics, which, as several of this book's authors suggest, are prescribed much more frequently with physician dispensation than under separation of functions, the tendency toward excessive usage and harmful externalities may be particularly egregious. An antibiotic dispensed unnecessarily to one patient can lead to bacterial resistance, and the recipient may transmit the resistant bacteria to other individuals, requiring ever more high-powered antibiotics in a kind of arms race.

Several authors suggest that the use of generic drugs is encouraged by the integration of diagnosis with dispensation because absolute margins on generics tend to be higher, yielding the dispensing physician a higher margin. Doubts intrude on this, considering the relatively low generic usage rates achieved in Asian nations relative to the above 50 percent average now prevalent in the United States and parts of Europe.[15] The logic in favor of a generic bias follows the empirical findings of prior studies, notably in the United States, showing higher average profit margins on generics. However, I am unsure that relationship carries over into a world in which generics are dispensed more frequently than branded drugs. There are countervailing arguments. On the one hand, those who establish and/or reimburse prices may wish to set them in such a way as to encourage generic usage. It is not clear why branded drug manufacturers should desire this, nor is it obvious for drug retailers. The case for higher margins at the retail decision-making level follows a broader logic, prevailing for private-label goods more generally: they turn over less rapidly on the retailer's shelf, and therefore higher margins are required to induce their stocking.[16] But if generics are an incomplete subset of all pharmaceutical entities and if, in the aggregate, more generic pills are dispensed than branded ones, the turnover rate for the branded drugs with generic alternatives should be higher, not lower. Thus, the rationale for higher generic margins fades. This, it seems to me, is a fruitful area for careful new research both in Asia and the United States.

Another important point on generics needs to be emphasized. The best empirical studies on generic pricing in a more or less free market support Augustin Cournot's prediction that the lower the prices the larger is the number of competing sellers. Richard Caves et al. (1991) found, for example, that with one generic producer, the generic product's price averaged 68 percent of the preentry branded product's price. The average generic price dropped to 50 percent with three generic rivals, 29 percent with ten generics, and 17 percent with twenty generics.[17] This phenomenon could explain why generic product prices tend to be higher—relative to their branded counterparts—in the Asia-Pacific and Europe than is common in the United States. The United States is a huge market, and so, given the typically modest fixed costs required to enter generic production, there is often room in the market for numerous suppliers, which in turn leads to low prices. Many Asian national markets on the other hand are much smaller, and in China, they may be fragmented inter alia by provincial organizations and other barriers to internal trade. Therefore, it may be more difficult to realize fully the benefits of generic competition. An escape hatch could be to import generics from specialist firms in nations such as India and Brazil. But if national or provincial health authorities express preferences in favor of domestically supplied products, the dilemma of small market size persists. Here, too, a much more comprehensive analysis is warranted.

Recognizing the disadvantages, on balance, of integrating diagnosis with drug dispensing, the nations on which this book focuses have taken a variety of measures to encourage the separation of these practices. The authors make it clear that progress has been made, but the transition has not been easy. Resistance appears to have been fiercest in South Korea, but is evident elsewhere too. Physicians have defended their traditional turf by emphasizing injectables—more difficult to administer outside the office—over pills, and they have entered profit-sharing arrangements with nearby (seemingly independent) pharmacists to whom they steer their patients. Kwon's suggestion (chapter 1) that governments raise the pay of generic-prescribing physicians suggests a degree of micro-management that might horrify more market-oriented Americans. Even more surprising is his report that when generic competition begins, government pricing authorities set the first generic entrant's price at 85 percent of the (reduced) branded drug price and that entrants 2 through 5 receive 85 percent of the first generic entrant's price.

Price Controls

These last two examples are merely the tip of an iceberg. In all the nations represented, it is customary for pharmaceutical prices to be regulated and/or fixed by government health-care authorities. A surprise to me is that no author mentions Patricia Danzon's (1997) authoritative work on the use and effects of government price controls in the pharmaceuticals industry.

Most of the well-known techniques are in evidence throughout the book: reference pricing against the prices charged in other nations, reference pricing against drugs in the same therapeutic category, arbitrary across-the-board percentage reductions within broad classes of drugs, cost-based percentage markups, variations in allowed margins to encourage drug innovations (which, the authors show, more often encourage minor "me-too" variants such as changes in the strength of active ingredients or even just name changes), flat aggregate budgets for drugs, and so on. The principal lacunae are (1) the uniquely British system of setting company-wide reimbursements to allow appropriate rates of return on investment, including R&D investment[18] and (2) targeting those drugs with the largest profit margins for percentage price reductions—a proposal for which Hillary Clinton came to grief in the early 1990s. Combined with physician-based dispensing, some of the methods used by Asian price controllers are so distortionary that, by encouraging overprescribing or inappropriate substitutions, they increase rather than reduce overall health-care expenditures.

Somewhat outside the realm of price controls, but equally controversial in U.S. political circles, is vigorous negotiation over prices by government health authorities with would-be pharmaceutical suppliers. Löfgren (chapter 6) provides an account of the Australian system, which, according to Kwon, has also been adopted in South Korea and proposed in Taiwan and China (see chapter 11, Sun and Meng). Similar negotiations are carried out by individual health maintenance organizations in the United States, although the success of their efforts has been curbed by federal legislation requiring any discounts they receive to be matched in the prices reimbursed by governmental authorities on pharmaceuticals dispensed under the Medicaid program.

What is left unclear by these authors is the hardest part: how a decision-maker—governmental or private—determines how much of a price premium is warranted by unique advantages a particular drug might offer. Australia appears to have made the most progress in this direction. Detailed case studies could enhance our understanding of how decision-makers cope.

Distribution Channels and Margin Policy in China

An important component of price controls is the determination of what margins will be allowed at each stage in the channels of distribution from manufacturer to patient. Here I was astonished more than by anything else I read in this book.

Chapters 10 (Li and Reimers) and 12 (Huang and Y. Yang) provide fairly consistent estimates of the share of retail drug prices obtained by various stages in the chain of distribution—that is, manufacturers, wholesalers, and retailers (the last including hospital pharmacies and physicians). Their general estimates are in ranges, which I have converted (in parentheses) so that the median stage shares sum to 100:

	Huang and Yang (%)	Li and Reimers (%)
Manufacturers	10–50 (32.7)	10–50 (32.7)
Wholesalers	3–20 (12.6)	3–10 (7.6)
Retail	30–70 (54.6)	30–80 (59.8)

Huang and Yang also provide a single example, for omeprazole (generic Prilosec):

- Manufacturer, 14 percent
- Wholesaler, 20 percent
- Retailer, 66 percent

The surprisingly high retail margins are said to cover physicians' dispensing fees, the profit margins of hospitals, brokerage paid to hospital administrators, and bidding expenses.

The accounts were surprising to me because I had worked with similar distribution channel breakdowns for the U.S. pharmaceutical system. During the mid-1970s, the average value chain share for retailers was 40 percent, for wholesalers 9 percent, and for manufacturers 51 percent.[19] By the late 1990s, several important changes had been wrought. At the retail level, resale price maintenance arrangements were outlawed, forcing retailers to compete for business on the basis inter alia of their margins. Pressure was also brought to bear on them by insurance companies and health maintenance organizations and by the government's Medicaid administrators, reducing the average retail margin to 20 percent of the ultimate sales value.[20] Numerous efficiency-increasing measures reduced the average wholesaler margin to 4 percent, leaving 76 percent for manufacturers.

Figure 21.4 brings together these various channel share estimates. Clearly, in part because of physician dispensing and in part because Chinese health-care authorities use retail margins to pay physicians for their services, manufacturers in China receive a much smaller share of the pharmaceutical value chain than their counterparts in the United States. This evidence has two somewhat different but probably complementary implications: the distribution system in China is quite inefficient, and it leaves for manufacturers a relatively small share of ultimate pharmaceutical sales revenue realizations to reimburse such activities as R&D, testing, and quality control.

Figure 21.4 Percent Distribution of Value Chain Elements, United States and China

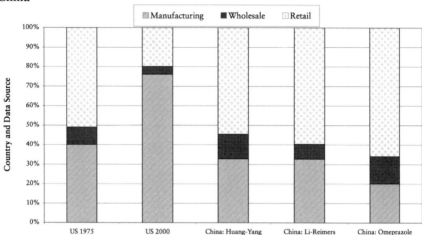

Sources: For the United States, F. M. Scherer 1997, p. 245, and "Profile of the Prescription Drug Wholesaling Industry," http://www.fda.gov/oc/pdma/report2001/attachmenttg/3.html. For China, data reported in Li and Reimers (chapter 10, this volume) and Huang and Y. Yang (chapter 12).

Li and Reimers report that, after a visit by a Chinese official to the United States, an electronic system for procuring drugs was implemented in diverse Chinese provinces beginning in the early 2000s. However, the use of electronics in China as compared to the United States seems to be quite different. In Beijing the system is apparently used to elicit price bids from manufacturers that are then reviewed by expert committees and either accepted, rejected, or subjected to renegotiation. The bid data are then apparently transmitted to using (that is, retail) agencies. In the United States, prices tend to be negotiated face-to-face between payers—hospitals, health maintenance organizations, and pharmacy benefit management companies—and the manufacturers. The bids are then entered confidentially into the computers of wholesalers, who take the merchandise from manufacturers, deliver it to dispensers at the negotiated prices, and then obtain a monetary "grantback" from the manufacturer to the wholesaler to reimburse the wholesaler for any discounts it gave to ultimate customers. Retailers, on the other hand, were usually served—at least during the 1990s—at posted and relatively invariant prices.[21] In China electronics serve to support a bidding and tracking system; in the United States, an accounting and reimbursement system.

I cannot pretend to understand fully the Chinese bidding system, which appears to generate a remarkably broad distribution of prices for products that must in many instances be similar. It seems also to offer transparency of successful bids to the various parties involved. But transparency is the antithesis of effective competition.[22] The free-market buyer who elicits a substantial discount and makes it public will compel other sellers to offer similar discounts, and knowledge that this will happen deters sellers from offering substantial discounts in the first place. Clearly, an analysis of the Chinese electronic bidding system that recognizes this important truth is in order.

Li and Reimers report that China has 8,000 active drug distributors (which, in the context, presumably means wholesalers), including 120 in the Beijing area alone. Sun and Meng report the number of wholesalers as 12,000. This too is remarkable. Efficient wholesaling entails a trade-off between (1) proximity to end customers and hence rapid delivery—which implies regional decentralization in a nation as large as China—and (2) concentration of supplies at relatively few nodes so as to achieve economies of scale aggregating inter alia random demand fluctuations.[23] That tradeoff drives market structures toward concentration of wholesalers. In the United States, 90 percent of all sales are made by 5 full-line drug wholesalers,[24] and the total number of wholesale drug establishments is estimated (with some reporting imprecision) at 3,283, among which 110 establishments with annual sales exceeding $50 million each accounted for 89 percent of total wholesale shipments.[25] From this I suspect that China has struck the wrong tradeoff and needs to make its drug wholesaling channels more efficient by concentrating individual units. Electronics cannot save the day unless they are accompanied by appropriate operations research analysis and structural rationalization. Doing so is a major challenge for China's future.

Chinese Production Facilities

Scale economy sacrifices are also implied by the large number of production facilities in the Chinese industry—estimated by Li and Reimers (chapter 10) and Zhang and X. Liu (chapter 13) at 5,000—30 percent of which are said to be running in the red. U.S. Census statistics do not permit an exact estimate of the number of U.S. manufacturers, since companies producing conventional pharmaceuticals, biologics, and other medicinals are reported in separate but possibly overlapping categories. A maximum estimate is that in 1997, the U.S. industry—presumably much larger than China's—included 1,286 companies, of whom the largest 20 originated 70 percent of total industry sales.[26]

There are economies of scale in manufacturing, and perhaps more importantly, economies of scale in quality control (see Scherer 2007).[27] Small plants are almost certain to have difficulty affording specialized quality-control staff and carrying out the tests needed to ensure product safety. And it is hard to imagine how a regulatory agency paralleling the U.S. FDA could reliably monitor manufacturing practices in 5,000 plants. This problem is likely to underlie the much-publicized safety problems experienced by Chinese pharmaceutical (and pharmaceutical ingredient) producers, highlighted in chapters 13 and 14.

Without an unsullied reputation for consistently high product quality, Chinese pharmaceutical makers will have great difficulty selling their products in world markets. And, given the complexity of the monitoring task, executing a corrupt regulator is not likely to provide a sufficient remedy.[28] Again, restructuring the industry to a more compact set of plants whose operations can be monitored consistently and thoroughly appears necessary. The relevant chapters leave unclear how this vital restructuring will be accomplished. Market processes would do so, weeding out the firms whose costs are too high or whose quality is too low. It seems doubtful that markets will be given this much scope for structural reform in China. But if the job is to be done through central planning or (more likely) decentralized provincial planning, it is far from clear how planners will obtain the information needed to determine which firms' costs are too high relative to quality or which firms offer exceptionally high quality. Only the cases of egregious quality-control failure appear susceptible to relatively easy structural decision-making.

Innovation and Patents

The pharmaceutical industry is one of the world's most technologically dynamic. The links to basic science are tight. Pharmaceutical companies in affluent economies have the highest company-financed R&D-to-sales ratios of any industries for which data are published; and, for nearly a century, new products have flowed out to raise human health standards materially.[29] One looks for recognition of these facts but, with the possible exception of chapters 19 (Grabowski, Ridley, Moe) and 20 (Barton), finds little emphasis on technological innovation. Will Asian companies continue (with a few exceptions, such as Japan and Singapore) to be technological followers or free-riders? Or will the future bring a great leap forward?

Private investment in pharmaceutical innovation is driven by the hope for substantial profit rewards. It is doubtful whether the price-control regimes deployed in most of the nations surveyed provide much incentive for R&D investments. To be sure, some price-control authorities adjust margins upward for newer, presumably more innovative, products. But the main effect appears to have been a stimulus for minor "me-too" product variants and size or compounding changes. One fundamental challenge is that the distribution of profit returns to new drug products successful enough to secure regulatory agency approval is highly skewed (Grabowski et al. 2002).[30] The top 10 percent of new pharmaceutical products in terms of profit returns garner roughly half of all new products' profits. Many marketed new products fail to cover the capitalized costs of their development and testing, including the costs of failed R&D efforts. In short, new product development is highly risky. In an entrepreneurial culture, and especially in newly emerging fields such as biotechnology, the skewness of rewards may actually encourage innovative risk-taking.[31] But it is rare for price controllers to allow the kinds of profit margins

Joseph A. Schumpeter (1942:73–74) had in mind when describing his model of capitalist dynamics:

> Spectacular prizes much greater than would have been necessary to call forth the particular effort are thrown to a small minority of winners, thus propelling much more efficaciously than a more equal and more "just" distribution would, the activity of that large majority of businessmen who receive in return very modest compensation or nothing or less than nothing, and yet do their utmost because they have the big prizes before their eyes and overrate their chances of doing equally well.

If price controls are to be the norm, there remain two main alternatives for attaining an innovative Asian pharmaceutical industry. For one, investments in innovation may be driven, as they are in some European countries, by the hope of a successful product launch in the (thus far) largely unregulated U.S. market. If so, Asian companies will have to develop their pharmaceutical export capabilities—something which, we have seen, has often eluded technologically progressive Japanese producers, but not (with a strategy emphasizing low generic prices rather than innovation) India. Or, alternatively, it may be possible to achieve a mix of government R&D subsidies, academic research, and private-sector production and marketing skills that sustains innovative performance. This is likely to be difficult, but not—as the experience of the U.S. weapon systems industry shows—impossible. Success would require solving two difficult problems. First, at the drug discovery stage, the uncertainties are formidable, and so it is necessary to ensure that many alternatives are explored—to follow Mao's maxim, "Let one hundred flowers bloom." But costs soar when clinical testing begins, and so there must be a decision-making process with strong scientific competence, freedom from political biases, and the willingness to take big calculated risks. One would like to know more about the strategies Asian science policymakers and companies in fact contemplate, if indeed they do so.

Except for Barton (chapter 19) the authors are largely silent on what I consider one of the great policy debates in recent years—whether nations that have long chosen not to award pharmaceutical product patents should be required under the Uruguay Round agreements to begin conferring them. The Treaty of Marrakech is a reality. India began issuing drug product patents in March 2005, nations such as Thailand and South Korea (earlier, in response to U.S. pressure) have joined the patent-granting parade, and all least-developed nations will be required to comply by the year 2016. What changes will their pharmaceutical industries have to make? How will the availability of low-cost medicines to the least affluent nations be affected? What incentives can be created, as chapters 19 and 20 ask, for the discovery and development of new medicines combating diseases prevalent mainly in parts of the world with too little purchasing power to offer much hope of high profits, contingent upon technological success?

Related to these questions is a question about the use of a potentially important escape clause allowed by the Marrakech treaty: compulsory patent licensing. Canada, the United States, Brazil, South Africa, and others have used the threat of compulsory licensing to win much lower prices for drugs combating AIDS and other lethal diseases. Thailand has been a leader in actually issuing compulsory licenses for the production of several important drugs, including the life-saving but egregiously priced protease inhibitor Kaletra. I was shocked to read, in chapter 4 (Ratanawijitrasin), that the U.S. government put Thailand on its priority watch list in 2007 for its compulsory licensing activities. A similar patent-linked action by the United States in 1991 led to proposed legislation in the Thai parliament precipitating a no-confidence vote and dissolution of the government. Will we Americans ever learn to let other governments make their own decisions freely, within the latitude allowed by international law?

I was also surprised to learn from Ratanawijitrasin that Thailand is producing generic erythropoietin (EPO). My surprise had nothing to do with compulsory licensing; Amgen's basic U.S. epoetin alpha patent expired in 2004 (although other patents continue to be disputed). But biologically engineered drugs are said to be much more difficult to produce than so-called small-molecule drugs, which are the only drugs on which a fast-track generic approval protocol was created under the U.S. Hatch-Waxman Act of 1984. In 2006 the EMA issued guidelines for the approval of "biosimilar" generics and granted two authorizations for the production of generic human-growth hormones. The U.S. Congress has been considering legislation to allow biological generic approvals, but was deadlocked on the issue and referred it recently to the U.S. FDA for consultation.

My surprise from the Thai evidence led to further investigation, revealing that the original alpha and other forms of EPO are in fact produced in many nations, including India, China, Japan, Hong Kong, Korea, and Vietnam, as well as Thailand.[32] A detailed case study of various nations' experience in producing generic EPO could make a significant contribution to the U.S. policy deliberations.

Conclusion

To sum up, the contributors to this book offer fascinating insights into how an important industry is emerging in the Asia-Pacific and how public policies have been structured to encourage it in some ways and hold it back in others. I have identified questions on which I should like to know much more. But I can also report that I have learned a lot from these authors and their book.

Notes

[1] An older source is Ballance et al. 1992.

[2] The report apparently came from Congressional testimony by witnesses from the Government Accountability Office (GAO). I was unable to find any

document among GAO reports posted electronically. Santoro's citation came from the *Wall Street Journal*, February 14, 2008; mine from the *Boston Globe*, February 3, 2008; and the *New York Times*, November 2, 2007. An earlier (2005) GAO report dealt only with drugs imported by mail, whose volume was believed to be "substantial and rising," although reliable data were unavailable.

[3] The data are from U.S. Census Bureau, "U.S. Imports from All Countries from 2002 to 2006 by 5-Digit End-Use Code," and "Shipments from Puerto Rico to the United States by Schedule B Commodity and Method of Transportation: Census Year 2006," both found on the Census Bureau Web site.

[4] For example, as active ingredients are produced at one or more sources and encapsulated in other factories.

[5] Puerto Rico was apparently treated as part of the Continental United States in the table 21.1 compilation. The Puerto Rican tax advantage under Section 936 of the U.S. tax code, implemented in 1976, was phased out as of December 31, 2005. But established plants continued to produce because of sunk costs, accumulated skills, and the continuation of provisions allowing duty-free importation into the United States. In addition to having the lowest corporate income tax rates of Western European nations, Ireland provided university-level education in science and engineering to an unusually large fraction of its youth.

[6] Cipla News Release dated June 12, 2007, at http://www.cipla.com/whatsnew/news.htm.

[7] "India Poised for Pharmaceutical Boom," *Christian Science Monitor*, January 2, 2007, found at http://www.csmonitor.com/2007/0102/p06s01-wosc.html.

[8] See Jean O. Lanjouw, 1997.

[9] http://www.ranbaxy.com/investorinformation/news.aspx (February 4, 2008).

[10] http://www.drreddys.com/innovations/nces_pipeline.htm (March 24, 2008).

[11] See also L.G. Thomas (2001).

[12] See Scherer (1996:351).

[13] See also Scherer (1977:38), which shows that between 1940 and 1975, Japanese firms originated only 1.1 percent of the new drugs listed in Paul de Haen's worldwide compilation. The leaders were the United States with 69.1 percent, Switzerland with 7.6 percent, and the United Kingdom with 5.7 percent.

[14] On new changes in Japanese firms' strategy, see "Bulking Up: Japan's Drug Makers," *Business Week* (June 30, 2008:32).

[15] Professor Iizuka describes how, beginning in 2002, the Japanese government tried to encourage generic prescribing by altering the parameters of prescription pads. How such changes affected the acceptance of generics in the United States is analyzed thoroughly in Masson and Steiner (1985). The transmission of economic knowledge appears to occur less completely than the transmission of biological knowledge!

[16] See National Commission on Food Marketing (1966:65–77).

[17] See also Grabowski, Henry, and John Vernon (1992).

[18] For a difficulty with the system, see F. M. Scherer (1995).

[19] F. M. Scherer (1997:245).

[20] "Profile of the Prescription Drug Wholesaling Industry," http://www.fda.gov/oc/pdma/report2001/attachmenttg/3.html.

[21] See again Scherer (1997).

[22] See Scherer (1980:208–10, 248–49, 449–53). See also the U.S. Supreme Court opinion in *Brooke Group Ltd. versus Brown & Williamson*, 509 U.S. 209, 238 (1993), discussing tacit coordination of oligopolistic pricing and observing that "Uncertainty is an oligopoly's greatest enemy."

[23] For a review of the substantial operations research literature on this point, see Scherer, et al. (1975:56–62).

[24] See again "Profile of the Prescription Drug Wholesaling Industry," http://www.fda.gov/oc/pdma/report2001/attachmenttg/3.html.

[25] U.S. Bureau of the Census, *Census of wholesale trade: 1997*, Subject Series, Table 21.4 (for industry category 4222101).

[26] From U.S. Bureau of the Census, *Concentration ratios in manufacturing: 1997*, table 21.3.

[27] See Scherer (2007).

[28] See "A Chinese Reformer Betrays His Cause, and Pays," *New York Times*, July 13, 2007.

[29] See my (forthcoming) survey.

[30] See, e.g., Grabowski et al. (2002).

[31] See Scherer (2001).

[32] "Erythropoetin," in the German language, *Wikipedia*, especially the section on "Nachahmerprepaerate" (imitator preparations).

References

Ballance, R. J., J. Pogany, and H. Forstner. 1992. *The world's pharmaceutical industries: An international perspective on innovation, competition, and public policy.* Cheltenham, UK: Edward Elgar.

Caves, Richard E., Michael Whinston, and Mark Hurwitz. 1991. Patent expiration, entry, and competition in the U.S. pharmaceutical industry. *Brookings Papers on Economic Activity: Microeconomics* 1–48.

Grabowski, Henry G., and John Vernon. 1992. Brand loyalty, entry, and price competition in pharmaceuticals after the 1984 Drug Act. *Journal of Law & Economics* 35: 331–50.

Grabowski, Henry G., John M. Vernon, and Joseph DiMasi. 2002. Returns on research and development for 1990s new drug introductions. *PharmacoEconomics* 20 (Suppl. 3): 16–27.

Lanjouw, Jean O. 1997. The introduction of pharmaceutical patents in India. National Bureau of Economic Research working paper 6366.

Masson, Allison, and Robert L. Steiner. 1985. *Generic drug substitution and prescription drug prices.* U.S. Federal Trade Commission staff report.

National Commission on Food Marketing. 1966. *Private label products in food retailing.* Technical study no. 10. Washington: USGPO.

Scherer, F. M. 1977. *The economic effects of compulsory patent licensing.* New York University Graduate School of Business Administration, Monograph Series in Finance and Economics 1977–2.

———. 1980. *Industrial market structure and economic performance.* Chicago: Rand-McNally.

———. 1995. U.S. industrial policy and the pharmaceutical industry. In *Industrial policy and the pharmaceutical industry*, ed. Adrian Towse. London: Office of Health Economics, 26–39.

———. 1996. *Industry structure, strategy, and public policy.* New York: HarperCollins.

———. 1997. How antitrust can go astray: The brand name prescription drug litigation." *International Journal of the Economics of Business* 4(2): 39–56.

———. 2001. The innovation lottery. In *Expanding the boundaries of intellectual property*, ed. Rochelle Dreyfuss, Diane Leenheer Zimmerman, and Harry. First edition. Oxford: Oxford Univ. Press.

———. 2007. An industrial organization perspective on the influenza vaccine shortage. *Managerial and Decision Economics* 28: 395–405.

———. Forthcoming. Pharmaceutical innovation. In *Handbook on the economics of technical change*, ed. Bronwyn Hall and Nathan Rosenberg. Oxford: Elsevier.

———. Scherer, F. M., Alan Beckenstein, Erich Kaufer, and R. D. Murphy. 1975. *The economics of multi-plant operation: An international comparisons Study.* Cambridge, MA: Harvard University Press.

Schumpeter, Joseph A. 1942. *Capitalism, socialism, and democracy.* New York: Harper.

Thomas, L. G. 1996. Industrial policy and international competitiveness in the pharmaceutical industry. In *Competitive strategies in the pharmaceutical industry*, ed. Robert B. Helms. Washington, D.C.: AEI Press, 107–29.

———. 2001. *The Japanese pharmaceutical industry: The new drug lag and the failure of industrial policy.* Cheltenham, UK: Edward Elgar.

U.S. Bureau of the Census. 2001. *Census of wholesale trade: 1997.* Washington: USGPO.

———. 2002. *Concentration ratios in manufacturing: 1997.* Washington: USGPO.

U.S. Government Accountability Office. 2005. *Prescription drugs.* Report GAO–05–372.

I

ABOUT THE CONTRIBUTORS

John H. Barton (1936–2009) died suddenly as this volume was going to press. He was a professor emeritus at the Stanford Law School, a senior fellow by courtesy of the Freeman Spogli Institute for International Studies, and an associate of the Center for Health Policy/Center for Primary Care and Outcomes Research. Barton taught at Stanford beginning in 1969 and led a variety of courses on international and technology law. His research and publications focused on international scientific research and cooperation, the relationship between intellectual property and antitrust law, and the transfer of technology—particularly vaccine production technology—to developing countries.

Barton recently published an article in the *Journal of the American Medical Association* on the pharmaceutical development process, and was a coauthor of a chapter on product development priorities in the 2006 revised edition of the book *Disease Control Priorities in Developing Countries*. He participated extensively in discussions on drug access for developing nations, and was interested in the marketing structure of the pharmaceutical industry and the impact of vaccine regulation on the structure of the international vaccine industry.

For the 2004–2005 academic year, Barton was a visiting scholar at the National Institutes of Health's Department of Clinical Bioethics. He chaired the U.K. Commission on Intellectual Property Rights in 2001–2002. He was a member of the National Research Council's committees on intellectual property and genetic resources, of the Nuffield Council on Bioethics committee on gene patenting, and of two working groups of the Sachs Commission on Macroeconomics and Health. He received an undergraduate degree from Marquette University in 1958 and a J.D. from Stanford in 1968.

Maarten Bode is a faculty member at the Medical Anthropology and Sociology Research Unit, University of Amsterdam, and adjunct research faculty at the Foundation for the Revitalisation of Local Health Traditions, Bangalore, India. Over the last decade he has published books and international scholarly articles on the modernization and commercialization of Indian medical traditions. In February 2008, his book *Taking Traditional Knowledge to the Market: The Modern Image of the Ayurvedic and Unani Industry, 1980–2000* appeared in the Orient Longman series titled New Perspectives on South Asian History. Bode is currently working on a new research project, "The Politics of Value: Medicines, Prescribers, and Patients, 1980–2010," which deals with the uses and representations of Ayurvedic medicines in Indian clinical contexts. Since 2002, Bode has served on the council of the International Association for the Study of Traditional Asian Medicine (http://www.iastam.org). He is also a member of the editorial board of the electronic *Journal of Indian Medicine* (http://indianmedicine.ub.rug.nl/).

Chirantan Chatterjee is a doctoral student in policy and management at Carnegie Mellon University, Pittsburgh. His ongoing dissertation work investigates the evolution of the Indian pharmaceutical industry and its post-TRIPS ramifications. Prior to joining Carnegie Mellon, Chirantan worked as a business journalist with India's leading business daily, *The Economic Times,* at the Mumbai office of the Times of India Group. He holds a B.Tech in civil engineering from the Indian Institute of Technology, Roorkee, and an M.B.A. from the Indian Institute of Management, Kolkata.

Karen Eggleston joined the Walter H. Shorenstein Asia-Pacific Research Center in the summer of 2007 to lead the center's Asia Health Policy Program. She is also a fellow at the Stanford Center for Health Policy. She holds a B.A. in Asian studies from Dartmouth College, an M.A. in economics and another in Asian studies from the University of Hawaii, and a Ph.D. in public policy from Harvard University (completed in 1999). Eggleston studied in China for two years and was a Fulbright scholar in South Korea. In 2004, she was a consultant to the World Bank on health service delivery in China. Eggleston has been a research associate at the China Academy of Health Policy at Peking University, Beijing, since 2003, and an adjunct professor at Xi'an Jiaotong University, Xi'an, since 2008.

Henry G. Grabowski has been at Duke University since 1972, where he is professor of economics and director of the Program in Pharmaceuticals and Health Economics. He received his undergraduate degree in engineering physics from Lehigh University in 1962 and Ph.D. in economics from Princeton University in 1967. He has also served on the faculty of Yale University and held visiting appointments at the Health Care Financing Administration in Washington, D.C., and the International Institute of Management in Berlin.

Grabowski has published numerous studies on the pharmaceutical industry; his principal research involves the economics of the innovation process, business regulation, and industrial organization. He has investigated the economics of pharmaceutical research and been an adviser and consultant to several organizations, including the National Academy of Sciences, the Institute of Medicine, the Federal Trade Commission, the General Accounting Office, and the Office of Technology Assessment.

Chee-Ruey Hsieh is a research fellow in the Institute of Economics at Academia Sinica. He received his Ph.D. in economics from Vanderbilt University in 1990. Hsieh has a long-standing interest in health economics and policy, and has published in several areas, including medical malpractice, demand for medical care, smoking behavior, the hospital industry, and pharmaceutical policy.

One of Hsieh's hobbies is organizing academic conferences. In 1999 he organized the Taipei International Conference on Health Economics. This conference led to the publication of two books, *The Economic Analysis of Substance Use and Abuse* and *The Economics of Health Care in Asia-Pacific*

Countries, coedited with Michael Grossman and Teh-Wei Hu, respectively. In 2005 he organized an international conference on pharmaceutical innovation and coedited the resulting book, *Pharmaceutical Innovation,* with Frank Sloan.

Yanfen Huang is a professor at the Institute of Public Finance, School of Public Administration, Renmin University of China. She earned her Ph.D. in economics at the University of Essen in Germany.

Huang's research focuses on price regulation policy, public sector economics, and econometrics. She is now working on a project on China's Price Regulation of Pharmaceuticals and Medical Services, which is supported by the National Natural Science Foundation of China under grant #70673109.

Toshiaki Iizuka is a professor in the Faculty of Economics at Keio University in Japan. Previously, he was a professor in the Graduate School of International Management (GSIM) at Aoyama Gakuin University in Japan. Iizuka's research interests are industrial organization and health economics. He has written several articles on the U.S. and Japanese pharmaceutical markets, published in the *RAND Journal of Economics* and the *Journal of Industrial Economics,* among others.

Before joining the GSIM in 2005, he was assistant professor of management at Owen Graduate School of Management, Vanderbilt University. Iizuka has also worked as a strategy consultant for multinational corporations. He holds a Ph.D. in economics from the University of California, Los Angeles, an M.A. from Columbia University, and an M.E. and a B.E. from the University of Tokyo.

Mark Johnston received his Ph.D. from Harvard's Kennedy School in 1990. Prior to completing his degree, he played a major role in the design and administration of the Australian Pharmaceutical Subsidy Scheme. In recent years, Johnston has been engaged in economic development work in Asia.

Soonman Kwon is a professor in the Department of Health Policy and Management at the School of Public Health, Seoul National University (SNU), Republic of Korea. He is also the director of the BK (Brain Korea) Center for Elderly Health Policy Research at SNU. After he received his Ph.D. from the Wharton School of the University of Pennsylvania, he was assistant professor of public policy at the University of Southern California from 1993 to 1996.

Kwon's major areas of interest are health economics and finance, comparative health policy and welfare states, pharmaceuticals, and aging and long-term care. He has served on numerous health policy committees of the government of South Korea, and has occasionally worked as a short-term consultant for the World Health Organization, the World Bank, and the German Technical Cooperation on health financing and policy in China, Mongolia, Pakistan, the Philippines, and Vietnam. Kwon serves on the editorial boards of *Social Science and Medicine* (Elsevier), *Health Economics Policy and Law* (Cambridge University Press), and many others. He is the editor-in-chief of the *Korean Journal of Public Health.*

Mingzhi Li is an associate professor at the School of Economics and Management, Tsinghua University, Beijing, China. He received a Ph.D. in economics from the University of Texas at Austin in 1999.

Siaw-Teng Liaw, an academic family physician and clinical researcher, is professor of General Practice at the University of New South Wales, Australia. His expertise is in multimethod research applied to health services, systems, and informatics research and education. His interests center on the safety, quality, and integration of health care across primary and secondary care settings, particularly in the quality use of medicines, with a focus on indigenous health. Other projects include patient record linkage and decision support applications to promote better clinical care, quality use of medicine, clinical audits, research, and community health.

He was a member of the Australian National Electronic Decision Support Taskforce, involved in the implementation and evaluation of such large-scale programs as the Victorian Clinicians' Health Channel, MediConnect, and HealthConnect, and has conducted a number of studies on e-health and electronic decision support. He consults and advises on a number of health informatics, primary care, and health terminology issues. He is a member of the Australian National Health and Medical Research Council Human Genetics Advisory Committee and the National Prescribing Service Pharmaceutical Decision Support Working Group.

Caitlin M. Liu is a research fellow at Rutgers Business School and a journalist specializing in business, law, and public policy. Formerly a staff writer at the *Los Angeles Times*, Liu also has written for the *New York Times*, the *Washington Post, Condé Nast Portfolio, Health Affairs*, and the *University of Chicago Law School Roundtable*. Liu received her B.A. from Stanford University and holds joint degrees in law (J.D.) and public policy (M.P.P.) from the University of California at Berkeley School of Law (Boalt Hall) and the Kennedy School of Government at Harvard University, where she was editor-in-chief of *The Citizen* and editing team leader for *Asian American Policy Review*. In 2007 Liu served as a consultant to the United Nations Development Programme's *Human Development Report*.

Xue Liu is a professor of strategy at Guanghua School of Management, Peking University. He holds a Ph.D. in economics from Peking University, where he also completed his postdoctoral training. Before coming to Peking University, he was associate dean at the School of Business Administration, Shenyang Pharmaceutical University. Liu's research interests are technology innovation and health-care management, and he has published extensively in various renowned management journals.

Hans Löfgren is a senior lecturer in politics and policy studies at Deakin University in Melbourne, Australia, and director of its Master of Politics and Policy Program. His Ph.D. dissertation, completed at the University of Melbourne in 1997, was titled "Globalization of the Pharmaceutical Industry and the Australian State: The Transformation of a Policy Network."

Löfgren's research specialization is the political economy of the biopharmaceutical industries of Australia, India, and the world. He has published articles on these topics in journals such as *Social Science and Medicine, Australian Journal of Political Science, Australian Health Review, Labour & Industry, Australian Journal of Social Issues, Australia and New Zealand Health Policy,* and *New Political Science.* He is presently engaged in research on the role of consumer groups in Australian health policy and on TRIPS and the future of the pharmaceutical industry in the developing world.

Qingyue Meng is professor and dean of the Shandong University School of Public Health. He obtained his M.D. from Shandong University in 1986, his masters in public health from Fudan University in 1989, his M.A. from the School of Economics of the University of the Philippines in 1995, and his Ph.D. from Karolinska Institute in Sweden in 2006. He serves as a member of the Advisory Committee of Health Policy and Management to Ministry of Health; the Advisory Committee of Tuberculosis Control to Ministry of Health; and the Steering Committee of Social, Economic, and Behaviour Studies, Training in Tropical Diseases (TDR), World Health Organization (WHO). He is also a council member of the Federation for International Cooperation of Health Services and Systems Research Centres (FICOSSER).

Meng's research interests include health financing and cost-effectiveness analysis of public health programs. Over the past decade, he has led a team conducting dozens of research projects supported by the WHO, the World Bank, the Department for International Development (DFID), and the Chinese government. He has published a number of peer-reviewed papers in international and Chinese journals, and provides a number of consultancy services focusing on health policy and systems for Chinese national and local governments, the World Bank, and DFID-funded projects. In recent years, Meng's work has focused on rural public health-care systems in poor areas, particularly developing policy recommendations to national and local governments to establish an equitable health-care system for vulnerable populations.

Jeffrey L. Moe is executive in residence and adjunct associate professor at the Fuqua School of Business, Duke University. He joined the Health Sector Management program at Fuqua in 2001. His research interests include new incentives for neglected disease research, private-sector responses to the global health-care worker shortage, and the use of business intelligence as a basis of competitive advantage among life sciences firms.

Moe was coauthor of "Developing Drugs for Developing Countries" (*Health Affairs,* March/April 2006) which led to the Sec. 524 amendment in the Food and Drug Administration (FDA) Amendments Act of 2007. The article recommended, and the legislation now makes into law, a new incentive for neglected tropical disease medicines: the priority review voucher (PRV). A PRV is awarded for U.S. registration of a new medicine (new chemical, biological or diagnostic) for a tropical disease (sixteen diseases, including TB and malaria), called a "tropical drug." The voucher is exercised by receiving priority review of a second drug, the "voucher drug," for FDA approval to market to U.S. patients. The FDA issued its guidance in October 2008 to administer the new voucher program, and Novartis made the first tropical drug application for its Coartem product, which was awarded the first in 2009.

Moe is the chief executive of the Institute for Global Disease Medicines, Inc. (IGDM) a spin-out of Duke University technology. IGDM utilizes a proprietary proteome-capture discovery technology that combines focused chemical libraries with parallel affinity capture screens. The drug discovery engine enables new drug candidates to be identified in large combinatorial chemical libraries en masse and rapidly progressed to Phase I clinical trials through directed iterative chemistry. IGDM is structured as a not-for-profit/for-profit hybrid business model and will become a self-sustaining biotechnology organization that is founded with philanthropic donations and grants. IGDM's initial research program will focus on malaria and cancer.

Before coming to Duke, Moe was an executive at GlaxoSmithKline. Over a fifteen-year career he held positions in business development, corporate strategy, marketing, market economics, and human resources. He received his Ph.D. in organization development and behavior from the University of North Carolina at Chapel Hill in 1981. He graduated from the Executive Development Program, the Kellogg School, Northwestern University, in 1997.

Sauwakon Ratanawijitrasin is an associate professor on the faculty of social sciences and humanities, Mahidol University, Thailand. She was a Fulbright scholar (1988–1993) and a Takemi Fellow in International Health at Harvard School of Public Health (1995–1996). Her education includes a B.S. in pharmacy and an M.A. and Ph.D. in public administration. Her dissertation won the best dissertation award from the U.S. National Association of Schools of Public Affairs and Administration in 1993.

Sauwakon's teaching and research are in the areas of pharmaceutical and health systems policy and management, health insurance and financing, drug utilization, and system thinking. Her publications include books on health insurance and *Effective Drug Regulation: A Multi-country Study*, published by the World Health Organization.

In addition to academic responsibilities, Sauwakon also works on systems development and management. She currently directs the Pharmaceutical System Research and Intelligence Center (PSyRIC). Previously, she served as deputy executive director of the Association of South-East Asian Nations (ASEAN) University Network and associate dean of the College of Public Health at Chulalongkorn University. She also served as adviser to the Thai Parliamentary

Special Commission on National Health Insurance Bill and to the World Health Organization, among others.

Michael R. Reich is Taro Takemi Professor of International Health Policy at the Harvard School of Public Health. He is a leading researcher on global health policy, particularly the political dimensions of public health policy and pharmaceutical policy. He serves as director of the Takemi Program in International Health at Harvard, and previously served as director of the Harvard Center for Population and Development Studies. He received his Ph.D. in political science from Yale University in 1981, and has been a member of the faculty of Harvard University since 1983. His research activities include the politics of health system reform, access to health technologies in poor countries, and shaping global health policy. During 2008–2009, he worked with the Japanese government and the Takemi Working Group on Global Health Challenges, on the global health agenda for the G8 Summit (held in July 2008 in Toyako, Japan). He has provided policy advice to many organizations around the world, including national governments, international agencies, nongovernmental organizations, private foundations, and private corporations. His books include *Access: How Do Good Health Technologies Get to Poor People in Poor Countries* (with Laura J. Frost, 2008); *Getting Health Reform Right: A Guide to Improving Performance and Equity* (with M. J. Roberts, W. Hsiao, and P. Berman, 2004); and *Public-Private Partnerships for Public Health* (2002).

Kai Reimers is currently a professor of information systems at RWTH Aachen University, Faculty of Business and Economics. From 1998 to 2003, he worked as a visiting professor at the School of Economics and Management, Tsinghua University. He earned a doctorate in economics from Wuppertal University and a venia legendi at Bremen University. He has published in many international journals, including *European Journal of Information Systems*, *Electronic Markets*, *Electronic Commerce Research*, *Communications of the AIS*, and *Journal of Information Technology*. He has authored or coauthored five books in the field of information systems. His main fields of research are interorganizational systems, IT management, and IT standards.

David B. Ridley is an assistant professor at Duke University's business school. Duke University is also where he earned a doctorate in economics. In his research Ridley examines business strategy regarding innovation, entry into new markets, differentiation, and the effects of government policy. Most of his work has applications in health care, especially pharmaceuticals. To encourage more pharmaceutical innovation for treatments for neglected diseases, Ridley, together with Henry G. Grabowski and Jeffrey L. Moe, proposed a priority review voucher prize. Their proposal became law in 2007.

Dennis Ross-Degnan is associate professor in the Department of Population Medicine (DPM) at Harvard Medical School and director of research at Harvard Pilgrim Health Care, a nonprofit health insurance plan in the United States. He holds a doctorate in health policy and management from the Harvard School of Public Health.

Ross-Degnan is one of the global leaders in improving use of medicines. His career has focused on improving health systems in the United States and developing countries, including research on the factors underlying use of medicines, impacts of pharmaceutical policies on utilization and clinical outcomes, interventions to improve quality of care, and appropriate methods for pharmaceutical research. In 1990 he cofounded the International Network for Rational Use of Drugs (INRUD), a global network of academics, health managers, and policymakers involved in developing and testing interdisciplinary interventions to improve use of medicines. In recognition of his efforts to build capacity for improving pharmaceutical situations around the world, he was awarded the 2005 Harvard Medical School Klaus Peter International Teaching Award and the 2009 Clifford A. Barger Excellence in Mentoring Award. Ross-Degnan has consulted extensively with the World Health Organization (WHO) on issues related to pharmaceutical access and appropriate use, and codirects the WHO Collaborating Center in Pharmaceutical Policy, based jointly at the DPM and the Boston University Center for International Health.

Michael A. Santoro is an associate professor (with tenure) of business ethics at the Rutgers Business School. He holds a Ph.D. in public policy from Harvard University , a J.D. from New York University, and an A.B. from Oberlin College. He has also been a Fulbright Fellow at the University of Hong Kong. Santoro's first book, *Profits and Principles: Global Capitalism and Human Rights in China* (2000), was widely praised and formed the basis of his testimony to the U.S. Senate Finance Committee in support of China 's entry into the World Trade Organization. He is the coeditor of *Ethics in the Pharmaceutical Industry* (2005). His most recent book is *China 2020: How Western Business Can—and Should—Influence Social and Political Change in the Coming Decade* (2009).

F. M. Scherer is Aetna Professor Emeritus at the John F. Kennedy School of Government, Harvard University. He has also taught at Princeton University, the University of Michigan, Northwestern University, Swarthmore College, Haverford College, the Central European University, and the University of Bayreuth. In 1974–1976 he was chief economist at the Federal Trade Commission. Scherer's undergraduate degree was from the University of Michigan; he received his M.B.A. and Ph.D. from Harvard University. His research specialties are industrial economics and the economics of technological change, leading to books on *Industrial Market Structure and Economic Performance* (3rd edition with David Ross); *The Economics of Multi-Plant Operation: An International Comparisons Study* (with three coauthors); *Innovation and Growth: Schumpeterian Perspectives*;

The Weapons Acquisition Process (two volumes, one with M. J. Peck); *Industry Structure, Strategy, and Public Policy*; *New Perspectives on Economic Growth and Technological Innovation*; and, most recently, *Quarter Notes and Bank Notes: The Economics of Music Composition in the 18th and 19th Centuries.*

Qiang Sun is a senior lecturer at the Center for Health Management and Policy at Shandong University, China. Sun has an M.D. and an M.A. in public health and is currently pursuing a Ph.D. His research areas include health economics and policy.

Naoko Tomita is a researcher in the Pharmacoeconomics Education Program at Keio University's Graduate School of Health Management. She is also a Ph.D. candidate in public health and policy at the London School of Hygiene and Tropical Medicine, University of London. She received her M.A. in political science and L.L.B. from Kobe University. Her doctoral dissertation focuses on the policymaking process in the separation of prescribing and dispensing in Japan and South Korea. Tomita's current research includes comparison of health technology assessment policies in Asia and the pharmacoepidemiological analysis of mental illness using prescription data. Her major areas of interest are the politics of health policy, comparative health policy, pharmaceutical policy, pharmacoeconomics, and patient decision-making.

Anita Wagner is assistant professor in the Department of Population Medicine at Harvard Medical School. A clinical pharmacist, pharmacoepidemiologist, and health services researcher, she seeks to improve population health and well-being through applied research on the effects of policy interventions to improve equitable medicines access, affordability, and use, and through building capacity for evidence-based policy decision-making in the United States and internationally.

As a core member of the World Health Organization's Collaborating Center in Pharmaceutical Policy, she coleads the global Medicines and Insurance Coverage (MedIC) Initiative, which aims to improve the health of the poor by supporting the design, implementation, evaluation, and routine monitoring of evidence-based medicines benefit policies for vulnerable populations across the world. Wagner directs MedIC's capacity-building activities and codirects the Harvard Medical School Fellowship in Pharmaceutical Policy Research. She holds a German masters'-equivalent degree in pharmacy, a doctorate in clinical pharmacy from Massachusetts College of Pharmacy, a masters of public health/ international health degree, and a doctorate in epidemiology from Harvard School of Public Health.

Bong-Min Yang has been the dean of the School of Public Health at Seoul National University since 2004, where he also teaches courses in health policy and management. Yang earned his Ph.D. in economics from Pennsylvania

State University in 1982. Yang has served as an adviser to the South Korean government, the World Bank, and the World Health Organization.

Yiyong Yang is the director-general of and a professor at the Institute of Social Development Research, National Development and Reform Commission, China. He also serves as vice president of the China Labor Academy Society. He earned a Ph.D. in economics at Renmin University. His main research topics include labor economics, public services, public health policy, social security, labor relations, and social development. He is now undertaking a research project entitled "Study on Equalization of Regional Public Health Services in China."

Richard Zeckhauser is the Frank P. Ramsey Professor of Political Economy at Harvard's Kennedy School of Government. He is an elected fellow of the Econometric Society, the American Academy of Arts and Sciences, and the Institute of Medicine (National Academy of Sciences). His work focuses on situations of uncertainty and the provision of incentives. Often working with others, he is the author of 250 professional articles and 5 books.

Wei Wilson Zhang is assistant professor of management at the China Europe International Business School in Shanghai. He received a Ph.D. in health policy from Harvard University (an interfaculty program of the Graduate School of Arts and Sciences, Business School, Kennedy School of Government, and Medical School) and an M.D. from Peking Union Medical College. He is also a Bing Fellow of Health Economics at RAND, and an affiliated member of Sloan Industry Studies Program. Previously, he was assistant professor of health economics and management in the Guanghua School of Management, Peking University.

RECENT AND FORTHCOMING PUBLICATIONS OF THE WALTER H. SHORENSTEIN ASIA-PACIFIC RESEARCH CENTER

Books (distributed by the Brookings Institution Press)

Rafiq Dossani, Daniel C. Sneider, and Vikram Sood. *Does South Asia Exist? Prospects for Regional Integration in South Asia.* Stanford, CA: Walter H. Shorenstein Asia-Pacific Research Center, forthcoming 2009.

Jean C. Oi, Scott Rozelle, and Xueguang Zhou. *Growing Pains: Tensions and Opportunities in China's Transformation.* Stanford, CA: Walter H. Shorenstein Asia-Pacific Research Center, 2009.

Donald A. L. Macintyre, Daniel C. Sneider, and Gi-Wook Shin, eds. *First Drafts of Korea: The U.S. Media and Perceptions of the Last Cold War Frontier.* Stanford, CA: Walter H. Shorenstein Asia-Pacific Research Center, 2009.

Steven Reed, Kenneth Mori McElwain, and Kay Shimizu, eds. *Political Change in Japan: Electoral Behavior, Party Realignment, and the Koizumi Reforms.* Stanford, CA: Walter H. Shorenstein Asia-Pacific Research Center, 2009.

Donald K. Emmerson. *Hard Choices: Security, Democracy, and Regionalism in Southeast Asia.* Stanford, CA: Walter H. Shorenstein Asia-Pacific Research Center, 2008.

Henry S. Rowen, Marguerite Gong Hancock, and William F. Miller, eds. *Greater China's Quest for Innovation.* Stanford, CA: Walter H. Shorenstein Asia-Pacific Research Center, 2008.

Gi-Wook Shin and Daniel C. Sneider, eds. *Cross Currents: Regionalism and Nationalism in Northeast Asia.* Stanford, CA: Walter H. Shorenstein Asia-Pacific Research Center, 2007.

Stella R. Quah, ed. *Crisis Preparedness: Asia and the Global Governance of Epidemics.* Stanford, CA: Walter H. Shorenstein Asia-Pacific Research Center, 2007.

Philip W. Yun and Gi-Wook Shin, eds. *North Korea: 2005 and Beyond*. Stanford, CA:Walter H. Shorenstein Asia-Pacific Research Center, 2006.

Jongryn Mo and Daniel I. Okimoto, eds. *From Crisis to Opportunity: Financial Globalization and East Asian Capitalism*. Stanford, CA: Walter H. Shorenstein Asia-Pacific Research Center, 2006.

Michael H. Armacost and Daniel I. Okimoto, eds. *The Future of America's Alliances in Northeast Asia*. Stanford, CA: Walter H. Shorenstein Asia-Pacific Research Center, 2004.

Henry S. Rowen and Sangmok Suh, eds. *To the Brink of Peace: New Challenges in Inter-Korean Economic Cooperation and Integration*. Stanford, CA: Walter H. Shorenstein Asia-Pacific Research Center, 2001.

Studies of the Walter H. Shorenstein Asia-Pacific Research Center
(published with Stanford University Press)

Jean Oi and Nara Dillon, eds. *At the Crossroads of Empires: Middlemen, Social Networks, and State-building in Republican Shanghai*. Stanford, CA: Stanford University Press, 2007.

Henry S. Rowen, Marguerite Gong Hancock, and William F. Miller, eds. *Making IT: The Rise of Asia in High Tech*. Stanford, CA: Stanford University Press, 2006.

Gi-Wook Shin. *Ethnic Nationalism in Korea: Genealogy, Politics, and Legacy*. Stanford, CA:Stanford University Press, 2006.

Andrew Walder, Joseph Esherick, and Paul Pickowicz, eds. *The Chinese Cultural Revolution as History*. Stanford, CA: Stanford University Press, 2006.

Rafiq Dossani and Henry S. Rowen, eds. *Prospects for Peace in South Asia*. Stanford, CA: Stanford University Press, 2005.